Private Secretaries to the Prime Minister

The importance of the Prime Minister in British foreign policy decision-making has long been noted by historians. However, while much attention has been given to high-level contacts between leaders and to the roles played by the premiers themselves, much less is known about the people advising and influencing them. In providing day-to-day assistance to the Prime Minister, a Private Secretary could wield significant influence on policy outcomes. This book examines the activities of those who advised prime ministers from Winston Churchill (1951–55) to Margaret Thatcher during her first administration (1979–83). Each chapter considers British foreign policy and assesses the influence of the specific advisers. For each office holder, particular attention is paid to a number of key themes. Firstly, their relationship with the Prime Minister is considered. A strong personal relationship of trust and respect could lead to an official wielding much greater influence. This could be especially relevant when an adviser served under two different leaders, often from different political parties. It also helps to shed light on the conduct of foreign policy by each premier. Secondly, the attitudes towards the adviser from the Foreign Office are examined. The Foreign Office traditionally enjoyed great autonomy in the making of British foreign policy and was sensitive to encroachments by Downing Street. Finally, each chapter explores the role of the adviser in the key foreign policy events and discussions of the day. Covering a fascinating 30-year period in post-war British political history, this collection broadens our understanding of the subject, and underlines the different ways influence could be brought to bear on government policy.

Andrew Holt taught at the University of Nottingham, King's College London and the University of Exeter, and held a visiting fellowship at Churchill College, Cambridge, before joining the Civil Service. He is the author of *The Foreign Policy of the Douglas-Home Government: Britain, the United States and the End of Empire* (2014).

Warren Dockter is a Lecturer in International Politics at Aberystwyth University, having previously been a Junior Research Fellow at Clare Hall, Cambridge. He is the author of *Winston Churchill and the Islamic World: Orientalism, Empire and Diplomacy in the Middle East* (2015) and edited *Churchill at the Telegraph* (2015).

Routledge Studies in Modern British History

https://www.routledge.com/history/series/RSMBH

12 The Chartist General
Charles James Napier, The Conquest of Sind, and Imperial Liberalism
Edward Beasley

13 The Great Church Crisis and the End of English Erastianism, 1898–1906
Bethany Kilcrease

14 Opening Schools and Closing Prisons
Caring for Destitute and Delinquent Children in Scotland 1812–1872
Andrew Ralston

15 Charles Pelham Villiers: Aristocratic Victorian Radical
Roger Swift

16 Women, Mission and Church in Uganda
Ethnographic encounters in an age of imperialism, 1895–1960s
Elizabeth Dimock

17 British Politics, Society and Empire, 1852–1945
Essays in Honour of Trevor O. Lloyd
David W. Gutzke

18 Deprivation, State Interventions and Urban Communities in Britain, 1968–79
Peter Shapely

19 Private Secretaries to the Prime Minister
Foreign Affairs from Churchill to Thatcher
Edited by Andrew Holt and Warren Dockter

20 Liberal Reform and Industrial Relations: J.H. Whitley (1866–1935), Halifax Radical and Speaker of the House of Commons
Edited by John A. Hargreaves, Keith Laybourn and Richard Toye

Private Secretaries to the Prime Minister

Foreign Affairs from Churchill to Thatcher

Edited by
Andrew Holt and Warren Dockter

LONDON AND NEW YORK

First published 2017
by Routledge
2 Park Square, Milton Park, Abingdon, Oxon OX14 4RN

and by Routledge
711 Third Avenue, New York, NY 10017

Routledge is an imprint of the Taylor & Francis Group, an informa business

© 2017 selection and editorial matter, Andrew Holt and Warren Dockter; individual chapters, the contributors

The right of Andrew Holt and Warren Dockter to be identified as the authors of the editorial material, and of the authors for their individual chapters, has been asserted in accordance with sections 77 and 78 of the Copyright, Designs and Patents Act 1988.

All rights reserved. No part of this book may be reprinted or reproduced or utilised in any form or by any electronic, mechanical, or other means, now known or hereafter invented, including photocopying and recording, or in any information storage or retrieval system, without permission in writing from the publishers.

Trademark notice: Product or corporate names may be trademarks or registered trademarks, and are used only for identification and explanation without intent to infringe.

British Library Cataloguing-in-Publication Data
A catalogue record for this book is available from the British Library

Library of Congress Cataloging-in-Publication Data
A catalog record for this book has been requested

ISBN: 978-1-4094-4180-9 (hbk)
ISBN: 978-1-315-60223-3 (ebk)

Typeset in Bembo
by Taylor & Francis Books

In memory of John Alan Holt and Albert W. Dockter, Jr

Contents

List of contributors		ix
Foreword		xi
Acknowledgements		xiv
	Introduction CHARLES POWELL	1
1	Managing a giant: Jock Colville and Winston Churchill WARREN DOCKTER	8
2	Advising the un-advisable: The Number 10 Private Office and the Suez Crisis KEVIN RUANE	34
3	Philip de Zulueta PETER CATTERALL	55
4	Oliver Wright ANDREW HOLT	81
5	Michael Palliser JOHN W. YOUNG	97
6	'Sound and comfortable men': Peter Moon, Lord Bridges and Britain's entry into the EEC NICK THOMAS	118
7	Patrick Wright and Bryan Cartledge JOHN SHEPHERD	136
8	Margaret Thatcher's Private Secretaries for Foreign Affairs, 1979–1984 AARON DONAGHY	166

Conclusion: The Prime Minister's Private Office from John Martin
to Chris Martin   187
ANTHONY SELDON

*Appendix I: Private Secretaries to the Prime Minister with responsibility
for foreign affairs, 1945–2015*   208
*Appendix II: Principal Private Secretaries to the Prime Minister,
1945–2015*   209
Index   210

Contributors

Peter Catterall is Professor of History and Policy at the University of Westminster and the editor of Harold Macmillan's diaries, published in two volumes in 2003 and 2011. His recent work includes chapters on Churchill as Chancellor of the Exchequer and Churchill and the General Strike for Richard Toye's *Winston Churchill: Politics, Strategy and Statecraft* (Bloomsbury, 2017) as well as 'Prime Minister and President: Harold Macmillan's Accounts of the Cuban Missile Crisis', in Len Scott and R. Gerald Hughes (eds), *The Cuban Missile Crisis: A Critical Reappraisal* (Routledge, 2015). He is the founding editor of *National Identities* and has just completed *Labour and the Free Churches 1918–1939: Religion, Radicalism and Righteousness* (Bloomsbury, 2016).

Warren Dockter is a Lecturer in International Politics at Aberystwyth University, having previously been a Junior Research Fellow at Clare Hall, Cambridge. He is the author of *Winston Churchill and the Islamic World: Orientalism, Empire and Diplomacy in the Middle East* (IB Tauris, 2015) and edited *Churchill at the Telegraph* (Aurum, 2015).

Aaron Donaghy is an EU Marie Curie Global Fellow at Harvard University, and a Visiting Scholar at Harvard's Center for European Studies. Previously, he held visiting fellowships at Cornell University, New York, the University of Cambridge, and a Government of Ireland postdoctoral fellowship at University College Dublin, where he also lectured in modern history. He is author of *The British Government and the Falkland Islands, 1974–79* (Palgrave Macmillan, 2014).

Tom Fletcher, CMG, is a Visiting Professor of International Relations at New York University, and Visiting Professor of Diplomatic Practice at the Emirates Diplomatic Academy. He was British Ambassador to Lebanon (2011–15), and the Downing Street foreign policy adviser to three Prime Ministers (2007–11). He is an Honorary Fellow of Oxford University, and the Global Strategy Director for the Global Business Coalition for Education, which seeks to harness private sector efforts to get 59 million children into school. He chairs the International Advisory Council of the Creative Industries Federation, promoting Britain's most dynamic and magnetic sector overseas. Tom has recently led a review of British diplomacy for the UK Foreign Office, and is currently working on a report on the future of the United Nations for the next UN Secretary General. He is the author of *Naked Diplomacy: Power and Statecraft in the Digital Age* (HarperCollins, 2016).

Andrew Holt taught at the University of Nottingham, King's College London and the University of Exeter, and held a visiting fellowship at Churchill College, Cambridge, before joining the Civil Service. He is the author of *The Foreign Policy of Douglas-Home Government: Britain, the United States and the End of Empire* (Palgrave Macmillan, 2014).

Charles Powell is an international businessman. After the excitement of the Downing Street years, he decided to try his luck in business rather than return to conventional diplomacy. He serves as a director of a number of leading international companies and as a strategy adviser to others. He combines this with, among other things, membership of the House of Lords, chairing the British Museum Trust and the Trustees of Oxford's Business School, and honorary fellowships of Somerville College Oxford and the Ashmolean Museum.

Kevin Ruane is Professor of Modern History at Canterbury Christ Church University. He has been researching and writing on international history for 30 years, including books on Cold War Europe, the Anglo-American 'special relationship', and the Vietnam War. His latest book is *Churchill and the Bomb in War and Cold War* (Bloomsbury, 2016).

Anthony Seldon is the author of multiple volumes on the premiership from Edward Heath to David Cameron, and is considered one of Britain's pre-eminent political biographers and contemporary historians. He is the former head of one of the country's leading independent schools, Wellington College, and is now Vice Chancellor of Buckingham University.

John Shepherd is Visiting Professor in Modern British History at the University of Huddersfield. His recent publications include *George Lansbury: At the Heart of Old Labour* (Oxford University Press, 2002); *Britain's First Labour Government*, with Keith Laybourn (Palgrave, 2006); and *Crisis? What Crisis? The Callaghan Government and the British 'Winter of Discontent'* (Manchester University Press, 2013). Currently he is completing a biography of Jon Cruddas MP to be published by Manchester University Press.

Nick Thomas is Assistant Professor in Twentieth Century History at the University of Nottingham.

John W. Young is Professor of International History at the University of Nottingham. His most recent books include *Twentieth Century Diplomacy: A Case Study of British Practice, 1963–76* (Cambridge University Press, 2008) and *David Bruce and Diplomatic Practice: An American Ambassador in London, 1961–69* (Bloomsbury, 2014).

Foreword

I served three very different Prime Ministers – Tony Blair, Gordon Brown and David Cameron. I do not possess the wisdom, distance or career certainty to be as candid as the eminent historians and former practitioners whose recollections form this fascinating account of life behind the black door. The 'Private' remains more important than the 'Secretary'.

The role of 'Private Secretary for Foreign Affairs to the Prime Minister' did not involve, as once translated to bewilderment, being the 'Intimate Typist for the Prime Minister's Affairs overseas'. It was a combination of policy adviser, journalist, negotiator, bag carrier and relationship manager. Occasionally therapist, translator, recruitment consultant and even bodyguard, as when President of Zimbabwe Robert Mugabe emerged from a corner of a UN Summit to seek a handshake with Gordon Brown. I wrote speeches, dreamt up policies and procured ProPlus from President Obama. Sometimes I had to tell white lies, as when a Middle Eastern monarch asked what was written on all the 'nice placards' being waved at him in London by 'friendly crowds'. The first voice I heard each morning, and the last each night, was the relentlessly cheerful Number 10 switchboard.

Many things about the Private Secretary's role are unchanged. We no longer cut the dash of the impresarios of Nico Henderson's memoirs, but we do have more influence than our age or rank would normally permit. We work in an atmosphere of creative tension with the departments from which we come. Output matters more than process. We succeed if we master the art of using leverage. We inhabit the grey but productive area between communications, policy and diary. We don't need to know everything about everything, but we do need to know something about everything. We cannot be control freaks, but we do have to create the illusion of freakish control. We rely as ever on the extraordinary good grace and professionalism of the duty clerks, switchboard operators and garden room staff who really run Number 10. The 30 seconds walking to the front door with the PM are more important than the two hours rewriting his brief. We have to think fast, but never bluff. When the door is closed, we can be a licensed heretic, impertinent irritation, devil's advocate. But not all the time, not in front of others, and never once the PM has reached a decision. If you appear too close to 'The Boss', you'll be seen as a threat. If not close enough, as irrelevant. As ever, the PS must navigate between civil servants and special advisers, drawing the best from both while sidestepping unnecessary scraps. You need a thick skin – I still wake at night to recall one prime ministerial ticking off accompanied by the strains of 'Don't Stop Me Now, I'm Having Such a Good Time' on a nearby loudspeaker. Just as the Private Secretaries of the past had to read Stalin or Kennedy, we have to know our Prime Ministers' interlocutors inside out. Some were easier than others – the success of meetings with one leader could be judged by how often he tapped his crotch. We have to understand how to get the most out of our leaders, including by building in moments to watch the football or beat us at tennis.

Yet many aspects of our roles have changed dramatically. I worked for the last paper and pen PM, the first email PM, and the first iPad PM. When I started, we had to consider how policy would look on the Sky ticker. By the time I left, by how it would look on Twitter. We have had to become more media-savvy than our predecessors, always with a good story in the back pocket. Preparations for PMQs or press conferences have become the sweet spot in which to debate and hone policy. We have become more focused on 'deliverables' – announcements designed, more in hope than expectation in my experience, to prevent the media from writing negative alternatives. We have to think more about the visuals, as demonstrated by our often grim experiences over bilaterals with successive US Presidents – there were few I can recall where the media judged us on the substance of the exchange rather than the length of the press conference.

Even the physical nature of the job has changed. Traditionally, the smaller the desk and the closer to the throne, the better. But under Gordon Brown, we had a period in open-plan, a u-shape of desks around the Prime Minister. We now have blackberries attached to our wrists – leading to a painful version of repetitive strain injury (or No10donitis). The pace of international diplomacy has quickened. Often at a 'three-shirter' EU budget discussion or climate change summit, I would long for the days when Churchill's PS, Jock Colville, could write in his diary: 'war declared, rode on Hampstead Heath for three hours'. We are probably more paranoid about leaks and inquiries – the minute to the PM that looks brilliant and witty in the PM's red box will seem reckless to a parliamentary committee armed with hindsight and media outrage. Recent inquiries have shown that no one comes out with much credit when their real-time communications are put under an intense spotlight. We're more 'The Thick of It' than 'Yes Prime Minister'.

In my experience, leaders are more decent and more human than their reputations suggest. They arrive planning to delegate, but end up centralising. On issues of core national interest, they tend to make similar calls. The stereotypes are flawed: those seen as gunslingers were smarter; those seen as steely were more subtle; those seen as gloomy could be hilarious; and those seen as too relaxed were driven. Someone said that JFK inspired America, RFK challenged America, and Ted Kennedy changed America. The best leader has to do all three: set the vision, engage people to believe in it, and put systems in place to deliver it. Most leaders master two out of three. Tactics often get in the way of strategy, but most calls are 51/49 and lonely. So all value judgement over intellect.

Few jobs in government are more gruelling than PS – during one demanding period, my wife interrupted a conference call between the Prime Minister and a head of state to inform us all of how fed up she was. But few can be as exciting, and such a privilege. They give you an extraordinary insight into moments of history, and the characters that shape them. I woke the Prime Minister to tell him of President Obama's election. I was in the car with Gordon Brown as he left Chequers for the last time, and with David Cameron as he arrived there for the first time.

All of this makes this book more interesting and relevant than ever. It is interesting that the Private Secretaries who are now best remembered are those who wrote most down. The code of *omerta* remains strong among most of us, but as government evolves it is right to shine a light into the corridors in which we operate.

Tom Fletcher

Acknowledgements

The editors would like to thank the contributors for their hard work and cooperation in bringing this volume to fruition. Acknowledgement is especially due to Professor John Young, whose conversations with Dr Holt inspired the idea for this project. We would also like to express our gratitude to FCO Historians Dr Richard Smith and Professor Patrick Salmon; Allen Packwood, Director of the Churchill Archives Centre; and to Tom Gray, Rob Langham, Michael Bourne, and the team at Routledge. Finally, we are particularly grateful for the support of our respective close family members.

Introduction

Charles Powell

This collection of pen-portraits of those who have served as the Prime Minister's Private Secretary for foreign affairs in the decades from 1950 to 1983 when I took up the post also examines and explains the role itself: its scope, its influence and its position in the Whitehall power structure.

That is not a straightforward task. The first problem is the paucity of raw material. Members of ministerial private offices have long been prohibited from keeping diaries so there is nothing to be gleaned from the horse's mouth. Ministerial memoirs have generally observed the principle that they should not comment on individual civil servants beyond the occasional bouquet. Interviews given by former Number 10 foreign affairs Private Secretaries provide some material but not a great deal. Moreover the secrets of success in a Number 10 Private Secretary's role are anonymity and discretion so as to avoid any public perception of supplanting Cabinet ministers as the Prime Minister's principal source of advice. As with much British constitutional practice appearances deceive: indeed the very title Private Secretary is a classic bit of British under-statement. A Private Secretary's daily proximity to his or her minister inevitably confers greater influence than a bald job-description implies. But for heaven's sake don't tell anyone!

This all presents the historian with quite a problem in trying to assess the real role of successive foreign affairs Private Secretaries in Number 10. To a degree it can only be done by re-capitulating the diplomatic history of the time and making assumptions about the Private Secretary's contribution to it, drawing on whatever can be found in the Number 10 archives. They perforce omit the daily, sometimes hourly, face-to-face discussions between the Private Secretaries and the Prime Minister which is actually the key to the extent of that influence. Within these considerable constraints the book nonetheless provides many fascinating insights.

In career terms, the Number 10 foreign affairs Private Secretaries have been pretty much stereotypes: male, invariably public school, Oxbridge, middle-ranking officials in the FCO for whom the Number 10 assignment was a brief – generally two to three years – way-station on the road to top ambassadorial or Permanent Under-Secretary appointments. But as characters they emerge as very different, and consequently their relationships with Prime

Ministers of the day no less so. Anthony Eden and Edward Heath regarded their Private Secretaries as members of an extended family with whom to gossip and exchange personal letters, supreme examples being Guy Millard under Eden and Freddie Bishop under Macmillan. Others maintained a more formal, almost arm's length relationship.

Interestingly the recruitment process seems always to have been haphazard. Oliver Wright defined the only necessary qualifications for the job as an iron constitution and an understanding wife. Generally the Foreign Office simply served up a candidate or candidates whom it believed appropriate – and no doubt guaranteed to be loyal to their alma mater, a point to which I will return. Michael Palliser appears to have been the only candidate put forward for interview by Harold Wilson. In my own case I had been tipped off by a friend in Number 10 that Margaret Thatcher tended to talk incessantly during such interviews and then conclude that the candidate was useless because he never said anything. I went on the offensive and gabbled away myself, whereupon she is reported to have said 'he won't do, he never stops talking'. I got the job all the same, from which I can only conclude there were no other candidates.

Several factors govern the Number 10 foreign affairs Private Secretary's role once appointed. The most obvious is the continuously growing involvement of Prime Ministers in foreign affairs. There is nothing new in this: all Prime Ministers for several decades now have found themselves steadily more drawn in. What is new is the continuity and the scale of their involvement. It is in particular a function of the multiplication of international summits of every description – UN, EU, NATO, environmental and so on – in which heads of government are expected to play the lead role. Successive British Prime Ministers complain the process is out of control but are powerless to stop it.

The growing involvement is also a subject of permanent discord in the Number 10 Private Office with the Private Secretaries dealing with domestic affairs raging against the demands of foreign affairs on the Prime Minister's time, not to speak of the Government Whips who want Prime Ministers to spend more time coddling their back-benchers. Yet the attractions are hard for a Prime Minister to resist whatever their private lamentations: the perpetual television coverage, the press conferences, the scope for logging national triumphs such as the Falklands victory or the British rebate in Europe, and the opportunities to put one over Johnny Foreigner in the eyes of the *Sun* or the *Daily Mail*.

The result has been that the foreign affairs Private Secretary has over the years had a growing share of the Prime Minister's time and attention span, and an expanding volume of work. That was further enhanced as the portfolio grew to embrace defence, Northern Ireland, development aid, trade and intelligence – in other words a substantial slice of government business. Despite this, the do-it-yourself staffing persisted. Until the Blair years, which lie beyond the scope of this book, these matters were handled by a single Private Secretary in Number 10 with no deputy or assistant, let alone support staff. This puzzled the more profligately staffed White House, Élysée Palace and Bundeskanzleramt, but personally I never felt it a disadvantage. The perceived imbalance was addressed in Tony Blair's time by moving the Leader of the Cabinet Office's defence and foreign affairs and European secretariats into Number 10 to serve as prime ministerial advisers. In David Cameron's time the answer has been the creation of a national security adviser and staff. Both have involved inflating the number of bodies dealing with the Prime Minister's involvement in foreign affairs, let alone inflating the grade of the civil servants concerned. Some would doubtless claim it works better. My own observation is that large numbers in other heads of governments' offices did not improve the speed or clarity of their decisions, and that Number 10s previous unprecedentedly short chain of command – in effect the foreign affairs Private Secretary sticking his head round the PM's door to get an answer – had many advantages.

What did the foreign affairs Private Secretary actually do? In graphic terms, you sit at what is the very heart of government in an office adjoining the Cabinet Room, shared with the Principal Private Secretary. At least that was the case for decades until Tony Blair took the office for himself and David Cameron has kept it. Looking back 20 years later on my own time in Number 10 I am posthumously impressed both by the volume of work and the pace at which we had to do it. The flow of paper was immense and Margaret Thatcher's appetite for it legendary. Every paper sent on to her needed to have a clear question written on the front, sometimes with a summary of the main arguments. It might simply be 'agree?', or ask her to choose between alternatives, or recommend she contest the advice provided. These annotations could produce spectacularly explosive comments.

There was preparation for Prime Minister's Questions, at that time twice a week, which involved early morning and lunch-time briefing sessions predicting questions, suggesting smart answers and generally psyching her up to crush the current Leader of the Opposition with some withering put-down. There was attendance at her meetings of relevant Cabinet Committees and Cabinet itself as well as her weekly bilateral with the Foreign Secretary, never an easy occasion as he struggled to get a word in edgeways.

There was making sure she was fully briefed for meetings with visiting foreign leaders, more and more of whom flocked to Number 10 as her fame or notoriety spread. These could often take an unpredictable course: a Japanese trade minister who burst into floods of tears on receiving condolences for the death of his mother and had to be mopped up: a visiting President from the (then) French Congo, a communist whom I had unsuccessfully advised the Foreign Office not to insist on her seeing and whom she greeted with the words 'I hate Communists', astutely rendered into French by a very alarmed Congolese interpreter as 'Madam the Prime Minister says that on the whole she has not always found herself in agreement with the doctrines of Karl Marx': and a disconcerting habit of climbing on to a window seat during a meeting to test whether the windows had been dusted.

There was speech-writing, both for parliamentary occasions, for the annual Lord Mayor's banquet which traditionally concentrated on foreign affairs, and for other public events, most notoriously the Bruges speech. There was preparing for and accompanying her on all her foreign visits and sitting in to take a note of her discussions with foreign leaders, almost invariably as the only other person in the room as she had a rooted dislike of delegations and refused to be accompanied by Whitehall panjandrums. These had to be followed by late-night dictation sessions with relays of incomparable Garden Room girls – the Number 10 secretaries – to ensure an accurate account of what had been said. This was crucial given that Margaret Thatcher characteristically remembered everything she said herself but very little of what the other party had said. There was accompanying her to European Councils and other summits where I took to walking into the head of government sessions to refuel her with a whisky despite protestations from other leaders that I was making her more difficult. (That was the whole point.) There were the seminars which she wanted organised so as to tap the wisdom on foreign affairs of a wider circle than just the Foreign Office itself, inviting academic experts, businessmen and others. Above all there was constant and boisterous argument with Britain's surely most argumentative Prime Minister. Weekends brought little respite: we simply adjourned to Chequers rather than Number 10. I marvel in retrospect at what she got through, bearing in mind all this was just on foreign affairs.

But that is only part of the story, as the various accounts in this volume illustrate. There are many other aspects of the job which lead Private Secretaries into zones of controversy.

The first is whom you are actually working for. Bernard Donoughue, working in Number 10 in Harold Wilson and Jim Callaghan's time, recorded that foreign affairs Private Secretaries somehow never ceased to be the Foreign Office representatives to the Prime Minister. That was probably what the Foreign Office hoped and indeed the temporary nature of the Number 10 assignment served to remind the occupants of the post that their longer-term future lay with the FCO, and they had better remember that in the way they conducted themselves in Number 10. I recall being summoned by an FCO Permanent Secretary and being told: 'Remember I am your boss', not a claim which I thought sustainable. You cannot sustain divided loyalties: you serve the Prime Minister and no two ways about it. Michael Palliser also recognised the problem of being 'totally loyal to the Prime Minister who is your boss and who you are there to serve while at the same time preserving a relationship with the Foreign Secretary which is actually crucial to the national interest'. In my experience that is a counsel of perfection and in practice hard to fulfil, particularly when a Prime Minister is at odds with his or her Foreign Secretary, as was Harold Wilson with George Brown or Margaret Thatcher with Geoffrey Howe. The best you can do is attempt to play a marriage counsellor role.

What is most important is to keep the FCO and the rest of Whitehall meticulously informed, sometimes under strict security caveats of what the Prime Minister is up to in foreign affairs and what he or she says to leaders. Failure to do that can lead to the pitfalls of separate foreign policies, with Suez the classic example where, as the chapter on Eden's Private Secretaries recount, only one of the three (let alone the Foreign Office itself) was made aware of his collusion with the French and the Israelis. Better to expose differences than conceal them.

Another sensitive border-line is how far the foreign affairs Private Secretary acts as an adviser to the Prime Minister not just as a transmitter of the advice of others. Different views of this emerge in these essays. Guy Millard, one of Eden's Private Secretaries, defined their role as 'intermediaries not advisers' and some of his successors tried to abide strictly by that definition. But by no means all of them did so. Michael Palliser in particular saw his role to advise and was clearly an important influence on policy particularly on Europe. In practice it is impossible not to act as an adviser if you are in constant contact with the Prime Minister, discussing the issues, attending the meetings with other heads of government and understanding what the Prime Minister wants. The advice should never be a substitute for the advice of the Foreign Secretary or other Cabinet ministers of which the Prime Minister should always be aware, but it can point out difficulties with following their advice or wider considerations which are not fully taken into account.

Closely allied to this is how far you speak on the Prime Minister's behalf. Number 10 is not the White House where presidential advisers easily trump Cabinet Secretaries, and nothing gives an unelected civil servant the right to take decisions in the Prime Minister's place. Yet even the most workaholic of Prime Minister's cannot decide everything. Especially in fast-moving situations, a Private Secretary who knows the Prime Minister's mind has to be able to act on their behalf. During the first Gulf War I frequently slipped notes under John Major's bedroom door seeking retrospective endorsement of decisions reached with President Bush's national security adviser during the night hours – and always received it. But the perception that Private Secretaries exercise too much influence causes resentment in the Foreign Office. Freddie Bishop was accused of exercising influence out of all proportion to his formal responsibilities in Harold Macmillan's time and of 'government by private secretary' – a charge which he rashly dismissed by suggesting that was better than government by politicians.

Yet another area of controversy is the degree to which the Number 10 foreign affairs Private Secretary establishes his own foreign affairs network, independent of the Foreign Office itself. There are several examples in these accounts of foreign affairs Private Secretaries being used as prime ministerial envoys. There has long been a direct relationship with the US President's national security adviser, though the latter holds a much more powerful position. In my time that was supplemented by a direct secure telephone line to his desk. Similar relationships have developed over the years with those managing foreign policy issues in the offices of the French President and the German Chancellor and in my time we sometimes met as a threesome, the differences in our status reflected in Jacques Attali's penchant for arriving in a presidential jet while I would trudge over to Paris or Bonn in BA economy class, a good way to keep a sense of proportion about one's relative importance in what could be heady circumstances. The meetings were useful as a means of coordinating policy on major issues, though they did not always succeed as in the case of German reunification. But they were not welcome to foreign ministries in any of the capitals. Once again the key was to ensure that foreign ministries were kept fully informed. I am confident that was more the case in Britain than in our partners.

A temptation to be resisted is being drawn – overtly or identifiably at least – into political activity. As with most temptations it's hard not to succumb sometimes. I found it impossible to resist tinkering with foreign policy and defence passages in party conference speeches or Conservative manifestoes where it seemed to me either that they departed from what the Prime Minister wanted or – more often – strayed into the realm of fantasy foreign policy-making. I do not regard that as becoming politicised. Nor was there ever any pressure in Margaret Thatcher's time to become so. Indeed she seemed to regard civil servants as political eunuchs.

I have been spared dissection in this collection of essays, as the papers for the period I was foreign affairs Private Secretary at Number 10 are not fully open. My own experience was different to most of my predecessors: I was younger on appointment to the role, stayed longer (around seven years) and decided at the end to leave the foreign service altogether. I thought I had enjoyed the best job which government service offered, to which an embassy would never match up – in other words quit while you are ahead – but also because of the perception of others that I had become politically 'tainted' or 'gone native' after such a long stint in Number 10. (It was far from the longest. The record was, I believe, held by Sir Philip de Zulueta.) Above all I wanted to see if I could make it in life outside the Civil Service cocoon. So I was ready to move on and the powers that be in Whitehall could not wait for me to do so.

Yet like others I found the Number 10 experience exhilarating. I was more fortunate than others: for much of the period covered by this volume Britain was on the defensive, fighting seemingly remorseless decline in its world standing and influence and rejection by Europe. My own experience was of a resurgent Britain with the country's self-confidence restored, the special relationship with the US as close as it has ever been, our money back in Europe and the Single Market launched, the Falklands conflict won, Hong Kong's future assured, Rhodesia brought belatedly to independence, apartheid in South Africa defeated and Mandela freed, Germany united and the Cold War lain to rest. 'Twas bliss to be alive, though it did not always feel like that at the time.

Looking back do I have any claim to responsibility for any of that? No, of course not. It was the result of strong forceful leadership from a remarkable Prime Minister supported by able ministers who first knocked the country back into shape and then used its economic recovery to rebuild Britain's role in the world. But it was invigorating to be along for the ride: to have a hand in prime ministerial speeches, to engage in daily argument with Britain's most tempestuous Prime Minister, to sit in on meetings with President Reagan, President Gorbachev, Deng Xiaoping, President Mandela and many many others, while feeding Margaret Thatcher's ammunition belt for battles in Europe and (too often) in Whitehall. It was the ultimate trainspotter's dream.

Just as the Civil Service itself has changed and is probably about to change much more, the classic foreign affairs Private Secretary will probably become extinct, to be replaced by the full-fledged and more politicised Prime Minister's Department in Whitehall which has been looming on the horizon for some time, with a large foreign affairs and defence component. It would be pointless to mourn the passing of the Private Secretary role. But there is everything to be said for celebrating those who performed it as recorded in this book.

1 Managing a giant
Jock Colville and Winston Churchill

Warren Dockter

After just arriving home on a holiday from the British Embassy in Lisbon where he had been working as Head of the Chancery, Jock Colville and his wife Margaret Egerton were invited to a dinner party on 25 October 1951, the day of the general election. While he was in London he was pleased to run into some familiar faces from his days at Downing Street where he served as Churchill's Assistant Private Secretary during the Second World War. Among those he saw was Sir Norman Brook, who inquired if Colville was home on leave or for a more extended period. The next day Colville, his wife and his mother-in-law stopped at the Cesarewitch horse races en route to Scotland, where they planned to continue their holiday. As Colville watched the races and partook of some much needed relaxation, an official from the Jockey Club informed him that he had a phone call from the Prime Minister. Aware that this might condemn the holiday, Margaret told him that, 'Whatever he asks you to do, say no'.

On the phone, the familiar voice of Winston Churchill reported to Jock that Sir Norman Brook had told him that he was home on leave and asked him 'Would you, if it is not inconvenient (but pray say if it is), take a train to London to come see me?' Eager to fulfil his duty and happy to see his old friend, Colville happily replied in the affirmative and perhaps hoping to impress Churchill with his immediate availability proposed a meeting for 'tomorrow morning'. Churchill said, 'No, this afternoon'.[1] Though it prematurely finished his holiday with Margret and her mother, the meeting proved fruitful as Churchill invited Colville back into the Private Office as his Principal Private Secretary, where Jock would serve Churchill until the end of his government in 1955.

Sir John 'Jock' Colville is a figure who is well known to any historian of British politics and the Second World War. Born into an affluent and well-connected family, Colville, like Churchill, was educated at Harrow and, unlike Churchill, went on to senior scholarship at Trinity College, Cambridge. Though Colville initially joined the Foreign Office in 1937, in just two years he was appointed to Assistant Private Secretary to Neville Chamberlain. After Chamberlain's resignation, Colville decided to stay on at the Private Office and work for Churchill. Thus an enduring friendship was born. Lady Jane Williams (one of Churchill's secretaries and Rab Butler's niece) remarked that Colville really became a part of Churchill's family as 'a surrogate son'.[2]

Perhaps remembered as the most imminent 'Churchillian', Colville was the Churchill's devoted Private Secretary, first as Assistant Private Secretary (1940–1941 and 1943–1945) and then as Joint Principal Private Secretary (1951–1955). He remained Churchill's loyal friend and confidant until Churchill's death in 1965. Churchill's daughter Mary Soames said that Colville was a 'close friend and witness of my father's private and public life from 1940 until his death in 1965, he is and will remain, among the most important sources of accurate information'.[3] This wealth of accurate information to which Lady Soames referred was Jock Colville's published diaries, *The Fringes of Power: Downing Street Diaries 1939–1955* (1985). These diaries, combined with a host of articles, editorials, and other books Colville wrote, provide an intimate view of the inner workings of Churchill's administration during the Second World War and, to a lesser degree, during Churchill's peacetime government (1951–1955). While his diaries during Churchill's last government were, by his own admission, 'spasmodic', he regularly recorded foreign journeys.[4] He also recorded his account of Churchill's last government in his essay in *Action this Day* (1968) and his own memoir *Footprints in Time* (1976).

However, these accounts are at times at odds with one another and with his diary, illustrating that while it remains and excellent source of information, his retrospective account is often biased, unbalanced and overly protective of Churchill. For instance, *Action this Day* was published as a reaction and defence against Lord Moran's book, *Churchill: The Struggle for Survival* (1966). Lord Norman Brook, the editor of *Action this Day*, wrote that he and the contributors of the book could not leave 'Moran's assessment as it stands. We believe that in some respects it is incorrect and in others incomplete and on both counts misleading'.[5] Unfortunately, this rebuke over corrects the narrative and errs too far the other way. 'Few notes of criticism were permitted to interlude on the traditional picture and in some cases this involved not just putting a favourable spin on events but departures from the strict truth'.[6] This certainly applied to Colville whom historian John Ramsden noted only 'devoted about eighty pages to the four years of Churchill's second premiership' in his published diaries, while he devoted over six hundred to the war years'. Had Colville more fully disclosed Churchill's later years, he would have almost certainly confirmed some of Moran's 'gloomier strictures on Churchill'.[7] Despite such irregularities, Colville's accounts and diary have been examined and re-examined by various historians looking to understand Churchill's war strategies, political tactics and all-around thinking on numerous topics.

For this reason, Colville's diary is considered something of a lens on Churchill, often forgetting that Colville was himself a player in the action and just not any player, but a very influential one. Lord Moran, Churchill's doctor and confidant, contemplated just how much influence Colville and other secretaries had on Churchill's policy decisions because:

the manner in which anything is presented to Winston before he has made up his mind — that is the crucial point — and the time chosen to bring it forward surely plays a part in shaping things. It would be easy, I think, to underrate the part they [Colville and other secretaries] have played in the shaping of events.[8]

Although political historian Anthony Seldon has pointed out that judging Colville and other secretaries' sway on Churchill's thinking is very difficult, because so many of their exchanges are unrecorded and Colville never imposed his judgements on affairs of state,[9] Anthony Montague Brown, Churchill's last PS, said that it was possible for 'the private Office to express its opinion, if clear and concise'.[10]

In any case, the role of Private Secretary has often been overlooked by historians and political scientists, largely because of its mercurial nature and oscillating functions between the political and the administrative, but which holds remarkable influence due to its proximity with the Prime Minister. Describing the multifaceted role of a PS, G.W. Jones, explained that they 'work behind the scenes; they are entrusted with secrets; they are confidential advisers; they are the depository of [the PM's] records; they write and speak on his behalf and transact business for him'.[11]

In no instance was this truer than in the case of Colville and Churchill, especially during Churchill's peacetime government. This had owed, partly, to the complexities of foreign affairs in the post-war world and partly to the nature of Churchill and Colville's relationship. The Cold War, advances in nuclear weaponry, decolonisation, balancing the 'special relationship' with the United States and Britain's place in Europe had all increased the pressure on Churchill's government. This was further complicated by Churchill and Eden's deteriorating relationship which often put the Prime Minister (and by extension, the Private Office) at odds with the Foreign Office. But in addition to the typical duties of the PS, new problems in foreign affairs, and the infighting with the administration, Colville had to manage the decline of a giant who refused to admit that his faculties were waning.

Churchill's Private Office

Though Churchill was past his prime when he entered the premiership in October 1951, he was still a considerable force. For instance, as soon as Churchill had entered Number 10, he immediately sought to change the staff that he inherited from Attlee.[12] According to Colville, when Churchill first returned to Downing Street in 1951, 'he flung open the door connecting the Cabinet Room to the Private Secretaries' Offices ... He gazed at them, closed the door without saying a word, shook his head and proclaimed to Norman Brook: "Drenched in socialism."'[13] One of those secretaries he inherited was David Pitblado who worked as Attlee's PS and stayed on in the Private Office after power had changed to the Conservatives.

By all accounts David Pitblado was a 'highly competent and highly contentious Civil Servant' but Churchill was not particularly interested in having him serve as PS,[14] in part because of his association with the Attlee Government but also because Churchill increasingly disliked learning new faces as he grew older and his temperament hardened.[15] Pitblado was 'not personally known to Churchill and was not on the same wave length'.[16] Initially, Churchill tried to install his old Principal PS Leslie Rowan but Edward Bridges, the Permanent Secretary to the Treasury and Head of the Civil Service, would not allow it because Rowan had just been made Head of the Overseas Finance Division at the Treasury, thus giving him too senior a position to be moved to PS.[17] Churchill then came to the idea of appointing Colville which would reunite him with his old friend. Churchill did not pay heed to those who murmured about nepotism or Colville being 'too young' to be appointed as Principal Private Secretary. Though David Hunt, another secretary in the Private Office, argued that Churchill was 'deeply attached to the British tradition of a politically impartial Civil Service', Churchill was happy to disregard any such notions and insisted that he should have Colville.[18]

But Colville was fearful that dismissing a 'highly qualified incumbent' for a 'largely unqualified one' would insult Pitblado and send the wrong kind of message. So he instinctively declined Churchill's first offer.[19] But Churchill characteristically refused, bellowing out, 'Rubbish!' This instantly dismissed Colville's trepidations, on the grounds that while, 'Pitblado was doubtless an excellent man', Churchill wanted someone he knew.[20]

In 1951, Colville was the obvious choice. Churchill had already become acquainted with Colville when he served as an Assistant Private Secretary during the Second World War. But perhaps more importantly Colville knew Churchill and understood that to remain in his employ meant long hours, sleepless nights, intense pressure and little or no private life. Colville had learned this lesson in 1940. On the very first day he worked for Churchill, Colville was permitted to leave at 1 a.m. Perhaps Churchill feared that this lesson might prove more difficult for those like Pitblado who were unfamiliar with his irregular work methods. This was undoubtedly true, as Pitblado seemed to find working at Chartwell rather distracting, with Churchill's tropical fish 'pebbling away' and his 'smelly dog Rufus around'.[21]

Furthermore, Colville noted that Churchill had kept his habit of unusual methods and long hours but that 'he was slower, less impetuous, much less irascible and much more inclined to delegate'.[22] Demonstrating he could still be impetuous when it suited his ends and making the notion he had a deep attachment to an impartial Civil Service seem farcical, Churchill divided the role of PPS, much to the dismay of Edward Bridges and others in the in the civil service. This 'exceptional arrangement' was something which had never been done before and has never been done since.[23]

Colville's diaries offer the official story, that while the creation of a joint PS 'should have been a recipe of ill-will and mismanagement' that actually the joint office 'worked well'.[24] David Hunt equally reported that 'it was a solution that satisfied every need'.[25] However, Anthony Montague Browne, another of Churchill's secretaries, recorded that though the agreement 'sounded all right ... it didn't work very well, in spite of the civilized manners of both those involved'.[26]

Though he was reluctant, Pitblado acquiesced in the 'rather odd arrangement' of 'running in double harness' because he believed, like Eden and many others, that Churchill would stand down in a short time. Unable or unwilling to recognise that Churchill had other plans, Pitblado thought the situation was 'not a good arrangement to go on forever' and supposed Churchill's alteration of the Private Office was little more than a stop-gap measure. Pitblado reflected later that Churchill 'really did not need a PPS in the way that Prime Ministers often have in the past'. That is to say Pitblado believed Churchill did not need a 'confidant' and that while he was 'happy to talk' to Cabinet ministers 'on downward', that there were very few people indeed Churchill would listen to.[27]

Undoubtedly, one of Churchill's confidants was Colville with whom Churchill spent the majority of his time. This owed partly to Churchill's and Colville's friendship, but was also the result of Colville's background in foreign affairs and defence, the primary issues on Churchill's agenda. Pitblado's background was in the Treasury and subsequently he was given a portfolio for home affairs and economics. These concerns were, comparatively, of little interest to Churchill, who primarily left the day-to-day running of the government to his ministers. As Montague Browne noted, 'Thus Pitblado was relegated to a less exciting, less intimate and indeed less significant role than was desirable and his due'.[28] Colville even confessed that Churchill's favouritism made him slightly uncomfortable:

> The position as far as I am concerned is getting a little difficult: W. Complains he sees very little of me, but I can't push myself more to the front without hurting my colleagues' feelings. But W. Says he has nothing in common with any of them ... and won't have them to Chartwell if he can avoid it.[29]

Ironically, the joint arrangement gave Pitblado freer range and more authority over policy than Colville. This was the general rule unless, as Pitblado said, there was something Churchill was 'brooding about, in which case one would ... assist in his brooding, not advise him, but listen to his brooding'. Pitblado knew that Churchill was going to spend most of his time 'thinking about defence and Foreign Affairs'. As a result, the Churchill's peacetime government became a 'Cabinet Government' which Pitblado explained was 'a Government in which ministers did their own responsibilities and only brought matters to Cabinet which *needed* to go to Cabinet'.[30] As Seldon put it, 'as Churchill was absorbed increasingly in foreign affairs, those close to him to him were able to bring more influence to bear on domestic policy matters'.[31]

This was further compounded by the fact other Private Secretaries who were responsible for home affairs and Parliamentary questions, E.G. Gass (who left in

1952) and P.G. Oats (who left in 1954), were also civil servants like Pitblado and were unknown to Churchill. Thus, like Pitblado, they remained outside Churchill's inner circle and remained relatively unsupervised. Despite this, Pitblado praised them and their work with R. A. Butler, the Home Secretary, who helped accomplish their goals with 'the normal number of banana peels a Home Secretary has'.[32] Additionally, Churchill's peacetime government was 'short on political input' as Churchill did not formally appoint a Parliamentary Private Secretary until February 1953.[33] This imbalance was relatively redressed when in 1953 Churchill appointed his son-in-law Christopher Soames to the role, despite the familiar, re-occurring charges of nepotism.

Close to Churchill and ever under his watchful eye, Colville had none of freedom Pitblado had. However, he did have access to ministers as Churchill's emissary and was often approached by ministers who wished to know Churchill's mind. This was especially true regarding foreign policy, as many knew that Colville had worked in the Foreign Office before moving to Number 10 and because he was considered 'exceptionally able' with 'vast knowledge of foreign affairs'.[34] While Colville's proximity to the PM kept him near the power centre, other civil servants felt that Colville had 'become overtly identified with the Prime Minster personally' and that was he was 'spoiled as a civil servant'.[35] This helps explain, to some degree, why Colville resigned his position in 1955 when Churchill retired. Regardless of inter-office jealousies, Churchill's blatant preference for Colville and Pitblado's increased marginalisation, this remained the set-up of Churchill's Private Office during his peacetime government.

The special relationship

Churchill's primary concern for his last government was foreign affairs and he thought none more important than the Anglo-American relationship. Colville recorded that one of the major priorities for Churchill's second administration was 'to concentrate on the partnership with the USA'.[36] Churchill immediately and publicly advertised that the American Ambassador in London had direct access to Number 10, allowing the Americans to bypass the Foreign Office, much to the chagrin of Anthony Eden. Even Colville was slightly dismayed by this arrangement since the American Ambassador had this privilege 'alone of other foreign representatives'.[37] Churchill clearly wanted to replicate his wartime approach to the American alliance, resetting Labour's approach to the special relationship.

Attlee's Labour Government, under the direction of Ernest Bevin, had itself 'maintained close links' with the Truman administration. But there were still issues with Churchill suspicious of Labour's commitment to the alliance and which might cause a rift between the powers.[38] Churchill knew that Bevin and Attlee were far more pragmatic about the 'special relationship', and that they saw it as a means to 'prop up Britain's crumbling position in the Middle East in the face of Russian encroachment'.[39] Undoubtedly Churchill understood Britain's declining role in world affairs and saw the Anglo-American alliance as a means to mitigate the effects of the power shift towards the United States.

But the harsh reality of the post-war world was not lost on Churchill's closest advisers Rab Butler and Colville. Butler argued in October 1952 that, 'We were all agreed when we took office that the defence programme which we inherited was beyond the nation's means. It was based on assumptions about American aid and the strength of our economy which have since been proved false'.[40] Colville echoed this in his diary entry for 13 June 1952: 'It is foolish to continue living with illusions. One may bury one's head in the past … but the facts are stark. At the moment we are just paying our way'.[41]

Churchill's understanding of Anglo-American relations was far more ideological. Churchill actually believed his rhetoric of 'Anglo-Saxonism' and saw the alliance as an end in itself. Colville recorded that Churchill and his scientific adviser Lord Cherwell believed in the possibility of common citizenship with the United States, and that through this means Britain might even come to dominate the United States.[42] Beyond an ideological motive, other questions over tariffs, nuclear weapons, international security, and the Korean War all led Churchill to believe 'that Anglo-American relations were still not intimate enough for his satisfaction'.[43] So Churchill arranged to visit the USA as quickly as he could once he re-entered the office of PM.

The first journey to the US Churchill embarked upon during his second premiership was in early January 1952 aboard the *Queen Mary*, to see the Truman administration. Naturally, Colville joined Churchill on his trips to the US. Churchill greatly enjoyed having Colville along for such trips, despite Colville's repeated attempts to actually get Churchill do some work while he was away. Colville complained that he 'found it difficult to persuade Churchill to read the array of briefs and memoranda' which Colville had 'laboriously prepared'. Churchill defended his lackadaisical attitude, telling Colville that, 'he was there to re-establish relations, not transact business'.[44] Perhaps as a light-hearted revenge, Colville recorded that the PM had become 'often quite lazy'.[45]

Colville's account of the first trip to the US in his memoir recorded that the meeting was 'a success' because 'military matters relating to NATO and the Korean War were fruitfully discussed' and 'Churchill won a long, loud and standing ovation' from Congress.[46] To some degree this was undoubtedly true. By August 1952, Churchill had convinced Truman to write a joint letter with him addressed to Mohammad Mosaddegh, the Prime Minister of Iran. As Colville noted in his diary, it greatly pleased Churchill because it was 'the first time since 1945 that the Americans have joined up with us in taking overt action against a third power'.[47]

Despite these gestures, the reality of the Anglo-American relationship was rather different. While Truman undoubtedly had a personal affection for Churchill, his administration remained 'cool and detached' during policy discussions.[48] Truman's Secretary of State, Dean Acheson, recorded in his memoirs that while Truman wanted 'Churchill to go home in a good mood', in matters of policy Truman and he wanted to bring Eden and the Foreign Office in to line with American thinking.[49] This led to very serious tension between Acheson and Eden, that became so obvious that in April 1952 *Newsweek* ran an article entitled 'A Clash of Personalities: Eden vs Acheson'.[50]

Aware of the reality of the situation, Colville noted in his article in *Action this Day* the futility of Churchill's dream of perfect Anglo-American relations, recording that though the meetings were friendly they 'fell short of the almost miraculous recreation of the earlier connexion for which [Churchill] was hoping'.[51] He even recognised that Acheson and other officials met Churchill's party with reserve, if not suspicion, because they wanted to insulate Truman from Churchill's persuasive and overt calls for Anglo-American camaraderie.[52] Colville was little help on this front, probably because he was slightly contemptuous of his American hosts. He recorded that he found President Truman to be 'affable but not impressive' and Acheson to be nothing 'out of the way'.[53]

Colville's feelings toward his hosts had not improved by their second visit to Washington in January 1953. Churchill wanted to say goodbye to Truman, and to try to rekindle his wartime relationship with the incoming President, Eisenhower. Colville reflected that Truman had been a political 'novice' and had President Roosevelt lived he 'would have checked American policy' towards the Soviets.[54]

Eisenhower's election did nothing to improve Colville's impressions. Both Churchill and Colville seemed to have a distrust of Republicans, despite Churchill and Eisenhower's war connections and Eisenhower's pledge that if here were elected 'he would pay just one visit outside the United States and that would be to the United Kingdom' to bolster the special relationship.[55] When Churchill referred to Eisenhower as 'a real man of limited stature'; Colville, retorted that 'he thought that 'just about sums up the new president'.[56] Colville's suspicions of the Eisenhower administration led him to be increasingly guarded around officials who were associated with Eisenhower. On 8 January, after a major goodbye Gala for Truman, Colville thought Churchill's remarks about Israel, the European Defence Community and Egypt were rather remiss in the presence of officials at the White House who would be staying on with Eisenhower.[57]

Colville's distrust of Eisenhower and the Republican Party undoubtedly had an effect on Churchill, causing him to adopt the same approach, though less diplomatically. At the afternoon meetings on 7 January, Churchill thought the exchanges with Eisenhower were going well. Colville recorded that Churchill said he had got the better of Eisenhower because 'Ike seemed to defer to his greater age and experience'.[58] However, as Churchill began to become aware of the fact Eisenhower's colleagues had little intention of taking his positions seriously, Churchill became frustrated by the situation. Later that night Churchill and John Foster Dulles, Eisenhower's Secretary of State, became engaged in a serious row over dinner regarding Churchill's influence on economic talks. Afterwards, Colville diplomatically explained to the Dulles and Governor Thomas Dewey that a 'sharp debate was the PM's idea of a pleasant evening'.[59] After the others left, Colville recorded that Churchill said 'some harsh things about the Republican Party and Dulles in particular' which Colville believed was 'unjust and dangerous'.[60]

The Republicans felt similarly suspicious and contemptuous of Churchill and his party. Eisenhower, like Truman, wanted Churchill to remember the good old days but did not actually feel that his input was very useful in policy-making. Eisenhower's estimation of Churchill's abilities had already dropped from the war years. In December 1951, Eisenhower recorded in his diary that thought that Churchill was incapable of 'think[ing] in terms of today' and that he 'no longer absorbs new ideas'.[61] By 1953, Eisenhower's thinking became less forgiving of Churchill. He recorded in his diary that he wished Churchill would turn over leadership to 'younger men' because he has 'developed an almost childlike faith that all of the answers are to be found merely in British-American partnership'.[62]

In this reticent environment, Colville acted as an emissary between Eisenhower who did not want to offend his old friend and Churchill, who continually pushed for stronger links with America. For instance, after delivering a message to Eisenhower at the Commodore Hotel for Churchill, Eisenhower kept Colville engaged in conversation for some time about the dangers of the appearance of collusion between the United States and Britain. He explained to Colville that he was 'in favour of it clandestinely, but not overtly, since it was important for the Unites States not to offend other nations'.[63] Colville, of course, reported this back to Churchill, who was increasingly discouraged with the Eisenhower administration's stance on the special relationship.

However, in some small way Colville's diplomacy both with Dulles and Dewey and then again relaying messages between Eisenhower and Churchill almost certainly had a positive effect on Anglo-American relations at the highest possible level. In fact, overtime a softening of 'Eisenhower's original rigid conception of the special relationship could be detected'.[64] Moreover, Colville certainly contributed to Churchill's powerful relationship with the US public. On the trip over to the US, Colville helped Churchill prepare for possible press questions. Colville asked around 30 questions and Churchill's job was to perfect and rehearse his responses, each more charming and erudite than the last. Colville recorded that one of his favourite remarks was a response to a question regarding the justification of 'such great expenditure' for the Queen's coronation during especially austere times. Churchill's witty (if not practised reply) was 'Everybody likes to wear a flower when he goes to see his girl'.[65] The American press and public found Churchill as appealing as ever.

The Cold War

One of the major features of Churchill's peacetime government was his desire to facilitate an end to the hostilities between the US and the USSR. The first hints of this plan came in November 1951 when Churchill sent Stalin a message of 'greetings'[66] and explained to the House of Commons that he and the heads of the states or governments should 'still hold to the idea of a supreme effort to bridge the gulf between the two worlds, so that each can life its life, if not in friendship, at least without fear, the hatreds and frightful wastes of the cold war'.[67] But the Truman administration spurned the idea. However, the goal manifested itself again for Churchill once Eisenhower was elected President in 1952. Churchill believed he would be able to bring the 'big three' to the conference table and 'preside over the ending of the Cold War'.[68] However, Churchill found the Eisenhower administration (not to mention the Foreign Office) considerably hesitant on the notion of a summit meeting. This was further complicated by the fact that when the possibility of a summit was mentioned by Eisenhower, nothing was mentioned about British involvement.[69]

But with the death of Stalin in March 1953, Churchill once again saw a chance to focus on his final ambition. He confessed to Lord Moran that he felt that 'Stalin's death may lead to a relaxation of tension'.[70] Though Colville believed Churchill was suffering from 'a degree of wishful thinking', Churchill thought Malenkov would be open of the notion of a summit meeting.[71] Colville noted that this marked a turning point for Churchill who was 'increasingly absorbed' by his mission to end the Cold War.[72] To that end, Colville helped Churchill draft a speech on foreign affairs, in which Churchill argued that the new, post-Stalin government of the Soviet Union had made a 'series of amicable gestures' and that these should be met with an open mind by those in the West. Illustrating his faith in high-power summits, Churchill continued that a conference 'should not be overhung by a ponderous or rigid agenda, or led into mazes and jungles of technical details, zealously contested by hoards of experts and officials drawn up in vast, cumbrous array'. Further underlining his devotion to the power of summits to change the political landscape Churchill pointed out, 'It might well be that no hard-faced agreements would be reached, but there might be a general feeling among those gathered together that they might do something better than tear the human race, including themselves, into bits'.[73] Despite Colville's acknowledgement that Churchill's plan was at best hopeful, he undoubtedly supported Churchill's plan, owing to his background in diplomacy and foreign policy.

Following the speech, Churchill made plans to go to Bermuda to discuss such a meeting with Eisenhower, but Churchill suffered a stroke on 23 June 1953 and as a result the Bermuda conference was cancelled. As Churchill convalesced, Lord Salisbury visited the United States and reported back to Colville and Churchill that he found Eisenhower to be 'violent in his hostility to Russia'.[74] Though Churchill found this 'distressing', he continually pushed for a meeting with Eisenhower.

The initial idea was to meet with the Eisenhower administration at the Azores but Eisenhower refused, knowing that if Churchill came he would demand a summit with the Russians. This refusal pleased Eden and Foreign Office, which, perhaps ironically, aligned more closely with the US State Department on this issue than with Churchill. Colville noted that Dulles and Eden were probably more reasonable in arguing that the recent shift in Russian attitude, with their 'amiable gestures', owed more to 'constant pressure and increased strength displayed by the Western powers' than Stalin's death.[75]

18 *Warren Dockter*

Churchill wanted to relentlessly pursue the US for a conference. However, demonstrating the power of his position (and negating his claims of an inability to influence Churchill), Colville convinced Churchill to let the matter rest a while. Colville asked Churchill what he planned on saying when he arrived at the proposed meeting. Colville then recorded that:

> It suddenly dawned on [Churchill] that everything he might say to the President would necessarily be met with a negative response and that on other topics such as Egypt ... he would have nothing to offer but criticisms and complaints of the US attitude. To bring the US president 1,000 miles for that seemed unfair and discourteous.[76]

Colville's cooler judgement prevailed.

But Churchill did not have to wait that long for his conference with the President. He and Colville left for Bermuda on 1 December 1953. Once the President arrived, Churchill whisked him away from Dulles and from Eden, so the two could engage in private talks, much to the 'indignation of Anthony Eden and John Foster Dulles neither of whom trusted their Chiefs alone together'.[77] While Churchill was able to 'get a good deal out of Ike' he still found that he recoiled at the thought of a meeting with the Soviets.[78] Colville recorded Eisenhower's statement, that 'Russia was a woman of the streets and whether her dress was new or the old one patched, it was still the same whore'. Eisenhower's colourful language did not dissuade Colville's already unimpressed view of the President. Colville recorded that he thought no such language had ever before been heard at an international conference.[79]

Colville once again took up the task of acting as a messenger between Churchill and Eisenhower. On the 6 December, Colville returned a draft of Eisenhower's speech which Churchill had reviewed and found 'two spilt infinitives and a double past-participle.[80] Colville was sent to help Eisenhower with corrections and found him sitting in a chair going through a speech but noted that he 'never smiled' which marked a change from the Ike of 'war days or even, indeed of last January'. It was in this setting that Eisenhower shared his thoughts with Colville, a remarkable act demonstrating the power of proximity, which is an intrinsic part of the role of the PS. The first thing which Colville thought was noteworthy was that President Eisenhower saw atomic weapons as conventional weapons, which is to say just the latest improvement in military weapons. This shocked Colville, who noted that this represented a fundamental difference of public opinion between US and UK and that was a juxtaposition of what Churchill believed.[81] But Colville believed it was not his place to argue such a 'delicate subject' with the President and returned to discussing the split infinitives.[82]

However, Colville was all too happy to discuss colonialism with the President, even lecturing him about India. After noting Churchill's comments and gathering his own on Eisenhower's draft speech, Colville mentioned to Eisenhower that his reference to 'the obsolete Colonial mould' would offend. Upon Eisenhower's dismissal of this, Colville angrily retorted that 'a lot of people in England thought India had been better governed by the viceroy and the British Government than at present'. Eisenhower demurred, arguing that he agreed with that notion but that to Americans, 'liberty was more precious than good government'.[83] Colville of course reported this to Churchill who later met with Eisenhower and convinced him to remove the phrase which had so upset Colville. This was perhaps the only time in history a British civil servant literally changed the President of the United States' speech.

The conference, however, was not a successful one and with the exceptions of the Berlin conference (February 1954) and the Geneva conference (April 1954), both of which were diplomatic negotiations based around settling problems in Indo-China, little had been done to bridge the gulf between the US and the USSR, at least from Churchill's perspective. In fact, the Geneva Conference was something of a bridge, as Anthony Eden co-chaired the conference with the Soviet Union's Vyacheslav Molotov, who was promoted to Minister of Foreign Affairs in early 1953. Yet Churchill became increasingly restless. According to Lord Moran, Churchill seemed disinterested in Eden's account of the Geneva Conference.[84] This was because Churchill believed that only a personal summit between himself, Eisenhower and Soviet Premier Georgi Malenkov would facilitate the peace process. This became 'an article of faith' for Churchill and was an idea which had 'taken possession of his mind'.[85] Luckily for Churchill, Christopher Soames had been approached by Jacob Malik, the recently appointed Soviet Ambassador for Britain, in the hopes that the Kremlin would be able to meet the Prime Minister. As a result, secret talks between Churchill's 'private envoys' John Colville and Christopher Soames and the Soviets took place at the Soviet Embassy in London.[86] Eventually, through the secret work of Colville, Soames and Malik it became apparent that 'Malenkov would welcome a meeting with the Prime Minster'.[87] In Churchill's government, Colville's remit as PS had grown to include secret diplomat.

Churchill, of course, welcomed the news and arranged a state visit to feel out Eisenhower's position on the notion in late June 1954. Nearly everyone but Churchill thought little would come from the visit.[88] Much to Colville's surprise Eisenhower immediately agreed to talks with the Soviets which Colville said Churchill hoped to achieve after only 'long talks'. Colville was further surprised that talks on 'Indo-China, Europe, and atoms' were 'immediately satisfactory and while the world in general believes that there is at this moment greater Anglo-American friction than ever in history'.[89] Eisenhower's initial enthusiasm for talks with the Soviets was supported by his planning to attend such a conference in the first day and then leaving only to return for the last five days.[90]

However, on the next day Colville was worried that the Churchill's peace project might be thwarted by Dulles who had constantly been 'getting at the president' and he also noted that increasingly Eden supported Dulles at dinner conversations.[91] Of course Eisenhower's initial enthusiasm might be explained by the fact that he knew Churchill would pursue talks anyway so he might help manage Churchill during the talks. As the visit went on it became apparent that Eisenhower, most likely influenced by Dulles, was still hesitant to have a summit with the Russians, though Churchill had still won his tacit approval for bilateral talks with Malenkov.[92] That was enough for Churchill. He was pleased with the state of Anglo-American relations and, equipped with Eisenhower's approval, Churchill grew more and more impatient for a summit, making Colville's job of managing Churchill more and more difficult.

Churchill and Eden

The journey home after the Washington conference revealed another major aspect of Colville's position: his role as a mediator between Winston Churchill and his heir apparent, Anthony Eden. Tension had been building between the two for some time. Since the beginning of Churchill's last government, Churchill often followed his own foreign policy initiatives and rarely consulted with the Foreign Office resulting in the 'two men acting as Foreign Secretary at the same time'.[93] This was especially true of Middle Eastern Policy. On questions of Sudanese independence, Persian oil rights, and the Suez base in Egypt, their opinions differed radically. Eden was so steadfast in his support for Sudanese independence he threatened to resign unless Churchill supported him.[94] Churchill was far more fearful than Eden that in the event of withdrawal from Suez: the Soviets would take advantage of the situation. By 1953, this tension became a major sticking point for both men and even led Anthony Montague Brown to later confide to Anthony Seldon that Churchill and Eden's relationship was 'never quite the same after the Government began to consider seriously the Suez Agreement'.[95]

To compound these disagreements, Eden was plagued by ill health – especially in 1953, when he was debilitated by a botched gall bladder operation – which perhaps 'coloured his judgement'.[96] This was undoubtedly true. Eden was regularly prescribed Benzedrine, an amphetamine and Drinamyl, a dangerous mixture of amphetamines and barbiturates.[97] Both drugs had terrible side-effects including impaired judgement, violent mood swings, and (in the case of Drinamyl) paranoia.[98] Increasingly, after 1953 Churchill doubted Eden's judgement and confided to Colville that he believed Eden was 'sometimes very foolish' arguing with the Americans over 'petty issues' rather than seeing the larger picture.[99] This, combined with the heavy workload Eden required of his overworked staff, made Eden fairly unpopular, even amongst his own Foreign Office colleagues, a fact of which Colville was made aware after he filed a complaint regarding a diplomatic bag which was sent to the wrong embassy. After filing the complaint, Colville received a 'virulent, five page' handwritten letter from a member of Eden's staff. Though Colville destroyed the letter, it made it very apparent that Eden was putting 'great strain' on his people.[100] This notion was also echoed by Churchill's literary assistant, Denis Kelly, who had been offered the opportunity to assist Eden with memoirs. Kelly recorded that Eden was 'smitten by ill health and disappointment and tormented by the failure at Suez. I found him beyond my power to serve and to help and after three months I, too, resigned'.[101]

But the real animosity between Churchill and Eden was not between their staff or differing views foreign policy; it lay in the latter's ambition to be Prime Minister. According to the historian, Anthony Adamthwaite, 'The old monarch's procrastination drove the heir apparent demented'.[102] Churchill had originally promised Eden that he would only hold office for a year. This stretched into two, then three years, all the while making the nervy Eden all the more anxious to assume the premiership. Even Colville thought that Churchill was being unfair with Eden on this count. He noted that while Churchill promised to step aside for Eden after the coronation of Elizabeth II, 'he never had any intention of doing so'.[103] Churchill, who was clearly aware of Eden's intent, often referred to Eden's 'hungry eyes' and as the government entered its last year, Churchill 'began to form a cold hatred of Eden'.[104]

Fully aware of this increasing rift, Colville was caught in the middle. He recorded that Eden's only real intention in going back with Churchill by sea aboard the *Queen Elizabeth* was to talk over a firm date with Churchill on the handover. However, Eden was unsure how to broach the subject and sought Colville's counsel. Colville noted that he thought Eden was 'boxing boastful' and he told Eden he thought it was a shame that 'two men who knew each other so well should be hampered by shyness'.[105] It is remarkable that Eden confided in Colville. Of course Eden may have been planting the information as a way for Colville to raise the subject for him. Either way, Eden got a tentative date out of Churchill: the 21st of September. However, Eden's reprieve from worry was short-lived.

Churchill had dictated to Colville a long telegram to Molotov, proposing talks with the Soviets 'in which the Americans would ... participate'.[106] By the afternoon, Churchill sent Colville to Eden with a draft of the telegram. Eden explained to Colville that 'he disliked the whole thing anyway' and that he had been weighing the pros and cons. Eden believed that such an action would create a 'serious Anglo-American rift', throw Western Europe out of balance, and destroy the united front which had 'built up against Russia'. But what angered him most was Churchill's intention of 'dispatching the telegram without showing it to the Cabinet'. Eden instructed Colville to deliver a message to his master, 'that if he insisted, he could do as he wished but ... but it would be against [Eden's] strong advice'.[107]

Acting as the bridge between the Prime Minister and his Foreign Secretary Colville did as he was bid. Churchill dismissed Eden's concerns as 'nonsense'. Colville tried to explain that this all put 'the Cabinet on the spot' because they would not have time to form a contrary opinion. Churchill became blustery and defiant. He said if the Cabinet would not back his play, that would 'give him a good occasion to go to' Russia. Colville further tried to talk Churchill down, insisting that would create a division in the country and the Conservative Party, 'from top to bottom'.[108] Ultimately, Eden agreed to the compromise of sending the telegram to the Cabinet but with his endorsement, which Colville noted put Eden 'on the spot' because he did not agree with the telegram. In this matter, even Colville felt that Churchill had been 'ruthless and unscrupulous in all this' and Colville acknowledged there was tremendous pressure on Eden who had confessed to Colville that 'he had considered resigning'.[109]

Eden and Colville had been correct. Once news had reached the Cabinet of Churchill's intention of sending a telegram, the Cabinet broke out in indignation. Lord Salisbury and Harry Crookshank immediately threatened to resign, while Lord Swinton declared this is the 'end of the voyage' with Winston. Harold Macmillan went to see Lady Churchill and confess the Cabinet was on the verge of breaking up over the issue. Afterward, Clementine rang up Colville and 'begged' him to help bring up the issue at a luncheon with Churchill.[110] This was a fairly regular occurrence for Colville because he had become close 'friend and confidant' of Clementine.[111] They often shared a correspondence and saw each other socially for many years.

Churchill was obstinate and even snapped at Clementine (something Colville noted Churchill seldom did).[112] However, Colville and Clementine seemed to make Churchill understand the significance of the situation, whereas previously upon being informed of Lord Salisbury's intention to resign, Churchill simply said 'he didn't give a damn'.[113] Unsurprisingly, Colville was quick to excuse Churchill's behaviour in all this saying, 'The stakes in this matter are so high and as he sees it, the possible benefits so crucial to our survival that he was prepared to adopt any methods to get a meeting with the Russians arranged'.[114]

As it became increasingly obvious it was time for Churchill to resign, tension between him and Eden got worse. Colville chronicled the growth of Churchill's 'cold hatred' for Eden and his repeated attempts to delay his resignation of the premiership. Churchill continually charged that 'he saw no reason why he should go' and Eden's furious retorts. Colville intervened as an intermediary on at least two occasions. The first was after Churchill received a telegram in March 1955, which suggested the Americans might go to Paris on the tenth anniversary of VE Day to ratify the London–Paris agreements. Churchill suspected this meant there might be a meeting with the Russians so he would 'stay on and with Eisenhower, meet the Russians'. Colville tried to explain nothing had been said about meeting the Russians but Churchill 'brushed it aside' and adressed Eden the next morning during the Cabinet meeting. Colville went with Norman Brook to personally warn Eden to stick solely with 'merits of the American proposal'. But Eden could not be stayed and asked about his succession near the end of meeting. Colville noted Churchill's livid response, that 'this was not a matter on which he required guidance or on which Cabinet discussion was usual', which elicited shock and embarrassment form his colleagues.[115]

The second time Colville tried to intervene was after the French government spoke favourably of four-power talks. For Churchill, this, combined with the forthcoming budget, date of the general election and two serious strikes, meant that 'he could not possibly go at such a moment just to satisfy Anthony's personal hunger for power'. Colville came to Eden's defence by reminding Churchill he would have had to call a party meeting to decide such a thing and that would such an action would 'make an unhappy last chapter to his biography if it told how he had destroyed the party of which he was the leader'.[116] Colville convinced himself that this was little more than a 'late night fantasy, a rather pathetic indication' of Churchill's grief at leaving office. But when Churchill woke the next morning he was still determined not to leave. Once again, Colville used the back channel of Eden's Principal Private Sectary, Anthony Humbold, to warn that 'Amiability must be the watch word'.[117] This apparently made its way to Eden. After meeting the Queen on the 30 April 1955, Churchill met with Rab Butler and Eden to say he was going to resign. Churchill confessed to Colville that he had been altered by Anthony's amiable manner'. Colville was pleased his advice was the right path for Eden and that the outcome was 'in the best interest of all'.[118] Churchill, of course, remained unconvinced and confessed to Colville that he didn't believe Eden was up to the task. Later, even Christopher Soames pointed out that Churchill said that 'only as a justification of his own delayed exit'.[119]

Relations had become so bad that, just before Churchill's resignation, Colville was forced to work his diplomatic magic in the Churchill family between Clarissa Churchill (Eden's wife and Winston's niece) and Randolph Churchill, Winston's son. This was particularly difficult for Colville because, while he liked and was impressed by Clarissa, he was never 'an admirer of Eden's' and he was not fond of Randolph.[120] He once remarked to Churchill's grandson, Winston, that he was not 'exactly a fan' of Randolph 'particularly in regard to his treatment to his father from 1940 onwards' and was quick to point out Randolph's 'rudeness and complete lack of self control'.[121]

Randolph, who had a vendetta against Eden and refused to support his ascendancy to PM, approached Clarissa at a dinner and said that he would be 'against the new regime' and that he was planning to write an article in *Punch* which declared his distrust of Eden. The next day, she wrote to Randolph to rebuke his behaviour and then asked Colville to intervene on Eden's behalf (Colville was making preparations for the handover at the time). Colville complied and 'did his best to defuse the cousinly feud'. He wrote to Randolph warning him that his father had chosen Eden and supported him and that 'by attacking Anthony if that is what you intend, you will distress [Churchill] and embarrass him'.[122] This seemed to mollify Randolph into backing down and the article he published on Eden was far tamer than he had originally intended.

Despite Colville's role as the Churchill family therapist and his window into the slow, agonising split between Churchill and Eden, he also provided an intimate picture of their great friendship, even at this late stage in Churchill's second government. One evening, during the trip to the US in December 1953, Christopher Soames read Eisenhower's draft speech on atomic energy aloud. Colville sat in a chair, while Christopher read and paced back and forth in the Churchill's bedroom. Listening intently, Churchill and Eden were 'still fully dressed in their dinner jackets laying side by side flat on the P.M.'s bed'.[123] Clearly, the two men had been great friends.

Churchill's health

The state of Churchill's health remained a constant theme during his last government. Though Churchill had suffered a mild heart attack during the Second World War, while he was in Washington, his health really began to falter after he suffered a minor stroke in August 1949 while he was on holiday in Monte Carlo. Though he recovered fairly quickly, Churchill's doctor Lord Moran recorded:

> This is the beginning of trouble. He will not give in without a great struggle, but there can only be one end to it. How long it will last is only guesswork; he might hang on for some years yet, but this is certain: my task is just beginning.[124]

Lord Moran was happily surprised at Churchill's victory in the 1951 general election but remained unsure if Churchill was up to the task of premiership and increasingly noted his faltering health, particularly his deafness. Of course this did not bother Colville, who 'liked to argue that a good deal of [Churchill's] deafness was due to inattention'.[125] Colville, however, was concerned because he felt that Churchill was slowing down. He recorded that Churchill's periods of 'lowness' were increasing and his age was beginning to show.[126] It was during this low period that Churchill confessed to Colville that 'The zest had diminished' and by that November, Colville believed that Churchill found it difficult to 'compose a speech'.[127] Increasingly, he and Anthony Montague Brown wrote larger parts of Churchill's speeches, which he would approve and then convert to his own prose.[128] Likewise, Denis Kelly, Churchill's post-war literary assistant, later recorded that after Churchill's stroke in 1949, he almost never wrote an 'original composition' on his histories.[129]

The slow decline of old age certainly took its toll on Churchill during his second government but it was perhaps made more pronounced by Churchill's increasingly frequent bouts of depression. Though he could have been more clear on this point, Lord Moran believed the 'black dog' affected Churchill's ability and clouded his judgement.[130] Colville's diaries also record Churchill's depressions even before his major stroke in 1953.[131]

Despite this, Colville later argued later that Churchill did not suffer from depression. In his article, in *Action This Day*, Colville took the position that while Churchill (like most people) got down at times, he did not suffer from prolonged melancholia.[132] Colville (along with Lady Churchill) seemed to believe that 'the black dog' was little more than a Victorian expression which Winston learned from Lady Everest as a child.[133] While this may have been a component of Churchill's understanding of his own depression, the overwhelming evidence, including stories from his contemporaries (and his own children) indicate that Churchill did indeed suffer from some form of depression.[134] It may have been a less dominant characteristic than his 'exceptional resilience', but it was always there in the background.[135] In any case, Colville was too close to Churchill to be impartial in this matter, which goes some way in explaining his constant efforts to call into question Moran's published diaries as a historical source. It seems that it was too painful a truth for Colville to admit that Churchill was, at times, a deeply melancholic figure.

Churchill's physical and mental health remained a constant background concern, until the evening of 21 February 1952. Churchill became convinced he might have had another stroke because he 'couldn't think of the words' he wanted to use in a phone call. After checking him over, Lord Moran was concerned that Churchill had experienced a small arterial spasm in which 'circulation to the speech centre was diminished'.[136] This clearly wasn't life-threatening but Moran saw it as a sign of stress.

The next day Moran went to Colville to see if Churchill's workload could be lightened. Colville's diary briefly covers this meeting with Moran and subsequent meeting with Lord Salisbury, saying that Lord Salisbury thought 'W[inston] might go to the Lords, leaving Eden to manage the Commons and thus remain P.M. till after the Coronation in May 1953'. Colville then says such an unorthodox arrangement would 'nowadays be impractical' but quickly sidesteps this idea by noting that 'Winston is not an ordinary person, the country as a whole would not like to see him go'.[137]

However, Moran's account is far more detailed and illustrates the struggle of managing Churchill behind the scenes. According to Moran, after saying his piece about taking work from Churchill, Lord Salisbury simply said, 'A Prime Minster cannot shed his responsibilities'. Colville immediately scrambled to find small ways to lift Churchill's burden, suggesting the budget proposals could be 'simplified and summarized' and that the honours and ecclesiastical preferment might be taken on by Salisbury.

Salisbury remained reticent. Revealing his frustration with Churchill, Colville exclaimed that he hated to be 'disloyal, but the PM is not doing his work'.[138] Then the three men, including Colville, hatched a scheme to send Churchill to the Lords but Colville feared Churchill would never acquiesce in such a request having suggested it on a previous occasion. They agreed that the only person who could convince him to go to the Lords was the Queen. So Colville and Moran approached Tommy Lascelles, the Private Secretary to the Queen. He agreed the Prime Minister should resign or go to the Lords, but that he could not ask the Queen to request such a thing and if she did Churchill 'would say charmingly: "It's very good of you, Ma'am, to think of it –" and then he would very politely brush it aside'.[139] So without a formal plan on how to get Churchill to either resign or act as a ceremonial PM in the Lords, the plan fizzled out, but only after Colville further pursued it on 23 February by suggesting that Anthony Head handle the defence speech. Churchill 'turned on him like a flash'.[140]

It is no surprise that Colville left the deeper scheming of this quiet coup out of his diaries, for it was unsuccessful. But it is remarkable that Colville was the one to push it the furthest. Colville clearly believed Churchill was under too much stress to continue as PM unaided. The only way Colville believed

Churchill could continue was for him to lighten his workload considerably or for his position to become completely ceremonial, all against Churchill's wishes. Colville's task of managing Churchill was becoming more and more difficult and his fears of a worst-case scenario were soon realised.

On 23 June 1953 Churchill suffered a massive stroke while hosting a dinner party for the Italian Prime Minister at 10 Downing Street. Luckily it happened near the end of the evening and any slurring of Churchill's speech was generally thought to be related to Churchill's drinking. As guests were leaving, Colville helped Churchill back to his bedroom. Ever determined to remain unencumbered, Churchill presided over the Cabinet the following day and, though Colville noticed the Churchill's 'slurred speech and his mouth drooping', others only seemed to notice he was more quiet than usual.[141]

However, Churchill's health quickly deteriorated and as Colville rode with him to Chartwell, Churchill gave him 'strict orders not to let it be known that he was temporarily incapacitated'.[142] If Colville's narrative is to be believed, it was in the capacity that he helped pull off something of a miracle for he was able to 'gag fleet street'. He wrote to eminent press barons Lord Beaverbrook, Brendan Bracken and Lord Camrose and explained the situation. They were all friends of the convalescing Prime Minister and quickly joined Colville at Chartwell where they 'paced the lawn in earnest conversation'.[143] They were discussing the nature of the health bulletin which needed to be issued, explaining why Churchill would not attend his imminent trip to Bermuda to meet President Eisenhower. Lord Moran and Dr Russell Brain, Churchill's specialist, drew up a memo which included the phrase 'disturbance in the cerebral circulation'. However Lord Camrose feared that such a phrase would indicate a stroke had happened and that 'there would be an immediate call for Churchill to resign'. So he redrafted the statement to be much more ambiguous saying that Churchill was 'in need of complete rest'.[144] According to Colville, together they were able to keep Churchill's incapacitation quiet and 'not a word of the Prime Minister's stroke was published until he himself casually mentioned it'.[145]

However, this was not strictly true. It is clear from the Cabinet minutes that R.A. Butler, who chaired the Cabinet during Churchill's absence, was aware. In the notes of the first Cabinet meeting after Churchill's stroke Butler explains that 'The P.M. is better and more cheerful today … He still finds difficulty with speech and movement'.[146] It is reasonable then to assume that the Cabinet at least knew something was seriously wrong with Churchill. Naturally, this would not have been made public but rumours of the stroke were published in the *Daily Mirror* which was controlled by Cecil King, no friend of Churchill's. Lord Hartwell, Lord Camrose's biographer, described Colville's memory as being 'at fault' and that his account was 'nonsense'.[147]

Beyond Churchill's health, a serious issue was the constitutional situation Churchill's stroke created. With Eden recovering from his surgery in the US, there was no one to properly succeed Churchill. Originally, there was to be a caretaker government which would be overseen by Lord Salisbury until Eden

Managing a giant 27

was healthy and the country could choose between him and Butler. But Churchill's recovery seemed to push this solution out of the room. There was still a lag time in which the government continued to function without a legal leader. Butler, Sir Norman Brook, Colville and Churchill's son-in-law, Christopher Soames played major parts in running the show while the ring master was unavailable. Colville described the situation:

> My colleagues and I had to handle requests for decisions from Ministers and Government departments entirely ignorant of the Prime Minister's incapacity. Discussion of how best to handle such inquiries, whether by postponement, by consultation with the Minister or Under Secretary responsible or, in some cases, by direct reply on the Prime Minister's behalf were the subject of daily discussions ...[148]

Colville also seemed aware of the dubious legal position in which this placed the government. He explained that he and his colleagues had to be careful 'not to allow their own judgment to be given Prime Ministerial effect' and if this happened there 'would have been a constitutional outrage'.[149] Many years later, Colville was asked if Churchill deliberately misled the public. He responded saying 'No. He would have resigned if he thought he would have been incapacitated. But the interviewer described the situation as a 'conspiracy of silence' and pushed Colville's colleague and Under-Secretary of State for Foreign Affairs, Anthony Nutting, by asking if the government behaved 'dishonourably'. He aided Colville saying, 'The government acted honourably enough. It would have been incorrect if Churchill had not recovered'.[150]

Of course, Churchill did recover and continued to lead the government until April 1955, though for Colville this increasingly meant playing bezique with Churchill. In fact, this became a game which everyone in the Private Office played with Churchill at some point. Colville was even instructed to teach Anthony Montague Browne how to play and afterwards it became 'rather central to his life'.[151]

Conclusion

Once Churchill did resign, Colville's relationship with him rather shifted; instead of being his Private Secretary he became something of a guardian for Churchill's legacy. The first and most obvious example of this was his enormous effort to help push forward the founding of Churchill College, Cambridge.[152] One would surmise that the logical home for Churchill College would have been at Oxford, given the proximity to Blenheim Palace and Lord Randolph's matriculation at Merton College, Oxford. Though the original plans were to create a school which might rival MIT in the US,[153] eventually Cambridge offered to host 'a new college devoted to science and technology' which would 'be called after Churchill and be a national memorial to him'.[154] To fund this, Colville, who left the Civil Service to become an investment banker after Churchill resigned, used his numerous contacts and business connections in the City. In this role Colville acted as a mediator between the University of Cambridge and Churchill. For instance, on 14 June 1958, Churchill wrote to Jock supporting the idea that women should be involved in the College. Churchill went on to say he was 'disturbed at our not having a woman on the council. I see no reason why women should not participate'.[155] Colville replied that undertaking a 'co-educational' approach might lead to the university rejecting the scheme for the college because it was already outside of the typical collegiate approach because it a specialist college. Colville said that if women joined 'it would be like dropping a hydrogen bomb in the middle of a University'.[156] Ultimately, Churchill College was one of the first all-male colleges to admit women in 1972.

Colville further acted as a guarantor of Churchill's legacy by acting as a trustee of both Sir Winston and Lady Churchill's estates, by aiding Randolph Churchill and Martin Gilbert in the official biography of Winston Churchill, publishing his own memoirs and diaries, and by defending Churchill in the press. During the late 1970s, Colville was involved in controversy with Bob Boothby – still bitter at his treatment during the Second World War when a scandal had forced his resignation as a junior minister – who claimed in an interview that Churchill had been 'gaga' when he returned to office in 1951.[157] Colville defended his former boss in *The Times* saying that Churchill had barely set eyes on Boothby during that period and had not been 'remotely interested in his views'.[158] Boothby wrote back to *The Times*, claiming that Colville had for many years been 'boasting, and boring everyone in talk and print, about his relationship with Sir Winston Churchill', yet was in fact 'of no importance at all'.[159] In turn, Mary Soames and Martin Gilbert rushed to Colville's defence.[160]

Colville passed away rather suddenly in 1987. He had done remarkable work on behalf of the various Churchill trusts and for the Archives Centre itself. Though more research is needed to fully appreciate the influence of Colville on Churchill's legacy, it is clear that he played a significant role, not just as a Private Secretary but also as Churchill's friend and loyal supporter. Colville's role as PS in Churchill's peacetime government was unique and remarkable. Churchill valued his opinion and trusted him with tasks rarely trusted to members of the Private Office. However, this also illustrates the fundamental paradox of Colville's tenure as PS. He was capable of remarkable feats above and beyond the role of Private Secretary, acting as a secret diplomat or working as a family mediator, but ultimately his loyalty was not with the Civil Service or even the British government but rather it lay with Churchill. While this probably did 'spoil Colville as a civil servant' it also allowed for a unique position where Colville could work inside Number 10 and also report on its processes in his diary. Had he been a straight-arrow civil servant, more like Pitblado, he would have not kept a diary and he certainly would never have published it. But in addition to being Churchill's PS, Colville was something more: he was Churchill's friend.

Notes

1 John Colville, *The Fringes of Power: Downing Street Diaries 1939–1955* (London: Hodder & Stoughton, 1985), 593.
2 Interview with Lady Jane Williams, 19 February 2013.
3 *The Times*, 23 October 1978; Churchill Archives Centre, Cambridge [henceforward CAC]: SOAM 7/7c.
4 Colville, *Fringes*, 635.
5 Lord Normanbrook quoted in John Ramsden, *Man of the Century: Winston Churchill and his Legend since 1945* (London: HarperCollins, 2002), 535–7.
6 Ibid., 536.
7 Ibid., 536.
8 Lord Moran, *Winston Churchill: The Struggle for Survival* (London: Sphere Books, 1968), 775.
9 Anthony Seldon, *Churchill's Indian Summer: The Conservative Government 1951–1955* (London: Hodder & Stoughton, 1981), 33.
10 Interview with Anthony Montague Browne, 3 September 1986, CAC: CHOH 2/4.
11 G. W. Jones, 'The Prime Minister's Secretaries: Politicians or Administrators', in *From Policy to Administration: Essays in Honour of William A. Robson*, ed. J. A. G. Griffith (London: Allen & Unwin, 1976), 14.
12 Denis Kavanagh and Anthony Seldon, *The Powers Behind the Prime Minister: The Hidden Influence of Number Ten* (London: HarperCollins, 1999), 56.
13 John Colville, *The Churchillians* (London: Weidenfeld & Nicolson, 1981), 64.
14 Anthony Montague Browne, *The Long Sunset: Memoirs of Winston Churchill's Last Private Secretary* (London: Indgo, 1995), 108.
15 Colville, *Churchillians*, 64.
16 Kavanagh and Seldon, *Powers behind the Prime Minister*, 56.
17 Seldon, *Churchill's Indian Summer*, 28.
18 David Hunt, *On the Spot: An Ambassador Remembers* (London: P. Davies, 1975), 50.
19 Colville, *Fringes*, 594.
20 Ibid., 594.
21 Interview with David Pitblado, CAC: WCHL 15/2/88.
22 John Colville, *Winston Churchill and His Inner Circle* (New York: Wyndham Books, 1981), 87.
23 Seldon, *Churchill's Indian Summer*, 513. See also Jones, 'Prime Minister's Secretaries', 31–2.
24 Colville, *Fringes*, 632.
25 Hunt, *On the Spot*, 50.
26 Montague Browne, *Long Sunset*, 108.
27 Interview with David Pitblado, CAC: WCHL 15/2/88.
28 Montague Browne, *Long Sunset*, 108.
29 Colville, *Fringes*, 645.
30 Interview with David Pitblado, CAC: WCHL 15/2/88.
31 Seldon, *Churchill's Indian Summer*, 33.
32 Interview with David Pitblado, CAC: WCHL 15/2/88.
33 Kavanagh and Seldon, *Powers behind the Prime Minister*, 56–7.
34 Ibid., 57, 306.
35 Ibid., 9–10.
36 John Colville, 'John Colville', in *Action this Day: Working with Churchill*, ed. John Wheeler-Bennett (London: Macmillan, 1968), 128.
37 John Colville, *Footprints in Time: Memories* (London: Century, 1976), 233.
38 Seldon, *Churchill's Indian Summer*, 388.

39 John Charmley, *Churchill's Grand Alliance: The Anglo-American Special Relationship 1940–1957* (London: Hodder & Stoughton, 1995), 292.
40 Memorandum by Butler, C. (52) 320, 3 October 1952, The National Archives, Kew [henceforward TNA]: CAB 129/55.
41 Colville, *Fringes*, 650.
42 Ibid., 651.
43 Colville, 'Colville', 126.
44 Colville, *Footprints*, 234.
45 Colville, 'Colville', 124.
46 Colville, *Footprints*, 234.
47 Colville, *Fringes*, 654.
48 Seldon, *Churchill's Indian Summer*, 389.
49 Dean Acheson, *Present at the Creation: My Years in the State Department* (New York: Norton, 1969), 595.
50 *Newsweek*, 14 April 1952.
51 Colville, 'Colville', 128.
52 Colville, 'Colville', 128.
53 Colville, *Fringes*, 637.
54 Colville diary, 1 January 1953, CAC: CLVL 1/7.
55 Colville, *Footprints*, 234.
56 Colville, *Fringes*, 665.
57 Colville diary, 8 January 1953, CAC: CLVL 1/7.
58 Colville, *Fringes*, 660.
59 Ibid., 662.
60 Colville diary, 7 January 1953, CAC: CLVL 1/7; Colville, *Fringes*, 664.
61 Dwight D. Eisenhower, *The Eisenhower Diaries*, ed. Robert H. Ferrell (New York: Norton, 1981), 208.
62 Ibid., 223.
63 Colville diary, 7 January 1953, CAC: CLVL 1/7. See also, Colville, 'Colville', 130.
64 Seldon, *Churchill's Indian Summer*, 391.
65 Colville diary, 3 January 1953, CAC: CLVL 1/7.
66 Churchill to Stalin, 4 November 1951, TNA: FO 371/94841/134.
67 Speech by Churchill, 6 November 1951, in *WinstonS. Churchill: His Complete Speeches*, vol. VII, ed. Robert Rhodes James (New York: Chelsea House Publishers, 1974), 8297.
68 Colville, *Footprints*, 234.
69 John W. Young, 'Churchill and East-West Detente', *Transactions of the Royal Historical Society*, 6th ser., 11 (2001): 381.
70 Moran, *Churchill*, 403.
71 Colville, *Footprints*, 238.
72 Colville, 'Colville', 130.
73 *The Parliamentary Debates (Hansard): House of Commons Official Report* (London: HMSO, 1944–) [henceforward *H.C. Deb.*], 5th ser., vol. 515, cc. 883–1004.
74 Colville, *Footprints*, 239.
75 Ibid., 239.
76 Colville, *Fringes*, 679.
77 Colville, *Footprints*, 240.
78 Colville, *Fringes*, 682–3.
79 Colville diary, 4 December 1953, CAC: CLVL 1/8.
80 Colville, *Footprints*, 241.
81 Colville, *Fringes*, 685.
82 Colville, *Footprints*, 241.
83 Colville, *Fringes*, 686.

84 Moran, *Churchill*, 559.
85 Ibid., 562.
86 Seldon, *Churchill's Indian Summer*, 399, 618.
87 Moran, *Churchill*, 540. See also Young, 'East-West Détente', 386.
88 Moran, *Churchill*, 560.
89 Colville diary, 25 June 1954, CAC: CLVL 1/7.
90 Seldon, *Churchill's Indian Summer*, 405.
91 Colville, *Fringes*, 693.
92 Young, 'East-West Détente', 387.
93 Evelyn Shuckburgh, *Descent to Suez: Diaries, 1951–1956* (London: Weidenfeld & Nicolson, 1987), 126.
94 Seldon, *Churchill's Indian Summer*, 413.
95 Ibid., 412, 622 n. 27.
96 Shuckburgh, *Descent*, 14.
97 See David Dutton, *Anthony Eden: A Life and Reputation* (London: Arnold, 1997) and Nigel Morris, 'Eden "was on purple hearts during Suez crisis"', *Independent on Sunday*, 4 November 2006.
98 See Nicolas Rasmussen, *On Speed: The Many Lives of Amphetamine* (New York: New York University Press, 2008).
99 Colville diary, 28 June 1954, CAC: CLVL 1/7.
100 Robert Rhodes James, *Anthony Eden* (London: Weidenfeld & Nicolson, 1986), 390.
101 Kelly memoirs, CAC: DEKE 2.
102 Anthony Adamthwaite, 'Overstretched and Overstrung: Eden, the Foreign Office and the Making of Policy, 1951–55', *International Affairs*, 64 (1988): 250.
103 Colville, *Fringes*, 704.
104 Colville, *Fringes*, 704, 706. See also Oscar Nemon's unpublished memoirs, 72, CAC: NEMO 3/1.
105 Colville diary, 2 July 1954, CAC: CLVL 1/7.
106 Colville, *Fringes*, 697.
107 Ibid.
108 Ibid.
109 Ibid.
110 Mary Soames, *Clementine Churchill*, 2nd edn (London: Doubleday, 2002), 491.
111 Ibid., 469.
112 Colville, *Fringes*, 702.
113 Ibid.
114 Colville diary, 16 July 1954, CAC: CLVL 1/7.
115 Colville, *Fringes*, 706.
116 Ibid., 707.
117 Ibid., 707.
118 Ibid., 708.
119 Soames to Seldon, CAC: SOAM 7/8.
120 D. R. Thorpe, *Eden: The Life and Times of Anthony Eden, First Earl of Avon* (London: Chatto & Windus, 2003), 376.
121 Colville to Churchill, 13 January 1984, RDCH 1/1/7.
122 Winston S. Churchill, *His Father's Son: The Life of Randolph Churchill* (London: Weidenfeld & Nicolson, 1996), 332.
123 Colville diary, 5 December 1953, CAC: CLVL 1/8.
124 Moran, *Churchill*, 336.
125 Ibid., 740.
126 Colville, 'Colville', 123.
127 Colville, *Fringes*, 651; Colville, 'Colville', 123.
128 Montague Browne, *Long Sunset*, 176; Additionally, Pitblado and David Hunt also wrote parts of Churchill's speeches, though Churchill typically rearranged their

contributions to match his style. See also Martin Gilbert, *In Search of Churchill: A Historian's Journey* (London: HarperCollins, 1994), 196.
129 Interview with Denis Kelly, n.d., CAC: DEKE 11.
130 Moran, *Churchill*, 181–2. For more on Churchill's 'black dog' see Wilfred Attenborough, *Churchill and the 'Black Dog' of Depression: Reassessing the Biographical Evidence of Psychological Disorder* (Basingstoke: Palgrave, 2014).
131 Colville diary, 13–15 June 1952; Colville, *Fringes*, 650–1.
132 Colville, 'Colville', 116–17.
133 Gilbert, *In Search of Churchill*, 209–10.
134 For Churchill's daughter's view of his depression see Soames, *Clementine Churchill*, 77–8 and for the various types of depression and anxiety from which Churchill suffered, see Wilfred Attenborough, 'Churchill's Black Dog at the Home Office 1910–1911: The Evidential Reliability of Psychiatric Reference', *History* 98 (2013): 390–405.
135 Gilbert, *In Search of Churchill*, 209.
136 Moran, *Churchill*, 373–4.
137 Colville, *Fringes*, 642.
138 Moran, *Churchill*, 375–6.
139 Tommy Lascelles, quoted in Moran, *Churchill*, 378.
140 Moran, *Churchill*, 379.
141 Colville, *Fringes*, 668.
142 Ibid., 668.
143 Ibid., 669.
144 Lord Hartwell, *William Camrose: Giant of Fleet Street* (London: Weidenfeld & Nicolson, 1992), 338. In Lord Moran's account, it was Lord Salisbury and R. A. Butler who altered the text, not Lord Camrose. Moran, *Churchill*, 411.
145 Colville, *Fringes*, 669.
146 CC (53) 37, 29 June 1953; TNA: CAB 195/11.
147 Hartwell, *Camrose*, 337–8.
148 Colville, *Fringes*, 669.
149 Colville, *Fringes*, 668–9.
150 Interview with Jock Colville, 'Winston Churchill's Stroke', BBC Radio 4, 15 September 1970, BBC Archives, www.bbc.co.uk/archive/churchill/11015.shtml (accessed 3 March 2015).
151 Montague Browne, *Long Sunset*, 137–8.
152 Colville's enormous task of pushing this forward is documented in CAC: CHUR 2/568A-B.
153 Colville to Churchill 14 May 1956, CAC: CHUR 2/268A.
154 Colville, *Footprints*, 258.
155 Churchill to Colville 14 June 1958, CAC: CHUR 2/268A.
156 Colville to Churchill 16 June 1958, CAC: CHUR 2/268A.
157 *The Times*, 14 October 1978.
158 *The Times*, 19 October 1978.
159 *The Times*, 23 October 1978.
160 *The Times*, 24 October 1978; *The Times*, 27 October 1978.

References

Acheson, Dean, *Present at the Creation: My Years in the State Department* (New York: Norton, 1969).
Attenborough, Wilfred, *Churchill and the 'Black Dog' of Depression: Reassessing the Biographical Evidence of Psychological Disorder* (Basingstoke: Palgrave, 2014).

Attenborough, Wilfred, 'Churchill's Black Dog at the Home Office 1910–1911: The Evidential Reliability of Psychiatric Reference', *History* 98(2013): 390–405.

Charmley, John, *Churchill's Grand Alliance: The Anglo-American Special Relationship 1940–1957* (London: Hodder & Stoughton, 1995).

Colville, John, *The Fringes of Power: Downing Street Diaries 1939–1955* (London: Hodder & Stoughton, 1985).

Colville, John, *The Churchillians* (London: Weidenfeld & Nicolson, 1981).

Colville, John, 'John Colville', in *Action this Day: Working with Churchill*, ed. John Wheeler-Bennett (London: Macmillan, 1968).

Colville, John, *Winston Churchill and His Inner Circle* (New York: Wyndham Books, 1981).

Dutton, David, *Anthony Eden: A Life and Reputation* (London: Arnold, 1997).

Eisenhower, Dwight D., *The Eisenhower Diaries*, ed. Robert H. Ferrell (New York: Norton, 1981).

Gilbert, Martin, *In Search of Churchill: A Historian's Journey* (London: HarperCollins, 1994).

Hartwell, Lord, *William Camrose: Giant of Fleet Street* (London: Weidenfeld & Nicolson, 1992).

Hunt, David, *On The Spot: An Ambassador Remembers* (London: P. Davies, 1975).

Jones, G. W., 'The Prime Minister's Secretaries: Politicians or Administrators', in *From Policy to Administration: Essays in Honour of William A. Robson*, ed. J. A. G. Griffith (London: Allen & Unwin, 1976).

Kavanagh, Denis and Anthony Seldon, *The Powers behind the Prime Minister: The Hidden Influence of Number ten* (London: HarperCollins, 1999).

Montague Browne, Anthony, *The Long Sunset: Memoirs of Winston Churchill's Last Private Secretary* (London: Indgo, 1995).

Moran, Lord, *Winston Churchill: The Struggle for Survival* (London: Sphere Books, 1968).

Ramsden, John, *Man of the Century: Winston Churchill and his Legend since 1945* (London: HarperCollins, 2002).

Rasmussen, Nicolas, *On Speed: The Many Lives of Amphetamine* (New York: New York University Press, 2008).

Rhodes James, Robert, *Winston S. Churchill: His Complete Speeches*, vol. VII (New York: Chelsea House Publishers, 1974).

Seldon, Anthony, *Churchill's Indian Summer: The Conservative Government 1951–1955* (London: Hodder & Stoughton, 1981).

Soames, Mary, *Clementine Churchill*, 2nd edn (London: Doubleday, 2002).

Young, John W., 'Churchill and East–West Detente', *Transactions of the Royal Historical Society* 6th ser., 11(2001): 373–392.

2 Advising the un-advisable

The Number 10 Private Office and the Suez Crisis

Kevin Ruane[1]

The Eden succession

On 4 April 1955, Winston Churchill hosted a grand dinner party at 10 Downing Street. The occasion was his imminent retirement as Prime Minister after three-and-a-half years at the head of his peacetime administration. Alongside the guests of honour, the young Queen Elizabeth and the Duke of Edinburgh, were sundry family, friends, political colleagues and social grandees. '10 Downing Street can seldom if ever have looked so gay', John Colville, Churchill's joint Principal Private Secretary (PPS), wrote in his diary, 'or its floorboards … have groaned under such a weight of jewels and decorations'. Also present was the Foreign Secretary, Anthony Eden, who had spent more than a decade as Churchill's designated successor but who was now tantalisingly close to securing the keys to Number 10. The evening was a 'splendid occasion', Colville recorded, although not without its incidents, one of which involved Eden and his wife Clarissa (Churchill's niece) who tried to jump the queue advancing to shake hands with the Queen. In the ensuing kerfuffle the Duchess of Westminster put her foot through Clarissa's train. 'That's torn it, in more than one sense', quipped the Duke of Edinburgh in a flash of the mordant humour for which he would become famous.[2]

Given our knowledge of what would befall Eden over the next 21 months – the disaster of Suez, the collapse of his health, and the humiliating end to his political career – there is always a temptation to read history backwards and look for ominous portents. Whether a torn dress falls into this category is debatable, but at the very least the impatience, frustration and indeed vanity which combined to produce the queue-jumping incident hinted at a politician already living on his nerves, overly anxious to get on with the job and prove himself after such a lengthy apprenticeship.[3] Moreover, thanks to Colville, we know that Churchill, too, wondered whether his anointed successor was temperamentally equipped to cope with the premiership. That same night, after the Queen and his other guests had left, Churchill went upstairs to his bedroom, and there, still wearing his Garter, Order of Merit and knee-breeches, he sat down on his bed. Colville watched him closely. 'For several minutes he did not speak and I, imagining that he was sadly contemplating that this was his last night at Downing Street, was silent. Then suddenly he stared at me and said with vehemence: "I don't believe Anthony can do it"'.[4] The following day, Churchill went to Buckingham Palace. 'I tendered my resignation to The Queen, which Her Majesty accepted', he wrote afterwards. 'She asked me whether I would recommend a successor and I said I preferred to leave it to Her. She said the case was not a difficult one and that She would summon Sir Anthony Eden'.[5]

The Number 10 private office

Alongside the priority of constructing his government, Eden set about staffing his Private Office. Immediately there was a change at the top when Colville, after almost nine years of dedicated service to Churchill in war and peace, decided to take up a new career in merchant banking. In his vividly drawn diary, published in 1985, Colville also did history a great service. Alas, the 1955–1957 Tory government possessed no strategically positioned insider-chronicler to do a similar job of 'Boswellization' (as Roy Jenkins has termed it) on Eden.[6] Then again, even if he had wished to stay on, it is unlikely that Colville would have been retained: he did not hold Eden in especially high regard, and Eden probably knew it.[7] To begin with, David Pitblado, the 'canny, unruffled Scotsman' who shared PPS duties with Colville, became head of the office in his own right.[8] Pitblado had begun his public service in the 1930s in the Dominions Office, where he was junior Private Secretary to Lord Stanley and Malcolm MacDonald, before a temporary secondment to the Treasury turned into something more permanent. In 1945 he was an economic adviser to the British delegation at the founding conference of the United Nations and went on to join Edwin Plowden's Central Economic Planning Staff where he stayed until July 1951 when, aged 39, he was transferred to Downing Street to become Clement Attlee's PPS. Three months later, when the Conservatives won the general election, Churchill wanted to resurrect his wartime partnership with Colville but came up against civil service protocol which protected Pitblado from being dismissed or demoted on a prime ministerial whim. Happily a compromise was quickly worked by which Churchill enjoyed the ministrations of two Principal Private Secretaries working in double harness, an arrangement that endured until Eden took over.[9] 'I suspect he thought I was still a Churchillian', Pitblado said of Eden, 'but I wasn't'. Be that as it may, it was natural that Eden should want his own man as PPS and it was agreed that Pitblado would stay on until a replacement was found.[10]

In the event this transition phase lasted nine months, but when Pitblado finally took his leave of Number 10 in January 1956 to join the economic section of the Washington Embassy, the man chosen to succeed him was Frederick ('Freddie') Bishop. Born near Bristol in 1915, Bishop joined the Civil Service straight from school and secured his first position in the Estate Duty Office in Somerset House. Ambitious for promotion, the prerequisite of which was a qualification in law, he enrolled as a part-time student at the University of

London and graduated from there with a law degree in 1938. For a time after the outbreak of war he continued with the Inland Revenue but in 1942 he left to join the RAF. Demobilised in 1946, he passed into the administrative grade of the Civil Service, was appointed to the Ministry of Food, and there became PPS to a succession of ministers. In 1953 he left to join the Cabinet Office as an assistant secretary responsible for coordinating the economic business of the Cabinet, and it was during this time that he formed a close working relationship with the powerful Cabinet Secretary, Sir Norman Brook. It was on Brook's recommendation that Eden agreed to Bishop replacing Pitblado.[11]

When he took over the Private Office, Bishop inherited three assistant secretaries, all of whom came in with Eden in 1955. Guy Millard, one of Eden's Private Secretaries during the war, was seconded from the Foreign Office where he had been Deputy Head of the African Department. Millard shared responsibility for foreign affairs with Philip de Zulueta, another FO man who had recently spent two years in the Moscow Embassy. Neil Cairncross, transferred from the Home Office to look after the domestic side of things, completed the team.[12] Unfortunately, historians attempting to assess the degree of influence that any of these individuals had on the shaping of Eden's foreign policy are hampered by a lack of personal diaries or private papers. True, there are the memoirs of William Clark, Eden's press secretary in 1955–1956, and, within them, extracts from his contemporary diary, but the recollections of this fringe spectator, whose office was semi-detached from that of Bishop and his colleagues, does not compensate for the absence of a Colville-esque chronicler at the very heart of Number 10. Nor do the large number of Private Office (PREM) files housed at the UK National Archives offer much insight into the advisory contribution of Eden's staff. This is partly due to the fact that, as Millard defined their role, 'Private Secretaries are intermediaries, not advisors', and partly because Eden, a diplomatist of great experience, tended to back his own judgement on international affairs and at times seemed to be acting as his own Foreign Secretary.[13]

In any event, the main task of the Number 10 team was to ensure the efficient running of the office machine and to help the Prime Minister manage his workload. Accordingly, while Bishop and his colleagues generated a lot of paper, most of it was given over to summaries of meetings, reminders to the Prime Minister of matters requiring attention, formal communications with ministers, including the conveyance of the prime ministerial will, and myriad other mundane but necessary chores. '[I]t was quite an adjustment coming from the FO or the Treasury, where you were expected to have a view on things', Pitblado recalled, 'then to find, when you got to Downing Street, that you were just a functionary. Some people found it a bit emasculating, professionally speaking'.[14] This may be so, but the day-to-day proximity of these officials to Eden undoubtedly encouraged him to use them as informal sounding boards or even lightning conductors when he needed to give vent to his legendary temper. Sadly from the standpoint of history, such moments were seldom if ever recorded. 'It was very much a relationship in which he felt he could say anything that he wanted to say and could rely on it not going any further unless it were appropriate', Bishop later commented.[15]

The policy context

Although international affairs dominated and ultimately defined the Eden government, de Zulueta rejected the claim that this was indicative of a lack of interest or experience in domestic matters on the part of the Prime Minister: '[H]e had after all been a senior Cabinet Minister and Deputy Leader for some 20 years and he had also enjoyed, while out of office, quite extensive involvement in commercial affairs'. Eden's ideas on a property-owning democracy, originating in the 1930s, developed in opposition in 1940s, and promoted in government the 1950s, represented 'a true ideal', and de Zulueta remembered Eden's bitterness towards 'the insensitive and selfish attitude of some of the older Tories' who sought to thwart his reformist agenda. 'His concentration on foreign affairs during his premiership was due much more to the pressure of outside events than to preference'.[16] Of these external factors, the Cold War was patently the most pressing. Despite a slight thaw in East–West relations following the death of Stalin, by the mid 1950s tensions were rising along with the danger that cold war could give way to hot war with all its doom-laden nuclear and thermonuclear destructiveness. In July 1955, Eden attended a Four-Power (UK, USA, USSR, France) summit at Geneva, the first heads of government conference since Potsdam. Although the shared fear of nuclear war that prompted the meeting in the first place failed to produce hard agreements, for the next year there was some hope that the 'spirit of Geneva', as President Eisenhower put it, would lead to real détente.[17]

However, while the great powers sought to improve their relations at the apex of the Cold War pyramid, at its base, particularly in the developing world, local crises continued to harbour the potential to escalate into prestige-engaging showdowns. The Middle East was among the most volatile areas, although until 1955 the instability of the region owed more to the incendiary Arab-Israeli conflict and to the clash between Arab nationalism and residual European imperialism than to Moscow mischief-making. This all changed in September 1955 when the Egyptian leader, Colonel Gamal Abdel Nasser, concluded an arms deal with Czechoslovakia, a Soviet satellite state. Leaving aside Nasser's need to defend his country against Israeli menaces, to the USA as much as to the UK this development appeared to signal the start of a more proactive Kremlin effort to extend its influence in the Middle East via locally recruited proxies.[18] In July 1956, when Nasser went on to nationalise the Suez Canal Company, Clarissa Eden famously – even notoriously – remarked that there were times during the ensuing crisis when it 'felt as if the Suez Canal was flowing through my drawing room'.[19] That was upstairs at Number 10. We may be sure that downstairs, too, the canal flowed equally strongly through the Private Office and, this being so, it will also flow through the remainder of this study of how Eden's staff, especially his PPS, Freddie Bishop, and his closest

38 *Kevin Ruane*

lieutenant, Guy Millard, handled the crisis. As for the story of Suez itself, this has been told so many times and in so many ways that there is no need to rehearse it here other than to sketch a bare-bones chronology as a point of reference for the succeeding discussion.

Animated by an admixture of strategic, economic, political and prestige considerations, as well as Eden's marked personal animus towards Nasser, the British government was committed from the outset to recovering control of the canal, if necessary through the use of force, and to the collateral objective of bringing down Nasser's government. During August and September, as UK military preparations proceeded, various diplomatic options for peacefully resolving the crisis were tried and failed, but then, in early October, and defying expectations on all sides, an Anglo-Egyptian *modus vivendi* appeared to be in the offing. At the same time, with the canal functioning well under Egyptian jurisdiction, Eden and the other proponents of force in the government – with the possible exception of Chancellor of the Exchequer Harold Macmillan – reluctantly accepted that military action could no longer be justified to public opinion either at home or abroad unless Nasser offered a new provocation. The crisis, it seemed, was about to blow itself out. Then, on 14 October, secret messengers from the French government brought Eden the news that Israel was prepared to attack Egypt if it could be assured of French and British support. A war between Egypt and Israel, the French suggested, would provide a pretext for Anglo-French intervention; officially, this would be presented as an altruistic move to maintain the security of a vital international waterway, but unofficially the goal was to reassert control over the canal and, if possible, topple Nasser.

Eden was gradually seduced by the siren songs of the French proposal, and the following week, in more highly secret talks at Sèvres, the French and British, joined now by the Israelis, solemnised their collusive arrangements. On 29 October, the agreed date, Israel launched its assault on Egypt. At the United Nations, the British and French promptly vetoed a US-sponsored resolution calling on Israel to desist and instead issued a joint ultimatum to both Egypt and Israel to halt the fighting on pain of Anglo-French military intervention to separate the combatants and protect the canal. When the ultimatum was rejected, on 31 October Anglo-French bombing of Egyptian air bases commenced. Over the next few days, the US government's criticism of the action intensified while wider international condemnation, voiced by and through the UN, steadily mounted. On 5 November, Anglo-French paratroops landed at Port Said at the northern end of the canal, followed at dawn the next day by larger seaborne forces. Later on 6 November, the USSR threatened to launch rocket weapons against Britain and France if they refused to abandon their campaign, while the USA ratcheted up its own pressure, diplomatic and economic, to the same end. When the Israelis and Egyptians then announced a ceasefire, the Anglo-French intervention immediately lost its *raison d'être*. At midnight (London time) on 6 November, the British downed arms: faced with the collapse of the UK economy as a result of a US-inspired run on the pound and with

UN economic sanctions in prospect, the government felt it had no other option. The French were angered at the collapse of British resolution when the success of the operation to take the canal was within sight but grudgingly followed suit. Pressured and cajoled by a still disapproving United States, over the next six weeks the humiliated British and French undertook the unconditional withdrawal of their forces.[20]

Freddie Bishop and Suez

Looking back on the events surrounding Suez, Bishop remembered Eden being punctilious about never asking any of his Secretaries for their views, and at one point, at the height of the crisis, the Prime Minister actually 'told me he mustn't ask me for advice, although he went on to say that he would be very interested in what I thought'.[21] A forthright character, Bishop was no mere functionary (to invoke Pitblado's term), and while it may be true that Eden seldom solicited his advice, this did not stop him from volunteering it. Although he 'never kept any personal diary or other record of my association with Ministers', his outlook on foreign affairs – described by William Plowden as 'hawkish' – still left its mark in some at least of the routine PREM files.[22] In August 1956, he wrote to Eden strongly endorsing his estimate of 'the risks of letting Nasser "get away with this"' and encouraged him to hold fast to his faith in the use of force to recover the canal.[23] As preparations for military action continued over the summer, he warned the Prime Minister against informing the Americans – whose declared preference was for a negotiated solution – of plans to furnish the UK task force with equipment supplied under the Mutual Defence Assistance Programme lest the Eisenhower administration impose unacceptable conditions.[24] And when the fighting erupted and the government began weighing the merits of transferring responsibility for the Anglo-French 'police action' to the United Nations, he insisted that 'whatever we say on this … must leave us free to continue to occupy key points on the Canal'.[25]

Nor was Bishop beyond offering the Prime Minister advice on how to handle the Cabinet at key junctures, one of which occurred towards the end of August 1956. A month on from nationalisation, with the early intensity of the crisis ebbing, the governmental consensus in support of military action, albeit as a last resort, had started to unravel. Sir Walter Monckton, the Minister of Defence and a member of the Egypt Committee, the small but high-powered sub-committee of the Cabinet formed in late July to manage the crisis, was a principal doubter. At a noon meeting on 24 August, he delivered an impassioned appeal for further and sincere efforts to achieve a diplomatic outcome. The previous day, 18 of the 22 powers represented at the First London Conference of Maritime Nations at Lancaster House had approved proposals which, if accepted by Cairo, would make the running of the canal an international rather than an Egyptian concern. In the Egypt Committee, Macmillan opined that if Nasser rejected the principle of international control (which was likely), and if the UN then endorsed that same principle, the diplomatic track would have run its course.[26] According to Brook, who took the minutes, it was when Macmillan began 'speaking as though we were deciding there and then on the date of the [military] operation' that Monckton was compelled to speak out.[27] For his part, Eden was well aware of the need to delimit the diplomatic process in view of the impossibility of maintaining indefinitely British armed forces, including reservists, in a heightened state of military readiness without a war to fight. But given that war would require the sanction of the full Cabinet, the Prime Minister and his more hawkish supporters grew nervous lest Monckton attract majority support for his conciliatory line, the more so as Rab Butler, the Lord Privy Seal and a powerful figure in the government, seemed to share his outlook.[28] In her diary, Clarissa Eden, channelling her husband's perturbation, wrote that 'Rab is wobbling to the point of lobbying' and had found 'seven members of the Cabinet who agree with him'.[29]

As it happened, 24 August was Bishop's last day in the office prior to taking annual leave. He certainly needed a break. A fortnight earlier, he had witnessed 'terrible tantrums' at Chequers and at one point he had the 'PM bouncing out of bed to shout at him' for being too noisy.[30] When he learned of what had occurred in the Egypt Committee that day, he immediately penned a long note to Eden expressing 'remorse at going away' at such a crucial moment but offering some 'simple thoughts' on how to deal with the Cabinet when it met four days hence and when (as Brook told him) Eden intended 'to put squarely' to ministers 'the issue of using force if diplomatic methods fail to get us a satisfactory solution'. Although the matter was 'hypothetical' until Nasser pronounced on the London proposals, Bishop thought it 'unwise to wait much longer before binding all your colleagues into our present policy'. The Cabinet had previously expressed itself as broadly in favour of using force if or when the diplomatic option failed, but there was 'a real dilemma here', Bishop suggested, 'because while the pursuit of diplomatic methods may improve the moral basis' for military action, 'the passage of time saps the national resolution (because of inertia and the natural love of a quiet life)'. The question, therefore, was whether Nasser's rejection of international control would justify recourse to force or whether further diplomatic hoops must be jumped through. He continued:

> This leads me to the view that, in putting the Government's policy to the Cabinet, *you should emphasise that the military plans, although precise and well-advanced, do not themselves govern the diplomatic timetable* [original emphasis] ... On this basis, I feel the Cabinet would be bound to confirm that the use of force is justified if it is necessary to prevent the worst risk of all, which is 'to let Nasser get away with it'. But the Cabinet would have to realise that a point must come at which the pursuit of diplomatic methods is no longer in our interests, because it would weaken our power to resort to force which we must in the last resort be able to do. If on these arguments you can get the Cabinet's support, as I feel sure you can, I see no reason why you should not steadily follow the policy of firmness, even if this in the end entails giving the signal for military action.

Bishop was suggesting that Eden give Cabinet doubters a reassurance that the diplomatic option was by no means spent, and that they, in turn, should be asked to rededicate themselves to the principle of the use of force. However, as the ultimate arbiter of what constituted the national interest, the Prime Minister should reserve the right to determine when the moment of 'last resort' had arrived – and that could well be, Bishop implied, before events at the United Nations or elsewhere had run their course. This was an extraordinary recommendation for a career civil servant to make with regard to the handling of the elected members of a national government, but then again, Bishop had always possessed that 'precious gift of a mandarin – an astute political sense, without in himself being political'.[31]

When the Cabinet assembled on 28 August, Monckton, supported by Butler, duly aired his worries, and to the extent that ministers agreed to look to the United Nations for succour if Cairo rejected international control – which it did the following week – he scored a success. But in Eden's carefully measured summation of the meeting there is more than a hint of Bishop. It had become 'evident', he said, 'that the Cabinet were united in the view that the frustration of Colonel Nasser's policy was a vital British interest which must be secured, in the last resort, by the use of force'. At the same time he 'fully recognised that, before recourse was had to force, every practicable attempt should be made to secure a satisfactory settlement by peaceful means'. But 'we could not allow these efforts to impose an undue delay … weaken our resolution or to reduce the weight of our pressure on the Egyptian Government'.[32] Monckton had been outmanoeuvred, and though he stayed on at the Ministry of Defence he continued to be one of the 'key Suez doubters', eventually resigning his portfolio to become Paymaster General in mid October.[33] As he confided to the US Ambassador to London, Winthrop Aldrich, an attack on Egypt would 'be a great blunder' and he was unable to 'remain as Minister of Defense and take the actions necessary if force be used'.[34]

Force, of course, was used, though little good it did Eden. Exhausted and ill, on 19 November he bowed to doctor's orders and cancelled all engagements. Four days later, he and his wife flew to Jamaica for a rest-cure ('I thought if we didn't go … he was going to drop down dead, literally', Clarissa recalled) leaving Butler in charge of the government.[35] After a fortnight, Bishop wrote to Eden at his Caribbean retreat to say that he was feeling 'a bit rudderless' in the Private Office.[36] Eden knew the feeling: with his health apparently improving, he was restless and keen to return to London. 'My greetings to Freddie, Neil & Philip as well as to yourself', he wrote to Millard on 8 December. 'I am feeling much better … Looking forward to seeing you'.[37] As we know, Eden's comeback was short-lived. A combination of new and harrowing medical prognoses about his health if he continued to carry the burden of high office and political manoeuvrings by senior ministerial colleagues led to his resignation on 9 January 1957.[38]

Bishop was devastated, and it took him a full six months before he felt able to write to Eden, and even then he struggled to control his emotions. 'My dear

Anthony', he began. 'You said that I might so call you, and I do … [W]hen you left … it was the end of a drama, or a tragedy – the sort in which fate overwhelms the good, but without in any way destroying the validity of the good'. He went on to berate himself for not being 'clever enough to help you through all your great work here' and admitted that 'I feel rather weary … one of the appalling things about Number 10 is that it goes on, and on, and on'.[39] Yet despite his great upset, Bishop was rejuvenated under Macmillan and went on to flourish as a foreign policy adviser in ways that would have been impossible had Eden remained in power. He began sitting in on Cabinet meetings (on Macmillan's insistence), played a key role in the policymaking process over the next two years, and generally exercised an influence out of all proportion to his formal responsibilities.[40] Macmillan proved far readier than Eden to seek the views of all his officials, employing them in a manner akin to national security advisers in the American system and developing the Private Office into a policy think tank, but it was Bishop whom he singled out for his 'exceptional brilliance'.[41] As a measure of his trust in his PPS, in September 1957 Macmillan sent him on a secret mission to Washington armed with a letter for the US Secretary of State, John Foster Dulles, avowing that its bearer was 'one of only two or three men in London' who knew his mind on Syria, the urgent matter he wanted the American's view on. Afterwards, Macmillan wrote again to Dulles, this time to thank him for 'giving so much of your confidence to one of my confidants' and to pronounce the Bishop mission 'a very good plan' since 'it was as near as we could get to talking together ourselves'.[42] The Foreign Office, however, increasingly resented Bishop's influence. Selwyn Lloyd nicknamed him 'Sir Horace', a pointed reference to Sir Horace Wilson, Neville Chamberlain's personal foreign policy adviser at the time of Munich, and on one occasion told him to his face of his distaste for 'government by private secretary'. Bishop brushed him off in characteristically bluff fashion: 'Well', he countered, 'the only alternative is government by politicians'.[43]

As for the rest of the Eden 'team', Clark, always an outsider-insider, had become disillusioned with his job even before the Suez crisis broke, while the Prime Minister, for his part, considered Clark too indiscreet to be a good press secretary. On 29 October, the day that Israel attacked Egypt, Clark's diary recounts a meeting with Bishop, who 'looked completely worn out and very jumpy'. This was partly due to events in the Middle East, and partly because of what he had to say. '[T]he PM has told me that I must keep you out of the Private Office; you must stay down at your end of the building', Bishop explained. 'I know that's very difficult but there is so much going on about the Middle East now that is peculiarly secret; in fact I don't know it all myself'. Bishop was 'sympathetic but firm and begged me not to make a fuss'. Although in practice the exclusion order proved impossible to uphold, Clark's resignation was inevitable and came on 6 November, the day that hostilities ceased.[44] Cairncross, who despite his domestic brief was often dragooned into helping with foreign affairs, stayed at Number 10 for another 18 months after Eden left, writing regularly to his old boss to keep him informed of the doings of 'Freddie

& Philip' and to emphasise 'the great privilege I had in being here while you were PM', before returning to the Home Office in late 1958.[45] De Zulueta has left little trace in the PREM files of his contribution to policymaking under Eden, though the Prime Minister seems to have used him – as he did Bishop – as his 'eyes and ears' about Whitehall.[46] However, in a an April 1957 letter to Eden in which he insisted that time and history would vindicate his Suez policy, de Zulueta gives us a clue as to his personal view on the events of 1956.[47] Another is to be found in his later public admonishment of Monckton and the Chiefs of Staff for their slowness in organising a military response to Nasser's coup: Eden, he declared, 'should have sacked the lot, especially the Minister of Defence'.[48] De Zulueta held Eden in great affection – he recalled shedding tears when he relinquished the premiership – but, like Bishop, he would only truly come into his own as a foreign policy adviser under Macmillan who later praised him as 'a tower of strength', commended his loyalty, calmness in time of crisis, and great knowledge of international affairs, and praised his flawless Russian and French (the latter often put to use as translator during Macmillan's meetings with de Gaulle).[49]

Guy Millard and Suez

Guy Millard was the official rightly regarded as the closest to the Prime Minister at this time.[50] Possibly because jealousy towards political contemporaries made it difficult for him to form close personal attachments, Eden had few real friends in politics. In consequence, and notwithstanding his marriage to Clarissa in 1952, Anthony Nutting thought him 'a very lonely man'. Although he made sure that he was rarely without company, 'his choice of companions generally fell on men much younger than himself who could not possibly represent any threat to his supremacy', and who, as the FO's Pierson Dixon described them, 'were more like "buddies" than real and enduring friends'.[51] In 1955, de Zulueta and Millard were both in their 30s – some 20 years younger than Eden – and fell easily into the buddy category, although Pitblado and Bishop were themselves only in their early 40s. Still, as David Owen tells us, Millard was *primus inter pares*; he was 'not only present at all [the PM's] most important meetings on international affairs, but would see him late at night, early in the morning, read his notations on documents and listen in on many of his telephone conversations'.[52] The personal as well as the professional bond was a very close one – the master and servant relationship did not prevent genuine friendship from forming, with Eden becoming godfather to Millard's son, Nicholas – but this did not mean that Millard necessarily enjoyed his work as a Number 10 functionary. In January 1956, after just nine months, he confessed to a friend that he 'loathes his job, and has tried to get out of it', but when he asked Norman Brook for a transfer he was told to see it through to the end of the year. 'We had Suez in between', he later wryly noted.[53] Millard finally got to submit his resignation on New Year's Eve, 1956, and his disappearance from the office a few weeks later was much regretted by his colleagues: 'Guy's departure was a very sad loss to us', Cairncross wrote to Eden, '& it is very often that we wish he was back'.[54]

Millard has left few fingerprints on the official record in terms of his outlook on events or the nature of the advice he may have offered to the Prime Minister. Nor did he keep a diary, has left no private papers, and in his rare interviews in the decades since Suez he has been the soul of diplomatic discretion.[55] Accordingly, the idea that he was 'a key figure' during the crisis is rooted more in the ubiquity of his presence at Eden's side than in what he said or did as counsellor, confessor or 'buddy'. To coin a cliché, he was there for Eden.[56] Indeed Millard's place in the story of Suez is assured for two 'being there' moments in particular. On the night of Thursday 26 July 1956, when the news reached London of Nasser's daring démarche, it fell to Millard as duty secretary to interrupt a dinner at Downing Street for King Faisal II and members of the Iraqi government to inform the Prime Minister of what had occurred.[57] As the man who whispered in the PM's ear the fatal word-combination of 'Nasser', 'Suez Canal Company', and 'nationalised', he thus unwittingly set in motion the countdown to the end of Eden's political career. Next, on Sunday 14 October 1956, he was present at Chequers when Eden received Major General Maurice Challe, deputy to the Chief of the French General Staff, and Albert Gazier, French Minister of Social Affairs, emissaries of French premier Guy Mollet, who brought with them the news that France and Israel had been secretly planning an attack on Egypt and were looking for British participation in the enterprise. Anthony Nutting, Minister of State at the Foreign Office and the fifth member of the Chequers quintet that day, recalled Eden '[d]oing his best to conceal his excitement'. When Millard, as was his wont, reached for pen and paper to take a record, the Prime Minister gently restrained him: 'There's no need to take notes, Guy'.[58]

For Nutting, this was a depressing epiphany: with a pretext for intervention secured, Eden now seemed determined to re-plot his course for war in company with France and Israel. Nutting, though, would not go with him and resigned from the government soon after.[59] In contrast, Millard's career continued uninterrupted for another two decades before he retired from his final post as Ambassador to Italy in 1976. Ten years on from that, he was prevailed upon by Peter Hennessy to break his silence about the fateful Chequers meeting. Eden had been 'intrigued', Millard felt, rather than excited (as Nutting claimed), by the Challe–Gazier proposal.

> I think he was clutching at straws in a sense; he was looking for a pretext. The problem was that the operation, which had been planned for a long time, had either to go ahead or be scrapped altogether. The reservists had been called up, the shipping had been mobilised and so on. You couldn't disperse all that without abandoning the whole idea of the use of force. Therefore ... this plan, originally worked out by the French and the Israelis, came at a convenient moment and he saw it as a handy pretext.[60]

The aftermath of Suez

In December 1956, Norman Brook commissioned an internal history of the Suez affair based on the documentation available in the Number 10 Private Office.[61] Millard was given the task of researching and writing the study, an implicit acknowledgement of his intimacy with the Suez story in all its forms. A first draft was completed in February 1957, just before his period of notice ended, and over the next few months, while working at the Foreign Office on the European Free Trade Area project, he undertook various revisions until a final version was complete in August and committed to Confidential Print in October.[62] The main conclusion of the study, which was given a very small circulation in Whitehall, now reads as a statement of the obvious. 'For Britain', Millard wrote, 'Suez was a climacteric. It had severely shaken the basis of Anglo-American relations and exposed the limitations of our strength. This fact defined the conditions within which British foreign policy must henceforth operate ... [W]e could never again resort to military action, outside British territories, without at least American acquiescence'. According to its own terms of reference, the study did not attempt 'to give a complete account of the crisis' and took little account of military planning and operations, public opinion in the UK and abroad, the diplomatic exchanges between the concerned governments, and the ebb and flow of negotiation, procedure and debate at the United Nations.[63] Small wonder then that historians looking to the Millard history for official confirmation of Nutting's claims about collusion in his 1967 book *No End of a Lesson* — a 'malevolent as well as inaccurate' work, according to Eden — will be disappointed.[64] Eden, though, when shown a copy of Millard's memorandum in October 1957, pronounced it 'a remarkable piece of work', a comment that can sustain multiple interpretations.[65] 'I used my own judgement', Millard explained in 1987 in connection with the blanket omission of collusion. 'I left that out because I didn't think it would be discreet at that time to write about that aspect of it'.[66] Yet even in 2006, half a century on from Suez, Millard (then in his late 80s) was still being discreet, insisting in a television interview that 'Eden had not had any prior warning that Israel was going to be involved'.[67]

Millard's side of Suez is clearly of great interest, but apart from Bishop's occasional interjections the Prime Minister's Private Office team rarely operated as foreign policy advisers in any formal sense.[68] In the light of Eden's vast experience and expertise in foreign affairs, it may be that awestruck officials considered him impossible to advise, or else, as Clark recalled, they worried that they might give the wrong advice and trigger an 'explosion ... at the back of everything was the fear that he would lose his temper and we should be sworn at'.[69] Pitblado later suggested that if Churchill had been Prime Minister at the time of Suez he would never have acted without careful prior coordination with the United States, and at the first hint of Anglo-American disunity 'Winston would have appeared in Washington' to smooth matters.[70] Whether Pitblado, a civil servant of high ability but by all accounts an unassertive personality, would have offered Eden advice along these lines if he had still been PPS is another matter. Bishop possessed the self-confidence to do so, but as has already seen, he was in agreement with the Prime Minister both on the use of force and, so far as we can tell, on keeping a querulous United States at arm's length.[71]

In the entire run of PREM files on foreign and defence policy for the 1955–1957 period there is only one clear example of Millard abandoning the role of functionary to offer a value judgement. Yet that judgement is of more than passing interest. In October 1955, Downing Street received a summary of a secret CIA assessment of Soviet Cold War policy. With the Kremlin still talking about the 'spirit of Geneva', US intelligence analysts suspected a tactical shift in Soviet policy, with Moscow's public promotion of détente likely to be accompanied by greater levels of subversion in Western Europe. After reading the summary, the Prime Minister asked for Millard's opinion ('GM. Pretty Good?'), an unusual occurrence in itself. Yet what Eden received in reply cohered so closely to his own attitude towards both the Middle East and the United States that he might have written it himself. (Frustratingly, a small portion of Millard's minute, indicated below by parentheses, remains classified after nearly 60 years). 'Yes', Millard agreed, the CIA report was valuable, 'but it doesn't take full account of the possibility that the Geneva spirit is intended primarily to mask an offensive against the ME [Middle East]'. He continued:

> Communism has failed, temporarily, in Europe. In the ME the prize is almost as great – W. oil supplies, a vast uncommitted area ripe for Communism, the possibility of separating us from India, Pakistan + SE Asia. Our weakness is correspondingly great. British + American policies are nationally divergent, and even our own hands are tied because we cannot abandon Israel. If this is Soviet policy, we might have to defend our ME policy much more vigorously – with men, money … + if necessary bring the Americans along in our wake. But we should also have to try to work with Arab nationalism, + not, as so often in the past, against it.[72]

Here, then, is a possible indication of the kind of counsel Millard may have given Eden in all those many informal and unrecorded conversations during Suez. And as with Bishop, we may infer that in most respects he was four-square behind his master's handling of the situation. This is also the conclusion to be drawn from his public statements. 'There is a lot of humbug about Suez quite honestly', he said in 1991. 'People forget that the policy at the time was extremely popular. It only became slightly less popular when it failed'.[73] As for the issue of collusion, Millard has been as evasive in public over the last four decades as he was in his secret internal history. Still, one cannot but wonder what he made of Eden's last ever performance in the House of Commons on 20 December 1956 when he declared: 'I want to say this on the question of foreknowledge, and to say it quite bluntly to the House, that there was not foreknowledge that Israel would attack Egypt – there was not'.[74] What many suspected, Millard knew for a fact: this was a lie. After all, he had been there, at

Chequers, on 14 October, and had also been fully briefed on the two follow-up meetings at Sèvres.[75] Did Millard ever consider resigning when the Prime Minister lied to Parliament? Or is the ethical dilemma different for an official, particularly a Number 10 secretary, compared with a politician? Does it even exist?[76] Millard was asked these kinds of questions in an interview for the BBC Radio 4 documentary *A Canal Too Far*, broadcast in 1987. 'I didn't feel the need to strike political or moral attitudes', he said. 'I don't somehow see that as the function of a civil servant'. When pressed – 'presumably you were distressed by your boss lying to the House of Commons[?]' – there was a pregnant pause before the reply: 'Not unduly'.[77] With this, Millard came close to articulating the principle 'My political master right or wrong', but this, perhaps, is how it should be for a civil servant. At any rate, this is how it was for Millard who wrote to Mark Laity, the producer of *A Canal Too Far*, thanking him for 'drawing my attention to an ethical dilemma of which I appear to have been unaware at the time'.[78]

How much did Eden's other Number 10 foreign policy advisers know of collusion? At one level, it seems hard to believe that thrown together in close daily contact, and probably sharing something of a siege mentality during the crisis, Bishop and de Zulueta were given no hints by Millard. On the other hand we must be cognisant of Millard's oft-remarked upon discretion and his utter loyalty to the Prime Minister. Moreover, Bishop later denied any personal awareness of collusion: 'Something was obviously taking place', he recalled, but information was disseminated 'very much on a need to know basis'.[79] When the 'collusion witch-hunt' (as Brook termed it) began in earnest in November 1956, Bishop's first instinct was assume the Prime Minister's innocence.[80] A demand by David Astor, the editor of the *Observer*, that the government 'clean up our national reputation' by adopting a policy of full disclosure, 'made me feel quite sick', Bishop wrote to Eden.[81] Even when collusion was later confirmed it does not seem to have affected Bishop's view of Eden with whom he maintained a regular, affectionate and lifelong correspondence.[82] This is instructive. So, too, is the fact that following Eden's death in January 1977, Bishop became was one of the Trustees (along with Lady Avon, as Clarissa became when Eden was raised to the peerage in 1961, and Lord Head) with responsibility responsible for the disposal of Eden's estate and papers.[83]

Eden's health has long been the subject of debate. In a note written at the time of his resignation, and probably with future biographers in mind, Eden confirmed that since 1953, when the slip of a surgeon's scalpel during a routine gall bladder operation had severed his bile duct and brought him close to death, he had only managed to function 'with the aid of drugs and stimulants', and that in the period following Nasser's coup 'I have been obliged to increase the drugs considerably & also increase the stimulants necessary to counteract the drugs'.[84] David Owen has shown that amongst these drugs was Drinamyl, which, in combination with other medication Eden was known to be taking, could well have caused insomnia, restlessness, anxiety, irritability, over-stimulation and over-confidence.[85] Historians have long debated the impact of Eden's drug regimen on his decision-making without ever reaching any definitive conclusion, though Clarissa, who ought to have known better than anyone, has wholly rejected the idea of a link between his health and his policy choices.[86] Owen, however, is convinced that in three areas – the decision on collusion, the assumption that the Americans would complain but ultimately acquiesce in the Anglo-French action, and the lying to Parliament – 'his judgement was seriously impaired and his illness and treatment made the major contribution to that impairment'.[87] To the extent that his Private Office team have commented on this issue, they are with Clarissa. 'He was very highly strung and the pressures on him at that time were enormous', Millard observed. 'He was undoubtedly much less well physically than he had been before. Under pressure he tended to get very nervy but to say he was not in command of himself is an exaggeration'.[88] Bishop agreed. 'I don't think this affected his performance. On occasion he was short-tempered and irritated, but there was nothing new in that. This was in his nature'.[89] In any event, Millard concluded, 'I doubt whether things would have changed very much even if he had been in full possession of his health'.[90]

Conclusion

From the standpoint of history it is a matter of considerable regret that Eden lacked a Downing Street insider-chronicler. Yet he might have had one if Evelyn Shuckburgh, his PPS at the Foreign Office from 1951 to 1954, had been able to continue with him to Number 10, as he might have done had Churchill stepped down earlier. In *Descent to Suez*, his diaries published in 1986, Shuckburgh offered a richly textured portrait of Eden, emphasising his qualities as a man and a statesmen, but never shying away from recording his personal failings (especially his temper tantrums and debilitating health issues) or critically scrutinising his policy choices. Immediately recognised as one of the most important diplomatic diaries to emerge in the post-war era, *Descent to Suez* has become essential reading for students and historians working on British foreign policy in the 1950s in general and on the origins of Suez in particular.[91]

Shuckburgh began keeping a diary shortly after Eden returned to the Foreign Office, initially as a form of therapy. 'You took on yourself a great deal of his emotional burdens', he later explained. Eden 'laid them on his Private Secretary' and the diary thus became 'a sort of prophylactic'.[92] But he was also very conscious of his position as an eye-witness to history and came to regard his diary as a source to be mined by historians in the future.[93] In 1965, when the Whitehall mandarinate attempted to ban the keeping of diaries by ministerial advisers, Shuckburgh, then UK Permanent Representative to NATO, reacted with fury. In a letter to the Head of the Diplomatic Service he decried 'a serious step in the down-grading and de-vitalisation of civil servants'. He went on:

> Ministers expect to have advisers of the highest quality, capable of contributing to their thought, sharing their official and even personal preoccupations

and adding to their political stature. They cannot expect these men at the same time to be lay figures, without memory or judgment, in whose presence the talk and behaviour of the Minister are to be as if they had never been. A man is responsible for his acts and his statements wherever he makes them and must learn to judge what confidence he can place in others and to use discretion. Politicians surely cannot be given a kind of blanket exemption from this human condition. There is also History to consider, and the claims of truth. Is it right to assist the establishment of a 'public image' for a Minister, to be protected even after his death from the intrusion of 'indiscreet' recollections? We are glad enough to be able to read, after a suitable delay, what public men have written to their wives and mistresses, and we consider this to be the stuff of History. Is what they say in front of senior civil servants to be considered more privileged than that?

'If we are not careful', he ended, 'we shall turn ourselves into intellectual eunuchs and un-men and create in our politicians a wholly erroneous idea of their immunity from the normal human responsibilities'.[94]

What would historians give for a Millard diary covering Eden's time at Number 10 to complement Shuckburgh's diary of his post-war Foreign Secretaryship? Oddly enough, the answer may be 'not a lot'. Everything we know about Millard indicates that he regarded the bond of trust between minister (and even more so Prime Minister) and official as sacred, and even if we accept, for the sake of argument, that he was indiscreet enough to keep a personal record while working with Eden, it would be unlikely to contain the kind of delicious and damning detail to be found in Shuckburgh's diary. And if even if it did record faithfully his experiences of working with the Prime Minister, it is hard to imagine that Millard – a genuine friend of Eden's – would have allowed it ever to enter the public domain. In the end, the difference between Millard and Shuckburgh, and the reason why the former served Eden but the latter served Eden *and* history (or at least his version of history), may hinge on their contrasting sense of 'duty'. Millard probably knew more of Eden's Suez secrets than anyone else apart from Clarissa,[95] but leaving aside his personal feelings of warmth and friendship for the Prime Minister, he clearly felt (as did Bishop) that duty and loyalty were synonymous concepts. For Millard, the rules of the confessional applied. Shuckburgh, in contrast, never accepted that duty involved aiding and abetting a politician in maintaining his public image unto and even beyond death and argued instead that there 'should be a limit to the subservience expected of officials by politicians'.[96] Accordingly, in *Descent to Suez*, he made his contribution to history, but in publishing his diaries he committed what Eden's family considered to be a gross and hurtful act of disloyalty.[97] Historians, however, have reason to be grateful to Shuckburgh, though Prime Ministers would undoubtedly prefer their Private Office staff to follow the Millard code.

50 *Kevin Ruane*

Notes

1. I would like to thank Canterbury Christ Church University for financial assistance in the researching of this chapter, and David Carlton, David Dutton, Peter Hennessey, Richard Thorpe and Geoffrey Warner for their help and advice.
2. John Colville, *The Fringes of Power: Downing Street Diaries 1939–1955* (London: Hodder & Stoughton, 1985), 708.
3. 'The trouble with Anthony Eden', Harold Macmillan later observed, 'was that he was trained to win the Derby in 1938; unfortunately, he was not let out of the starting stalls until 1955'. Cited in D. R. Thorpe,*Eden: The Life and Times of Anthony Eden, First Earl of Avon* (London: Chatto & Windus, 2003), 430.
4. Colville, *Fringes*, 708.
5. Note by Churchill, 6 April 1955, quoted in Martin Gilbert, *Never Despair: Winston S. Churchill, 1945–1965* (London: Heinemann, 1988), 1125.
6. Roy Jenkins, *Churchill* (London: Macmillan, 2001), 843. In truth, Lord Moran's diaries come closer than Colville's to a true act of 'Boswellization'. Lord Moran, *Churchill: The Struggle for Survival, 1940–1965* (London: Constable, 1965).
7. Colville to Shuckburgh, 12 October 1986, Cadbury Research Library, Birmingham [henceforward CRL]: MS191/4/3.
8. William Clark, *Memoirs: From Three Worlds* (London: Sidgwick & Jackson, 1986), 151.
9. Colville, *Fringes*, 631–2.
10. Interview with David Pitblado, Liddell Hart Centre for Military Archives, King's College London [henceforward LHCMA]: SUEZOHP 15.
11. *Daily Telegraph*, 14 March 2005; William Plowden, 'Bishop, Sir Frederick Arthur (1915–2005), *Oxford Dictionary of National Biography: 2005–2008*, ed. Lawrence Goldman (Oxford: Oxford University Press, 2013), 105.
12. Thorpe, *Eden*, 443; Plowden, 'Bishop', 105; Max Egremont, 'Zulueta, Sir Philip Francis de (1925–1989)', in *Oxford Dictionary of National Biography: From the earliest times to the year 2000*, ed. H. G. C. Matthew and Brian Harrison (Oxford: Oxford University Press, 2004), vol. LX, 1023; *Daily Telegraph*, 7 May 2013; *The Times*, 16 May 2013.
13. Interview with Guy Millard, LHCMA: SUEZOHP 14; Peter Catterall, ed., *The Macmillan Diaries*, vol. I:*The Cabinet Years, 1950–1957* (London: Macmillan, 2003), 482.
14. Interview with David Pitblado, LHCMA: SUEZOHP 15; Pitblado to the author, 13 March 1996.
15. Interview with Freddie Bishop, LHCMA: SUEZOHP 3.
16. Philip de Zulueta, 'Thirty years on', *The Spectator*, 11 October 1986, 33.
17. Speech by Eisenhower, 24 August 1955, *Public Papers of the Presidents: Dwight D. Eisenhower, 1955* (Washington, D.C.: USGPO, 1959), 807.
18. Keith Kyle, *Suez* (London: Weidenfeld & Nicolson, 1991), 72–8.
19. Clarissa Eden, *A Memoir: From Churchill to Eden* (London: Weidenfeld & Nicolson, 2007), 258.
20. On Suez, in addition to Keith Kyle, see Simon C. Smith, ed., *Reassessing Suez: New Perspectives on the Crisis and its Aftermath* (London: Ashgate, 2008); Jonathan Pearson, *Sir Anthony Eden and the Suez Crisis: Reluctant Gamble* (Basingstoke: Palgrave, 2003); W. Scott Lucas, *Divided War Stand: Britain, the US and the Suez Crisis* (London: Hodder & Stoughton, 1991); David Carlton, *Britain and the Suez Crisis* (Oxford: Blackwell, 1989); and Hugh Thomas, *The Suez Affair* (London: Weidenfeld & Nicolson, 1967).
21. Alistair Horne, *Macmillan*, vol. II: *1957–1986* (London: Macmillan, 1989), 161; Interview with Freddie Bishop, LHCMA: SUEZOHP 3.
22. Bishop to Helsby, 5 May 1965, The National Archives, Kew [henceforward TNA]: BA 19/58; Plowden, 'Bishop', 105.

23 Minute by Bishop and enclosure, 24 August 1956, TNA: PREM 11/1100; Memorandum by Millard, August 1957, TNA: FO 800/728.
24 Bishop to Eden, 20 August 1956; Minute by Millard, 20 August 1956, TNA: PREM 11/1093.
25 Bishop to Eden, 2 November 1956, TNA: PREM 11/1105; CM (56) 77, 2 November 1956, TNA: CAB 128/30.
26 Catterall, *Macmillan Diaries*, 590.
27 Brook to Eden, 25 August 1956, TNA: PREM 11/1152.
28 Ibid.; Salisbury to Eden; Home and Lennox-Boyd, 24 August 1956, TNA: PREM 11/1152.
29 Clarissa Eden diary, 27 August 1956, quoted in Clarissa Eden, *Memoir*, 240.
30 Clark, *Three Worlds*, 173.
31 Minute by Bishop to Eden and enclosure, 24 August 1956, TNA: PREM 11/1100; *The Times*, 5 April 2005.
32 CM (56) 62, 28 August 1956, TNA: CAB 128/30.
33 Thorpe, *Eden*, 445.
34 London to State, 23 October 1956, *Foreign Relations of the United States* [henceforward *FRUS*] *1955–1957* (Washington, DC: United States Government Printing Office, 1985–1992), vol. XVI, 774.
35 Cherie Booth and Cate Haste, *The Goldfish Bowl: Married to the Prime Minister, 1955–1997* (London: Chatto & Windus, 2004), 29.
36 Bishop to Eden, 4 December 1956, TNA: PREM 11/1548.
37 Eden to Millard, 8 December 1956, TNA: PREM 11/2195.
38 Thorpe, *Eden*, 542–8.
39 Bishop to Eden, 29 July 1957, CRL: AP23/10/1.
40 Plowden, 'Bishop', 105; *Daily Telegraph*, 14 March 2005; *The Times*, 5 April 2005; Interview with Freddie Bishop, LHCMA: SUEZOHP 3.
41 Robert McNamara, *Britain, Nasser and the Balance of Power in the Middle East, 1952–1957* (London: Cass, 2003), 66; Harold Macmillan, *Tides of Fortune 1945–1955* (London: Macmillan, 1969), 303–4.
42 Macmillan to Dulles, 30 August 1957, *FRUS 1955–1957*, vol. XIII, 670, note 3; Macmillan to Dulles, 12 September 1957, TNA: PREM 11/2190.
43 D. R. Thorpe, *Selwyn Lloyd* (London: Jonathan Cape, 1989), 304; *The Times*, 5 April 2005.
44 Clark diary, 29 October 1956, quoted in Clark, *Three Worlds*, 196.
45 Cairncross to Eden, 4 April 1957, CRL: AP24/10/1; 16 August 1957, CRL: AP24/10/2; 17 December 1957, CRL: AP24/10/8; 8 June 1958, CRL: AP24/10/14.
46 Thorpe, *Eden*, 498.
47 De Zulueta to Eden, 24 April 1957, CRL: AP23/67/1.
48 De Zulueta, 'Thirty years on', 33–4.
49 Macmillan, *Riding the Storm*, 192; Egremont, 'Zulueta', 1023.
50 Peter Hennessy, *The Prime Minister: The Office and its Holders since 1945* (London: Allen Lane, 2000), 235.
51 Anthony Nutting, 'Sir Anthony Eden', in *The Prime Ministers*, vol. II:*From Lord John Russell to Edward Heath*, ed. Herbert Van Thal (London: Allen & Unwin, 1975), 338.
52 David Owen, *In Sickness and in Health: Illness in Heads of Government during the Last 100 Years* (London: Methuen, 2008), 397.
53 Evelyn Shuckburgh, *Descent to Suez: Diaries 1951–1956* (London: Weidenfeld & Nicolson, 1986), 326; Interview with Guy Millard, LHCMA: SUEZOHP 14; *The Times*, 16 May 2013.
54 Cairncross to Eden, 4 April 1957, CRL: AP24/10/1; 16 August 1957, CRL: AP24/10/2. Millard later said that had he known how ill Eden was he would have stayed on. Pearson, *Reluctant Gamble*, 125–6.

55 The Millard papers, so-called, in the Bodleian Library in Oxford, contain only the transcript of an interview he gave as part of the United Nations Career Record Project.
56 Thorpe, *Eden*, 274.
57 Peter Hennessy, *Having it So Good: Britain in the Fifties* (London: Allen Lane, 2006), 417. D. R. Thorpe suggests that de Zulueta brought Eden the news. See *Supermac: The Life of Harold Macmillan* (London: Chatto & Windus, 2010), 333. However, the next day, 27 July, *The Times* listed Millard (but not de Zulueta) amongst the guests, and Millard himself later insisted 'I was on duty that night'. Interview with Guy Millard, LHCMA: SUEZOHP 14.
58 Anthony Nutting, *No End of a Lesson: The Story of Suez* (London: Constable, 1967), 93; Thorpe, *Eden*, 513.
59 *Guardian*, 26 February 1999.
60 Hennessy, *Having it So Good*, 434.
61 Ironically, Brook may have had a hand in destroying key documents. See Edward Heath, *The Course of My Life: My Autobiography* (London: Hodder & Stoughton, 1998), 176–7, and letter from Hugh Greene, *The Listener*, 25 September 1986.
62 Memorandum by Millard, October 1957, TNA: FO800/728; Millard to Eden, 9 October 1957, CRL: AP24/49/1A.
63 Memorandum by Millard, August 1957, and note by Selwyn Lloyd, n.d., CRL: AP24/49/1A; Brook to Eden, 9 November 1957, CRL: AP23/50/10.
64 Eden to Salisbury, 6 May 1967, CRL: AP24/60/13.
65 Eden to Millard, 8 October 1957, CRL: AP24/49/1.
66 Peter Hennessy, 'The Scars of Suez: Reopening the Wounds of the End of Empire', *The Listener*, 5 February 1987, 8.
67 Owen, *Sickness*, 124 n.
68 Denis Kavanagh and Anthony Seldon, *The Powers behind the Prime Minister: The Hidden Influence of Number Ten* (London: HarperCollins, 2000), 58–9.
69 Clark, *Three Worlds*, 164.
70 Gilbert, *Never Despair*, 1222 n. 2.
71 Colville, *Fringes*, 632 n. 1.
72 Washington to FO, No. 2489, 14 October 1955; Minute by Millard to Eden, 18 October 1955, TNA: PREM 11/1079. (Eden acknowledged the memo by noting 'Thank you. No easy task'.) Peter Hennessey suspects that the redaction relates to clandestine operations. See *Prime Minister*, 228.
73 Interview with Guy Millard, LHCMA: SUEZOHP 14.
74 *The Parliamentary Debates (Hansard): House of Commons Official Report* (London: HMSO, 1944–) [henceforward *H.C. Deb.*], 5th ser., vol. 562, c. 1518.
75 Hennessy, 'Scars of Suez', 9.
76 Two junior ministers, Nutting and Edward Boyle, Economic Secretary to the Treasury, resigned over Suez, along with three junior officials at the FO.
77 Hennessy, 'Scars of Suez', 9.
78 Peter Hennessy, *Whitehall* (London: Secker & Warburg, 1989), 168–9. This chimes with what Bishop told Clark on 29 October 1956.
79 Interview with Freddie Bishop, LHCMA: SUEZOHP 3.
80 Diary, 15 November 1956, Clarissa Eden, *Memoir*, 257.
81 Astor to Macleod, 14 November 1956, Bishop to Eden, 16 November 1956, Cairncross note, 17 November 1956, TNA: PREM 11/1127.
82 See the CRL: AP23/10 series, with Eden's last letter to Bishop written from the USA just one month before his death.
83 Cabinet Office meeting, 3 March 1977; Head to Palliser, 31 May 1977, TNA: FCO 12/1220.
84 Note by Eden, n.d. [January 1957], CRL: AP20/23/11.
85 Owen, *Sickness*, 118–21.

86 Clarissa Eden, *Memoir*, 260.
87 Owen, *Sickness*, 140.
88 Interview with Guy Millard, LHCMA: SUEZOHP 14.
89 Interview with Freddie Bishop, LHCMA: SUEZOHP 3.
90 Interview with Guy Millard, 20 April 1991, Bodleian Library, Oxford: MS. Eng. c. 4729.
91 For example, William Roger Louis, 'A prima donna with honour', *Times Literary Supplement*, 31 October 1986, 1207; Ritchie Ovendale, Review of *Anthony Eden* by Robert Rhodes James, and *Descent to Suez: Diaries 1951–1956* by Evelyn Shuckburgh, *International Affairs*, 63 (1987), 669; Peter Hennessy, 'Through Egyptian eyes', *New Statesman*, 14 November 1986.
92 Interview with Evelyn Shuckburgh, LHCMA: SUEZOHP 20.
93 Shuckburgh to Wilkinson, 11 October 1969, CRL: MS191/2/6/3/2; Shuckburgh, *Descent to Suez*, introduction, 3, 154.
94 Shuckburgh to Garner, 23 June 1965, TNA: FO366/3547.
95 In 1980, a review of the Suez records at the UK National Archives, authorised by Prime Minister Margaret Thatcher, confirmed that Millard was one of only three officials fully in the know with regard to the story of the crisis. The other two were Sir Donald Logan, Assistant Private Secretary to Foreign Secretary Selwyn Lloyd, and Sir Patrick Dean, Assistant Under-Secretary at the Foreign Office and Chairman of the Joint Intelligence Committee. See The National Archives, 'Release of Suez record', www.nationalarchives.gov.uk/releases/2006/december/release.htm; also *The Times*, 16 May 2013.
96 Shuckburgh to Wilkinson, 11 October 1969, CRL: MS191/2/6/3/2.
97 Private information.

References

Catterall, Peter, ed., *The Macmillan Diaries*, vol. I: *The Cabinet Years, 1950–1957* (London: Macmillan, 2003).

Carlton, David, *Britain and the Suez Crisis* (Oxford: Blackwell, 1989).

Clark, William, *Memoirs: From Three Worlds* (London: Sidgwick & Jackson, 1986).

Colville, John, *The Fringes of Power: Downing Street Diaries 1939–1955* (London: Hodder & Stoughton, 1985).

Eden, Clarissa, *A Memoir: From Churchill to Eden* (London: Weidenfeld & Nicolson, 2007).

Gilbert, Martin, *Never Despair: Winston S. Churchill, 1945–1965* (London: Heinemann, 1988).

Heath, Edward, *The Course of My Life: My Autobiography* (London: Hodder & Stoughton, 1998).

Hennessy, Peter, *Having it So Good: Britain in the Fifties* (London: Allen Lane, 2006).

Hennessy, Peter, *The Prime Minister: The Office and its Holders since 1945* (London: Allen Lane, 2000).

Hennessy, Peter, *Whitehall* (London: Secker & Warburg, 1989).

Horne, Alistair, *Macmillan*, vol. II: *1957–1986* (London: Macmillan, 1989).

Jenkins, Roy, *Churchill* (London: Macmillan, 2001).

Kavanagh, Denis, and Anthony Seldon, *The Powers Behind the Prime Minister: The Hidden Influence of Number ten* (London: HarperCollins, 2000).

Kyle, Keith, *Suez* (London: Weidenfeld & Nicolson, 1991).

Lucas, W.Scott, *Divided War Stand: Britain, the US and the Suez Crisis* (London: Hodder & Stoughton, 1991).

Macmillan, Harold, *Tides of Fortune 1945–1955* (London: Macmillan, 1969).

McNamara, Robert, *Britain, Nasser and the Balance of Power in the Middle East, 1952–1957* (London: Cass, 2003).

Moran, Lord, *Churchill: The Struggle for Survival, 1940–1965* (London: Constable, 1965).

Nutting, Anthony, *No End of a Lesson: The Story of Suez* (London: Constable, 1967).

Nutting, Anthony, 'Sir Anthony Eden', in *The Prime Ministers*, vol. II: *From Lord John Russell to Edward Heath*, ed. Herbert Van Thal (London: Allen & Unwin, 1975).

Owen, David, *In Sickness and in Health: Illness in Heads of Government During the Last 100 Years* (London: Methuen, 2008).

Pearson, Jonathan, *Sir Anthony Eden and the Suez Crisis: Reluctant Gamble* (Basingstoke: Palgrave, 2003).

Smith, Simon C., ed., *Reassessing Suez: New Perspectives on the Crisis and its Aftermath* (London: Ashgate, 2008).

Thomas, Hugh, *The Suez Affair* (London: Weidenfeld & Nicolson, 1967).

Thorpe, D. R., *Eden: The Life and Times of Anthony Eden, First Earl of Avon* (London: Chatto & Windus, 2003).

Thorpe, D. R., *Selwyn Lloyd* (London: Jonathan Cape, 1989).

Thorpe, D. R., *Supermac: The Life of Harold Macmillan* (London: Chatto & Windus, 2010).

3   Philip de Zulueta

Peter Catterall[1]

It is perhaps one measure of the perceived importance of the position of Private Secretary for foreign affairs to the Prime Minister at the time that the first mention of Sir Philip Francis de Zulueta in *Who's Who*, that listing of the great and good, was in 1964 after he had moved on from that situation to more lucrative opportunities in the City.[2] This, however, is not necessarily surprising. Being a Private Secretary had, after all, long been a very junior position in the Diplomatic Service, often combining the duties of secretarial support with those of a general factotum.[3] What won Philip the attention of *Who's Who* was not his job, but the knighthood he was given in 1963: within the hierarchy of the Foreign Office he remained a comparatively young man in a commensurate role. Philip had only just turned 39 when he embarked on what turned out to be a high-flying second career in business.

Having been born on 2 January 1925 in Oxford, both diplomacy and business might be said to have been in Philip's blood. The de Zuluetas were a Basque family who became established as bankers and traders in the southern Spanish port of Cadiz in the mid eighteenth century. There they became embroiled in the tumultuous Spanish politics during and immediately after the French revolutionary wars. Philip's great-great-grandfather, Pedro Juan, was briefly president of the *Cortes de Cadiz* in the summer of 1823 just before a French invasion enabled Ferdinand VII to repudiate the liberal constitution of 1812 and turn on his enemies.[4] Pedro Juan fled to Liverpool and re-established his banking and shipping interests there and in London. At the end of the 1820s there was an application for British citizenship on the grounds that Zulueta & Co was now well-established in the City, whence they had come in order more effectively to carry on their commerce with the newly independent colonies of South America than was then possible from their native Spain.[5] After Ferdinand's death in 1833, however, Pedro Juan came back into favour in Spain, being appointed Condé de Torre Diaz in 1846.

By then Zulueta & Co was being run by his eldest son, Philip's great-grandfather, Pedro José. He had become a British subject in 1836, the year he married Sophie Anna Wilcox, the daughter of Brodie Wilcox, one of the founders of the P&O shipping line, in 1834. Pedro José was clearly well-connected in the City, but also had some more dubious contacts, including his cousin

Julian, who acted for the firm in Havana and was the largest slave-trader in the Spanish empire. The slave trade had been outlawed in Britain in 1807 and consolidating legislation in 1824 further made trading with slavers illegal, but only if conducted with prior knowledge. It was this proviso which proved instrumental in securing Pedro José's acquittal in 1843 when he was arraigned at the Old Bailey in a celebrated trial for his firm's role in financing and equipping the voyage of the *Augusta* via Cadiz to the notorious slaving station of Gallinas on behalf of the equally notorious slaver Pedro Martinez.

Pedro José's somewhat cynical view expressed in his subsequent publication about the trial was that laws to control the end-use of commerce were impossible to police and, in an age when slavery was still legal in many territories, in any case undesirable. These views had some resonances in Philip's time, considering American attempts to discourage British trade with communist states like Cuba. They were clearly widely shared amongst Pedro José's fellow bankers in the City, where Zulueta & Co remained active until closed for family reasons in 1915.[6] Meanwhile, his second son and Philip's grandfather, Pedro Juan, moved into a different field. He served in the Spanish Diplomatic Service from 1866 to 1888 and was first secretary of the Spanish Embassy in London in the 1870s when he married Laura Mary, the daughter of Sir Justin Sheil, a former British Ambassador to Persia.[7] It was in that Embassy, and thus on Spanish soil, that Philip's father, Francis, was born on 12 September 1878.

Francis, unusually, was neither a businessman nor a diplomat. He was instead a distinguished classicist, academic and Egyptologist. At the time of Philip's birth he was Fellow of All Souls in Oxford and also Regius Professor of Civil Law at that university.[8] Spanish citizenship had been no hindrance to such advancements. It did, however, prevent Francis from identifying with his adopted country by rallying to the colours in 1914. It was in this emergency that Francis now applied for naturalisation, urging haste before he became too old for military service and writing 'I do not see how one can avoid army service as a matter of honour'.[9] He served in the Worcestershire Regiment throughout the First World War, rising to the rank of captain in 1916, before returning to Oxford in 1919.

Philip inherited a number of useful skills from his father. Francis was linguistically gifted and gregarious. He also passed on his devout Catholicism to his only child. One of his cousins was Cardinal Rafael Merry del Val, the secretary of the Congregation of the Holy Office from 1914 until his death in 1930. Another, Rafael's elder brother Alfonso, was Spanish Ambassador to the Court of St James, 1913–1931.[10] These familial connections with Catholic and royalist Spain were clearly important both to Francis and to Philip and help to explain Francis' support for Franco during the Spanish Civil War (1936–1939). Philip accordingly grew up in a very conservative household and followed his father's footsteps via the Jesuit private school of Beaumont College in Berkshire – where he was head boy – to New College, Oxford. By then the Second World War was already raging. While Francis pursued good works, aiding Polish and Jewish refugees, Philip began his studies not in law but modern history. As soon as he was able, in 1943, he joined the Welsh Guards. For the rest of his life he shared with his future boss, Harold Macmillan, who had served in the Grenadier Guards in the First World War, a strong identification as a guardsman.[11] As a tank commander he participated in the liberation of the Netherlands. Like his father, Philip rose to the rank of captain in 1945. After two years' service in occupied Europe Philip left the army in 1947 and returned to Oxford to complete his degree, leaving with a third class in jurisprudence in 1948. It was not that he lacked Francis's brilliance so much as the difficulty of returning to university life after the war.[12] With his father's encouragement, Philip still read for the Bar, but his aptitude lay elsewhere.[13] Luckily for him there was heavy recruitment to the Foreign Service in the aftermath of the war: instead of the second class honours degree normally required as standard for entrants to Branch A – the senior ranks of the service known as the administrative class – candidates had to demonstrate their capability to pass this and to acquire linguistic competence. Philip spoke flawless French but still had to pass the written examination and surmount the various personality tests during the country house weekend used to assess entrants.[14] Having done so, he was appointed a grade 9 officer, also known as a Third Secretary, on 13 October 1949.[15]

In common with about half the new entrants of the period, Philip swiftly was given his first overseas posting, being sent to Moscow on 28 January 1950.[16] There he served as Private Secretary to the Ambassador, Sir David Kelly. A later diplomat opined that Third Secretaries are 'treated as skivvies' by their ambassadors.[17] It is likely that Philip's experience was little different. Certainly, in the lengthy memoir Kelly wrote immediately at the end of what was his last diplomatic posting, while he comments in some detail on the Russian secret service bodyguards who accompanied him – and indeed Philip on his one attempt to see something of Russia – everywhere, there is no discussion of any of his staff.[18] On the other hand, as Sir Evelyn Shuckburgh noted of his experiences skivvying for Sir Miles Lampson in Egypt in the 1930s, private secretaries nevertheless 'are given responsibilities well beyond their years and enjoy the acquaintance of interesting people in every walk of life long before they could otherwise expect it'.[19] Such experiences no doubt helped to prepare Philip for when he later succeeded to Shuckburgh's sometime role as Private Secretary to Sir Anthony Eden. So did the knowledge of Russian he acquired. Language education was then the main form of training the Foreign Office provided.[20] Philip, however, had little time to enjoy the £100 a year allowance granted him for his Russian skills on 31 October 1951. These allowances were only payable when serving in the field, and Philip returned to London on 4 February 1952.[21] The only overseas posting of his diplomatic career had ended.

The Foreign Office back in London was then divided into some 30 departments which had functional, territorial, administrative or miscellaneous responsibilities. Philip was placed in the General Department, whose role was to advise the Foreign Secretary on broad policy relating to civil aviation, shipping, telecommunications, international post, meteorology, fishing, safety at sea or locust control. These departments were small teams, in which junior responsibility was given to Second or even Third Secretaries. Having been promoted to Second Secretary (grade 8) on his 28th birthday, Philip was given responsibility for civil aviation.[22] He also, however, clearly acquired some miscellaneous duties as well, including an attachment to the Brazilian representative at the Coronation in June 1953. This seems to have given him on the grounds that his Spanish language would be useful in dealing with the lusophone Brazilians, though in practice all his conversations with them were in French. The appointment did, however, give him his first encounter with his future wife who, sharing his linguistic facility with French and Spanish, was also helping the Brazilians and literally ran into him on the stairs one day.[23] Then, on 1 September 1953, he became a Resident Clerk.[24]

Some years later Geoffrey Moorhouse noted that the six Resident Clerks of the 1970s were generally at the rank of First Secretary (grade 7), a rank Philip did not obtain until 5 March 1957. Philip may have risen more rapidly because of the war-induced gaps in the ranks. The four Resident Clerks of his day occupied flats in the eaves of the Foreign Office with spectacular views over St James' Park, taking it in turns to be on night duty dealing with any issues that might arise. Because of the unsocial nature of the job they were given a special allowance and necessarily expected to be unmarried.[25] Accordingly, it was not until after he left this role in 1955 that Philip married Marie-Louise, the eldest daughter of the 2nd Baron Windlesham. They proved a devoted couple, and Philip immensely valued his wife's judgement.[26]

It was this post as Resident Clerk that gave Philip some significant patrons. The Resident Clerks came under the Permanent Under-Secretary's Department established in 1948 which managed liaison with the Ministry of Defence, the Chiefs of Staff, the Joint Planning Staff and the Joint Intelligence Committee (JIC). The chairman of the JIC at the time was Patrick Dean, one of the two Assistant Under-Secretaries responsible for this department, while the head of department was Geoffrey McDermott.[27] The position also involved liaison at the highest level, for instance through passing on drafts to the Foreign Secretary; the resulting sense of policy influence helping to compensate for the unsocial hours.[28] It certainly must have given Philip a chance to attract attention at those highest levels such that, when the Foreign Secretary, Sir Anthony Eden, succeeded Churchill as Prime Minister on 12 April 1955 he took Philip with him to Downing Street. Philip, however, had not previously met Eden. It was Eden's Private Secretary, Anthony Rumbold, who recommended Philip for the position. Rumbold stayed at the Foreign Office to serve the new Secretary of State, Harold Macmillan, until replaced by P. F. Hancock in September 1955. Philip, meanwhile, was now officially seconded to the Treasury in order to serve in the Prime Minister's Private Office.[29]

Working under Eden

The Number 10 Private Office Philip then joined was four strong headed by David Pitblado.[30] Guy Millard, a future Ambassador to Italy, was the other member from a diplomatic background, having preceded Philip to Number 10 by six days. Millard was considerably senior to Philip in the Diplomatic Service, having served as an assistant Private Secretary to Foreign Secretary Eden in 1941–1945. He accordingly knew Eden – his son's godfather – well and had been invited to join him in Number 10. The other member of the team was Freddie Bishop. He had previously, in 1953–1955, been in the Cabinet Office dealing with the economic business of the Cabinet and the organisation of its committees. This was invaluable experience for the Private Office which stood Bishop in good stead when in early 1956 he succeeded Pitblado as Principal Private Secretary, being replaced in his turn by Neil Cairncross, who specialised in advising on answering Prime Minister's questions. Despite his background as a home civil servant Bishop played a major role in advising the Prime Minister on foreign affairs and accompanying him on overseas visits throughout his time in the Private Office until his move back to the Cabinet Office in the summer of 1959 as deputy secretary. Accordingly Philip was at the time only the most junior of several foreign policy advisers in the Private Office.[31]

Initially Philip's chances to shine in foreign affairs were accordingly limited. It was Millard who was taken to Geneva with Eden for the Indo-China talks in July 1955, while Philip merely managed correspondence between this delegation and the Far Eastern Department of the Foreign Office.[32] It was also Millard – having served in Ankara from 1949 to 1954 – who liaised in 1955 with Shuckburgh, the latter being then responsible for the Levant, Arabian and Eastern departments of the Foreign Office dealing with the Middle Eastern policy problems which were to so overshadow Eden's premiership. Furthermore, Philip was serving a Prime Minister who, as Shuckburgh noted, was himself something of a professional diplomat who could not forebear interfering in Foreign Office affairs, bombarding his successor with telegrams even when at home in Broadchalke 'where he has no room for a Private Secretary'.[33]

At the Foreign Office Eden had already acquired a reputation of relying on his own judgement and for irascibility.[34] His health problems certainly could make Eden a demanding master both in terms of the medications he required and his tendency to imitate Churchill's penchant for bedroom dictation to his staff.[35] It is clear that Shuckburgh felt that the situation became worse after Eden's translation to Number 10, noting in his diary on 31 January 1956: 'I can see no prospect of my ever being intimate with him again, and I don't think his present Private Secretaries like him enough to want to be'.[36]

Shuckburgh's source was presumably his friend Millard. Millard, however, has no recollection of such personal difficulties.[37] The warm personal correspondence both he and Philip kept up for years with Eden after the latter left office, including visits for lunch with the former Prime Minister whenever Eden's health permitted, certainly suggests sustained good friendship. Indeed, some months after Eden's resignation, Philip wrote to tell Eden: 'All your former private secretaries very much including Bobby [Allan MP], miss you greatly'.[38]

Millard also clearly had some influence on Eden's policy towards the Middle East: in the run-up to Eden's January 1956 Washington visit Millard stressed to the Prime Minister the need for economic counters to the Soviet penetration of the region marked by the Egyptian arms deal announced the previous September.[39] Shuckburgh was thus too critical of Eden's relations with the Private Office. Its standard roles continued unimpaired: of managing liaison with ministers and officials; keeping up records; preparing drafts of correspondence and speeches; and superintending the Cabinet committee system in conjunction with the Cabinet Office. An example of this last duty was Philip's advice to the Prime Minister that a Cabinet committee was not necessary on university expansion – demonstrating as well that his role was never confined to foreign affairs.[40]

Eden also used his private secretaries as occasional sounding-boards for ideas.[41] He seems to have taken Philip into his confidence even on some domestic matters, for instance on the mistake of combining the Leadership of the Commons with the Conservative Party chairmanship.[42] Eden would also allow them to express his sentiments: for instance, on the desirability of making sure that the Americans appreciated the importance to Britain of linkage between the 1955 Anglo-American Alpha Plan to tackle Israeli–Egyptian relations and the compensating offer of tanks for Iraq. Philip's expression of this, however, was regarded by the Foreign Secretary's assistant Private Secretary, Andrew Stark, as 'somewhat elliptical'.[43]

This was a relatively rare foray then by Philip into Middle East policy, which seems to have remained Millard's fiefdom until the end of the Eden premiership. Otherwise evidence of Philip acting as more than an efficient manager of communications and liaison between the Prime Minister and the Foreign Office – for instance in terms of drafting British views on Nehru's somewhat vacuous principles of international relations – is scant.[44] When this does start to appear there are hints of the significance of his Soviet experiences, for instance in influencing the distribution list for a telegram interpreting the latest Delphic utterances from Moscow.[45] He does not seem, however, to have been involved in the exploratory four-power talks that briefly flourished in 1955 following the conclusion of the Austrian State Treaty.[46] Such talks became for Eden even more expedient after the Soviet arms deal with Egypt and culminated in the visit to Britain of Bulganin and Khrushchev in April 1956. Previous private secretaries, notably Jock Colville during the Second World War, had been used as interpreters in such circumstances. Philip's Russian skills, however, were initially kept quiet, which enabled him to follow the visitors' conversation without their knowing and pass on any details to Eden. Other interpreters were used, with damaging outcomes as a result of drunkenness at the Foreign Secretary's lunch for the visiting dignitaries on 25 April 1956. Khrushchev, however, had picked up on Philip's mastery of Russian by the end of the visit.[47]

Philip also used his Russian later that year in response to Bulganin's letter implying that Britain was being dragged into the Suez imbroglio to help the French out in tackling their war against nationalists in Algeria. There was much truth in Bulganin's observations, but Philip's role was confined to suggesting, without fully checking the Russian, that there might be significance in the textual differences between the three versions of the letter received, a suggestion dismissed by his Foreign Office counterpart.[48] This might be an example of the rivalry sometimes detected between the Foreign Office and those who have left it to serve in Number 10 or the Cabinet Office, a rivalry which arguably grew with perceptions of Philip's influence the longer he stayed at the former.[49] At the time it hardly furnished evidence of his influence; in this whole long file on the background to the Suez crisis this exchange is the only sign of Philip's involvement.

Earlier that month Philip pithily summarised a seven-page telegram from Egypt's President Nasser on the crisis prompted by the Egyptian nationalisation of the Suez Canal on 26 July 1956: 'This is Nasser's reply. There is nothing new in it and it is an unequivocal rejection of international control'.[50] However, much of the policy support for Suez in the Private Office fell on Millard. Millard would interpret at meetings with the French Prime Minister and Foreign Minister, Guy Mollet and Christian Pineau, and was present on 14 October when General Challe came over from Paris to unfold for Eden the scheme of collusion with the Israelis. Eden also turned to Millard for guidance on the course of the Suez events for his memoirs.[51] This included advice on the atmosphere 'at Downing Street during the Suez time. Have you any comments to suggest, apart from bad language?'[52]

Neither Millard nor Philip had much sympathy with the doubts about the ensuing military operations against Egypt launched on 5 November 1956 expressed by the Prime Minister's press secretary, William Clark, who resigned on 6 November 1956.[53] Later that day, under enormous financial pressure from the Americans, Eden called the operations off, resigning the following year, when he was replaced as Prime Minister by Macmillan. Writing privately a few months later to welcome Eden's apparent return to health after the strains of Suez, Philip made clear his broad support for the Suez strategy:

> I believe the Americans are slowly and painfully being brought to accept facts and that the Israelis are naturally less jittery than they were before Nasser's power was broken ... But there is still no way of meeting Nasser's act of force by negotiation and one can only hope that in the end he will succumb to the pressures building up against him and that meanwhile he will fail to overthrow our friends.[54]

Despite his Russian background, however, Philip did not mention here the anxieties about Soviet penetration of the Middle East that featured so highly amongst Eden's concerns.[55]

By then Millard had resigned on 31 December 1956 for personal reasons. Partly because of a bad skiing accident at Kitzbuhl he had to endure nine months gardening leave and a two-year sabbatical in the Paymaster General's office supporting Reginald Maudling's abortive attempts to negotiate a European Free Trade Area (FTA) before resuming his diplomatic career.[56] It did not take Millard long correctly to surmise that these efforts would achieve little.[57]

62   *Peter Catterall*

Philip, in contrast, seems to have been one of those encouraging the new Prime Minister to continue to believe – even with the return of Charles de Gaulle to power in Paris – that German–French differences were such that these efforts had a realistic chance of success.[58]

Working under Macmillan

Millard's departure meant that Macmillan inherited a depleted Private Office headed by Bishop and supported on the foreign policy side by Philip and on the domestic side (until 1958) by Cairncross. On 27 May 1957 Macmillan, having survived the post-Suez crisis, decided to strengthen this team by appointing his old wartime aide and friend, John Wyndham, as an unpaid supplementary Private Secretary who could take on the political as well as the administrative work. Wyndham regarded his new Civil Service colleagues as both loyal and effective and by all accounts it was a happy team. For Macmillan they were his eyes and ears, controlling access to the Prime Minister from their adjoining offices adjacent to the Cabinet room on the first floor of Number 10.[59]

There was 'a great volume and variety of business' with which all the private secretaries, regardless of specialism, required considerable familiarity. This was not least because of the duty rota, with the last one on duty each evening designated to close the box of papers from the day, which was then taken up to the Prime Minister's bedroom, to be returned the following morning with each paper duly annotated by Macmillan. There was also 'the Dip' – consisting of carbon copies of letters and minutes from the day before with which the Private Office were expected to be *au fait* – and Macmillan's 'Bits and Pieces Box', into which went quips and good material for future prime ministerial speeches. Macmillan was the first Prime Minister to travel abroad extensively and this Private Office set-up, usually including Philip, would accompany him on these journeys.[60] Indeed, the job of the Private Office, like that of courtiers to a peripatetic mediaeval king, was very much one of following their master on his travels or from Number 10 to Chequers to the Prime Minister's room in the Commons.

According to Wyndham, the Private Office could be quite as ruthless as Macmillan himself when interfering with the departments of state.[61] Harold Evans, who had replaced Clark as press secretary at Number 10, where he was physically located within the Private Office, certainly later described Philip as

> [P]ossessing a formidable array of gifts and talents – intellectual agility, charm, self-confidence to the point of arrogance and a readiness to be ruthless. Even the Prime Minister could be heard speaking jokingly of 'that bully Philip'.

Evans nevertheless closed this examination of Philip's qualities with 'From my point of view he was never anything but helpful and considerate'.[62]

Macmillan would use these various qualities for his own ends. He later observed, based on his own experiences, that 'every Foreign Secretary must accept a great measure of interest, or even interference, from the Prime Minister of the day'.[63] Philip's role included carrying this interference out on Macmillan's behalf, and sometimes justifying it to the Foreign Secretary afterwards. Selwyn Lloyd, who had succeeded Macmillan to that post in 1955, for instance, very much resented the way in which he felt Philip and Bishop influenced Macmillan's personal efforts – excluding him – to try to save the Paris summit in 1960.[64]

To play this role Philip had to acquire Macmillan's trust. This he clearly achieved, being described – alongside Bishop and Cabinet Secretary, Sir Norman Brook – as a 'tower of strength' in Macmillan's memoirs.[65] Wyndham explains this role by saying:

> The private secretary should seek to protect his Minister at all times and also to run a two-way traffic in ideas, which means having the confidence not only of the Minister but of everybody else with whom he has business. With all of them he must be absolutely straight. Above all he must understand his Minister's mind. When the Minister has a 'bright idea' the private secretary should know instinctively how best to deal with it ... This is where a good private secretary comes in. He touts the Minister's ideas around and with complete honesty he reports back on the reactions.[66]

That Philip did indeed deserve Macmillan's tribute and successfully played this role of liaising with the Foreign Secretary and Foreign Office was in the 1970s widely and unanimously confirmed by both ministers and officials.[67]

Specific examples of Philip acting as the influential 'tower of strength' of repute and the Macmillan memoirs are, however, not always easy to find. In the period up to the 1959 election for instance, during which Bishop continued to play a considerable role in foreign policy advice, Macmillan appreciated Philip's help in responding to the concerns of the Leader of the Opposition, Hugh Gaitskell, about the 1958 Quemoy crisis between the US and China. Macmillan also notes that Philip's Russian proved useful on his trip to the Soviet Union in 1959.[68]

Furthermore, there were clearly areas in which Philip had little direct role. There is no sign of Philip's input into Macmillan's efforts to reshape defence organisation and policy at the start and end of his premiership, despite its obvious relevance to the projection of foreign policy. He could, however, advise on mistakes, observing in 1958: 'By some extraordinary muddle the Chiefs of Staff in their paper have commended on the wrong Foreign Office paper. Consequently I am afraid that many of their remarks are irrelevant'.[69]

There was little Private Office involvement in the policy review exercise under Eden which in 1956 produced a paper – but little else – on 'The future of the UK in world affairs'. This policy review effort was led by Sir Norman Brook and the Cabinet Office, and the Private Office contribution consisted of little more than Bishop's doubt 'whether this grandiose exercise will really produce much additional help'.[70] This did not deter Macmillan from launching the even more grandiose 'Future Policy' exercise in 1959. This attempt to sketch in broad strategy for after that autumn's general election commenced with a Chequers meeting on 7 June 1959. The Cabinet Office, Foreign Office, Ministry of Defence and Treasury – the departments that would lead on the project – were all well-represented. The Prime Minister's Private Office was represented not by Philip but by Tim Bligh, a home civil servant who joined from the Treasury earlier that year.[71] One of the few contributions Philip seems to have made was the prescient observation that the TSR-2 strike aircraft might not be required, though cancellation of this project was left to the next Labour government.[72]

Philip in fact is not even mentioned in Macmillan's diaries – and then only *en passant* – before 23 October 1957. By the following summer, however, Philip seems to have become much more of a confidant, being invited with his wife to Chequers for a weekend of broad conversations.[73] It seems that their relationship had clearly blossomed into personal friendship by summer 1959, with Philip and Marie-Lou being invited down to Macmillan's private estate of Birch Grove in Sussex during a family weekend.[74]

By then Philip had proved his worth to Macmillan through his work on a specific policy problem the Prime Minister had been wrestling with earlier when Foreign Secretary in 1955. By 1957 Macmillan had moved to trying to solve the terrorism in Cyprus and related Graeco-Turkish tensions with the idea of a tridominium on the island preserving the British sovereign bases. Faced with intransigence from both Turks and Greeks in March 1958 Macmillan undertook to redraft the plan. He was aided by 'an excellent draft from de Zulueta'.[75] That summer Philip accompanied Macmillan on a visit to the island. He was party to the discussions at Chequers on 8 September 1958 with the Colonial Secretary Alan Lennox-Boyd, the Governor of Cyprus Sir Hugh Foot, Macmillan and John Addis of the Foreign Office about when to allow Archbishop Makarios to return to the island. He also played an important role in drafting statements about Cyprus for Parliament.[76]

Philip was if anything even more valuable as a steadying hand during the crisis precipitated by the coup in Iraq of 14 July 1958. This removed what had been the linchpin of Britain's position in the Middle East. Macmillan's son-in-law, Julian Amery, immediately advocated action to try to reconquer Iraq. As he had been a leading member of the Suez group of Tory MPs advocating action against Nasser's Egypt two years earlier, this was hardly surprising. Amery was, however, joined by the Colonial Secretary, Alan Lennox-Boyd, in enthusiasm for using figures like Colonel de Gaury – an old friend of the Iraqi royal family – to try to stir up counter-revolution.[77] Philip was instrumental in getting the Foreign Office to warn Macmillan against such adventures. Of a later Amery paper Philip noted: 'If he is right we shall I think have either to bring down Nasser by military means or lose all our favourable position over oil supplies from the Middle East'. But, he went on to advise, 'this is such an unattractive dilemma that we should seek to avoid it if we can and I do not believe that we are yet quite faced with it'.[78] It was this wise counsel that prevailed.

Philip was thus effective at weighing political risks for his chief. It is interesting that Millard described him as 'imaginative'.[79] Macmillan's supple mind was constantly probing for broad plans – what he called 'Grand Designs' – through which to tackle the issues he confronted. Those officials he invited periodically for general, wide-ranging discussions to address these were not necessarily the most senior, but those whose thinking he found congenial – Philip, for instance, felt that it was important to encourage contact with the Soviets, a view Macmillan had also developed when Foreign Secretary – and conducive to exploring the solutions he sought.[80] Their role was to help Macmillan to tease out the interlocking policy devices he tended to favour. Accordingly, these sessions acted like impromptu policy seminars, helping the Prime Minister to crystallise his thoughts on, for instance, responses to the connected problems of the Soviet threats to Berlin in November 1958 and the need to reduce tension in the Cold War when many in the West (wrongly) believed that the Russians had a nuclear lead and political problems were gathering through the related fear of the consequences of nuclear testing.[81] Philip was amongst those officials, including Bishop and Rumbold, Macmillan invited for one of these very long conversations over luncheon at Chequers in January 1959. The upshot was to help the Prime Minister to decide to address these issues through the device of the probing visit to Moscow on which Philip accompanied him the following month, with follow-up visits to Western capitals, including Washington.[82]

Before they left, Philip warned Macmillan of recent press reports suggesting that the West German people were becoming more favourable to neutrality as a means of securing reunification. Such reports could make it more difficult to secure concessions from the Russians. This indicates that part of Philip's job was to keep the Prime Minister abreast of the context in which his foreign policy was operating. It might have been helpful if he had also warned that this situation would make the West German Chancellor, Konrad Adenauer, much more sensitive to Macmillan's Moscow visit. Adenauer never really trusted Macmillan again.

This might suggest that there was a downside to having in such a central advisory role a figure sharing and reinforcing Macmillan's view that German reunification was a subsidiary problem of the Cold War and other wider global problems and disinclined to compensate for his master's tendency to underplay German anxieties.[83] Philip, like Macmillan, seems not to have readily noticed the way in which Anglo-German relations soured after de Gaulle in the autumn of 1958 set out to woo the aged Chancellor. He had recognised by December 1958 that the FTA negotiations were abortive, but continued to see the problem essentially in terms of threatening rather than persuading the Germans, in the hope of gaining leverage on the French. Thus at the end of the year he wrote to Macmillan 'If we alarm the Germans sufficiently we might, perhaps, cause them to put such pressure on the French that the Common Market would collapse or be very much watered down'.[84]

The scheme Philip subsequently put forward in October 1959 further compounded the offence caused by the Moscow trip in Adenauer's eyes. The idea of an Anglo-Soviet arms limitation agreement in central Europe he then raised had obvious strategic and pecuniary benefits for the overstretched British; however, far from proving, as Philip hoped, a means of bullying the Germans into supporting wider European unity, it was only likely to continue to drive Adenauer into the arms of de Gaulle.[85] As Macmillan astutely observed, the French liked to pretend that we are weak and defeatist, and that they are for 'being tough'. The purpose of this is to impress Chancellor Adenauer, and keep his support in their protectionist attitude towards European economic problems.[86]

Some sort of Anglo-Soviet rapprochement was nevertheless clearly desirable. Through reducing international tension it would reduce military expenditure. But it would also increase Britain's room for manoeuvre. In consequence British foreign policy would no longer be so dependent upon the US. The problem that 'Western policy on Germany is to a large extent a prisoner of the Federal Government', with concomitant stationing costs, would also be diminished.[87] Nuclear weapons were felt to have rendered redundant the large forces that Adenauer still demanded that his allies maintained in Germany. Furthermore, it might also help to slow Soviet penetration in both the Middle East and Africa. To combat this Macmillan advocated freer trade and greater Western unity. Indeed, his African tour of 1960 very much arose from this context, culminating in his warning in Cape Town in February that if the West did not respond to the 'wind of change' of nationalism blowing through the continent 'we may imperil the precarious balance between the East and West on which the peace of the world depends'.[88] All these factors, together with political imperatives regarding the October 1959 election and the personal inclinations of both Philip and Macmillan, ensured a growing emphasis on the need for a four-power summit after the Moscow visit.

In the process Philip could temper the Prime Minister's inclination to run ahead of what his allies would stomach, as is clear from their very private exchange of August 1959 in response to the latest Khrushchev letter about Berlin.[89] Nevertheless, Philip clearly also supported Macmillan's goals. Lloyd, who did not entirely share their enthusiasm, certainly seems to have felt that the policy which culminated in the Paris summit of May 1960 was at least as much Philip's as Macmillan's, hence his bitter comments then about 'government by private secretary'.[90] It was Philip, not Lloyd, who accompanied the Prime Minister on the key trips to Paris and Camp David on the road to the summit. He also helped Macmillan to respond to Khrushchev's communications after the shooting down of an American U2 overflying the Soviet Union on spying mission imperilled the impending meeting.[91] The following day, 11 May 1960, he sought to reassure his chief that the U2 incident was being used by the Soviet leader to sabre-rattle to keep in check his enemies at home and did not mean that the conference was doomed, in contrast to the gloomy prognostications coming from the British Ambassador, Sir Patrick Reilly, in Moscow. This overly sanguine, if not self-deluding, optimism suggests how much Philip had personally invested in success in Paris, a view reinforced by his part in Macmillan's last-ditch efforts to prevent a breakdown. His subsequent comment to Alistair Horne that, after this failure, 'I never saw [Macmillan] more depressed' is often quoted, but it is hard to escape the sense that Philip was here expressing his own sentiments as well.[92]

The turn to Europe

Thereafter the British not only had to try to pick out some alternative policy, but also respond to the impending change of President in the US. Eisenhower, Macmillan's wartime colleague, was coming to the end of his term. The Democrat candidate to replace him, John F. Kennedy, Philip warned in June 1960, had told a garden party in the South of France the previous year 'the British have made such a mess of things in the world and especially in the Middle East that the best thing they can do is keep out of it in future'.[93] Such attitudes presented a problem when Kennedy subsequently took the White House. Macmillan rapidly concluded that he could no longer rely on

> the link of memories and a long friendship. I will have to base myself now on trying to win him by ideas. I have started working on a memorandum wh[ich] I might send him – giving a broad survey of the problems wh[ich] face us in the world.[94]

It is not clear whether this approach was influenced by Philip, but a subsequent memorandum from the latter shows that he came to similar conclusions.[95]

He also seems to have come to similar conclusions regarding the ideas Macmillan then sketched out. This required something of a shift on his part. After the FTA failure Philip had felt French hostility to any kind of trade deal with Britain was such that 'our only course is either to try and break up the Common Market or watering it down'.[96] Although a great Francophile who wrote many position papers for Macmillan on Anglo-French affairs, Philip continued to feel of the French in October 1959 'At the moment I do not think they do want us at all'.[97] However, it was increasingly clear that the alternative course Macmillan had been pursuing, of some kind of accommodation between the Six and the Seven – the countries of the Common Market and the European Free Trade Association that Britain had formed as an alternative – was a non-starter. One of Macmillan's old friends from his days in the European League for Economic Co-operation, Juliet Rhys-Williams, wrote to Philip in December 1960 about the difficulties of achieving such an accommodation in the face of GATT rules.[98] Informal external advisers like Rhys-Williams had been important to Macmillan when out of power in the late 1940s and into the early 1950s, a period when Europe remained a fluid concept. Now, with the Hallstein tariffs of July 1960, the Common Market in contrast was a present reality which threatened British trade.

Macmillan's solution was to work up his initial ideas for Kennedy in December 1960 into a 'Grand Design' paper. This paper distilled various policy proposals in the aftermath of the summit failure. It sought to liberalise international trade and aid in order to provide a non-inflationary external stimulus to the UK economy, consolidate resistance to communism, and reduce military costs. These were largely consistent with earlier policy devices such as the FTA concept, but the means was now through an exploration of whether some kind of accommodation was possible with the Common Market created by the Treaty of Rome in 1957.[99]

The 'Grand Design' paper was drafted with the aid of a small circle of Philip, Bishop and Brook.[100] It was by no means exclusively about European entry. Reflecting the recurring significance of the Cold War in Philip's thought, he advised that the 'Soviet fear of Germany and the spread of nuclear weapons might come in useful in th[is] enterprise'.[101] This is because hopes of making progress with de Gaulle seem to have rested upon (a) persuading Kennedy to support the project, including by allowing nuclear information sharing with the French; and (b) reducing tensions over Berlin. On the first of these Macmillan recorded 'most satisfactory' progress when accompanied by Philip to the White House in April 1961. However, while Kennedy was certainly supportive over the envisaged Common Market entry negotiations, he was to oppose the nuclear information sharing with the French which Philip and Macmillan had dangled before de Gaulle at what the Prime Minister considered a successful meeting at Rambouillet in January.[102] Taking the view that de Gaulle was more interested in being the strongman of Europe than contributing usefully to tackling the Cold War, the Americans thus denied Macmillan a key means of leverage on the French.[103] The second goal proved no less tricky. Soviet fears were indeed evident in their desire to consolidate the division of Germany, reflected in the building of the Berlin Wall that summer. This, however, simply made de Gaulle even more reluctant to consider negotiations with the Soviets that were likely to prove unpalatable to Adenauer when Macmillan and Philip met with him at Birch Grove in November 1961.[104]

Philip was heavily involved with the gestation, development and communication of this Grand Design both to British and overseas audiences.[105] This suggests that he was, by this stage if not earlier, more than a Private Secretary or a policy adviser. He it was, rather than the Foreign Secretary (by then Lord Home) who generally accompanied the Prime Minister on the visits whereby the policy advanced. By May 1962, however, little had been achieved. The ministerial meetings in Brussels were deadlocked. Pessimistic views were also being presented to Philip to pass on to the Prime Minister. The American journalist Joseph Alsop, for instance, told Philip over lunch that he was convinced de Gaulle did not want Britain in Europe and that nor, in the aftermath of the Anglo-American handling of the Berlin Wall crisis, did Adenauer – a verdict Philip recorded as unduly unfavourable, though there might be a 'certain truth in what he says'.[106] Macmillan was coming to similar views about de Gaulle's attitudes, convening a dinner at Chequers on 27 May 1962 to discuss responses at which Philip joined Home, chief European negotiator Ted Heath, Sir Harold Caccia (Permanent Under-Secretary at the Foreign Office), Sir Frank Lee (Permanent Under-Secretary at the Board of Trade) and Sir Pierson Dixon (Ambassador to France). This was in preparation for his visit, accompanied by Philip and Dixon, to de Gaulle at Château des Champs on 2–3 June. Philip seems to have returned from this with a sanguine assessment.[107] Although Macmillan could not play the nuclear card, following earlier advice from Philip, he did emphasise military cooperation in Europe.[108] Macmillan also felt that he had convinced de Gaulle that Britain regarded it as in their interest to join the Six 'if reasonable terms can be made, esp[ecially] for the old Commonwealth countries'.[109]

The latter, however, were not necessarily any more enthusiastic about British entry than de Gaulle. Philip's next major task was therefore helping to draft Macmillan's speech for the upcoming Commonwealth conference at which he would try to sell the policy. His important role in drafting or improving such speeches illustrates that he contributed significantly to the articulation of Macmillan's policy.[110] However, not all his advice was heeded; for instance, his concern that the creation of Malaysia in 1962 would amongst other risks overburden military relations with Australia and New Zealand.[111] On the other hand, during the Cuban crisis that October his warning to American intelligence officer Chet Cooper of the likely scepticism of the British press seems to have been a significant factor in the American decision to publish photographs of the Soviet missile sites.[112] Philip was thus much more than a conduit (as in his communications with Kennedy's National Security Advisor, McGeorge Bundy, during the Cuban missile crisis), a bag-carrier or interpreter. He also offered an informal, plausibly deniable channel of information for representatives of other countries. Thus in February 1961 he was invited to luncheon by Alex Romanov, the minister-counsellor at the Soviet Embassy. For the Russians this was a means of exploring British attitudes to the Laos crisis that was then very much exercising the incoming Kennedy administration.[113] Splendid meals and vodka at the Ritz and Café Royal over the next two years became a regular means of sounding out Soviet and British positions on issues from the Congo or China to the nuclear test ban that Macmillan sought so persistently from 1959, even if Philip could complain to the Foreign Office that Romanov's 'detailed knowledge of the Soviet negotiating position was better than my understanding of ours'.[114]

Philip similarly dined informally and strategically for Britain with journalists like Alsop or the French and American ambassadors. For instance, following the Château des Champs meeting he arranged a couple of private dinners with Geoffroy de Courcel, the new French Ambassador. His predecessor, Paul Chauvel, had a reputation of being too anglophile to reliably transmit de Gaulle's views.[115] In contrast, although Philip was able to use these meetings to convey Macmillan's dismay at de Gaulle's remarks on his September 1962 visit to Adenauer, de Courcel – formerly de Gaulle's personal aide – kept his cards close to his chest.[116] They do not seem to have helped to prepare for the December 1962 meeting at Rambouillet with the General at which, as Macmillan puts it in his diaries, 'Philip de Z acted as my chief adviser and secretary'.[117] These talks, according to Macmillan, were 'as bad as they c[oul]d be from the European point of view'. The French President, taking the line that British entry would subordinate Europe both to America and the Commonwealth, was clearly bent on refusal.[118] Going into the talks Macmillan had continued to place hope in some nuclear agreement to give him leverage with de Gaulle. According to Philip, the problem was that the Prime Minister was not always as proficient at French as he liked to think, and the General – who he felt was only interested in nuclear weapons for prestige reasons – did not fully grasp the British offer.[119]

Nuclear relations

At the same time nuclear relations with the Americans were becoming critical. Almost straight after Rambouillet Philip accompanied Macmillan to Nassau for Anglo-American talks in which the future of the British deterrent bulked large. At issue was whether the British could acquire a credible missile to launch nuclear warheads, having cancelled their own Blue Streak development in 1960 in favour of the American Skybolt, a programme the administration had just decided to discontinue. Back then Philip had presciently argued in favour of the alternative submarine-based missiles, pointing out 'Unless we have an option to buy or build Polaris we ourselves get nothing out of giving the Americans [nuclear] facilities in Scotland'.[120] Britain had proved unable to secure an option on Polaris in 1960, but at Nassau a sleight of hand over the alignment of Britain's deterrent secured these missiles for the Americans' disgruntled ally. The Americans wished to present the Nassau deal as part of the Multilateral Force (MLF) through which they were trying to deter the West Germans from developing their own nuclear weapons.[121] When Alsop complained a few months later that everywhere in Europe British representatives were speaking against the MLF, Philip did his 'best to assure him this must be nonsense'.[122] His assurance was almost certainly disingenuous. Philip no doubt shared widespread British doubts about the MLF concept, which eventually ran into the sands in 1967. Instead the Nassau episode reinforced for Philip that

> our 'special relationship' with the United States is not worth much in real terms ... so that we had better start reinforcing ourselves vis-à-vis the Americans by an independent policy in concert with someone else, e.g. the French.[123]

Working over the weekend at Chequers with Philip on 28 January 1963, Macmillan sadly reflected on the lack of prospect of progress with the French as the entry talks ground to a halt. 'If it were not', he complained, 'for the fatal

Philip de Zulueta 71

survival of Dr Adenauer (the Pétain of Germany) we c[oul]d hope for a firm stand by the Germans'.[124] Macmillan, unlike Eden, had developed an uneasy relationship with Adenauer. Indeed, Eden noted of his dinner with the West German delegation during their November 1959 visit to Macmillan the Chancellor's bitter complaints about the lack of clear British policy towards his country.[125] Philip does not seem materially to have helped to tackle this deficiency, later approvingly recording the observations of Llewellyn Thompson, the American Ambassador to Russia, that 'American conversations with the Federal Government were becoming rather like their conversations with the Russians in that they had a stock series of arguments which they had to continually employ'.[126]

More success was in fact achieved in 1963 in conversations with the Americans and Russians than the French and Germans. Philip was part of the luncheon party Macmillan convened on 8 March 1963 to discuss how to break the deadlock in the test ban talks. With Philip's help in drafting proposals Macmillan proceeded to woo Kennedy's support for progress, culminating in the President's visit to Birch Grove on 29–30 June. The Prime Minister regarded this as a great success:

> 'We got all we wanted.
> Full steam ahead with Moscow talks – Test Ban to be no. 1 priority
> Go slow on Multi-Manned.[127]

Philip's duties over this weekend included taking his fellow Catholic, Kennedy, to Mass. He later told Richard Thorpe of his shock that the President only seemed interested in pumping Philip for the salacious details of the ongoing Profumo scandal.[128] This was by no means the only occasion when Philip's Catholicism proved useful. His personal and familial connections with the Catholic hierarchy meant he was well-placed to keep Macmillan abreast of developments within the Holy See and to represent the Prime Minister at the coronation Mass for John XXIII in 1958 and the requiem Mass after his death in 1963. So good were these connections that the *Sunday Express* could credibly, if mendaciously, allege to Evans prime ministerial involvement in the selection of a new Archbishop of Westminster in 1963.[129]

Philip meanwhile sought to help Macmillan to reopen some of the well-worn foreign policy objectives they had persistently pursued. For instance, following Birch Grove, Kennedy's letter to Macmillan drawing attention to the possibility of Franco-German objections to the test ban talks prompted the fertile minds of both Prime Minister and adviser to look again at nuclear relations with France. Thoughts of using American acquiescence at last to nuclear information sharing with the French as a means of persuading them to drop their objections to the proposed test ban led Macmillan to enthuse:

> We might even revise Europe – (Common Market) etc and start a new and hopeful movement to straighten out the whole alliance ... I put my

ideas through de Zulueta to a small drafting ctee (1 F.O. and 1 MofD man) wh[ich] he dominated.[130]

Philip, charged with drafting yet another paper on Anglo-French nuclear relations, sought to find a price in a memorandum written on September 1963 which 'we want, the French would give, and the Americans would not dislike'. The French reaction to the signing of the Test Ban Treaty on 25 July 1963 in Moscow, however, demonstrated that this remained an impossible proposition.[131]

Conclusion

Philip's perennial efforts to tackle Anglo-French relations thus ended in failure. A month later Macmillan, having at length decided to continue as premier until the next election, was stricken by the prostate problem that prompted his retirement. Two days before Macmillan's resignation Philip visited his hospital bed to tell the Prime Minister that he had decided to go to the City rather than return to the Foreign Office.[132] By kind permission of Rab Butler, who succeeded the incoming Prime Minister at the Foreign Office, a leaving party was held at Foreign Secretary's London residence, 1 Carlton Gardens, on 12 December 1963.[133] A month later Philip, having been knighted in Macmillan's resignation honours list, became a banker with Philip Hill-Higginson Erlanges.

There ensued some controversy both about the knighthood and about Philip's decision to leave the Diplomatic Service. His old chief, Geoffrey McDermott, later gave this as an example of the wastage of talent by the Foreign Office. Both John Wyndham and Macmillan's official biographer, Alistair Horne, felt this put a premature end to a career in which Philip could have risen to the top. The latter suggests that the length of his service in the Private Office, and resulting identification with Macmillan, was an obstacle to returning to diplomatic life.[134] Philip certainly stayed in Number 10 longer than any of the other private secretaries with whom he served. Indeed, the only other to rival him in length of service (and the only other to receive a knighthood courtesy of Macmillan) was Tim Bligh, who also joined Philip in moving to the private sector. This, however, was surely largely down to personal choice. In the Private Office he had a master who shared his views and valued and relied upon him, plus a roving ability to influence foreign policy broadly in a manner not generally possible for a lowly grade 7. Going back to the Foreign Office would mean resuming the slow climb to the top in a world made more competitive by the many diplomats of his age drafted in after the Second World War. As Moorhouse later noted, the age of 35 (Philip in 1963 was 38) is often a plateau in the diplomatic corps: after that the career structure becomes more pyramidal. The result, as Wyndham pointed out, is that promising civil servants like Philip could find it a long wait for advancement. Not many, either, were in Philip's position to instead get tempting offers to shift to the City. He turned down a Washington posting and formally left the Foreign Office on 17 January 1964.[135]

In addition to his City career, Philip became a trustee both of the trust set up to manage Macmillan's memoirs and literary legacy and the Kennedy Memorial Trust. In 1965 he wrote to Eden asking for his support in efforts to gain the Conservative nomination for the constituency of the Cities of London and Westminster 'since it was at your feet that I first became really interested in politics'. There had been suspicions that such political sympathies had also been a reason for his decision to leave the Civil Service. However, as Philip pointed out when ambushed by a television interviewer on this point in Lusaka in 1964, it was not he but his wife who had more problems stomaching the idea of him working for the Labour government which, following the 1964 election, was by then in office.[136] Party politics was not the reason for his departure from Whitehall. Nor did he pursue it strongly. Despite Macmillan's coaching, however, the attempt to win the nomination for this promising seat proved unsuccessful, while career considerations precluded him chasing others.[137] This episode, however, illustrates that Philip remained close to the former Prime Minister, advising him both on the international financial situation (useful in Macmillan's resumed role at the eponymous publishing firm) and the handling of misleading allegations made about Rambouillet by the Labour Prime Minister, Harold Wilson, during the 1966 general election.[138] Philip was well-aware of Wilson's position on the nuclear issue, having reported of a transatlantic conversation with the then Leader of the Opposition in November 1963, that Wilson's objection was not to British warheads but to the purchase of American missiles.[139]

Macmillan remained a would-be patron, unsuccessfully nominating Philip as a potential Ambassador to Washington in 1970. Macmillan's tribute says much about his continuing regard for the man who served him so closely:

> He is extremely able … and has made a considerable reputation in his knowledge of financial and economic affairs particularly in the European field. He knows a lot about both theoretical and applied economics. He has kept pretty close his friendships and connections with the diplomatic world. He has a charming and efficient wife … Here is a man who is still under fifty, known and respected in governing circles in almost every capital, with the unique experience of how No. 10 and the Foreign Office must work together.[140]

These virtues helped to make Philip a key asset to Macmillan, someone with whom during weekends at Chequers together they would clear their correspondence and crystallise views on foreign policy issues around the world. He thus served as much more than a Private Secretary, or even a special adviser. Philip became a confidant for a lonely Prime Minister who relied heavily on friendships in the Private Office to compensate both for an unhappy marriage and the gradual loss of political companions, particularly after the self-inflicted wounds of the botched Cabinet reshuffle of July 1962. To some extent Philip even became a co-producer of policy, as demonstrated by his contribution to

74 *Peter Catterall*

continuity in objectives both before and after the 1960 summit. This close-working relationship was based upon a similarity of view which meant that the Prime Minister could trust Philip to draft for him, represent him and be his eyes and ears in Whitehall and beyond. As Macmillan later reflected, 'Philip knows my mind'.[141] He could calm a sometimes overwrought premier. Philip also provided invaluable insights in subsequently reading drafts of Macmillan's memoirs.

Nevertheless, this meeting of minds was almost too symbiotic, amplifying some concerns such as the need to reduce tensions with Russia. Both men also held similar attitudes towards Germany. They shared not only policy imperatives, but also certain character traits. A common penchant for understated, ironic humour comes across in the relaxed correspondence that passed between them.[142] They were also both apt to express themselves elliptically on occasion. These similarities no doubt ensured Philip's indispensability as a companion to Macmillan. They also helped to reinforce Macmillan's foreign policy preferences. Arguably, however, Philip was not always as successful at putting forward alternatives to what Macmillan wished to achieve, partly because he shared so closely the Prime Minister's views. He was thus not an independent source of advice. Accordingly, therefore, Philip's very closeness to and importance as a foreign policy adviser for Macmillan also somewhat diminished his overall effectiveness in that role.

Notes

1. I am grateful for the assistance of Vernon Bogdanor, Max Egremont, Sir Guy Millard, Walter Rønning, D. R. Thorpe and Lady de Zulueta in the preparation of this chapter.
2. *Who's Who 1964: An Annual Biographical Dictionary with which is Incorporated 'Men and Women of the Time'* (London: A. & C. Black, 1964), 3389.
3. See Sir Evelyn Shuckburgh, *Descent to Suez: Diaries 1951–1956* (London: Weidenfeld & Nicolson, 1986), 4–6.
4. *British and Foreign State Papers 1822–1823* (London: J. Harrison, 1828), 981–2.
5. The National Archives, Kew [henceforward TNA]: HO 1/10/22.
6. *Trial of Pedro de Zulueta Jun. on a charge of slave trading* (London: C. Wood & Co., 1844), preface; Marika Sherwood, '"Oh, what a tangled web we weave": Britain, the slave trade and slavery 1808–43', *Shunpiking*, www.shunpiking.org/bhs2007/200-BHS-MS-britishStrade.htm (accessed 20 November 2012).
7. *The Catholic Who's Who & Year-Book 1908*, ed. F. C. Burnand (London: Burns & Oates, 1908), 115–16.
8. F. H. Lawson, 'Zulueta, Francis de (1878–1958)', in *Oxford Dictionary of National Biography: From the earliest times to the year 2000*, ed. H. G. C. Matthew and Brian Harrison (Oxford: Oxford University Press, 2004), vol. LX, 1021–1022; *Who's Who 1962: An Annual Biographical Dictionary with which is Incorporated 'Men and Women of the Time'* (London: A. & C. Black, 1925), 3163. According to Adrian Hastings, Francis was the leading Catholic in inter-war Oxford. Adrian Hastings, *A History of English Christianity 1920–1990*, 3rd edn (London: SCM Press, 1991), 138–9.
9. Francis de Zulueta to Bannatyne, 29 August 1914, The National Archives, Kew [henceforward TNA]: HO 144/104.

10   *The Catholic Who's Who & Year-Book 1936* (London: Burns, Oates & Washbourne, 1936).
11   On the camaraderie of this background see Peter Catterall, ed., *The Macmillan Diaries*, vol. I:*The Cabinet Years, 1950–1957* (London: Macmillan, 2003), 231; Simon Ball, *The Guardsmen: Harold Macmillan, Three Friends and the World They Made* (London: HarperCollins, 2004).
12   Interview with Lady de Zulueta, 24 October 2012.
13   Lawson, 'Zulueta', 1022; Max Egremont, 'Zulueta, Sir Philip Francis de (1925–1989)', in *Oxford Dictionary of National Biography: From the earliest times to the year 2000*, ed. H. G. C. Matthew and Brian Harrison (Oxford: Oxford University Press, 2004), vol. LX, 1023.
14   Lord Strang, *The Foreign Office* (London: Allen & Unwin, 1955), 79–80; Lord Strang, *The Diplomatic Career* (London: André Deutsch, 1962), 36–9, 45; Alistair Horne, *Macmillan*, vol. II: *1957–1986* (London: Macmillan, 1989), 161.
15   *The Foreign Office List for 1951* (London: Harrison & Sons, 1951), 506.
16   Strang, *The Diplomatic Career*, 42; *The Foreign Office List for 1952* (London: Harrison & Sons, 1952), 526.
17   Quoted in Geoffrey Moorhouse, *The Diplomats: The Foreign Office Today* (London: Jonathan Cape, 1977), 47.
18   Sir David Kelly, *The Ruling Few or the Human Background to Diplomacy* (London: Hollis & Carter, 1952), 369–72.
19   Shuckburgh, *Descent*, 7.
20   Moorhouse, *Diplomats*, 76.
21   *The Foreign Office List for 1953* (London: Harrison & Sons, 1953), 545; *The Foreign Office List for 1954* (London: Harrison & Sons, 1954), 126.
22   Strang, *Foreign Office*, 209; Strang, *Diplomatic Career*, 82, 87; *Foreign Office List for 1953*, 67; *Foreign Office List for 1954*, 481.
23   Interview with Lady de Zulueta, 24 October 2012.
24   *The Foreign Office List for 1956* (London: Harrison & Sons, 1956), 482.
25   *The Foreign Office List for 1958* (London: Harrison & Sons, 1958), 481; Moorhouse, *Diplomats*, 18–19; Strang, *Diplomatic Career*, 45.
26   Email from Lord Egremont, 18 September 2012.
27   *Foreign Office List* (1954), 45; Geoffrey McDermott, *The Eden Legacy and the Decline of British Diplomacy* (London: Leslie Frewin, 1969), 138; W. Scott Lucas, 'The Missing Link? Patrick Dean, Chairman of the Joint Intelligence Committee', in *Whitehall and the Suez Crisis*, ed. Saul Kelly and Anthony Gorst (London: Frank Cass, 2000), 118.
28   Shuckburgh, *Descent*, 20; Moorhouse, *Diplomats*, 18.
29   *Foreign Office List for 1956*, 45, 407, 482.
30   Apparently Kennedy could not believe that the Prime Minister got by with so few staff. Interview with Lady de Zulueta, 24 October 2012.
31   D. R. Thorpe, *Eden: The Life and Times of Anthony Eden, First Earl of Avon 1897–1977* (London: Chatto & Windus, 2003), 443; *Daily Telegraph*, 14 March 2005; Telephone conversation with Sir Guy Millard, 28 August 2012.
32   TNA: PREM 11/1310.
33   Shuckburgh, *Descent*, 11–12, 277, 314.
34   Avi Shlaim, Peter Jones and Keith Sainsbury, *British Foreign Secretaries since 1945* (Newton Abbot: David & Charles, 1977), 87.
35   Shuckburgh, *Descent*, 10, 14, 326.
36   Shuckburgh, *Descent*, 331.
37   Telephone conversation with Sir Guy Millard, 28 August 2012.
38   De Zulueta to Eden, 24 April 1957, Cadbury Research Library, Birmingham [henceforward CRL]: AP 23/67/1. Allan was Eden's Parliamentary Private Secretary.

39 Millard to Eden, 3 January 1956, TNA: PREM 11/1334.
40 De Zulueta to Eden, 22 February 1956, TNA: PREM 11/2283.
41 Thorpe, *Eden*, 498.
42 De Zulueta to Macmillan, 28 May 1962, Weston Library, Oxford [henceforward WL]: MS Macmillan, dep. c. 310.
43 Quoted in Richard Lamb, *The Failure of the Eden Government* (London: Sidgwick & Jackson, 1987), 167.
44 TNA: PREM 11/1303.
45 Ward to de Zulueta, 13 January 1956, TNA: PREM 11/1341.
46 On the principles behind these see Peter Catterall, ed., *The Macmillan Diaries*, 2 vols (London: Macmillan, 2003–2011), vol. I, 420.
47 Interview: Lady de Zulueta, 24 October 2012; Thorpe, *Eden*, 470–1.
48 De Zulueta to John Graham, 14 September 1956; Graham to de Zulueta, 25 September 1956, TNA: FO371/119138.
49 Moorhouse, *Diplomats*, 134; Anne Deighton, 'British Foreign Policy-Making: The Macmillan Years', in *British Foreign Policy 1955–1964: Contracting Options*, ed. Wolfram Kaiser and Gillian Staerck (Basingstoke: Macmillan, 2000), 5–6.
50 Lamb, *Failure of the Eden Government*, 204.
51 Eden to Millard, 8 October 1957, CRL: AP24/49/1.
52 Eden to Millard, 1 July 1958, CRL: AP24/49/6. Any comments Millard gave do not seem to have survived on paper.
53 Thorpe, *Eden*, 498, 532; Lamb, *Failure of the Eden Government*, 261; telephone conversation with Sir Guy Millard, 28 August 2012.
54 De Zulueta to Eden, 24 April 1957, CRL: AP23/67/1.
55 See diary entry, 2 January 1957, CRL: AP20/5.
56 De Zulueta to Eden, 24 April 1957, CRL: AP23/67/1; Millard to Eden, 20 July 1958, CRL: AP24/49/7; telephone conversation with Sir Guy Millard, 28 August 2012.
57 Millard to Eden, 22 May 1958, CRL: AP24/49/5.
58 Horne, *Macmillan*, 35; Martin P. C. Schaad, *Bullying Bonn: Anglo-German Diplomacy on European Integration 1955–1961* (Basingstoke: Macmillan, 2000), 93.
59 Horne, *Macmillan*, 11–12, 160; Lord Egremont, *Wyndham and Children First* (London: Macmillan, 1968), 162–3, 165–6.
60 Egremont, *Wyndham and Children First*, 168–9, 177.
61 Egremont, *Wyndham and Children First*, 167.
62 Harold Evans, *Downing Street Diary: The Macmillan Years 1957–1963* (London: Hodder & Stoughton, 1981), 30.
63 Harold Macmillan, *Tides of Fortune 1945–1955* (London: Macmillan, 1969), 529.
64 D. R. Thorpe, *Selwyn Lloyd* (London: Jonathan Cape, 1989), 303–4.
65 Harold Macmillan, *Riding the Storm 1956–1959* (London: Macmillan, 1971), 192.
66 Egremont, *Wyndham and Children First*, 189.
67 Shlaim, Jones and Sainsbury, *British Foreign Secretaries*, 240.
68 Macmillan, *Riding the Storm*, 553, 615.
69 De Zulueta to Macmillan, 19 March 1958, TNA: PREM 11/2347.
70 Bishop to Hunt, 18 October 1956, TNA: PREM 11/1778; Brook to Macmillan, 25 November 1957; Bishop to Macmillan, 26 November 1957, TNA: PREM 11/2321.
71 Meeting at Chequers, 7 June 1959, TNA: CAB134/1929.
72 De Zulueta to Brook, 31 August 1960, TNA: PREM 11/2946.
73 Macmillan diary, 31 August 1958, WL: MS Macmillan, dep. d. 33.
74 Macmillan diary, 4 July 1959, WL: MS Macmillan, dep. d. 36.
75 Macmillan diary, 8 March 1958, WL: MS Macmillan, dep. d. 31.
76 Catterall, *Macmillan Diaries*, vol. II, 149, 157, 482; Macmillan diary, 10 December 1958, WL: MS Macmillan, dep. d. 33.

77 Amery to Macmillan, 15 July 1958, TNA: PREM 11/2397; Lennox-Boyd to Macmillan, 16 July 1958, TNA: PREM 11/2416.
78 TNA: PREM 11/2416, de Zulueta to D. C. Symon, 19 July 1958, to Macmillan, 29 July 1958; de Zulueta to Macmillan, 10 September 1958, TNA: PREM 11/2397.
79 Telephone conversation with Sir Guy Millard, 28 August 2012.
80 Richard Aldous, *Macmillan, Eisenhower and the Cold War* (Dublin: Four Courts Press, 2005), 31; Catterall, *Macmillan Diaries*, vol. I, 420–5.
81 Catterall, *Macmillan Diaries*, vol. II, 323 n.
82 Macmillan diary, 18 January 1959, WL: MS Macmillan, dep. d. 34.
83 De Zulueta to Macmillan, 18 February 1959, TNA: PREM 11/2708; Sabine Lee, *An Uneasy Partnership: British-German Relations between 1955 and 1961* (Bochum: Universitätsverlag Dr. N. Brockmeyer, 1996), 71.
84 De Zulueta to Macmillan, 30 December 1958, TNA: PREM 11/2826.
85 Lee, *Uneasy Partnership*, 71–84; Schaad, *Bullying Bonn*, 128; Peter Mangold, *The Almost Impossible Ally: Harold Macmillan and Charles de Gaulle* (London: I.B.Tauris, 2006), 91.
86 Macmillan, *Riding the Storm*, 637.
87 'British Policy on Germany and European Security', January 1958, TNA: PREM 11/2347. Philip reiterated concerns about these costs in a letter to *The Times*, 9 November 1976.
88 Cited in Peter Catterall, 'Identity and Integration: Macmillan, "Britishness" and the Turn towards Europe', in *Angleterre ou Albion, Entre Fascination et Repulsion*, ed. Gilbert Millat (Lille: Université Lille 3 Charles de Gaulle, 2006), 175.
89 Macmillan to de Zulueta, 15 August 1959, de Zulueta to Macmillan, 18 August 1959, TNA: PREM 11/2703.
90 Thorpe, *Selwyn Lloyd*, 303–4.
91 HMD 12 March 1960, 29 March 1960, 10 May 1960.
92 Aldous, *Macmillan, Eisenhower*, 134–5, 148–9, 158; Horne, *Macmillan*, 231.
93 De Zulueta to Macmillan, 1 June 1960, TNA: PREM 11/3169.
94 HMD: 11 November 1960.
95 Aldous, *Macmillan, Eisenhower*, 168.
96 De Zulueta to Macmillan, 30 December 1958TNA: PREM 11/2826.
97 De Zulueta to Macmillan, 30 October 1959TNA: PREM 11/2985; Aldous, *Macmillan, Eisenhower*, 117; Mangold, *Almost Impossible Ally*, 97. Philip later chaired the British section of the Franco-British Society from 1981 until his death in 1989.
98 Rhys-Williams to de Zulueta, 19 December 1960; notes of speech by Maurice Schumann, 16 December 1960, London School of Economics and Political Science Library, London [henceforward LSEL]:RHYS WILLIAMS J/5/4/11.
99 Catterall, 'Identity and Integration', 176.
100 Catterall, *Macmillan Diaries*, vol. II, 353.
101 Macmillan to de Zulueta, 24 January 1961, WL: MS Macmillan dep. c. 353.
102 Catterall, *Macmillan Diaries*, vol. II, 358, 372; Mangold, *Almost Impossible Ally*, 155.
103 'Background and Objects of Visit', 21 March 1961, John F. Kennedy Presidential Library, Boston, MA, United States [hereafter JFKL]: NSF174A.
104 Catterall, *Macmillan Diaries*, vol. II, 429–31.
105 Ibid., 372; Evans, *Downing Street Diary*, 153.
106 De Zulueta to Macmillan, 14 May 1962, TNA: PREM 11/4575.
107 Catterall, *Macmillan Diaries*, vol. II, 473; Evans, *Downing Street Diary*, 199.
108 Mangold, *Almost Impossible Ally*, 158; N. Piers Ludlow, *Dealing with Britain: The Six and the First UK Application to the EEC* (Cambridge: Cambridge University Press, 1997), 120–1.
109 Catterall, *Macmillan Diaries*, vol. II, 475.

110 Macmillan diary, 30 August 1962, WL: MS Macmillan, dep. d. 46; Evans, *Downing Street Diary*, 217.
111 Christopher Staerck and Gillian Staerck, 'The Realities behind Britain's Global Defence Strategy', in Kaiser and Staerck, *British Foreign Policy*, 49.
112 L. V. Scott, *Macmillan, Kennedy and the Cuban Missile Crisis: Political, Military and Intelligence Aspects* (Basingstoke: Palgrave, 1999), 118.
113 On Laos see Nigel Ashton, *Kennedy, Macmillan and the Cold War: The Irony of Independence* (Basingstoke: Palgrave, 2002), chapter 2.
114 De Zulueta to Samuel, 9 February 1961, TNA: PREM 11/4495.
115 Beddington-Behrens to Thorneycroft, 17 May 1959, LSEL: RHYS WILLIAMS J/5/4/11.
116 De Zulueta to Wiggins, 21 September 1962, TNA: PREM 11/3791. See also Catterall, *Macmillan Diaries*, vol. II, 577.
117 Catterall, *Macmillan Diaries*, vol. II, 525.
118 Ibid., 526; Mangold, *Almost Impossible Ally*, 182–6.
119 Minutes of meeting, 20 November 1962, TNA: PREM 11/3859; Horne, *Macmillan*, 431; email from Lord Egremont, 18 September 2012.
120 Cited in Richard Lamb, *The Macmillan Years: The Emerging Truth* (London: John Murray, 1995), 293.
121 Peter Catterall, 'Roles and Relationships: Dean Acheson, "British Decline" and Post-War Anglo-American Relations', in *The Special Relationship*, ed. Antoine Capet and Aissatou Sy-Wonyu (Rouen: Université de Rouen, 2003), 115–17.
122 De Zulueta to Wright, 26 March 1963, TNA: PREM 11/4575.
123 Cited in Lamb, *Macmillan Years*, 292.
124 Catterall, *Macmillan Diaries*, vol. II, 536.
125 Note by Eden, 1 May 1968, CRL: AP23/3/18; Catterall, *Macmillan Diaries*, vol. II, 258.
126 De Zulueta to Douglas-Home, 14 November 1963, TNA: PREM 11/4578.
127 Catterall, *Macmillan Diaries*, vol. II, 575.
128 Email from D. R. Thorpe, 13 September 2012.
129 See TNA: PREM 11/4427, PREM 11/4594.
130 Kennedy to Macmillan, 10 July 1963, JFKL: NSF174; Macmillan diary, 18 July 1963, WL: MS Macmillan, dep. d. 49.
131 Mangold, *Almost Impossible Ally*, 207–10.
132 Catterall, *Macmillan Diaries*, vol. II, 608.
133 Invitation card, CRL: AP23/67/40.
134 McDermott, *Eden Legacy*, 217; Egremont, *Wyndham and Children First*, 191; Horne, *Macmillan*, 571.
135 Strang, *The Diplomatic Career*, 45; Moorhouse, *Diplomats*, 93–5; Egremont, *Wyndham and Children First*, 191; *The Foreign Office List for 1964* (London: Harrison & Sons, 1964), 449; Interview with Lady de Zulueta, 24 October 2012.
136 Interview with Lady de Zulueta, 24 October 2012.
137 *The Times*, 22 January 1964; Macmillan diary, 2 April 1964, WL: MS Macmillan, dep. d. 51; Macmillan diary, 3 October 1965, WL: MS Macmillan, dep. d. 53; de Zulueta to Eden, 25 September 1965, CRL: AP23/67/41.
138 Catterall, *Macmillan Diaries*, vol. II, 660, 677–9.
139 Note by de Zulueta, 24 November 1963, TNA: PREM 11/4332.
140 Macmillan to Douglas-Home, 23 July 1970, WL: MS Macmillan, dep. c. 539.
141 Cited in Egremont, *Wyndham and Children First*, 1023.
142 For instance, on a memorandum noting that Labour would oppose British nuclear tests but not American ones Philip noted 'Not a very courageous attitude' to which Macmillan replied 'Nor very logical'. Minute, 4 January 1962, TNA: PREM 11/3858.

References

Aldous, Richard, *Macmillan, Eisenhower and the Cold War* (Dublin: Four Courts Press, 2005).
Ashton, Nigel, *Kennedy, Macmillan and the Cold War: The Irony of Independence* (Basingstoke: Palgrave, 2002).
Ball, Simon, *The Guardsmen: Harold Macmillan, Three Friends and the World They Made* (London: HarperCollins, 2004).
Catterall, Peter, 'Identity and Integration: Macmillan, "Britishness" and the Turn towards Europe' in *Angleterre ou Albion, Entre Fascination et Repulsion*, ed. Gilbert Millat (Lille: Université Lille 3 Charles de Gaulle, 2006).
Catterall, Peter, ed., *The Macmillan Diaries*, 2 vols (London: Macmillan, 2003–2011).
Catterall, Peter, 'Roles and Relationships: Dean Acheson, "British Decline" and Post-War Anglo-American Relations', in *The Special Relationship*, ed. Antoine Capet and Aissatou Sy-Wonyu (Rouen: Université de Rouen, 2003), 109–126.
Deighton, Anne, 'British ForeignPolicy-Making: The Macmillan Years', in *British Foreign Policy 1955–1964: Contracting Options*, ed. Wolfram Kaiser and Gillian Staerck (Basingstoke: Macmillan, 2000), 3–18.
Egremont, Lord, *Wyndham and Children First* (London: Macmillan, 1968).
Evans, Harold, *Downing Street Diary: The Macmillan Years 1957–1963* (London: Hodder & Stoughton, 1981).
Hastings, Adrian, *A History of English Christianity 1920–1990*, 3rd edn (London: SCM Press, 1991).
Horne, Alistair, *Macmillan*, vol. II: *1957–1986* (London: Macmillan, 1989).
Kelly, Sir David, *The Ruling Few or the Human Background to Diplomacy* (London: Hollis & Carter, 1952).
Lamb, Richard, *The Failure of the Eden Government* (London: Sidgwick & Jackson, 1987).
Lamb, Richard, *The Macmillan Years: The Emerging Truth* (London: John Murray, 1995).
Lee, Sabine, *An Uneasy Partnership: British-German Relations between 1955 and 1961* (Bochum: Universitätsverlag Dr. N. Brockmeyer, 1996).
Lucas, W.Scott, 'The Missing Link? Patrick Dean, Chairman of the Joint Intelligence Committee' in *Whitehall and the Suez Crisis*, ed. Saul Kelly and Anthony Gorst (London: Frank Cass, 2000).
Ludlow, N.Piers, *Dealing with Britain: The Six and the First UK Application to the EEC* (Cambridge: Cambridge University Press, 1997).
Macmillan, Harold, *Riding the Storm 1956–1959* (London: Macmillan, 1971).
Macmillan, Harold, *Tides of Fortune 1945–1955* (London: Macmillan, 1969).
McDermott, Geoffrey, *The Eden Legacy and the Decline of British Diplomacy* (London: Leslie Frewin, 1969).
Mangold, Peter, *The Almost Impossible Ally: Harold Macmillan and Charles de Gaulle* (London: I.B.Tauris, 2006).
Moorhouse, Geoffrey, *The Diplomats: The Foreign Office Today* (London: Jonathan Cape, 1977).
Schaad, Martin P. C., *Bullying Bonn: Anglo-German Diplomacy on European Integration 1955–1961* (Basingstoke: Macmillan, 2000).
Scott, L. V., *Macmillan, Kennedy and the Cuban Missile Crisis: Political, Military and Intelligence Aspects* (Basingstoke: Palgrave, 1999).
Shlaim, Avi, Peter Jones and Keith Sainsbury, *British Foreign Secretaries since 1945* (Newton Abbot: David & Charles, 1977).

Shuckburgh, SirEvelyn, *Descent to Suez: Diaries 1951–1956* (London: Weidenfeld & Nicolson, 1986).
Staerck, Christopher, and Gillian Staerck, 'The Realities behind Britain's Global Defence Strategy' in *British Foreign Policy 1955–1964: Contracting Options*, ed. Wolfram Kaiser and Gillian Staerck (Basingstoke: Macmillan, 2000), 33–60.
Strang, Lord, *The Diplomatic Career* (London: André Deutsch, 1962).
Strang, Lord, *The Foreign Office* (London: Allen & Unwin, 1955).
Thorpe, D. R., *Eden: The Life and Times of Anthony Eden, First Earl of Avon 1897–1977* (London: Chatto & Windus, 2003).
Thorpe, D. R., *Selwyn Lloyd* (London: Jonathan Cape, 1989).

4 Oliver Wright

Andrew Holt

Introduction

Sir Oliver Wright had a long and distinguished diplomatic career. Spanning five decades, it reached its pinnacle with his appointment to the post of Ambassador to the United States in 1982. Wright was 'a tall, handsome man, with the erect posture and slightly military bearing that recalled his years in the Royal Navy'.[1] Fellow diplomat Sir Alan Campbell later wrote that 'There was something of the actor about him. His dark good looks and five o'clock shadow seemed to suggest the stage, or politics, rather than the public service'.[2] Born on 6 March 1921, John Oliver Wright was educated in the West Midlands – excelling at languages at school – before moving on to Christ's College, Cambridge. He served as a Royal Navy Voluntary Reserve officer from 1941 to 1945, earning a Distinguished Service Cross as commander of a motor torpedo boat. With the Second World War at an end, Wright returned to civilian life and joined the Foreign Office. His diplomatic career initially progressed haphazardly, with postings taking him from New York to Bucharest to Singapore; from Berlin to Pretoria; and back to London in 1959 to attend the Imperial Defence College (now the Royal College of Defence Studies).

Wright's big break came the following year. In July 1960, Prime Minister Harold Macmillan's controversially appointed a peer, the Earl of Home, as Foreign Secretary. With Edward Heath tasked with speaking on foreign affairs in the House of Commons, there became a need for another Private Secretary in the Foreign Office. Wright became assistant Private Secretary to Home, helping particularly with speech writing – something for which Wright had shown skill while in South Africa.[3] The two men developed a strong relationship, working together on issues such as the security of Berlin, the Cuban missile crisis, and the deal by which Britain secured Polaris nuclear weapons from the United States. Wright quickly came to admire his new political master, later describing Home as 'the nearest thing to a Saint in Politics as possible' and 'a superb Foreign Secretary' whose 'judgement was impeccable'.[4]

Relations with the Prime Minister

Wright's path to Number 10 opened up when Home unexpectedly succeeded Macmillan as Prime Minister in October 1963. The new premier asked Wright to go with him to 10 Downing Street, reflecting the confidence that he placed in his Private Secretary. By the mid 1960s the role of the Private Secretary to the Prime Minister had become something of a young man's post. Wright's immediate predecessor, Philip de Zulueta, was almost four years his junior and had left office before turning 40; Wright was almost 43 upon succeeding him. He joined a team headed by Principal Private Secretary Tim Bligh, who was himself replaced by Derek Mitchell in April 1964.

Wright and Sir Alec Douglas-Home – as the Prime Minister was known after renouncing his peerage – continued their working relationship at Number 10. The strong sense of propriety and the separation of government and party management had been established while at the Foreign Office. On one occasion, after resolving a matter of departmental policy on Europe with Heath, Douglas-Home asked the officials to leave the room as the ministers discussed how to present the decision to the Conservative Party.[5] Nevertheless, Wright was involved in the full range of issues affecting Britain's world position. Surprisingly in the context of the Cold War, relations with the Soviet Union were relatively calm. As Douglas-Home told his Italian counterpart in April 1964, there had been 'a distinct improvement in East–West relations which dated from the time of the Cuba crisis'. He attributed this to the risk of nuclear war, American nuclear preponderance, increased tension with China and agricultural issues.[6] Instead, 'the main problems we had at Number 10 ongoing were Rhodesia and Vietnam, lesser order problems than East-West relations or European problems, problems of the second order'.[7] Despite being 'second order' concerns, however, many of these issues were still of grave concern to Britain's foreign policymakers.

One of the major controversies in Anglo-American relations under Douglas-Home was a contract held by Leyland Motors to supply buses to Fidel Castro's Cuba. In the wake of the disastrous Bay of Pigs operation in 1961 and the October 1962 Cuban missile crisis, President Lyndon B. Johnson and his administration vehemently opposed any Western trade with the small communist state. From a British perspective, however, there was merit in closer economic cooperation with Cuba. Douglas-Home believed that trade would weaken Communism, and British policy was traditionally sceptical of boycotts. Moreover, as Cuba was trying to increase her imports from the West, there was a chance that Britain could obtain a significant share of heavy equipment orders worth £10 million. In relation to the political arguments, Cabinet Secretary Sir Burke Trend saw 'no obvious reason why … we should yield to them in the future'.[8] The deal also came with other benefits beyond the immediate economic ones. A report noted that Cuba 'did us a number of small favours' – releasing four political prisoners and exercising restraint on propaganda.[9]

As Douglas-Home's Private Secretary, Wright was involved in advising the Prime Minister throughout the deliberations over how to handle the deal.

Initially he was optimistic and saw little need to change course. In early 1964, less than a month before Douglas-Home visited Washington for a summit meeting with the President, Wright wrote that 'I am sure we can ride this'.[10] He was encouraged by American press coverage. While the *Washington Daily News* described it as 'grabbing a fast buck in careless disregard for the obvious long-term interests of Britain', and warned of a 'new and sterner' US policy on the issue, other voices were less hostile. The *Baltimore Sun*, for example, argued that 'It is hardly reasonable for the United States to offer its wheat to Moscow, but to dispute Britain's right to sell civilian vehicles to Havana'.[11]

Wright's optimism soon dissipated, however. US Ambassador to London David Bruce, back in the US for Christmas, noticed 'trouble brewing' almost instantly. Johnson was said to be personally outraged. Secretary of State Dean Rusk 'bitterly denounced the action' and some members of Congress were equally angry.[12] State Department officials also left Britain's Ambassador to Washington, David Ormsby Gore, under no illusion that the deal and the credit guarantee 'had … caused very serious concern at the highest levels in the administration and in Congress'.[13] At the root of this sentiment was the administration's view that the buses deal was 'a major setback to our program to deny critical commodities to Cuba'.[14] The President personally telephoned London to vent his frustration, only to be told by the Prime Minister that the buses did not endanger the US, and that British trade with Cuba had already fallen from £15 million in 1959 to £1.9 million in 1963. Furthermore, the Cuban press exploited the deal as an example of disagreement amongst the United States' allies. They pointed out that French and German companies also tendered for the contract and highlighted the futility of the blockade.[15] By February, Wright had come to think that 'This is a "no win" situation for us in the States'.[16] He later concluded that 'Unfortunately, Americans are not rational about Cuba'.[17]

Wright continually demonstrated his concern for American opinion and the importance of the special relationship. In late April, Rusk explained to Foreign Secretary Rab Butler that the US intended to continue surveillance overflights of Cuba. The risk with such a policy was that a U2 aircraft could be shot down, provoking an American attack on the responsible surface-to-air missile site.[18] Wright took the view that 'The point about this exercise is not really consultation, but support. Whether or not you are consulted by the President I am quite sure that you must support him'. He continued 'This is a fundamental question of confidence between the British Prime Minister and the American President'. Highlighting Johnson's support over the British attack on Fort Harib in Yemen in March 1964 and disagreements over Cuban trade, he argued that 'Your support will therefore be decisive in the context of your personal relations with the President'.[19] Douglas-Home himself was more circumspect. Although he agreed that 'if there is an incident we would support', he complained about the U2 missions and that 'They deliberately over fly at a shootable level'.[20]

Wright's professional relationship with Douglas-Home came to an end after less than a year in Downing Street. In the October 1964 general election,

Labour narrowly defeated the Conservatives and Harold Wilson became Prime Minister. It was common that a change of government would also signal a change of personnel in the Private Office. Given Wright's long association with Douglas-Home, this seemed even more likely the autumn 1964. Wilson, however, 'decided to keep him on, having recognised his ability and suitability'.[21] He also retained other members of the team, which also comprised Mitchell as Principal Private Secretary, P. J. Woodfield (Parliamentary and Home Affairs) and M. H. M Reid (Home Affairs and General).[22] Wilson was a very different character from his predecessor. As Wright later reflected, in contrast with Douglas-Home:

> his best friend would not have described Harold Wilson as a Saint in politics. Here was a man who was a political animal to his fingertips and, of course, the difference between the Labour Party and the Conservative Party is not merely a difference of policy. They are different animals altogether ... All parties are difficult to manage but the Labour Party's difficulty is in spades.[23]

His institutional memory was helpful from the outset. He knew of the sensitivity of handling the problems in Cyprus, and asked the Foreign Office for a memorandum summarising the position on the issue almost immediately after Wilson took office.[24] He went on to warn Wilson about the risk of Lord Mountbatten becoming too involved in politics 'having exceeded his instructions and somewhat embarrassed the previous Administration' when discussing Cyprus during an earlier visit to Greece.[25] He also used his connections with the Foreign Office. In relation to the Accra plan, which entailed removing British bases form Cyprus, Wright was sceptical. He suggested that Wilson would not wish to volunteer any comment when meeting Turkish Foreign Minister Feridun Cemal Erkin, but should focus on the threat to the role of the mediator and the belief that Turkey welcomed the bases. Should the matter be raised in an immediately preceding meeting with the Foreign Secretary, Wright had arranged to be tipped off by the FO.[26]

Given that this was a new relationship, Wright was initially more circumspect in his tone when communicating with Wilson and his notes in this period tend to give less opinion. Nevertheless, he still advised the Prime Minister on sensitive issues like changes to the NATO naval command structure in the Mediterranean that might need to be raised with other ministers.[27] He would also prepare drafts for the Prime Minister. In July 1965, Wright produced an amended reply to Soviet Foreign Minister Alexei Kosygin after Wilson was not happy with the FO's original.[28] With Wilson absent from London, Wright authorised the despatch of the message.[29] He also advised on which meetings Wilson might need to arrange. In response to Cypriot Foreign Minister Spyros Kyprianou's plan to visit London, Wright wrote in November 1964 that 'There is no need for you to bother with Mr. K.' Wilson agreed.[30] Other tasks were more mundane. For example, he could be responsible for the

Commonwealth Relations Office that previously prepared telegrams could be dispatched.[31] Another aspect of his role was monitoring the media, such as providing the Prime Minister with a clipping of a *Spectator* article in early 1965.[32]

As Wilson's Private Secretary, Wright attended relevant meetings between the Prime Minister and visiting foreign leaders and liaised with the Foreign Office, over Congo, for example.[33] He also accompanied the Wilson on overseas visits. He went on the trip to the US and Canada in December 1964, though he did not attend every meeting.[34] When accompanying Wilson on his visit to Moscow in February 1966, Wright attended a private meeting with Leonid Brezhnev.[35] In April he went with the Prime Minister to meet French President Charles de Gaulle. The intention was for him to interpret for Wilson, but in the event Prince Andronikov, the General's interpreter, performed the role for both leaders.[36] Wright sometimes met visiting officials and statesmen on his own. National Security Council staffer Robert Komer asked to see Wright while in the country with Averell Harriman, using the meeting to emphasise matters of particular concern to the US.[37] Visiting Italian Foreign Minister Giuseppe Saragat met Wright before seeing Wilson, allowing Wright to try to persuade Saragat not to take a decision on the MLF proposal until the British had put forward their own ideas. He asked that Wilson reinforce this.[38] Wilson also trusted Wright to liaise with the Americans over Vietnam. The Prime Minister dispatched Wright to talk to National Security Adviser McGeorge Bundy. Wright later recalled that 'There was no question of saying "don't do that"'. Instead, his purpose was 'to maintain a public stance of reasonable solidarity with the Americans … But certainly not to give the Americans what they really wanted which was to have a British force on the ground. We knew it was a disastrous policy'.[39]

From the outset, the Wilson government faced arguably the most challenging of its foreign policy problems: Rhodesia. Discussion of the terms under which Rhodesia, which was ruled by a white minority, might become independent like its former partners in the Central African Federation, dated back to the previous administration. Mindful of the need to avoid unnecessary controversy in the run-up to the impending general election, Douglas-Home had succeeded in delaying any decision until after the poll. This luxury was not afforded to Wilson. Nevertheless, Douglas-Home had followed a bipartisan policy towards the issue and been keen to maintain the Labour Party's support. Wilson took a similar line, but was unable to prevent Rhodesia's Unilateral Declaration of Independence (UDI) in November 1965. As Britain considered ways to convince Ian Smith's government to reverse its decision, Wright's role was not without criticism. According to Austen Morgan, Wilson's assertion at the January 1966 Commonwealth conference that oil sanctions would bring Rhodesia to its knees in 'weeks not months' was based on Wright's advice.[40] 'We did think', Wright later said, 'not that we would bring [Smith] to his knees, but that this might lead him to negotiate'.[41]

Wright had also been involved, alongside Douglas-Home, in dealing with the process of transitioning British Guiana to independence. Britain had been keen to grant independence quickly. The US government, however, was concerned that such a move could result in Cheddi Jagan, whom they believed to be a communist, winning power. Colonial and Commonwealth Secretary Duncan Sandys resolved the matter by granting independence on the basis of a constitution based on proportional representation, thereby hindering any one party from gaining overall control of the government. Here was an area where the approach was much less bipartisan and Wilson was frustrated that 'we've been on the run ever since the [British Guiana] constitution was fiddled'.[42] When the matter came up again, Wright backed Foreign Secretary Patrick Gordon Walker's view that proposing a coalition between Jagan and Forbes Burnham – the Johnson administration's preferred candidate – would antagonise the US and damage Anglo-American cooperation on the issue.[43] The Prime Minister agreed with Wright's suggestion that he have 'a preliminary run over the ground' with Gordon Walker, Colonial Secretary Anthony Greenwood and Sir Burke Trend, before referring the matter of holding a constitutional conference for British Guiana to the Defence and Oversea Policy Committee.[44]

Oliver Wright remained a firm believer in the special relationship during his time with Harold Wilson. He was not, however, afraid to be blunt with the Prime Minister regarding the Americans. Less than a month after the Labour leader entered Number 10, Wright wrote that 'It is clear that some of the blinkered whizz-kids have been eliminated from the White House'.[45] In this context, he thought that 'To my mind the overriding purpose of your visit to Washington is to secure a broad meeting of minds between yourself and the President on what the world is going to look like from 1965 onwards and what the United States and United Kingdom jointly should do about it'. Wright even argued that 'What we need in fact is a sort of new "Fulton" speech' to chart the course for the next decade. 'The occasional uproar every ten years or so is a good thing if it makes people take a fresh look at the world', he concluded.[46] Wilson described it as 'the best memo I have seen on this. I'll have it out … ready for quick reference'.[47] Unfortunately, hopes for renewed Anglo-American cooperation were not sustained. In February 1965 Wright wrote that 'The fact that we have to deal with is that the man who is at present at the head of the United States is basically not interested in Foreign Affairs … The conduct of American foreign policy is, therefore, likely to be left to the professionals in the State Department'. As such, Wright lamented 'that we are in for a period of the reduction of American committedness'.[48]

Wright was a firm believer in the reunification of Germany, and pressed this view on Harold Wilson. He suggested that Britain should promote the reunification of a peaceful, non-nuclear Germany as a means to help unite the continent. This could be achieved through détente with the USSR, with France then coming to see the need for closer ties with Britain as Germany grew stronger. In order to achieve this, he argued that 'the time is coming for a bit of British "haute politique"' in order to modify the nature of the Six and create a Europe more amenable to Britain, to defuse the German problem and to put Britain back at the heart of events.[49] Wright argued that 'it seems to me utterly lunatic to base a European policy on sucking up to the Germans and doing down the French'.[50] The former risked alienating the USSR and hindering attempts to secure détente.[51]

He was, however, more sceptical about the EEC.[52] Wright later reflected that 'the French and the Germans at Messina invented a Europe that took no account of our interest at all and created the sort of Europe which we could not be comfortable with, but which the Germans were prepared to be comfortable with to assuage their guilt'. 'The idea' he continued, 'was that the Germans should pay and every month the other five should go to the bank and cash the cheques. And then there was the CAP from which we are still suffering'.[53] In the 1990s, he identified himself as 'an anti-Maastricht [Treaty] Europhile'.[54] In contrast, Wright's successor, Michael Palliser, was known to be more positive. Given Wilson's scepticism, Palliser was therefore surprised to be chosen for the role, though he soon came to see that Wilson planned to push for British membership as a means of boosting British competitiveness.[55]

Relations with other policymakers and departments

Wright frequently found himself embroiled in issues that cut across departmental responsibilities. The American proposal to create a multilateral nuclear force (MLF) was one such case. The Ministry of Defence under Peter Thorneycroft vehemently opposed the scheme, which made little sense militarily. However, the vehemence of this sentiment was not replicated elsewhere within the government. The Foreign Office eventually concluded that the effect on relations with the US and the prospect of isolation would be too great if Britain remained outside the project, leading to an 'an unusually visible Whitehall dispute' between the two departments.[56] Downing Street tended to back the FO approach. As Foreign Secretary, Douglas-Home himself had supported joining the Paris talks, arguing to the Cabinet that to rule out the MLF might raise US antagonism and risked jeopardising the supply of Polaris missiles.[57]

Over time, Oliver Wright became increasingly frustrated and direct. Unimpressed with the renewed inter-departmental squabbling in the summer of 1964, he described how the minutes from Butler and Secretary of State for Defence Peter Thorneycroft did little more than 'rehearse all the old arguments for and against the M.LF. which we had in abundance when the Cabinet was debating the matter a year ago'. Wright felt that little more could be done. The Americans, Germans, and Italians were informed of the British position and he felt that Britain had been successful in ensuring that British ideas were given a fair hearing in the working group.[58] Having informed all interested parties that no action could be taken in advance of the election, the Prime Minister replied 'I do not think there is anything more to be done at present'.[59] Wright also advised that few minutes were sent on the subject given its sensitivity,[60] but became increasingly exasperated. When informing Douglas-Home that the Defence Secretary had 'added to his long list of minutes about the M.L.F', he wondered 'whether you will think it worth while keeping up with Mr. Thorneycroft's barrage of minutes'.[61]

In line with his belief in the special relationship, Wright became increasingly convinced that Britain must participate in the MLF. There was alarm when he told the Prime Minister that Germany had invoked vague statements from Secretary of State Dean Rusk, which hinted that the US might eventually withdraw their veto as part of a European clause as a sign to press ahead with a claim for majority voting, doing so 'in their usual ham-handed way'.

'What this means of course', he continued, 'is that the Germans and the Americans must not be allowed to go ahead with the M.L. F. on their own. We must be in on it in order to keep it safe. In other words, if we cannot break it, we must join it'.[62]

He also warned that Thorneycroft was right in pointing out that Germany hoped for the abolition of the US veto.[63] As the MLF looked increasingly likely to come into force come what may, Douglas-Home replied to one Thorneycroft minute by pointing out the 'cogent argument' that Britain should join the MLF to keep her finger on the trigger whatever the US may decide in the future.[64]

The MLF was not the only matter to arouse inter-departmental tension. One of the unique problems that Wright faced as Douglas-Home's Private Secretary was the confusion in policymaking within the government on colonial matters. The positions of Colonial Secretary and Commonwealth Secretary had been combined since 1962, but the merged Foreign and Commonwealth Office would not come into being until 1968. The CRO and the FO thus coexisted uneasily, with many important problems – Cyprus, Aden and Rhodesia – overlapping their respective jurisdictions. Most notably, Sir Patrick Dean, Ambassador to the UN, reported to the FO despite the colonial nature of many issues. That Britain effectively had two foreign ministries also created confusion among her allies. This ill-defined division of responsibilities led to tension between Duncan Sandys, the Commonwealth and Colonial Secretary, and Rab Butler at the Foreign Office.

Butler was not an especially active Foreign Secretary. Tired after 13 years of continuous Cabinet service and two failures to become Prime Minister, he made no major speech on foreign affairs from November 1963 to April 1964 and was frequently absent from Cabinet meetings, especially in the early part of 1964.[65] He even appeared insufficiently briefed on occasions.[66] In contrast, Sandys was of much more forceful character. As the *Daily Mail* stated, 'it is recognised that he has seized the initiative from the Foreign Office time and time again'.[67] The only burst of activity from the Foreign Secretary came in the spring of 1964. At this point, Butler also began taking the lead in smoothing over the damage caused by the raid in Aden, while Minister without Portfolio Lord Carrington's visits to Asia asserted FO primacy.[68] Only in June could it be said that Butler 'emerged … from the shadows of more than six months' curiously coy reticence' to deliver his first major Commons speech since arriving at the FO.[69]

The handling of the Confrontation between Indonesia and Malaysia clearly illustrated the friction. Wright found himself pitched in between the FO and the CO. The day after Douglas-Home requested help from Britain's Commonwealth partners in Oceania, Wright observed that 'the Australians and the New Zealanders seem to be getting cold feet about Indonesia', while Cabinet Secretary Sir Burke Trend warned that 'the situation is gradually getting worse, not better, and that the Australians and New Zealanders ought not to procrastinate much longer'.[70] This in turn prompted a deep reconsideration of the direction of British policy. Wright felt that 'We have got the negative aspect all right', but 'What is lacking is a positive aspect', especially since Britain's allies were probably more concerned with defending the general Western interest of keeping Indonesia non-communist.[71] Throughout January, Oliver Wright remained a dissenting voice. He was damning of 'our whole approach to the political solution to Sukarno's confrontation', warning that 'we are in danger of developing a Sukarno fixation of our own to match the Castro fixation we deplore in the Americans'. He referred to Britain's 'precious little success' in winning support from those with similar interests like Australia and New Zealand and 'almost none' from the likes of West Germany and Japan. He complained that 'We show very little understanding of the fact that the Americans have in fact done a good deal to help us so far' within the limits of preventing the spread of Communism. He therefore opposed the plan that emerged from the previous evening's talks with Sandys and Lord Head – 'to put the screws on the Americans' – on the basis that they had already applied a number of screws. Sukarno was not susceptible to reason and the Americans were ultimately going to prioritise keeping Indonesia non-communist. Trying to alter their view was therefore likely to be counter-productive. He proposed to make it clear that Britain had to support Malaysia, but to acknowledge the strategic differences and try to work together.[72]

President Johnson tasked Attorney General Robert Kennedy with trying to find a solution to the Confrontation. Kennedy's visit to the UK in January was therefore seen by Wright as important in setting the scene for Kennedy's visit to Indonesia.[73] Butler, Thorneycroft, Sandys and Carrington also comprised the British delegation. There was a productive discussion of foreign affairs, though the Prime Minister did not shrink from making some sharp criticism of US policy in Indonesia.[74] Wright thought that Kennedy 'appears to be on the verge of selling us down the river'.[75] Mindful of the potential for Anglo-American discord, the Cabinet resolved that Britain should continue to seek a political solution, but 'we must be on our guard against allowing the Government of Malaysia to pay too high a price for it'.[76] Kennedy found evidence of Sandys's unpopularity from the Tunku, while the US Ambassador to Malaysia also noticed this. Bruce warned Kennedy that he 'must stop criticising Duncan Sandys to the British, as he had in every capital he had visited'.[77]

A particular area of concern was the use of covert action. Peter Thorneycroft wrote to Douglas-Home in early May 1964 arguing that unless attacks on Indonesian communications were authorised, 'it may well be too late to influence the deteriorating situation'.[78] Wright, however, thought this idea 'dangerous, unnecessary and premature'.[79] The Lord Chancellor, Lord Dilhorne, wrote that 'I do not believe that if we do go into Indonesian territory, it will be possible to keep that secret. Nor do I think that any such false denial is in the least compatible with the position and reputation of the British government'. Instead, he argued that if such measures are necessary, they should be justified rather than denied.[80] Wright thought that 'The Lord Chancellor may have a point here'.[81] He also came to question the position of Lord Head. On 24 September, Wright wrote to Douglas-Home that 'It is clear that we must tidy this up by withdrawing authority from High Commissioner Lord Head and by your arrogating it to yourself'.[82] The Prime Minister suggested that a meeting be held the same day.[83]

Wright was also very critical of British policy over Yemen. The UN debate on Britain's bombing of Fort Harib both highlighted and exacerbated British isolation. Douglas-Home's Private Secretary noted that the action had 'left us friendless in the world'. Wright was damning of British policy in the Middle East for failing both to recognise the nature of the situation and to align with the United States. He believed Britain's only real interests were access to oil and overflying rights in order to access other parts of the Empire. As such, he argued that Kuwait and Aden as a means of defending it constituted 'secondary protection'. He thought that the US was not hostile to British interests in the region. Contrary to the earlier consensus, Wright argued that US policy had not failed. He urged that Britain should resist any temptation 'to have a bash at Nasser' and proposed a review of policy towards Yemen and the Federation to be conducted with the US. Such a review would come under the jurisdiction of the FO, 'which is the only Department in Whitehall which is making sense at the moment on this subject. The Colonial Office ought to be making Aden a better place to live in'.[84]

This analysis seemingly carried weight with the Prime Minister. At the Cabinet meeting the following day, Douglas-Home said that it was necessary to make renewed efforts to enlist US cooperation.[85] On 10 April, he wrote of the need 'to make a real effort to align our policies over the Yemen and Egypt' as had been done on the Confrontation and followed this with a personal letter to President Johnson thanking him for the US abstention and adding that 'I should now like to do for the Middle East what we did for South-East Asia last February'.[86] At the same time there were still voices arguing that Britain could hit back in the Yemen, with Sandys having put forward a number of targets. Wright doubted that this would succeed. 'It would require the wisdom of Solomon to know what is the best course to take', but he advised strongly against escalation, which he felt was 'bound to lead to disaster'. The US would not be supportive, there would be an Arab outcry 'And we should end up being booted out not only of Aden but out of Libya and Kuwait as well'.[87] Increasingly exasperated, Wright complained that 'the weakness of Sir Kennedy Trevaskis' policies is that his career has been among the feudal rulers and he seems quite unaware of the repercussions on British interests outside his area of what he does inside it'. Wright considered it imperative to avoid any more strain on relations with the US.[88] He remained a fierce opponent of Sandys's approach. He lamented the failure to recognise the Republican regime and wrote that 'I think that we should recognise that Nasser has been able to capture the most dynamic and modern forces in the area while we have been left, by our own choice, backing the forces which are not merely reactionary, but shifty, unreliable, and treacherous'. He also denounced the way in which the FO had been marginalised, as he did on Cyprus.[89]

Wright was particularly outspoken over Cyprus. By Christmas 1963, the situation on the island appeared dire. The Prime Minister wrote to Sandys in pessimistic mood. He thought the present constitution unworkable, with Archbishop Makarios unlikely to adhere to it but the Turkish community unable to accept any alterations. He predicted that any conference would end in deadlock and partition would result.[90] This reflected Wright's view that the failure of the constitution made partition likely, leaving Britain's Sovereign Base Areas (SBAs) unsustainable.[91] Controversially, Wright argued that the SBAs could be a liability, carrying the risk troops could be required to help maintain law and order if inter-ethnic violence erupted. Wright therefore thought Britain would be better with as few as possible. He even went so far as to minute the Prime Minister that 'our commitment in Cyprus is becoming both undesirable and unnecessary. It does us no good either at home or abroad and we should be considering ways of decently liquidating it'.[92] This seemingly had some effect on the Prime Minister, who enquired of Duncan Sandys about British military needs for the island, adding that 'They seem rather thin'.[93] However, the island was Britain's only major influence in the region after the loss of her position in Palestine and Egypt. Wright was therefore overruled by senior Cabinet members like Peter Thorneycroft who maintained that it was important to retain the presence in order to support any possible operations in the Near East and Mediterranean. Like Thorneycroft, Sandys also opposed the abandonment of the Cyprus bases. In addition to undermining British influence, Sandys pointed out that the loss of Cyprus would be subject to criticism at home.[94] The process of negotiation over the situation in Cyprus was slow. Clearly frustrated, Wright wanted to 'announce our intention to pack our hand in'. He complained that 'every single party in this crisis is indulging in an exercise in brinkmanship to see what they can get out of it, knowing that we are left to hold the baby while they intrigue'. He felt, however, that it was more likely that an 'ineffective' 'dribble into Cyprus of an international force' was a more likely outcome.[95]

Conclusion

In retirement, Oliver Wright modestly remarked that 'much of my career has been built on luck'.[96] In fact, he 'was one of those rare diplomats of whom British politicians of both major parties thought highly'.[97] He was unusual in that he served under two Prime Ministers, men of very different backgrounds, personalities and political views. He formed effective working relationships with both, and was able to be frank and forceful in expressing his views where necessary. He had a long and productive relationship with Alec-Douglas-Home. They had worked well together at the Foreign Office, and this transitioned to Downing Street. The Prime Minister valued Wright's contribution. Upon leaving office, Douglas-Home presented his former Private Secretary with two porcelain parrots, which Wright affectionately called Blood and Sweat.[98]

Wright's relationship with Wilson developed quickly. As Helen Parr argues, he 'attempted to anticipate and thus articulate what he perceived Wilson's wishes to be'.[99] He was effective in this, and his analysis of the international situation was often in tune with the Prime Minister's. Early in 1966, Wright penned a memo arguing that

> now that, post-Cuba, it is evident that the giants are not going to fight each other, the tiddlers have felt free to pursue their own interests and create their own troubles. So that whereas before 1962 one had a fairly stable world situation under the threat of nuclear power, now we have a danger of world anarchy because the threat is no longer believed in.

Wilson thought this 'fascinating' and 'ahead of the way I had been thinking'.[100] Shortly afterwards, Wilson sent Wright with a Colonial Office team to enter negotiations with Ian Smith over a return to constitutional rule and a possible independence settlement for Rhodesia.[101] As *The Times* noted, 'he has played a leading part in the secret diplomacy which has paved the way for the informal talks with Rhodesia'.[102]

The trust that Wilson placed in Wright became apparent again in August 1969. The Prime Minister asked him, unexpectedly and at short notice, to go to Northern Ireland. Wright himself 'never knew why I was selected for the job', as 'the only two essential qualifications I had for it were, one: I was on leave and therefore available and, two: I knew nothing about the problem at all and, therefore, could be held to be unbiased'.[103] As the Troubles worsened, he was sent to be close to Northern Ireland Prime Minister James Chichester-Clark. The intention was 'to thicken up the political relationship', acting as Wilson's eyes and ears, 'rather less than a governor and rather more than an ambassador'.[104]

Oliver Wright acted across the full range of foreign policy issues under both Douglas-Home and Wilson. Disputes between departments over colonial issues were not uncommon under Douglas-Home. As the debate over the MLF lingered during the summer of 1964, Wright became increasingly frustrated by the attitude of the Ministry of Defence and Secretary of State Peter Thorneycroft. Wright was also frequently critical of British colonial policy. This is visible in his attitude towards handling of the Confrontation between Indonesia and Malaysia, and the problems in Yemen and Cyprus. Despite Foreign Secretary Rab Butler's personal lethargy, Wright was generally supportive of the Foreign Office position. He also tended to be more sympathetic to American opinions on the issues.

Wright demonstrated a clear concern for maintaining the special relationship with the United States throughout his time in Downing Street. Douglas-Home was frequently in agreement despite the difficulty of dealing with a President more interested in domestic concerns. Wright accompanied Douglas-Home on his February 1964 visit to meet President Johnson in Washington, later recalling that 'I remember going and visiting him with Alec Home and afterwards Alec saying, "that man does not make sense on foreign affairs"'.[105] Nevertheless, Wright believed that the visit strengthened the Anglo-American relationship by imbuing an appreciation that Britain was the only global power on which the United States could rely.[106] In European matters, he was far-sighted in his support for détente and for a peaceful, re-unified Germany. He was less enthusiastic about the EEC.

By the time Wright left the role, he had become 'the longest toothed Private Secretary in the business'.[107] In contrast with his predecessor, de Zulueta, and his former master Bligh, Wright eschewed the private sector. Wilson helped ensure that his career progressed. As Wright later told the story:

> those who were responsible for my life thought it was the right thing after six years as a private secretary to take me down a peg or two and said, 'What about Deputy High Commissioner in Lusaka?' Well, when this proposition was put to the Prime Minister, Harold Wilson reacted in much the way I would have wanted him to react, without any prompting from myself I might add. And so the Permanent Under-Secretary was sent away with a flea in his ear and told to think again, that I had to be promoted and I had to have an Embassy of my own.[108]

Wright was soon dispatched to Copenhagen.

Wright's diplomatic career went from strength to strength. After his stint in Northern Ireland, Wright returned to the UK to become was Chief Clerk of the Diplomatic Service and then the Deputy Under-Secretary of State at the FCO responsible for European Affairs. In 1975 he became Ambassador to West Germany, holding the post until his retirement in 1981. Despite having been elected Master of Christ's College, Cambridge in May 1982, Margaret Thatcher called him back into action in July, appointing him Ambassador to the United States. He retired for the second and final time in 1986.

Notes

1. *Independent*, 22 September 2009.
2. *Guardian*, 9 September 2009. Rather confusingly Campbell added that Wright 'was thought to have a physical resemblance to Richard Nixon'.
3. Interview with Oliver Wright, 18 September 1996, Churchill Archive Centre, Cambridge [henceforward CAC]: DOHP 17.
4. Interview with Oliver Wright, 18 September 1996, CAC: DOHP 17.
5. N. Wright to author, 16 May 2014.
6. Record of conversation, 27 April 1964, The National Archives, Kew [henceforward TNA]: PREM 11/4788.

7 Interview with Oliver Wright, 18 September 1996, CAC: DOHP 17.
8 Trend to Douglas-Home, 26 February 1964, TNA: PREM 11/4695.
9 Memorandum by Watson to Butler, 'Cuba: Annual Review for 1963', 13 January 1964, AK 1011/1, TNA: PREM 11/4695.
10 Note by Wright, n.d, on Washington to FO, No. 89, 9 January 1964, TNA: PREM 11/4697.
11 Washington (Ormsby Gore) to FO, No. 89, 9 January 1964, TNA: PREM 11/4697.
12 Raj Roy and John W. Young, eds, *Ambassador to Sixties London: The Diaries of David Bruce, 1961–1969* (Dordrecht: Republic of Letters, 2009), 137.
13 Washington to FO, No. 102, 10 January 1964, TNA: PREM 11/4697.
14 'Talking Points Outline', Box 212, National Security File, Country File, LBJL.
15 Havana to FO, No. 2, 11 January 1964, TNA: PREM 11/4697.
16 Wright to Douglas-Home, 11 February 1964, TNA: PREM 11/4794; D. R. Thorpe, *Alec Douglas-Home* (London: Sinclair–Stevenson), 1997, 348.
17 Wright to Douglas-Home, 4 May 1964, TNA: PREM 11/4695.
18 Record of conversation, 27 April 1964, TNA: PREM 11/4696.
19 Wright to Douglas-Home, 1 May 1964, TNA: PREM 11/4696.
20 Douglas-Home, n.d.; Wright to Douglas-Home, 1 May 1964, TNA: PREM 11/4696.
21 *Guardian*, 9 September 2009.
22 *The British Imperial Calendar and Civil Service List 1965* (London: HMSO, 1965), col. 21.
23 Interview with Oliver Wright, 18 September 1996, CAC: DOHP 17.
24 Henderson to Wright, 16 October 1964, TNA: PREM 13/ 197.
25 Wright to Wilson, 25 November 1964, TNA: PREM 13/45.
26 Wright to Wilson, 14 January 1965, TNA: PREM 13/197.
27 Note by Wright, on Healey to Wilson, 3 December, 1964, TNA: PREM 13/20.
28 Wright to Wilson, n.d. [c. 9–16 July 1965], TNA: PREM 13/600.
29 Wright to Wilson, 16 July 1965, TNA: PREM 13/600.
30 Note by Wright, on Bishop to CRO, No. 2697, 20 November 1964, TNA: PREM 13/198; note by Wilson, on Bishop to CRO, No. 2697, 20 November 1964, TNA: PREM 13/198.
31 Wright to Minogue, 14 December 1964, TNA: PREM 13/4.
32 Wright to Wilson, 13 February 1965, TNA: PREM 13/692. For the article see *Spectator*, 12 February 1965, 193.
33 See Wright to Wilson, 13 November 1964, TNA: PREM 13/4.
34 See TNA: PREM 13/9.
35 Austen Morgan, *Harold Wilson* (London: Pluto Press, 1992), 292.
36 Harold Wilson, *The Labour Government 1964–1970: A Personal Record* (London: Weidenfeld & Nicolson; Joseph, 1971), 90.
37 Note for the record by Wright, 24 March 1965, TNA: PREM 13/664.
38 Wright to Wilson, PM/64/119, 3 November 1964, TNA: PREM 13/50.
39 Interview with Oliver Wright, 18 September 1996, CAC: DOHP 17.
40 Morgan, *Wilson*, 276.
41 Interview with Oliver Wright, 1 May 1990, quoted in Morgan, *Wilson*, 276.
42 Note by Wilson, on Stacpoole to Mitchell, 2 April 1965, TNA: PREM 13/137.
43 Wright to Wilson, 5 January 1965, TNA: PREM 13/137.
44 Wright to Wilson, 23 March 1965, TNA: PREM 13/137; Note by Wilson, on Wright to Wilson, 23 March 1965, TNA: PREM 13/137.
45 Wright to Wilson, 19 November 1964, TNA: PREM 13/108.
46 Memorandum by Wright to Wilson, 'Strategy for Washington', 2 December 1964, TNA: PREM 13/103.
47 Note by Wilson, on memorandum by Wright to Wilson, 'Strategy for Washington', 2 December 1964, TNA: PREM 13/103.

48 Wright to Wilson, 12 February 1965, TNA: PREM 13/316.
49 Wright to Wilson, 12 February 1965, TNA: PREM 13/316.
50 Wright to Wilson, 1 February 1966, TNA: PREM 13/905; Helen Parr, *Britain's Policy towards the European Community: Harold Wilson and Britain's World Role 1964–1967* (Abingdon: Routledge, 2005), 61.
51 Parr, *Britain's Policy towards the European Community*, 61.
52 See, for example, Wright to Wilson, 28 January 1966, TNA: PREM 13/905.
53 Interview with Oliver Wright, 18 September 1996, CAC: DOHP 17.
54 See Oliver Wright, *Britain, Europe and the United States: Reflections of an Anti-Maastricht Europhile* (London: Institute of Latin American Studies, 2000).
55 Saki Dockrill, *Britain's Retreat from East of Suez: The Choice between Europe and the World?* (Basingstoke: Palgrave Macmillan, 2002), 157–8.
56 Andrew J. Pierre, *Nuclear Politics: The British Experience with an Independent Strategic Force, 1939–1970* (London: Oxford University Press, 1972), 247.
57 Memorandum by Home, C (63) 151, 12 September 1963, TNA: CAB 129/114.
58 Wright to Douglas-Home, 2 July 1964, 30 June 1964, TNA: PREM 11/4740.
59 Douglas-Home to Butler, M.81/64, 2 July 1964, TNA: PREM 11/4740.
60 Wright to Douglas-Home, 16 July 1964, TNA: PREM 11/4740.
61 Wright to Douglas-Home, 24 July 1964, TNA: PREM 11/4740.
62 Wright to Douglas-Home, 16 July 1964, TNA: PREM 11/4740.
63 Wright to Douglas-Home, 24 July 1964, TNA: PREM 11/4740.
64 Douglas-Home to Thorneycroft, M.86/64, 27 July 1964, TNA: PREM 11/4740, TNA.
65 *People*, 26 April 1964.
66 Avi Shlaim, Peter Jones and Keith Sainsbury, *British Foreign Secretaries since 1945* (Newton Abbot: David & Charles, 1977), 176.
67 *Daily Mail*, 6 April 1964.
68 *Daily Mail*, 6 April 1964.
69 *Daily Mail*, 17 June 1964.
70 Note by Douglas-Home, on Wright to Douglas-Home, 17 December 1963; Trend to Douglas-Home, 18 December 1963, TNA: PREM 11/4905.
71 Wright to Douglas-Home, 17 December 1963, TNA: PREM 11/4905.
72 Wright to Douglas-Home, 22 January 1964, TNA: PREM 11/4906.
73 Wright to Douglas-Home, n.d. [January 1964], TNA: PREM 11/5196.
74 Thorpe, *Douglas-Home*, 346.
75 Wright to Douglas-Home, 20 January 1964, TNA: PREM 11/4906.
76 CM 6 (64) 3, 23 January 1964, TNA: CAB 128/38.
77 'Notes for WAH personal files', 1 February 1964, Library of Congress, Washington, D.C.: W. Averell Harriman Papers, Box 479; Matthew Jones, *Conflict and Confrontation in South East Asia, 1961–1965: Britain, the United States, and the Creation of Malaysia* (Cambridge: Cambridge University Press, 2002), 253.
78 Thorneycroft to Douglas-Home, 4 May 1964, TNA: PREM 11/4908.
79 Wright to Douglas-Home, 4 May 1964, TNA: PREM 11/4908.
80 Dilhorne to Douglas-Home, 5 May 1964, TNA: PREM 11/4908.
81 Wright to Douglas-Home, 6 May 1964, TNA: PREM 11/4908.
82 Wright to Douglas-Home, 24 September 1964, TNA: PREM 11/4910.
83 Note by Douglas-Home, on Wright to Douglas-Home, 24 September 1964, TNA: PREM 11/4910.
84 Wright to Douglas-Home, 8 April 1964, TNA: PREM 11/4679.
85 CC (64) 23, 9 April 1964, TNA: CAB 128/38.
86 Douglas-Home to Butler, M.36/64, 10 April 1964; Douglas-Home to Johnson, T.137/64, 10 April 1964, TNA: PREM 11/4679.
87 Wright to Douglas-Home, 22 April 1964, TNA: PREM 11/4680.
88 Wright to Douglas-Home, 6 May, TNA: PREM 11/4680.

89 Memorandum by Wright to Douglas-Home, 18 July 1964, TNA: PREM 11/4929.
90 Memorandum by Douglas-Home to Sandys, M. 440H/63, 27 December 1963, TNA: PREM 11/4139.
91 Wright to Douglas-Home, 27 December 1963, TNA: PREM 11/4139.
92 Wright to Douglas-Home, 27 December 1963, TNA: PREM 11/4139.
93 Memorandum by Douglas-Home to Sandys, M. 440H/63, 27 December 1963, TNA: PREM 11/4139.
94 Sandys to Douglas-Home, T.80H/63, 30 December 1963, TNA: PREM 11/4702.
95 Wight to Douglas-Home, 11 March 1964, TNA: PREM 11/4707.
96 Interview with Oliver Wright, 18 September 1996, CAC: DOHP 17.
97 *Guardian*, 9 September 2009.
98 N. Wright to author, 16 May 2014.
99 Parr, *Britain's Policy towards the European Community*, 31.
100 Wright to Wilson, 28 January 1966, TNA: PREM 13/905; Dockrill, *Britain's Retreat*, 105.
101 Wilson, *Labour Government*, 271.
102 *The Times*, 29 April 1966.
103 Interview with Oliver Wright, 18 September 1996, CAC: DOHP 17.
104 Interview with Oliver Wright, 1 May 1990, quoted in Morgan, *Wilson*, 276.
105 Interview with Oliver Wright, 18 September 1996, CAC: DOHP 17.
106 Wright to Douglas-Home, 17 February 1964, TNA: PREM 11/4794; Jones, *Conflict*, 304.
107 Interview with Oliver Wright, 18 September 1996, CAC: DOHP 17.
108 Interview with Oliver Wright, 18 September 1996, CAC: DOHP 17.

References

Dockrill, Saki, *Britain's Retreat from East of Suez: The Choice between Europe and the World?* (Basingstoke: Palgrave Macmillan, 2002).

Jones, Matthew, *Conflict and Confrontation in South East Asia, 1961–1965: Britain, the United States, and the Creation of Malaysia* (Cambridge: Cambridge University Press, 2002).

Morgan, Austen, *Harold Wilson* (London: Pluto Press, 1992).

Parr, Helen, *Britain's Policy towards the European Community: Harold Wilson and Britain's World Role 1964–1967* (Abingdon: Routledge, 2005).

Pierre, Andrew J., *Nuclear Politics: The British Experience with an Independent Strategic Force, 1939–1970* (London: Oxford University Press, 1972).

Roy, Raj, and John W. Young, eds, *Ambassador to Sixties London: The Diaries of David Bruce, 1961–1969* (Dordrecht: Republic of Letters, 2009).

Shlaim, Avi, Peter Jones and Keith Sainsbury, *British Foreign Secretaries since 1945* (Newton Abbot: David & Charles, 1977).

Wilson, Harold, *The Labour Government 1964–1970: A Personal Record* (London: Weidenfeld & Nicolson; Joseph, 1971).

Wright, Oliver, *Britain, Europe and the United States: Reflections of an Anti-Maastricht Europhile* (London: Institute of Latin American Studies, 2000).

5 Michael Palliser

John W. Young[1]

Michael Palliser was unique among the Private Secretaries to the Prime Minister discussed in this volume, in that he later held the highest position in the Foreign and Commonwealth Office, serving as Permanent Under-Secretary (PUS) for seven years, in 1975–1982. He arrived in Downing Street at a key point in March 1966, just as Labour was re-elected with a clear majority and shortly before a major economic crisis, which eventually led to swingeing overseas spending cuts and pushed the government towards a second application to join the European Economic Community (EEC).

In South East Asia, while the Vietnam War was turning into a quagmire for London's key ally, the United States, another conflict, the Confrontation between Indonesia and the former British colonies in Malaysia, was coming to an end, freeing the British to consider a military withdrawal from the region. In southern Africa, it was becoming clearer that it would not be possible to put an early end to the white supremacist regime of Ian Smith in Rhodesia, which had unilaterally declared its independence from Britain the previous year. Within Whitehall, the end of the Empire was symbolised by the winding-up of the Colonial Office in August 1966; the Commonwealth Office merged with the FO in October 1968, creating the Foreign and Commonwealth Office (FCO).

Nearer to home, the Cold War in Europe seemed less intense and there were hopes of engaging the Soviet bloc in a process of détente. However, in March 1966 the French President, Charles de Gaulle, pulled his country out of NATO, asserting his independence of Washington. Palliser's time as Private Secretary to the Labour Prime Minister Harold Wilson therefore proved a highly significant one for British foreign policy, when decisions were made that effectively ended Britain's world role and focused instead on a European future.[2]

Born in 1922, Michael Palliser was the son of an admiral. He was educated at Wellington College and Oxford University, and had five years' service in the Coldstream Guards before joining the Foreign Office in 1947. His early postings included Athens (1949–1951), in the wake of the Greek civil war, Paris (1956–1960), as the Fourth Republic disintegrated and de Gaulle established the Fifth, and Dakar (1960–1963), in the early years of Senegalese independence.[3] The American diplomat Philip Kaiser, who worked with Palliser in

Dakar and served as number two in the London Embassy in 1964–1969, later described his British colleague as follows:

> Tall, handsome and congenial, he was a superb public school-Oxford product. He combined a relaxed personal style with a thorough knowledge of international relations, a keen intellect, and an exceptional ability for easily and clearly articulating his ideas.

Kaiser was 'delighted but not surprised' when Palliser became Wilson's PS,[4] and they were able to have frank conversations about differences that arose between the two countries.[5]

Appointment to Downing Street

The reasons for appointing Palliser as PS were brought out, albeit briefly, in Wilson's memoirs: he 'was commended to me by officials and ministers alike as one of the high-flyers of the Diplomatic Service – and so he proved'.[6] Palliser later said that the summons to Downing Street came 'out of the blue'. He seems to have been the only candidate put forward by the FO for the post, though Wilson, smoking his trademark pipe, did give him an interview in the Cabinet Room before confirming the appointment. The Prime Minister also consulted George Thomson, who had been Minister of State at the FO since 1964 and who supported the idea, perhaps seeing Palliser as an ally in pressing EEC membership.[7] The appointment was announced in late February and, following some leave, Palliser took up the post in April. He wrote to his godfather, a former diplomat, George Rendel, 'My feelings are a little mixed, as you can imagine. But I know it will be a fascinating experience and most interesting'.[8] In 1954–1956, Palliser had already been Private Secretary to the PUS and, in 1964–1966, he was the first head of the Foreign Office's Planning Staff, which was set up to study long-term challenges.

The task of PS could be a gruelling one, especially for someone like Palliser who was married with three children, the last only a few years old. He liked to get 'regular box-loads of paper to work on at home [where] one can deal with it quietly and in orderly fashion', in contrast to Number 10, where 'the office is always a turmoil'.[9] Looking back on his career, he did not feel the Downing Street job was any more difficult in terms of time, energy and effort than his subsequent roles as Permanent Representative at the EEC or PUS, but that was only because those jobs, too, were so challenging. Oliver Wright told him, when handing over the job, 'There are only two qualifications for it, an iron constitution and an understanding wife'. Palliser was fortunate to have both. He could only recall being badly ill once, with a bad cold during a visit from Soviet premier Alexei Kosygin, and his wife learnt to cope with countless late evenings, when Palliser would stay in Downing Street until Wilson came back from the House of Commons, typically around 10.30.[10] When an urgent issue arose on overseas visits, Palliser might sometimes be the one who had to wake

Wilson up, even in the dead of night.[11] The disruption caused by the job extended to holiday planning: 'I have to plan to be away at the same time as the PM and he goes invariably in August ...'.[12] In August 1968, Palliser was holidaying in the Ardennes and Wilson was in the Scillies, when both had to return to Downing Street because of the sudden Soviet invasion of Czechoslovakia.[13]

Within Downing Street itself, Palliser was the primary, but not the only, individual working on foreign policy. The Principal Private Secretary was Michael Halls, who also joined the team in 1966 but stayed until 1970. He had served Wilson when the latter was President of the Board of Trade back in the 1940s and was generally felt to be over-promoted by the Prime Minister. It was a view Palliser shared[14] and Halls, who in any case was likeable enough, never became a rival in the foreign policy field. He did, however, sometimes became involved on the economic side of international policy, as when Wilson hoped to boost Anglo-Soviet trade[15] or when he was interested in organising a meeting of the Governor of the Bank of England with his EEC counterparts during Britain's second entry bid.[16] Halls would also become active in administrative matters, for example, when George Brown, the Foreign Secretary, failed to arrive to chair a ministerial meeting on the EEC talks in July 1967.[17] Sometimes, Palliser and Halls would unite to press a view on Wilson, as in March 1967, when they argued in support of Brown that it would be better to launch a fresh application for EEC membership than to revive the one made by the Conservatives in 1961.[18]

A more significant and impressive figure, who certainly influenced Wilson's view of world affairs on a regular basis, was the Cabinet Secretary, Sir Burke Trend. Although he was not physically based at Number 10, Trend was literally just around the corner in the Cabinet Office. He had enormous influence not only because of his acute intelligence, long experience and grasp of business across Whitehall, but also because Wilson respected him. It was in the nature of his role to provide the Prime Minister with a covering analysis to all memoranda that came before the Cabinet or its key ministerial committees.[19] Thus, Trend would give Wilson a view on how to handle the questions that came before the Defence and Oversea Policy Committee, the most important committee on international matters. Palliser himself later acknowledged Trend's enormous importance, talking of,

> the influence, discreet but ever present, of the Secretary of the Cabinet: someone who is always at the Prime Minister's right hand, lacking the power of a departmental Permanent Under-Secretary with a big Ministry behind him, but more than compensating for that by the influence flowing from his unique position at the heart of government.[20]

One of the points that emerges is that Palliser, too, was able to use a position, close to the Prime Minister, 'at the heart of government' to have an important influence on policy.

Day-to-day routine

Palliser's daily routine was much the same as his predecessors. As he put it, 'I had to ensure that the Prime Minister was fully informed about every aspect of foreign relations, to convey his ... comments to the Foreign Secretary and to ensure in turn that the latter's views ... were drawn fully to the Prime Minister's attention'.[21] He also provided advice of his own to Wilson and there were more mundane, if sensitive, issues such as recommending which foreign leaders should receive Christmas cards from the Prime Minister[22] or where precisely to sit guests at dinner.[23] As far as liaising with the FO is concerned, his most important contacts were the Private Secretaries to the Foreign Secretary, Murray Maclehose in 1965–1967 and Donald Maitland in 1967–1969. As 'the collision mats of the civil service',[24] they would keep each other informed of thinking in the FO and Number 10. Thus, in April 1966, Palliser wrote to Maclehose that, in contrast to de Gaulle, who had just pulled France out of NATO, Wilson was determined to pursue détente with the Soviet bloc on the basis of a *united* Atlantic alliance.[25] In November 1967, he warned Maitland that Wilson was 'decidedly allergic' to George Brown's idea of increasing arms sales to the apartheid regime in South Africa.[26]

Palliser came to realise, like others before and after, that a key problem as PS was 'precisely how to reconcile being totally loyal to the Prime Minister, who is your boss and who you are there to serve, while at the same time preserving a relationship with the Foreign Secretary ... which is actually crucial to the national interest'. With the calm, agreeable Michael Stewart, who was Foreign Secretary in Palliser's early months and again after March 1968, this was not a major challenge. But the relationship was fraught when Brown became Foreign Secretary. During one meeting, in Wilson's presence, Brown accused Palliser of effectively being a traitor to the FO. However, Palliser and his colleagues in the FO prevented any serious rupture. It helped that Palliser and Maclehose got on personally so well, having worked together in the Paris Embassy. They lunched together very week or so, trying 'to repair such bits of china as had been broken during the week ...'. Although, ultimately, Downing Street held the upper hand in any showdown, Palliser believed his job was 'not to dominate the Foreign Office or to run other Departments, it was to ensure the smooth liaison between the two while preserving the loyalty to the Prime Minister ...'.[27]

Since Palliser was also in post during the last years of the Commonwealth Office, he also had contact with the PS to the Commonwealth Secretary, Oliver Forster (1965–1967), and the latter's successor, John Williams (1967–1968). Downing Street and the Commonwealth Office had to cooperate on a wide range of issues, including Indian premier Indira Gandhi's visit to London in April 1966, and an Australian idea, in September 1966, for a renewed Commonwealth peace mission to end the Vietnam War, as well as the more persistent problem of Rhodesia.[28] In fact, there was a range of departments in Whitehall with which Downing Street had to cooperate on international policy. For example, Palliser was in contact with the Ministry of Technology, in October 1967, on ideas for technological cooperation in Western Europe.[29] However, Halls dealt most with his former department, the Board of Trade.[30]

In working with the Prime Minister, Palliser often simply appeared to pass messages back and forth. Some were designed to keep the right people informed about issues, not least the records of meetings that were exchanged between Downing Street and the FO. But he would also select the material that the Prime Minister, faced by a tight schedule, should or should not see. This included material from the so-called 'Red Book', submitted weekly by the Joint Intelligence Committee. Palliser sometimes found this 'long and boring' and many of the materials were not passed to Wilson, because 'the situation they are dealing with is not of concern to him at present'. At other times, however, 'there are several items which I find well worth showing to the Prime Minister, and ... he often sparks on them and throws up comments ...'.[31] Palliser was also expected to provide advice on how best to handle foreign policy challenges. 'A private secretary is not just there to shuffle papers – you're there to advise your minister; that is your job'.[32] Some were short-term and relatively simple. In December 1966, ahead of a visit by the Soviet premier, Alexei Kosygin, there was a delicate challenge posed by the need to deter him from criticising the Americans or Germans while he was in London. Palliser recommended that the matter should be raised with him verbally, after he arrived, and Wilson agreed.[33]

However, Palliser was quite capable of expressing strong views of his own on major questions. In early 1967, when London discovered that it had been kept uninformed about a US attempt to contact Hanoi using a Polish intermediary, the PS accused Washington of 'muddle, lack of confidence and incompetence'.[34] In an early memorandum to Wilson, Palliser revealed his own openness to détente and his willingness to criticise other foreign policy experts. Arguing that the erection of the Berlin Wall in 1961 had been an admission of Soviet defeat in its attempts to expand westwards and that Moscow had learnt lessons from the Cuban missile crisis, the PS argued:

> It seems to me that our Soviet experts spend so much of their time doing analyses of Soviet Holy Writ that they tend to ignore the actions of the Soviet Government. Which all goes to show that if war is too serious a matter to be left to Generals, East-West relations are too serious a matter to be left to Kremlinologists.[35]

Downing Street diplomacy

Another aspect of Palliser's work was to accompany the Prime Minister to meetings, at home and abroad. At the highest level, these included 'summit' conferences with foreign leaders, which were a growing phenomenon in the 1960s, as jet aircraft made it easier for heads of state and government to travel the world.[36] Palliser recognised that, thanks to summits, Prime Ministers were involved in foreign policy, 'not just ... because it's important but because he or she has now to handle much more of it personally'.[37] In May 1966, along with

Trend, Halls and various FO officials, Palliser was part of the British team that held talks with a German delegation under Chancellor Ludwig Erhard.[38] Several weeks later, Palliser sat in on a plenary meeting between Wilson and Lyndon Johnson at the White House, when Trend and Halls were again present.[39] Palliser might sometimes get involved with setting the agenda for summits, as when he talked to the Minister of the French Embassy about Wilson's planned summit with de Gaulle in mid 1967.[40] Wilson was impressed by Palliser's skills as an interpreter, especially when these proved more than a match for his French opposite number during a summit with de Gaulle in January 1967.[41] Some foreign ministers would also see the Prime Minister, when visiting London, including Israel's Abba Eban in February 1967 and Palliser would keep a record, later forwarded to the FO.[42]

There were other visitors to Downing Street, not least the ambassadors of key allies. These meetings, too, were recorded by Palliser and passed to the FO. Perhaps the most important were Wilson's quite frequent meetings with America's David Bruce. Within months of taking up his post, Palliser had sent Maclehose notes of meetings with Bruce about the Ambassador's pessimism about American progress in Vietnam, a possible visit by Wilson to Washington and the Johnson administration's determination that such a visit must be 'carefully prepared'.[43] Palliser also recorded meetings between Wilson and other Cabinet ministers where they were relevant to foreign affairs. Thus, in June 1966 he passed on to Maclehose a record of a meeting between Wilson and Stewart, about the upcoming US bombing of industrial targets in North Vietnam.[44] Sometimes, it was also worth making a record of telephone conversations, as when Wilson and Brown discussed their attitude towards a possible UN Resolution on an Arab-Israeli peace settlement in July 1967.[45]

Inevitably, the PS was also at the centre of any diplomatic exchanges that focused on Downing Street, perhaps the most famous in this period being the 'Sunflower' talks of February 1967 when there was an Anglo-Soviet attempt to bring Washington and Hanoi together. Palliser helped liaise with the CIA officer Chester Cooper, who was sent over by President Johnson, attended key meetings and, in the aftermath of Sunflower, helped prevent Wilson's criticisms of US tactics from damaging the transatlantic relationship.[46] In late 1968, Palliser was involved in planning for the somewhat ludicrous, secret mission to Rhodesia by Wilson's lawyer, Lord Goodman, and the press baron Max Aitken, in August 1968, which paved the way for a summit meeting with Rhodesian premier Ian Smith on board HMS *Fearless*.[47]

There were occasions when Palliser would conduct diplomatic business on his own. For example, in August 1966, in the wake of a major monetary crisis, he tackled a member of the French Embassy over Downing Street's suspicions that Paris had helped to destabilise the pound on the money markets.[48] A more delicate, clandestine meeting was with a representative of the breakaway 'Biafran' regime during the Nigerian civil war.[49] Palliser might also have direct communication with certain British ambassadors, like Patrick Dean in Washington who, in June 1966, passed on views about a possible Wilson visit to

Washington, based on conversations with the Secretary of State, Dean Rusk, and the National Security Advisor, Walt Rostow.[50] Soon afterwards, on the Prime Minister's instructions, Palliser also took up with Dean the question of a press leak, in the *Sunday Times*, about messages between Wilson and President Johnson.[51] Inevitably, the PS also played an important role in securing agreement between Number 10 and the FO on certain issues, as in June 1966 when Wilson wanted to issue a statement dissociating London from the US bombing of oil installations around urban centres in North Vietnam.[52]

Downing Street was frequently at the very centre of British foreign policy. One unusual example of diplomacy was the clandestine contact that took place between London and North Vietnam, using two supposed Vietnamese 'journalists', who were actually diplomats. Given that London did not recognise Hanoi's official existence, it was necessary to contact the pair via irregular channels, in this case a junior minister in the government, Harold Davies, who was both personally loyal to Wilson and knowledgeable about North Vietnam, having once met its leader, Ho Chi Minh.[53] Davies' conversations with the Vietnamese 'journalists' were reported directly to Downing Street, but Palliser kept the FO informed about them.[54] There are other cases of Palliser sharing delicate information with his former colleagues. In late 1966, for example, the American diplomat Averell Harriman visited Wilson and asked that no record be kept of the fact that, in pursuing a Vietnam peace settlement, President Johnson would be ready to accept Soviet assurances of North Vietnamese behaviour provided there was a guarantee of 'something positive'. However, Palliser did record the fact – and passed it on to Maclehose.[55]

Not all Palliser's overseas visits were in Wilson's company. In November 1968 he went with George Thomson to Rhodesia, to follow up the summit on HMS *Fearless*.[56] On certain occasions, the PS became involved in overseas visits of his own. He went to Washington just ahead of Wilson's June 1967 visit in order to sound out the Americans on British plans to withdraw from military bases East of Suez: he found both disappointment at the decision and resignation that it would be carried out.[57] Several weeks later, at a critical moment in the second EEC membership bid, he went to Brussels, where he found that the five members other than France were united behind a British application.[58] Perhaps most important of all, Palliser helped to establish links to the incoming Nixon administration, following the presidential election of November 1968. Initially, Wilson thought of sending his old friend John Freeman, who had been selected as the next Ambassador to Washington to do the job. But the incumbent Ambassador, Patrick Dean, argued against this. Among other considerations, Freeman was too high-profile a figure for the mission to remain secret. It was then that Palliser put his own case forward. Henry Kissinger, slated to become Nixon's National Security Advisor, was 'a very old friend of mine and we have been seeing each other 2 or 3 times a year. If you want a direct line to the President-elect ... I think I can do it for you ...'.[59] Palliser subsequently had a 'very friendly and relaxed' talk with Kissinger, in which they were able to discuss a possible visit by Wilson to

Washington key personalities in the new administration and pressing international questions.[60]

Spying on the Foreign Office

An intriguing aspect of Palliser's work was the creation of a kind of intelligence-gathering operation *inside* the Foreign Office so as to discover the likely policies of George Brown, the Deputy Leader of the Labour Party, when he became Foreign Secretary in August 1966. There was little warmth between Wilson and Brown. They stood on different wings of the Party, had competed for the leadership in 1963 and had rather different views on Britain's role in the world. In his memoirs, Brown complained about the 'troublesome arrangement' whereby a PS was appointed to Downing Street from the FO and claimed, without providing any concrete example, that this 'raised considerable conflict on occasions'.[61] Ironically, in many ways, Palliser's international outlook might be seen as similar to Brown's, who was a keen advocate of EEC membership and ready to wind down the position East of Suez. But Brown was also a controversial, volatile figure, fond of alcohol, who soon alienated many diplomats. The precise reasons for setting up an intelligence operation are nowhere set down but, given the distrust between Prime Minister and Foreign Secretary, Wilson's desire to play a leading foreign policy role and the unpredictability of Brown, it is clear that advance information on the latter's likely doings could be useful for Downing Street.

Palliser seems to have had no trouble in having colleagues in the FO pass information to him and, within months, he had established a means of obtaining key pieces of information. When passing to Wilson a telegram from Brown to the German Foreign Minister, Willy Brandt, in January 1967, Palliser added. 'I hope you will not reveal that you know of this message. My private line to the FO is very useful and I should not wish it to be cut off'.[62] In May 1967, having procured another 'private' copy of an FO document, he expressed the fear that 'in certain important matters the Foreign Office are being less than frank with us', but he assured Wilson that 'I am reasonably confident that I can keep us in the picture through my own network'.[63] This network clearly included individuals at the highest level in the FO, who could pass on documents intended for Brown himself. One was probably Lord Chalfont, who had been personally appointed to the role of Minister for Disarmament by Wilson back in 1964, who later focused on the EEC application and who seem to have remained personally committed to the Prime Minister. In July 1967, Palliser was able to obtain a memorandum from Chalfont to Brown for the 'private eye' of Downing Street; and in December he obtained a similar document, 'sent to me on the usual *personal* and *non-attributable* basis' [original emphasis], before Brown had even seen it.[64] Once established, the 'private line' continued to operate even after Brown suddenly resigned in March 1968, being replaced by the more dependable Stewart. Thus, Wilson received a minute from Chalfont to Stewart in May 1968 regarding policy towards the EEC[65] and the Prime

Minister was informed early on about the FO's consideration of an invasion of Anguilla, a former British colony in the West Indies that had slipped into political instability, although this time by Halls rather than Palliser.[66]

Despite such signs of distrust between Number 10 and the FO at ministerial level, the evidence is that relations between the two were generally good at a lower level, not least because of Palliser's relationship with his opposite numbers at the Office. Any problems that did spring up seem to have been quickly smoothed over. In May 1967, for example, Maclehose admitted that the FO, without consulting Downing Street, had issued a statement about an exchange of messages between Wilson and de Gaulle. Palliser wrote back that Downing Street certainly should have been consulted but he suggested 'we leave it at that'.[67] Palliser hoped that Wilson and Brown could be kept working in harness on the EEC application if the former focused on strategic questions, like winning over de Gaulle, while the Foreign Secretary handled details like agricultural policy. However, Brown was always likely to take initiatives of his own: at one point in June 1967, Wilson only learnt of the Foreign Secretary's latest plans to publicise Britain's EEC negotiating position when he read the newspapers.[68] Palliser also seems to have tried to avoid openly taking sides in the Wilson–Brown feud. The PS was present during the bitter row that took place in the Cabinet Room between the pair in March 1968, which was followed by Brown's resignation, because he had not been consulted over a decision to declare a Bank Holiday as a way of forestalling a financial crisis. Among all the shouting, Palliser was pointedly asked by Brown how long Wilson had spent trying to contact him, before taking the decision on a Bank Holiday. Palliser simply refused to answer.[69] Many individuals were caught up in the tension and uncertainties created by Brown's appointment but one of them, the PUS at the FO, Paul Gore-Booth, was generous enough to say that he thought Palliser's position had perhaps been 'the most difficult':

> [The] man at No. 10 ... has two loyalties; he is the servant of the Prime Minister but he is bound to keep closely acquainted with and reflect the thinking of the Foreign Office at all levels on the international situation. Palliser managed both with great skill.[70]

The 'second try'

Being at the centre of British government, with a wide remit over foreign affairs, the Prime Minister's Private Secretaries for foreign affairs found themselves involved in a vast array of issues. Palliser himself recalled, 'I had, so far as possible, to cover the globe'.[71] To give just a short selection of items, Palliser's work involved him in receiving reports on the dangers of a nuclear arms race in Asia (where India was concerned about the Chinese threat); the 'snail-like' advance of talks with the illegal regime in Rhodesia; and the attempts to bring an Arab-Israeli peace settlement following the June 1967 Six-Day War.[72] But his involvement in many of these issues was intermittent, partly because they were not so consistently important as to require the regular input of the Prime Minister. The main issue that illuminates Palliser's role in shaping foreign policy, and which certainly demanded a lot of Wilson's time, was the so-called 'second try' to enter the EEC. This was closely linked to the discussion about Britain's continued presence East of Suez where, in 1966, it still had a military presence in Malaysia-Singapore, Aden and the Persian Gulf.

Under Oliver Wright, it had seemed that Britain might remain East of Suez for many years. Military withdrawal *was* discussed, in the context of cuts in defence spending that were discussed from the moment Labour took office, largely thanks to the country's persistent balance of payments problems. Palliser himself later recalled that foreign policy under Wilson was carried out under 'a permanent economic thundercloud'.[73] But until 1966 the Confrontation with Indonesia made it impossible to contemplate a precipitate retreat from Malaysia-Singapore, the US government would have been upset by such a move (especially as it became increasingly entangled in Vietnam) and Wilson himself portrayed himself as an 'East of Suez man', seeing the bases as essential to Britain's role as a major power.[74] Wright believed that, with the Cold War stalemated in Europe, the challenges for the West in the 1960s lay in the less-developed world, where British efforts should be focused.[75] This outlook rapidly disappeared after he left Downing Street.

It is not the case that his friend and successor, Palliser, wanted a precipitate retreat from the world role. In March 1967, when ministers discussed plans for a rapid withdrawal from East of Suez, he was quite clear about the dramatic implications, telling the Prime Minister, 'we should be under no illusion that it is anything but the end of Britain's "world role" in defence'. The PS even struck a cautious note, warning that such a withdrawal could be seen as a reversal of Wilson's earlier policies and must be given very careful presentation, so that it would be wise to take more time over it.[76] This advice shows that, however much he may himself have favoured a shift towards Europe, Palliser preserved his loyalty to the Prime Minister. Subsequently, he also advised Wilson that, however difficult the process, London must consult Washington about the process of withdrawal. President Johnson would feel hurt if he found out about British intentions only at the last minute.[77] Palliser recognised that one danger of withdrawal from East of Suez was that it would reduce Britain's significance in the world and risk damaging relations with the US and other allies, like Australia, at a time when entry to the EEC was not yet secure. 'All of this means, I suggest, that the logic of our Far Eastern policy is to add considerably greater urgency to our European policy'.[78] But Palliser never stood in the way of a withdrawal from East of Suez; his concern was how to manage the process to minimise any deleterious side-effects.

As a corollary to his enthusiasm for the world role, Wright had been sceptical about another bid to enter the EEC.[79] Here the difference with Palliser was more marked. The latter was very much identified as a supporter of entry to the EEC. To some extent this may have reflected the FO opinion that membership was the best way to maintain Britain's international significance, Wright being something of an exception to the consensus. With Palliser, however, there was also a deep personal commitment to the cause. He traced this back to the destruction he witnessed as a tank officer in Europe in 1944–1945 and subsequently as a member of the occupation forces in Germany.[80] A Roman Catholic, in 1948 he married to Marie Marguerite, daughter of one of the so-called 'fathers of Europe', the former Belgian Prime Minister, Paul-Henri Spaak. As head of the Planning Staff, in early 1965 he had already pressed the government on the dangers of isolation from the growing power of the EEC and the need to develop a positive, coherent policy towards it.[81]

His enthusiasm for EEC membership had initially put some doubts in Palliser's mind about working with the Prime Minister, who always took an outwardly cool and calculating approach to the question. Many of Wilson's political allies, including Cabinet ministers like Barbara Castle and Richard Crossman, were sceptical about EEC membership, as were some of his Downing Street political staff, notably the economist Thomas Balogh. Indeed, Palliser was so concerned about possible differences with his new boss over the EEC that he raised the matter in their initial interview, telling Wilson, 'I'm a convinced believer in British membership ... and I wouldn't want you to take me under false pretences in a situation where you and I might find each other in disagreement over Europe ...'. But Wilson immediately told his new PS, 'we shan't have any problems over Europe'. Palliser soon became familiar with Wilson's strategy on Europe, moving 'in his usual devious crab-like fashion so it was almost impossible to know what his views were'.[82] Wilson later explained that he had been interested in the prospect of EEC membership 'for quite a long time. You've got to realise that the Labour Party is pretty hostile, and I can't sort of go out on a limb, without having the party behind me'.[83] But the clear majority in the March 1966 election freed the Prime Minister to take greater risks. Palliser's appointment has been seen, alongside the change in role of George Thomson, who now became the informal 'minister for Europe' inside the FO, as evidence that, 'Wilson shifted the personnel around him to facilitate any potential initiative towards the Community'.[84]

For Palliser, the decision on withdrawal from East of Suez was closely linked to the need to enter the EEC, but this too created a problem of managing the process. With an eye on British influence in international affairs, he advised Wilson in July 1967, as the withdrawal was announced, that, 'we cannot afford to reach a position where the Americans have discarded us as a useful world ally before we have managed to join the Community'.[85] This was one reason why the PS wanted to press on with an application promptly. Palliser's ability to influence the Prime Minister on European questions was obvious at an early date. In March 1966, the new PS took up the linked issues of détente and de Gaulle's withdrawal from NATO. He argued that the French President, while uncooperative, was not always mistaken in his views. There was little chance of war breaking out in Europe, so the withdrawal was not necessarily dangerous. Indeed, 'the French have given us all the opportunity to rethink on East-West relations and the problems of the Western alliance'. Palliser's preferred line was to seek détente on the basis of holding the rest of NATO together and, at the same time, to seek disarmament in Europe. Disarmament was already a favoured project of the Prime Minister and it may be that, to an extent, Palliser was exploiting some of Wilson's own ideas in this memorandum, but it is noteworthy that these views were subsequently sent on to Foreign Secretary Stewart and the Defence Secretary, Denis Healey, as recommended policy.[86]

Clearly, Palliser did not simply press for an EEC application in isolation: his argument that de Gaulle's views on détente made some sense were intended to show that London and Paris could work together. Palliser also encouraged Wilson's interest in the idea of technological cooperation with Europe as a way of encouraging the EEC members to welcome British membership. In September 1966, the PS was quick to draw to the Prime Minister's attention an Italian scheme for European action to match America's technological prowess and to urge the FO to stay informed about this.[87] It was another example of Palliser's ability to dovetail his own outlook with that of the Prime Minister, known as an enthusiast for technological investment. The dream of a European technological community eventually became part of Wilson's strategy for pressurizing France into accepting British membership. As Palliser explained to Maitland in November 1967, Paris 'should be confronted with a certain dilemma': it could not have the benefits of a technological community without letting Britain inside the EEC.[88]

Unlike some other observers, Palliser believed that Wilson's commitment to 'the second try' was more than some Machiavellian, tactical ploy. 'Harold Wilson was an extraordinarily complex human being, combining intellectual brilliance with political cunning ... Many of those closest to him found it difficult to divine his purposes ....' But his 'desire to see Britain join the EEC ... was indeed sincere ...'.[89] When it was announced that the Prime Minister and Foreign Secretary would make a tour of EEC capitals in early 1967, to prepare the way for an application, Brown himself was sceptical about what might result. But Palliser told him, 'You should be pleased. It means that Harold is committing himself to Europe'. The PS had no doubt that the Prime Minister was genuine in seeking membership.[90] At this point, Palliser became particularly important for advising Wilson on tactics to enter the EEC. The key challenge was to circumvent a likely veto from de Gaulle when Britain formally submitted a membership application. Looking back a generation later, Palliser said, 'I think I always made it clear to Wilson that I was very sceptical of his being able to get General de Gaulle to change his mind, but I do not think that I would ever have told him that there was no hope of success'.[91] Contemporary evidence confirms that Palliser continued to urge Wilson to press on with the 'second try' right down to – and beyond – the French veto of November 1967. In January 1967 he told Wilson that, rather than making common cause with the President on limiting supranational elements in the Community, an approach that could only alienate the other five members, it was better to appeal to his 'sense of history and monumental vanity', by arguing that only British membership would allow the EEC to match the superpowers.[92] Palliser also wanted to keep the other five members closely behind the membership bid and he spoke out against those, like Chalfont, who hoped to browbeat the West Germans into putting pressure on de Gaulle. It was better to win German Chancellor Kurt Kiesinger's sympathy by 'subtle', rather than 'crude' means.[93]

On 16 May, during a press conference, de Gaulle came close to a veto, saying that Britain would be better to apply for 'association' with the Community rather than full membership. Palliser, however, pressed Wilson to 'bash on, regardless'; the Prime Minister was engaged in 'a war of nerves – to see whether your nerve is as strong as the General's. My money is confidently on yours'.[94] Palliser still believed it could be possible to get into the EEC, 'provided we play our negotiating hand with skill and with speed', although there was always the danger that, if backed into a corner, de Gaulle could 'lash out in any case'.[95] In September, he seems to have been less certain of de Gaulle's purpose, telling Wilson that rumours of a forthcoming veto might be a 'War of nerves, truth, perfidy – who can tell?'[96] In October, more convinced that de Gaulle was on the defensive, Palliser felt this was 'a signal success for your policy up-to-date of not taking no for an answer'. Wilson should maintain this line, keep the other five EEC members on Britain's side and avoid giving de Gaulle any excuse for a veto.[97] Ahead of a visit from Kiesinger that same month, Palliser's remained a moderate voice. He did not want to back de Gaulle into a corner for fear of driving him to issue another veto; and Kiesinger would only resent being asked to put pressure on the French leader. British tactics should be built around undermining de Gaulle's claims that London was not ready for EEC membership. 'Surely this must continue to be our approach', he told Wilson, 'patient perseverance coupled with your refusal to take no for an answer'.[98] But around this time it became clear that the French had a potential excuse to try to kill the application, because of the weakness of the pound on international money markets.[99] Within weeks the pound was devalued and de Gaulle seized his chance to issue a veto. Reading over the General's 'ironical, not to say sarcastic' statement, Palliser was forced to conclude that he had 'not moved an inch in his general approach'.[100]

Yet this did mark the end of the second application. As well as urging Wilson to pursue an immediate application, Palliser was also responsible, at an early date, for developing the argument that London should continue pressing for membership in the long term. He argued that, even if de Gaulle did not want her, his successors might alter that policy, not least because Britain could help balance the growing economic might of West Germany. Thus, in October 1966, the PS said that Britain should 'prepare for a post-de Gaulle situation where our entry ... can become possible within the reasonably near future ... perhaps even before the next general election'.[101] This line of thought was highly significant because it meant that, when de Gaulle did issue his veto, Wilson said London must keep the second application 'on the table', waiting for it to be picked up[102] – as it eventually was in 1970, following de Gaulle's resignation. This explains why, during 1968–1969, Wilson, advised by Palliser, continued to look for ways to keep the pressure on the EEC to recognise

Britain's case. It was a strategy backed by Palliser's father-in-law, Spaak,[103] but it was not an easy process. In May 1968, only six months after the embarrassment of a veto, Cabinet ministers were extremely reluctant to take any initiative and even Palliser advised Wilson to await events although, 'If we simply withdraw into our shell ... it will become increasingly hard to make future progress ...'.[104] Such logic meant that Palliser encouraged the Prime Minister to continue regular meetings with EEC leaders, like Kiesinger, because 'the major hurdles, internally, have been taken', thanks to the 1967 application, and 'we are still in the best posture ... to take advantage of any sudden change in circumstances'.[105]

Palliser summed up his preferred tactics as 'skirmishing around the citadel' before finally breaking into the EEC.[106] The problem was that it was not easy to find any route forward. During the closing months of 1968 and into early 1969, Palliser suggested that London might propose an up-dated version of the Fouchet Plan, a French initiative of the early 1960s that would have developed foreign policy cooperation among the EEC members. But the FO feared that such an initiative would instead provoke divisions among Britain's supporters.[107] In November, Palliser was dismayed by the heavy pressure that ministers, led by Wilson, put on West Germany to revalue the Deutschmark, so as to relieve continuing pressure on the pound. He argued that, 'given present realities in Europe, we cannot attain our European objectives by ... being beastly to the Germans ...', who might turn against EEC enlargement.[108]

On 4 February 1969, came a rather different opening when de Gaulle himself suggested to the British Ambassador to Paris, Christopher Soames, that their two countries should work towards a free trade area in Europe, with agriculture included. This initiative fitted into established ideas that de Gaulle had for limiting the supranational element in the EEC and protecting French farmers, but it was likely to upset the other five members of the Community, on whose support Britain relied. With Wilson due to meet Kiesinger for another summit, the British were now faced with a dilemma about whether they should mention the Soames interview. If they did not, and word of it subsequently leaked, the Germans would be offended. However, if they did decide to reveal the details, they must forewarn the French leader, who was unlikely to welcome the prospect. The FO wanted to tell Kiesinger; Soames argued that this would betray de Gaulle's confidence. Typically, Palliser tried to keep both the French and Germans content, and was willing to differ from his colleagues at the FO. He advised Wilson to be very cautious in what he said to Kiesinger, warned of the dangers of upsetting de Gaulle and also feared that Soames might resign over the issue.[109] As it transpired, Wilson eventually followed FO advice and, while Soames remained at his post, de Gaulle was livid. Anglo-French relations reached a new low, though fortunately one that proved short-lived, since de Gaulle suddenly resigned, over a domestic setback, in April. It was around the same time, however, that Palliser left Downing Street.

Edward Youde

Palliser was succeeded as PS by Edward Youde, who only remained in the post until January 1970. Born in 1924, he had entered the Foreign Office in 1947, following wartime service in the Royal Navy. Educated at the School of Oriental and African Studies in London, he became a China specialist, serving in Nanking and Peking at the time of the Chinese civil war (1948–1950), as well as two later occasions (1953–1955 and 1960–1962). He had made his name early, when he was on *HMS Amethyst* in 1949 and took a central role in negotiating the ship's release, after Mao's Red Army attacked it on the Yangtze. He also had experience of the United States, working at both the Washington Embassy in the aftermath of the Suez crisis (1956–1959) and at the British Mission to the United Nations, where he was Head of Chancery at a difficult time (1965–1969), when the Communist bloc and newly independent states often allied to condemn British imperialism.[110] In 1967 he was considered as a possible PS to the Foreign Secretary, but George Brown preferred to appoint Donald Maitland.[111] As well as seeing improving chances to join the EEC, Youde's period as PS to Wilson was dominated by the closing stages of the Nigerian civil war.[112] Like Palliser, he was trusted by Wilson with delicate missions, going over to Washington to talk to Kissinger in September 1969,[113] but there are few major examples of long items of policy advice to the Prime Minister, such as his predecessor had produced.

The shortness of Youde's term in Downing Street was probably linked to the onset of heart disease that eventually led to a bypass operation.[114] It proved no setback to his career, which included four years as Ambassador to Beijing (1974–1978) and ended with his appointment as Governor of Hong Kong (1982–1986). He was there when the Sino-British declaration was signed that eventually returned the colony to Chinese sovereignty. He was the only one of the Colony's governors to die in office.[115]

Conclusion

After three years in Downing Street, it was Palliser himself who decided, around the time of the 'Soames Affair', that it was better to move on, fearing that, otherwise, he might be forced to remain through another election. He was more interested, he said later, 'in the nature of the job than in the status' it had.[116] Wilson offered to try to find him an ambassadorship, but Palliser preferred to return to Paris, as number two to Christopher Soames, because this offered such an 'interesting' challenge at the time. Palliser became Minister at the Paris Embassy in June 1969. While he was still there, negotiations finally began for enlarging the EEC. Palliser remained central to this process over the following years, as Ambassador to the Community in Brussels, in 1971–1973, and then as Britain's first Permanent Representative to the Community, in 1973–1975.[117] It was his continuing success in these challenging position that made him the natural choice to become PUS, at the relatively early age of 53.

In his rise to the top, Palliser's time in Downing Street had clearly been a major success. He had won the Prime Minister's trust and coped triumphantly with the intense pressures of the post; he had maintained a good working relationship with the FO, even during the challenging years when Brown was Foreign Secretary; and he had carried out some effective diplomacy of his own. Above all, though, he had a real effect on strategic decisions. The PS to the Prime Minister may only be a small part of a much larger foreign policymaking machine. The FCO, its embassies abroad, the Defence and Oversea Policy Committee, the Cabinet Secretary, the Prime Minister himself – all of these had important role to play. But Palliser's experience shows that the Private Secretary, by occupying a pivotal role between the Prime Minister and the rest of the machine, may help push policy in particular directions. True, Palliser was helped by what might be termed the march of events, with the retreat from a world role continuing, a need to cut costs abroad, persistent economic difficulties and a feeling that EEC membership was the only viable future if Britain wished to remain an important player on the world stage. He was also helped by the fact that Wilson himself seems to have recognised this shift and adapted himself to it. But Palliser was capable of stating the British dilemma in clear terms that could only help give confidence that the new direction, leading towards EEC membership, was the right one. In retrospect, Palliser viewed Wilson's international policy as 'one of failure', partly because of his inability to achieve entry into the EEC'.[118] But this is surely too negative a judgment. De Gaulle may have issued his veto but, by 1970, partly thanks to Palliser's strategy of leaving the second application 'on the table', Britain was on the brink of successful negotiation for EEC entry.

Notes

1. I am grateful to the British Academy for funding the archival research on which this chapter is based.
2. On the foreign policy of these years see John W. Young, *The Labour Governments, 1964–1970*, vol. II:*International Policy* (Manchester: Manchester University Press, 2003).
3. *The Diplomatic Service List 1971* (London: HMSO, 1971), 317.
4. Philip M. Kaiser, *Journeying Far and Wide: A Political and Diplomatic Memoir* (New York: Scribner's, 1992), 231–2.
5. For example, in the wake of the British decision to withdraw from 'East of Suez'. Palliser to Wilson, 15 August 1967, The National Archives, Kew [henceforward TNA]: PREM 13/2459.
6. Harold Wilson, *The Labour Government, 1964–1970: A Personal Record* (London: Weidenfeld & Nicolson, 1971), 334.
7. Interview with Michael Palliser, 28 April 1999, Churchill Archive Centre, Cambridge [henceforward CAC]: DOHP 13.
8. Palliser to Rendel, 22 February 1966, National Library of Wales, Aberystwyth [henceforward NLW]: RENDEL M6 (by kind permission of Miss Rosemary Rendel).
9. Palliser to Rendel, 17 October 1967, NLW: RENDEL M6.

10 Interview with Michael Palliser, 28 April 1999, CAC: DOHP 13. But note that Palliser also seems to have been ill at home in October 1967. G.F. (for Palliser) to Wilson, 6 October 1967, TNA: PREM 13/1485.
11 Wilson, *Labour Government*, 636.
12 Palliser to Rendel, 11 April 1968, NLW: RENDEL M6.
13 Wilson, *Labour Government*, 552–3.
14 Ben Pimlott, *Harold Wilson* (London: HarperCollins, 1992), 519.
15 Halls to Nicoll, 14 January 1967, TNA: PREM 13/1863.
16 Halls to Baldwin, 5 February 1967; Baldwin to Halls, 31 March 1967, TNA: PREM 13/1420.
17 Halls to Trend, 14 July 1967, TNA: PREM 13/1361.
18 Palliser to Wilson, 22 March 1967, TNA: PREM 13/1479.
19 See Philip Ziegler, *Wilson: The Authorised Life* (London: Weidenfeld & Nicolson, 1993), 184–5.
20 Michael Palliser, 'Foreword', in Saki Dockrill, *Britain's Retreat from East of Suez: The Choice between Europe and the World?* (Basingstoke: Palgrave Macmillan, 2002), xi.
21 Michael Palliser, 'Introduction', in Helen Parr, *Britain's Policy towards the European Community: Harold Wilson and Britain's World Role 1964–1967* (Abingdon: Routledge, 2005), x.
22 Palliser to Wilson, 29 November 1968, TNA: PREM 13/2308.
23 Interview with Michael Palliser, 28 April 1999, CAC: DOHP 13.
24 Geoffrey Moorhouse, *The Diplomats: The Foreign Office Today* (London: Jonathan Cape, 1977), 149.
25 Palliser to Maclehose, 4 June 1966, TNA: PREM 13/902.
26 Palliser to Maitland, 28 November 1967, TNA: PREM 13/2400.
27 Interview with Michael Palliser, 28 April 1999, CAC: DOHP 13.
28 Forster to Palliser, 26 April 1966, TNA: PREM 13/970; Palliser to Forster, 5 September 1966, TNA: PREM 13/1266; Palliser to Williams, 5 February 1968, TNA: PREM 13/2320. See also Forster to Palliser, 12 July 1967; Palliser to Forster, 17 July 1967, TNA: PREM 13/1372, regarding the dangers of a coup in Cyprus.
29 Palliser to Knighton, 25 October 1967, TNA: PREM 13/1851.
30 See, for example, Halls to Meynell, 9 April 1967, TNA: PREM 13/1479; and Halls to Meynell, 8 and 16 January 1968, TNA: PREM 13/2980.
31 Minute by Palliser, 4 November 1966, TNA: PREM 13/1343; and see Peter Hennessy, *The Prime Minister: The Office and its Holders since 1945* (London: Allen Lane, 2000), 292.
32 Anonymous official, quoted in Moorhouse, *Diplomats*, 149.
33 Palliser to Wilson, 13 December 1966, TNA: PREM 13/1221.
34 Palliser to Wilson, 4 January 1967, TNA: PREM 13/1917.
35 Palliser to Wilson, 4 April 1966, TNA: PREM 13/1043. On East–West relations see Geraint Hughes, *Harold Wilson's Cold War: The Labour Government and East–West Politics, 1964–1970* (London: Royal Historical Society, 2009).
36 See John W. Young, *Twentieth Century Diplomacy: A Case Study of British Practice, 1963–1976* (Cambridge: Cambridge University Press, 2008), chapters 6 and 7.
37 Palliser, quoted in Simon Jenkins and Anne Sloman, *With Respect Ambassador: An Inquiry into the Foreign Office* (London: BBC, 1985), 139.
38 Record of meetings, 23 and 24 May 1966, TNA: PREM 13/933.
39 Record of meeting, 29 July 1966, TNA: PREM 13/1083.
40 Palliser to Wilson, 26 May 1967, TNA: PREM 13/1521.
41 Wilson, *Labour Government*, 334–5.
42 Palliser to Morphet, 20 February 1967, TNA: PREM 13/1582.
43 Palliser to Maclehose, 11 May 1966, TNA: PREM 13/1273; Palliser to Maclehose, 2 June 1966, TNA: PREM 13/1083; Palliser to Maclehose, 4 July 1966, TNA: PREM 13/1276.

114 *John W. Young*

44 Palliser to Maclehose, 10 June 1966, TNA: PREM 13/1083.
45 Note for the record by Palliser, 1 July 1967, TNA: PREM 13/1622.
46 See Sylvia Ellis, *Britain, America and the Vietnam War* (Westport: Praeger, 2004), 222–4, 240–3, 278.
47 Minutes by Palliser, 30 July, 2 and 5 August 1967, TNA: PREM 13/2323; Palliser to Mackilligin, 22 and 26 August 1968, TNA: PREM 13/2324; and, on this mission, see Brian Brivati, *Lord Goodman* (London: Richard Cohen, 1999), 194–7.
48 Palliser to Maclehose, 3 August, TNA: PREM 13/917. See also de la Martiniere to Palliser, 8 August 1966, TNA: PREM 13/917.
49 Record of meeting, 11 January 1969, TNA: PREM 13/2817.
50 Dean to Palliser, 22 June 1966, TNA: PREM 13/1274.
51 Minute by Wilson to Palliser, 26 June 1966; FO to Washington, 26 June 1966; Dean to Palliser, 28 and 30 June 1966, TNA: PREM 13/1275.
52 Palliser to Maclehose, 3 June 1966, TNA: PREM 13/1273; Palliser to Wilson, 3 June 1966; Palliser to Maclehose, 17 June 1966; Palliser to James, 22 June 1966, PREM 13/1274.
53 On clandestine contacts with Hanoi and Davies's role see: John W. Young, 'The Wilson Government and the Davies Peace Mission to North Vietnam', *Review of International Studies* 24 (1998): 545–62.
54 See, for example, Palliser to Maclehose, 4 July 1966, TNA: PREM 13/1276.
55 Palliser to Maclehose, 8 November 1966, TNA: PREM 13/1277.
56 TNA: PREM 13/2330.
57 For discussions of this visit see Jonathan Colman, *A Special Relationship? Harold Wilson, Lyndon B. Johnson and Anglo-American Relations at the Summit, 1964–1968* (Manchester: Manchester University Press, 2004), 139–40; and P. L. Pham, *Ending East of Suez: The British Decision to Withdraw from Malaysia and Singapore, 1964–1968* (Oxford: Oxford University Press, 2010), 174–5.
58 Palliser to Wilson, 15 July 1967, TNA: PREM 13/1851.
59 Palliser to Wilson, 2 December 1968, TNA: PREM 13/2444. But this idea, too, was later presented as coming from Wilson. See Palliser to Gore-Booth, 9 December 1968, TNA: PREM 13/2097.
60 Record of meeting, 20 December 1968; Palliser to Wilson, 23 December 1968, TNA: PREM 13/2097.
61 George Brown, *In My Way: Memoirs* (London: Gollancz, 1971), 134.
62 Palliser to Wilson, 26 January 1967, TNA: PREM 13/1476.
63 Palliser to Wilson, 13 May 1967, TNA: PREM 13/1482.
64 Palliser to Wilson, 20 July 1967, TNA: PREM 13/1484; Palliser to Wilson, 2 December 1967, PREM 13/1487. On Chalfont's role as a 'minder' for Brown see Alun Chalfont, *The Shadow of My Hand* (London: Weidenfeld & Nicolson, 2000), 126.
65 Palliser to Wilson, 24 May 1968, TNA: PREM 13/2112.
66 Halls to Wilson, 16 March 1968, TNA: PREM 13/2517.
67 Maclehose to Palliser, 2 May 1967; Palliser to Maclehose, 3 May 1967, TNA: PREM 13/1518.
68 Parr, *Britain's Policy*, 161.
69 Pimlott, *Wilson*, 497.
70 Paul Gore-Booth, *With Great Truth and Respect* (London: Constable, 1974), 350. There were other clandestine activities in which Palliser participated as PS. Documents show that he was involved in discussing certain deliberate 'leaks' of information to the press, for example about arms supplies that were reaching the rebel Biafran regime in the Nigerian civil war or of information from inside the Rhodesian government about opposition to a settlement with Britain. Williams to Palliser, 2 and 30 October 1968, TNA: PREM 13/2260; Mackilligin to Palliser, 17 January 1969, TNA: PREM 13/2895.

71 Palliser, 'Introduction', x.
72 MacKilligin to Palliser, 2 June 1966, TNA: PREM 13/966; Wright to Palliser, 10 June 1966, TNA: PREM 13/1122; Day to Palliser, 12 and 13 June 1967, TNA: PREM 13/1621.
73 Michael Palliser, 'Foreign Policy', in *Looking Back: The Wilson Years*, ed. Michael Parsons (Pau: University of Pau Press, 1999), 23.
74 The best study of the whole question is Dockrill, *Britain's Retreat from East of Suez*.
75 Wright to Wilson, 2 December 1964, TNA: PREM 13/103.
76 Palliser to Wilson, 21 March 1967, TNA: PREM 13/1384.
77 Palliser to Wilson, 10 July 1967, TNA: PREM 13/1457.
78 Palliser to Wilson, 7 July 1967, TNA: PREM 13/2636.
79 See, for example, Wright to Wilson, 28 January 1966, TNA: PREM 13/905. In general on policy towards the EEC see: Oliver Daddow, ed., *Harold Wilson and European Integration: Britain's Second Application to Join the EEC* (London: Frank Cass, 2003); Parr, *Britain's Policy*; Melissa Pine, *Harold Wilson and Europe: Pursuing Britain's Membership of the European Community* (London: I.B.Tauris, 2007), which focuses on the years 1968–1970; Jane Toomey, *Harold Wilson's EEC Application: Inside the Foreign Office* (Dublin: University College Press, 2007) and James Ellison, *The United States, Britain and the Transatlantic Crisis: Rising to the Gaullist Challenge, 1963–1968* (Basingstoke, Palgrave, 2007), chapters 3–6.
80 Palliser, 'Introduction', x.
81 Palliser, 'Introduction', x; Parr, *Britain's Policy*, 41–2.
82 Interview with Michael Palliser, 28 April 1999, CAC: DOHP 13.
83 Interview with Michael Palliser, 12 July 2002, quoted in Pine, *Wilson and Europe*, 17.
84 Parr, *Britain's Policy*, 70; Ellison, *Transatlantic Crisis*, 63.
85 Palliser to Wilson, 7 July 1967, TNA: PREM 13/2636.
86 Palliser to Wilson, 11 March 1966; Wilson to Stewart, 15 March 1966, TNA: PREM 13/1043.
87 Palliser to Wilson, 23 September 1966; Palliser to Maclehose, 27 September 1966, TNA: PREM 13/1850. In general on the proposal see: John W. Young, 'Technological Cooperation in Wilson's Strategy for EEC Entry', in *Wilson and European Integration*, ed. Daddow, 95–114.
88 Palliser to Maitland, 10 November 1967, TNA: PREM 13/1851.
89 Palliser, 'Introduction', xi.
90 Interview with Michael Palliser, quoted in Pimlott, *Wilson*, 438. See also interview with Michael Palliser, quoted in Pine, *Wilson and Europe*, 20–1, 175Michael.
91 Palliser to Parr, 18 September 1999, quoted in Parr, *Britain's Policy*, 103.
92 Palliser to Wilson, 16 January 1967, TNA: PREM 13/1475.
93 See especially Palliser to Wilson, 21 October 1967, TNA: PREM 13/1527.
94 Charles de Gaulle, *Discours et Messages*, vol. V:*Vers le Terme, 1966–1969* (Paris: Plon, 1970), 155–73; Palliser to Wilson, 20 May 1967, TNA: PREM 13/1482. For an example of Palliser's views later being portrayed as the Prime Minister's own, see Palliser to Maclehose, 22 May 1967, TNA: PREM 13/1482.
95 Palliser to Wilson, 17 May 1967, TNA: PREM 13/2646.
96 Palliser to Wilson, 22 September 1967, TNA: PREM 13/1484.
97 G.F. (for Palliser) to Wilson, 6 October 1967, TNA: PREM 13/1485.
98 Palliser to Wilson, 21 October 1967, TNA: PREM 13/1527.
99 Palliser to Wilson, 25 October 1967, TNA: PREM 13/1486.
100 Palliser to Wilson, 27 November 1967, TNA: PREM 13/2646.
101 Palliser to Wilson, 13 October 1966, TNA: PREM 13/897. Palliser recognised that, in the long term, an extension of the EEC was likely to lead to a deepening of integration, in order to hold it together, a view he put to Wilson. Palliser to Wilson, 12 September 1967, TNA: PREM 13/1468.

102 Palliser to Maitland, 28 November 1967, TNA: PREM 13/2646.
103 Palliser to Wilson, 10 September 1968, TNA: PREM 13/2113.
104 Palliser to Wilson, 24 May 1968, TNA: PREM 13/2112.
105 Palliser to Wilson, 19 July 1968, TNA: PREM 13/2113.
106 Palliser to Wilson, 4 October 1968, TNA: PREM 13/2113.
107 See Pine, *Wilson and Europe*, 86–9, 100–1.
108 Palliser to Wilson, 22 November 1968, TNA: PREM 13/2586.
109 Palliser to Wilson, 10 February 1969, TNA: PREM 13/2628. On the details of the 'Soames affair' see Pine, *Wilson and Europe*, chapter 6.
110 *Diplomatic Service List 1971*, 394.
111 Interview with Donald Maitland, 11 December 1997, CAC: DOHP 27.
112 For his input into policy regarding Nigeria see, for example, Youde to Wilson, 3 June 1969, TNA: PREM 13/2820; Youde to Graham, 17 July 1969; Youde to Wilson, 25 July and 17 October 1969, TNA: PREM 13/2821; and Youde to Wilson, 5 December 1969, TNA: PREM 13/2822.
113 Washington to FO, 16 September 1969, TNA: PREM 13/2874.
114 See his obituary in *The Times*, 6 December 1986.
115 The fullest treatment of his career is Jason Tomes, 'Youde, Sir Edward (1924–1986)', in *Oxford Dictionary of National Biography: From the earliest times to the year 2000*, ed. H. G. C. Matthew and Brian Harrison (Oxford: Oxford University Press, 2004), vol. XL, 858–9.
116 Interview with Michael Palliser, 28 April 1999, CAC: DOHP 13.
117 On Palliser's role as Permanent Representative in Brussels see Young, *Twentieth Century Diplomacy*, 80–3.
118 Palliser, 'Foreign Policy', in *Looking Back*, ed. Parsons, 28.

References

Brivati, Brian, *Lord Goodman* (London: Richard Cohen, 1999).

Brown, George, *In My Way: Memoirs* (London: Gollancz, 1971).

Chalfont, Alun, *The Shadow of My Hand* (London: Weidenfeld & Nicolson, 2000).

Colman, Jonathan, *A Special Relationship? Harold Wilson, Lyndon B. Johnson and Anglo-American Relations at the Summit, 1964–1968* (Manchester: Manchester University Press, 2004).

de Gaulle, Charles, *Discours et Messages*, vol. V: *Vers le Terme, 1966–1969* (Paris: Plon, 1970).

Dockrill, Saki, *Britain's Retreat from East of Suez: The Choice between Europe and the World?* (Basingstoke: Palgrave Macmillan, 2002).

Ellis, Sylvia, *Britain, America and the Vietnam War* (Westport: Praeger, 2004).

Ellison, James, *The United States, Britain and the Transatlantic Crisis: Rising to the Gaullist Challenge, 1963–1968* (Basingstoke: Palgrave, 2007).

Gore-Booth, Paul, *With Great Truth and Respect* (London: Constable, 1974).

Hennessy, Peter, *The Prime Minister: The Office and its Holders since 1945* (London: Allen Lane, 2000).

Hughes, Geraint, *Harold Wilson's Cold War: The Labour Government and East–West Politics, 1964–1970* (London: Royal Historical Society, 2009).

Jenkins, Simon, and Anne Sloman, *With Respect Ambassador: An Inquiry into the Foreign Office* (London: BBC, 1985).

Kaiser, Philip M., *Journeying Far and Wide: A Political and Diplomatic Memoir* (New York: Scribner's, 1992).

Moorhouse, Geoffrey, *The Diplomats: The Foreign Office Today* (London: Jonathan Cape, 1977).

Palliser, Michael, 'Foreign Policy', in *Looking Back: The Wilson Years*, ed. Michael Parsons (Pau: University of Pau Press, 1999).

Parr, Helen, *Britain's Policy towards the European Community: Harold Wilson and Britain's World Role 1964–1967* (Abingdon: Routledge, 2005).

Pham, P. L., *Ending East of Suez: The British Decision to Withdraw from Malaysia and Singapore, 1964–1968* (Oxford: Oxford University Press, 2010).

Pimlott, Ben, *Harold Wilson* (London: HarperCollins, 1992).

Pine, Melissa, *Harold Wilson and Europe: Pursuing Britain's Membership of the European Community* (London: I.B.Tauris, 2007).

Toomey, Jane, *Harold Wilson's EEC Application: Inside the Foreign Office* (Dublin: University College Press, 2007).

Wilson, Harold, *The Labour Government, 1964–1970: A Personal Record* (London: Weidenfeld & Nicolson, 1971).

Young, John W., *The Labour Governments, 1964–1970*, vol. 2: *International Policy* (Manchester: Manchester University Press, 2003).

Young, John W., 'Technological Cooperation in Wilson's Strategy for EEC Entry', in *Harold Wilson and European Integration: Britain's Second Application to Join the EEC*, ed. Oliver Daddow (London: Frank Cass, 2003), 95–114.

Young, John W., *Twentieth Century Diplomacy: A Case Study of British Practice, 1963–1976* (Cambridge: Cambridge University Press, 2008).

Young, John W., 'The Wilson government and the Davies peace mission to North Vietnam', *Review of International Studies* 24(1998): 545–562.

Ziegler, Philip, *Wilson: The Authorised Life* (London: Weidenfeld & Nicolson, 1993).

6 'Sound and comfortable men'
Peter Moon, Lord Bridges and Britain's entry into the EEC

Nick Thomas

Sir Peter Moon was appointed as foreign affairs Private Secretary to the Prime Minister toward the end of Harold Wilson's first term of office. After two years of service with Wilson's successor, Edward Heath, he left for a series of diplomatic appointments. His replacement, Lord Thomas Bridges, remained at 10 Downing Street until just after Harold Wilson's return to the premiership in 1974. As Robert Armstrong, who as Principal Private Secretary to the Prime Minister from 1970 to 1975 was Moon and Bridges's immediate superior, noted, the relationship between the Prime Minister and the Foreign Secretary could potentially be fraught because of the overlap between the two roles. In his obituary for Moon, Armstrong argued that Moon was central to smoothing the course of this relationship since he

> saw his function as that of being a channel of communication between the Prime Minister and the Foreign Secretary and his office and sought to make it as clear, open and untroubled a channel as possible. He was a self-effacing man who did not seek to obtrude his own personality or prejudices on the conduct of the relationship.[1]

Both Moon and Bridges conformed to Lord Bernard Donoughue's view that 'Establishment culture is the culture of sound and comfortable men', with each enjoying similar backgrounds and following similar approaches to their role, with an emphasis upon quiet discretion and measured advice.[2] This chapter will explore the nature of their role by examining Britain's successful bid to enter the European Economic Community (EEC), a process in which the Foreign Secretary, Alec Douglas-Home, was sidelined not just by the Prime Minister but also by the appointment of successive Chancellors of the Duchy of Lancaster as the key players in the negotiating process. In a situation with considerable potential for fraught relationships over lines of demarcation, Moon and Bridges acted as conduits of communications and helped to push the negotiation and planning process along.

This chapter will concentrate upon people and processes rather than the events of the EEC bid, focusing in particular upon two people who operated 'behind the scenes' and who have largely been left out of accounts of the period. The historian will search in vain for a detailed view of Moon and Bridges in the secondary literature, such as those by Uwe Kitzinger and Simon Z. Young written at the time, and so without access to relevant documents, while other works, such as those by Christopher Lord and John W. Young, quite reasonably emphasise the substance of the negotiations rather than the mechanics and the personnel.[3] Unfortunately this trend is reflected elsewhere in the historical record and the historian is immediately confronted with the problem of actually locating these men in the sources. It is notable, for instance, that Edward Heath mentions Moon in his autobiography only once, and Bridges twice, and in each case these are simply passing references rather than insights into their role or views, such as the statement that Heath was 'exceptionally well supported by my private office team', a number of whom he then names, including Moon and Bridges.[4] Alec Douglas-Home makes no reference to Moon or Bridges at all in his memoirs, *The Way the Wind Blows*, and it is a telling indication of the extent of his role in the European Community bid negotiations that he devoted a mere two pages to the whole process.[5] Similarly, Douglas Hurd, who was Political Secretary to the Prime Minister from 1970 to 1974, also says nothing about Moon and Bridges in his account of the administration, *An End to Promises*.[6] Turning to biographies simply repeats the same tale, with John Campbell's biography of Heath remaining silent on Moon and Bridges and Philip Ziegler's official biography mentioning Moon just once in passing, while referring to Bridges several times, but not in connection with the European Community bid and only giving a brief insight into his function.[7] Further, neither man was interviewed for the British Diplomacy Oral History Programme (BDOHP) at the Churchill Archive Centre in Cambridge, and nor did they published diaries or write personal memoirs. There will be some reliance, then, upon the odd mention in other people's memoirs and diaries, but above all the bulk of the sources used for this chapter come from within the Prime Minister's Private Office held at The National Archives, notably the PREM 15 collection relating to the EEC negotiations, either in the form of documents which mention Moon or Bridges or which were produced by them.

In fact, despite difficulties, it is possible to gain a sense of Moon and Bridges as people and as civil servants. Their backgrounds highlight a number of wider issues and debates relating to the Civil Service in general. John W. Young's *Twentieth-Century Diplomacy* is one of the very few works to investigate the machinery and personnel of British diplomacy and he has argued that, alongside their upper-class Oxbridge backgrounds, members of the Foreign and Commonwealth Office (FCO) were often 'linked by family relationships, attendance at the same schools and membership of the same gentleman's clubs', with the Foreign Office increasingly 'accused of being an elitist, closed, snobbish institution, out of touch with the rest of society'. Young also notes that the Foreign Office 'had a professional ethos all of its own that smacked of a kind of freemasonry'.[8] Such a view is added to by Marcus Collins' analysis of the decline of the English gentleman within the context of wider debates on British decline since he has argued that 'the ideal gentleman of the mid twentieth century was upper or upper-middle class, with a good family and a public school and Oxbridge education', with an emphasis upon amateurism and character because of 'the equanimity and objectivity which amateurism ostensibly engendered'.[9] This rather fits with Nicholas Henderson's view that 'no particular qualities are required for appointment to a Private Office, though obviously some people are more suited to it by temperament than others. No training or instruction is provided for the post; you are meant to adapt and pick it up as you go along', which is a method he praised but which he feared 'will be regarded by some as yet another example of its unprofessionalism'. In terms of their background, training and attitudes both Moon and Bridges conformed to this model entirely.

Peter Moon was born in 1928 and so in common with most people who served in the Private Office in Downing Street he was in his early 40s when he became Private Secretary. In keeping with his gentlemanly urbanity Moon was fluent in French and married a Frenchwoman, Lucille Worms, in 1955. He was described as having an 'incisive intellect'.[10] Moon joined the Home Office in 1952 and went to the Commonwealth Relations Office in 1954, resulting in a posting to Cape Town in 1956 as Second Secretary. Various appointments followed, including positions in Colombo and with the United Nations Mission in New York, before his arrival at Downing Street in January 1970. After leaving Downing Street in 1972 Moon spent time at the NATO Defence College and was seconded to NATO's International Staff in Brussels until 1975. This was followed by a succession of appointments around the world, including Counsellor in Cairo, Ambassador to Madagascar, High Commissioner in Tanzania, High Commissioner in Singapore and finally Ambassador to Kuwait from 1985 to 1987. Moon was knighted in 1979 and died in 1991, just four years after his retirement, at the age of 63.[11] Lord Armstrong, who appears to have taken a close interest in Moon's career, described him as an 'eminently likeable man'. In an anecdote which spoke volumes about Moon's assured but understated presence at Number 10, Armstrong told of the visit of a senior member of the French government who was fluent in English but insisted upon speaking in French. Moon therefore acted as interpreter and, according to Armstrong, 'after the visitor had departed Peter apologised to the Prime Minister for not having laid on an interpreter, explaining why we had thought it unnecessary to do so. Even Peter was a little taken aback when Mr Heath replied, with an airy nonchalance: "Oh, were you having trouble with his French?"'[12] It is clear, then, that Moon was actively involved in assisting Heath's discussions with the French, that he could and would rise to the occasion when necessary, and that he possessed the calm in stressful situations that made him a reassuring presence.

Bridges' credentials were even more impeccable than Moon's. Bridges was the grandson of the Poet Laureate Robert Bridges (1844–1930) and was the son of Sir Edward Bridges, later the First Baron Bridges, who was Cabinet Secretary from 1938 to 1946. He was born in 1927 and so was only a few months older than Moon, his mother being the daughter of the 2nd Baron Farrer. He attended Eton and then New College, Oxford and entered the Foreign Service in 1951, marrying the daughter of Sir Henry Bunbury two years later. Bridges was the epitome of the Establishment figure, then, and was brought up with the ethos of the civil service as a central feature of his formative years. He went on to occupy posts in Bonn, Berlin, Rio de Janeiro, Athens, and Moscow before his time at Downing Street from 1972 to 1974. This was followed by a position in Washington as Deputy Under-Secretary of State at the Foreign and Commonwealth Office from 1979 to 1982, and appointment as Ambassador to Italy from 1983 to 1987. Following retirement, Bridges held positions on various boards and in 1999 was elected as one of the hereditary peers in the House of Lords, having succeeded his father as Baron Bridges 30 years earlier.[13] As with Moon, anecdotal evidence indicates an urbane and discreet gentleman who was comfortable in the corridors of power. For instance, Nicholas Henderson recounts that on a flight to Tokyo in 1964 with the then Foreign Secretary, Rab Butler, for whom Bridges was Assistant Private Secretary, that 'Mrs Butler talked to Tom Bridges about modern poetry, particularly Rupert Brooke'. Henderson felt Bridges was 'an appropriate audience because he was the grandson of the former Poet Laureate. He was also a model Private Secretary'.[14] Both Moon and Bridges had particular backgrounds which informed their assumptions about their role and played a part in the ways in which they carried out their duties.

As to the nature of the roles performed by Moon and Bridges, these very much entailed them standing in the shadows and in this respect the silence about members of the Private Office should come as no surprise. The Private Office consisted of two senior civil servants, one the Principal Private Secretary and the other the foreign affairs Secretary, which was the role occupied by Moon and Bridges. Alongside them were three more junior civil servants covering economics, home affairs and parliamentary issues, as well as a diary secretary.[15] Their role is summed up by Bernard Donoughue, who gives a valuable insight into the life of the Private Office which he described as:

> the single most important section of the administrative support services in No. 10. It is the communications centre of Downing Street, and is in regular contact with all the ministerial private offices. Virtually all official communications to or from the Prime Minister, written or verbal, are channelled through the Private Office. The Private Secretaries sift through the flow of papers and decide – based upon their experience of central government and upon their knowledge of a particular Prime Minister's interests and priorities – which to put before him urgently, which to delay, and which not to bother him with but to answer themselves. They fill the Prime Minister's red boxes for his nightly or his weekend reading. The Senior Secretaries will periodically sit with him in the study or in the flat discussing how to respond on certain issues. Usually a close bond of trust

builds up between the Prime Minister and his Private Office, which organises the whole routine of his governmental working day.[16]

This only gives part of the picture, however, and Nicholas Henderson's outline of the role of the Private Office and its various occupants is particularly useful in this respect. Henderson, himself a former member of the Diplomatic Service who was Private Secretary to the Foreign Secretary from 1963 to 1965, argued that for ministers 'it is impossible to exaggerate the importance to them of the members of their Private Offices, both personally and for the conduct of public business'.[17] In this respect it is notable that Peter Hennessy has said of Heath's Private Office that 'I used to think that it would probably be going too far to suggest that they became a surrogate family for him, but he himself described them in his memoirs as "a kind of extended family"'.[18]

Moon, Bridges and the role of the Private Secretary

In terms of the role of the Private Secretary, for Henderson the central feature of his position (and it was invariably a man) was his permanence, in that 'he does not necessarily come or go with the Minister. With a few exceptions he belongs to the department; he is appointed regardless of his political opinions; he is the hinge between the Minister and his Ministry, and his loyalty is really a double one – to both Minister and department'.[19] Nonetheless, this is rather qualified by the view put forward by Lord Donoughue, a member of Wilson's Downing Street team from 1974 onwards, that 'the Foreign Service Secretaries all seemed a little set apart from the rest of us in No. 10 ... somehow they never ceased to be the Foreign Office representatives to the Prime Minister. The other Private Secretaries were unreservedly the Prime Minister's men'.[20] Whatever their loyalties might have been, the permanence of Private Secretaries meant that they, along with every other civil servant, were not linked to political parties or patronage and this was central to the concept of the civil service as an apolitical administrative machine. The *Civil Service Code* stated that civil servants were to:

> discharge loyally the duties assigned to them by the Government of the day of whatever political persuasion. For the Civil Service to serve successive governments of different political complexions it is essential that ministers and the public should have confidence that civil servants' personal views do not cut across the discharge of their official duties.[21]

This selflessness, with its emphasis upon service, understatement, self-control, discretion and gentlemanly reticence, was central to the role of the Private Secretaries, but of course it also means that the individuals concerned, especially their personalities, often remain elusive in the primary sources.

Of course such a view of the civil service is an ideal and the reality was often somewhat more complex, if in quite subtle ways. The relationship between politicians and civil servants has been the subject of considerable comment and controversy, whether in terms of suggestions of political influence over particular policies or larger debates linking British post-war decline to a supposedly amateurish and self-serving civil service.[22] It is not intended for this chapter to become distracted by the declinism debate which has dogged the Civil Service for several decades. There is also no desire to impose value judgements on whether the Civil Service should be or is politically motivated, or on its potential influence upon the political process, whether through obstructionism or advice or any other mechanism, although the potential for Moon or Bridges to make a mark upon decision-making will be explored. The influence of individual civil servants can be overestimated, underestimated, misunderstood and misrepresented, according to one's political desires. In the context of the EEC negotiations under Heath, for instance, one might assume that, as senior civil servants, Moon and Bridges made regular and devastating interventions in the decision-making process, but this is far from the impression given by the primary evidence and in fact their task revolved around keeping the wheels of government turning, notably by acting as conduits for information. They drafted speeches, notes and telegrams, acted as intermediaries between departments, and sometimes can be found offering advice, albeit usually in rather guarded tones as though they are afraid of entering a potential minefield. As Private Secretaries, they were the people who got things done, who maintained contacts across Whitehall which allowed ministers to gain a sense of opinion in other departments. Henderson repeats Harold Macmillan's comment that 'if you want to get anything done in government it's no good going to the top. It only antagonizes the officials. You have to know someone who knows someone who really does the job'. Macmillan added that asking his Private Secretary to get something done meant 'he would have talked on an old-boy basis to his opposite number and the whole thing would have been fixed up'.[23] This often comes through in numerous of the documents relating to the EEC negotiations, although these documents only give a glimpse of the discussions, many of which were based upon verbal contacts. There is only occasionally a sense of personal views in these documents and never a view of political loyalties. Their role and influence was subtle, often played out through infinitesimally small adjustments to the wording of speeches or telegrams, minor adjustments to the accounts of meetings, and so on. This could give the impression of a kind of 'death by a thousand cuts' in the formation or obstruction of policy, but this is not to suggest deviousness, and alternatively nor is it to follow the ingenuous line that civil servants said they were politically neutral and so they must have been. Nonetheless, it is essential to recognise that there was a tension between an apolitical ideal and an environment in which the permanence and experience of civil servants meant they were sometimes called upon to provide advice to politicians. Moon and Bridges negotiated a delicate path between these competing demands.

The influence Moon and Bridges had on events can also be overestimated by a failure to recognise that they were cogs in a much larger machine in which many other people, both politicians and civil servants, played important parts. Heath, Douglas-Home and the successive Chancellors of the Duchy of Lancaster were the key actors in the EEC negotiations and each were supported by a number of advisers, including civil servants. Among the various politicians involved the potential for strained relationships was considerable. As Lord Privy Seal under Macmillan, for instance, Heath had been responsible for Britain's failed bid for EEC entry in the early 1960s and had occupied the unusual position of being deputy Foreign Secretary, making statements on foreign affairs in the Commons, since Douglas-Home as Foreign Secretary then sat in the Lords. Despite this potentially difficult situation Heath and Douglas-Home appear to have worked well together and Heath was appointed President of the Board of Trade when Douglas-Home became Prime Minister in 1964. After Heath took office in Number 10 in 1970 Douglas-Home was therefore serving as Foreign Secretary for a Prime Minister who had once been one of his Cabinet ministers so again this could have been an awkward relationship. Further possible tension was added by Heath's decision to give responsibility for the EEC entry negotiations to Anthony Barber as Chancellor of the Duchy of Lancaster. In many respects this was a logical decision since the workload of the Foreign Secretary meant that the EEC negotiations would be unlikely to receive the attention they required, and Douglas-Home had not been unhappy to be absolved of this responsibility when Foreign Secretary in the Macmillan government. With Iain Macleod's unexpected death just a month after the June 1970 election, however, the resulting reshuffle meant that Barber replaced Macleod as Chancellor of the Exchequer and Geoffrey Rippon was promoted from Minister for Technology to Chancellor of the Duchy of Lancaster. Rippon remained in this position until he had completed the negotiations for Britain's entry into the EEC in 1972 when he became Secretary of State for the Environment and John Davis took over as Chancellor of the Duchy of Lancaster. Rippon was therefore the key Chancellor of the Duchy of Lancaster during the negotiations, but he met regularly with Heath and Douglas-Home. To add even further to the potential for clashes Heath was the main negotiator with figures such as Pompidou and it was he who drove the process along. Yet Heath, Rippon and Douglas-Home were team players who worked well together, with Rippon readily deferring to the Prime Minister's judgement and with Douglas-Home behaving with considerable generosity of spirit in the name of supporting successful negotiations. If Douglas-Home felt any resentment he hid it well and in his memoirs he insisted that the success of the Britain's bid for entry into the EEC 'was much to the credit of Geoffrey Rippon and Edward Heath and the Conservative Party'.[24] It would also be easy to assume that neither Douglas-Home nor the FCO played any substantial role in Britain's entry bid, but this would be mistaken. The FCO was centrally involved in the negotiation process in multiple ways, whether through the participation of ambassadors, negotiators or advisers. Since the Foreign Secretary was the key link with the rest of the Commonwealth and Britain's non-European allies and trading partners, Douglas-Home was involved in reassuring these countries as well as occasionally becoming directly involved in the EEC negotiations. In April 1971, for example, Douglas-Home met with the Leader of the New Zealand Opposition in order to discuss New Zealand's economic problems, notably trade in products such as butter and lamb and especially the effect Britain's entry into the EEC might have upon them.[25] Similarly, in March 1971 Douglas-Home met with the French Ambassador, Baron Geoffroy de Courcel in order to discuss Sterling.[26] Douglas-Home's willingness to allow Heath and Rippon to play the central roles in the negotiation process clearly had implications for the foreign affairs Private Secretaries in Downing Street, notably in making the jobs less fraught, but he and his department were still centrally important to the success of the bid. The scale of this task is perhaps best summarised by Peter Hennessy who has argued that:

> in its way, the achievement of membership on 1 January 1973 is without parallel in British history. Neither the acquisition nor the disposal of Empire can be fixed to a particular man or moment. Yet EEC entry was an event of equal, probably greater, significance in the long term.[27]

The fact that the foreign affairs Private Secretaries were the conduits for communications between the multiple politicians and civil servants involved in the process means that they might appear to have been well placed to influence events but the very presence of numerous actors in the process, as well as the apolitical nature of the Civil Service, tended to dilute that influence.

The EEC negotiations

Among the various other civil servants regularly appearing in the archive material relating to the EEC negotiations were Pat Nairne, who was Second Permanent Secretary to the Cabinet Office from 1973 to 1975, and Antony Acland, the Principal Private Secretary to the Foreign Secretary from 1972 to 1973. Sir John Hunt was Nairne's predecessor as Second Permanent Secretary to the Cabinet Office from 1972 to 1973 before becoming Cabinet Secretary from 1973 to 1979. In this capacity Hunt was the most senior civil servant in Whitehall, but he was not based at Number 10.[28] Another regular contributor to discussions was Sir Douglas Allen, the Permanent Secretary to the Treasury from 1968 to 1974 and then Head of the Home Civil Service from 1974 to 1977. The Ambassador to France from 1968 to 1972, Sir Christopher Soames, played a key role in negotiations before becoming Vice President of the Commission of the European Communities in 1973, after Britain's entry to the EEC. These civil servants were just some of those involved in the EEC negotiations and because they rarely stayed in their posts for more than a few years the cast of characters often changed radically: Crispin Tickell, Sir William Nield and Sir Burke Trend were among many others who were involved in different aspects of the process at different times. So, for instance, in December 1970 Nield, at that time Permanent Secretary to the Cabinet Office, wrote to Moon asking him to highlight a letter from Soames and Sir Con O'Neill on the French view of the Sterling Area. Nield insisted that he tried 'hard to avoid sending the Prime Minister anything to read unless it is really important' but felt that the analysis of the situation 'totally confirms my own impression of the French position on sterling [sic]' and he went on to propose a summit with the French as a result. In the margin of the letter Heath wrote 'v. interesting'.[29] So in one brief letter it becomes clear that civil servants certainly did express opinions and that Moon acted as an intermediary, that there were multiple actors involved and that, in this and numerous other instances, Moon's voice was entirely absent. Among the few constants was Robert Armstrong who was involved in every aspect of the process because, although he was an Under-Secretary and so not as senior as the Cabinet Secretary, he was the senior civil servant in 10 Downing Street and had close contact with the Prime Minister. Indeed, it could perhaps be argued that Armstrong was far more important to the EEC negotiations than Moon or Bridges.

Moreover, some people could be involved in some meetings but not others and this certainly applied to Moon and Bridges. In John Young's account of Heath's summits on EEC entry he notes that while Heath was meeting Georges Pompidou only two interpreters were allowed into the meeting.[30] To take a further example from many other possibilities, in July 1970 Heath met with Trend, Nield and Armstrong to discuss their 'approach to Europe'. Armstrong wrote up the account of this meeting so that while there is an account of the views put forward by Trend and Nield, there is no mention of Armstrong's comments. Above all, though, it is striking that Moon was absent from such an important meeting.[31] Further, even when Moon did attend meetings he usually wrote up the official report and so it is impossible to establish the nature of his contribution. For instance, in March 1971 Moon reported to Crispin Tickell, the Foreign Office Private Secretary to Geoffrey Rippon, the Chancellor of the Duchy of Lancaster, on a meeting between Heath, Douglas-Home and Rippon. The letter simply reported on the content of the meeting, providing no interpretation, analysis or opinion and is similar to multiple other examples written and received by both Moon and Bridges throughout their time at Number 10.[32] Similarly, Bridges wrote a report in April 1972 about the meeting between Heath and West German Chancellor Willy Brandt in Downing Street in advance of the European summit to be held later that year. Bridges was among just six people present and his account, which was marked 'secret', gives the impression that Brandt was keen to work closely with Heath during the preparations for the summit. Again, Bridges expressed no direct opinions and offers up no analysis.[33] A further variation on this theme is the provision of précis of reports written by other people, such as that written in March 1972 by Michael Palliser, the Head of the UK Delegation to the European Communities in Brussels. Palliser's report referred to a meeting in Brussels between Foreign Ministers of the ten on the subject of the timing and agenda of the European Summit. Bridges had certainly not attended this meeting but instead acted as a gate-keeper to the Prime Minister's office, so that although he provided Palliser's report in full, he sought to save the Prime Minister's time by providing a brief summary of the report which covered just a little more than an A4 page.[34] This précis expressed no opinions and gave no advice, but instead Bridges concentrated upon providing Heath with a concise outline of the salient points. These letters, reports and reports on reports represented the oil which allowed the Whitehall machine to work, providing essential information to interested parties and clearly taking up a great deal of administrative time for those writing them. They were certainly centrally important to the roles performed by Moon and Bridges. The apparent objectivity of these letters and reports can be seductive, however, and of course they constitute just one person's view of a particular meeting or report, with only some of these documents written by Moon or Bridges being subject to review or approval by other people. It would have been possible for Moon or Bridges to overemphasise or ignore certain points, but at this stage the historian has to ask, 'to what end?' This is not to suggest that such editing did not take place, since of course it was essential to the process, but it is to say that identifying and following the progress of such intervention by civil servants, and particularly highlighting their motivations, is often impossible.

The differing personalities of individual civil servants also needs to be considered. It is all too easy to view the Civil Service as a block of faceless bureaucrats, with their non-political role adding to this sense of them as a group without ideas or personalities. Such assumptions do not withstand scrutiny and Hennessy even notes the differences in interpretation different civil servants such as Trend and John Hunt applied to their apolitical role. According to Hennessy, Trend 'took the apolitical nature of the British Civil Service so seriously that, throughout his Whitehall career, he never cast a vote in a general election' while in contrast Hunt, who replaced Trend as Cabinet Secretary in 1973, was 'never reluctant to give his views when asked'.[35] The same contrasts applied to Moon and Bridges, with the former reluctant to express personal opinions, at least in writing, while the latter occasionally became notably outspoken. The contrast was particularly clear when it came to discussions about the role of the Civil Service in supporting ministers dealing with EEC issues after entry had been secured. On 6 April 1971 Tickell wrote to Moon with reference to the Valedictory Despatch from the Head of the Delegation to the European Communities in Brussels and particularly pointed out the recommendation that 'we need to build up a body of experts on Community procedure'.[36] There is no comment from Moon among the sources, but then this is perhaps not surprising since the responsibility for discussions on this issue was held by much more senior members of the Civil Service. In fact, Trend wrote a document in May 1971 setting out some of the discussions which had been taking place at a senior level on this and other issues about personnel and structures, notably Willy Brandt's suggestion that member states should have a separate 'Minister for Europe' with Cabinet rank. This was resisted on the grounds that foreign policy should come under the aegis of the Foreign Secretary, but there was an acknowledgement that 'given the frequency of meetings in Brussels and the complexity of many of the issues involved, he would have to shoulder a heavy additional burden', so it was felt that it would be 'necessary to decide what relief could best be given him in these circumstances'. Part of this relief would come in the form of two Commissioners in Brussels, each with his own supporting team and in addition there would 'substantial staff requirements in Departments at home'. It was estimated that between 750 and 1,000 civil servants would be needed between 1972 and 1974 to deal with EEC issues. This was the limit of planning at this stage and Trend was reluctant to take the discussion further until it was clear that Britain's bid for entry would be successful.[37]

This was followed in April 1973 by a note to Armstrong from Hunt, marked 'personal and in confidence', in which he took stock of the 'first 100 days in the EEC'. This was a notably frank document in which Hunt put forward a number of positive points, but also set out his observations on several problems in robust terms. One of the largest ongoing problems remained ministerial responsibility for EEC issues, with Hunt noting that both the Foreign Secretary and the Chancellor of the Duchy of Lancaster were attending EEC Councils. Hunt proposed that the Chancellor of the Duchy should be the sole representative and in a reference to continuing jostling for position he insisted 'I do not myself believe (despite what Sir Christopher Soames said to the Prime Minister) that FCO officials would make difficulties over this provided that when the Foreign Secretary did not go another Foreign Office Minister did not go either'. Hunt felt that this confusion about responsibility continued into the ranks of the Civil Service. He was insistent that the creation of the European coordinating machinery in the Cabinet Office had not meant 'a lesser role in future for the Foreign Office' but he was 'increasingly beginning to suspect that they have got their role wrong'. The new coordinating section had been established because the EEC's policies impacted upon numerous domestic departments as well as the Foreign Office. Hunt noted that the previous Foreign Office role of coordinating Whitehall views on Europe had been taken over by the new team within the Cabinet Office but that the Foreign Office still sought to retain its former role. This, Hunt felt, caused 'unnecessary duplication and friction' and distracted from the Foreign Office role of advising 'Whitehall on the negotiability and impact of our proposed policies' and then once a decision had been taken, to 'assist with its presentation and actively to lobby on its behalf'. Hunt concluded his note with the blunt assertion that:

> I should however like, if the Prime Minister agrees, to take any other suitable opportunity to encourage the Foreign Office to concentrate more on the negotiability of our policies in the Community and on the marshalling of support for them and rather less on marking the cards of home departments.[38]

The following day Bridges responded with a note to Armstrong that was rather less positive about the diplomatic efforts during the initial period of the British presence within the EEC and which argued that in stubbornly arguing its case on minor issues the effect had been 'to dissipate a lot of the goodwill' toward Britain which had existed upon entry. Bridges attempted to be as diplomatic as possible when it came to Hunt's views on the role of the Foreign Office but his irritation is clear. While he felt that 'there are few Whitehall warriors in the F.C.O.', he conceded that 'people do not abandon very readily their training to argue the merits of other Departments' proposals, and this is still the F.C.O.'s function outside Europe'. Nonetheless, he felt that the new European policy unit within the Cabinet Office would be accepted more readily 'if there could be more senior representation of the F.C.O. in the Cabinet Office secretariat dealing with European affairs'. He concluded with the view that

> the most gnawing personal anxieties in the F.C.O. are not the 'loss of a role' for the Department, but sadness that so many of the key jobs in promoting a policy of which the Diplomatic Service wholeheartedly approves, have gone to younger men in other Departments who, however able, often know less about it.

While this hardly constitutes a polemic, this is an astonishing intervention in the discussion when compared with Moon's contribution. Moon was never remotely as forthright as this, but rather quietly got on with his job. Interestingly Heath wrote 'v. perceptive' at the top of the report.[39] There is certainly a sense of the Foreign Office representative within Downing Street flying the flag for his own department, defending it against accusations from the Cabinet Office and attempting to maintain its influence. Crucially, this was being done by civil servants rather than politicians. In some respects, of course, Bridges was fulfilling his role as an intermediary between the FCO and Downing Street, but his loyalty was clearly to the FCO and as for smoothing ruffled feathers, in this instance it appears that Bridges and his colleagues at the FCO were those whose feathers required smoothing. The comparison with Moon, who appears to have tended toward Trend's view of the apolitical role of the Civil Service, is startling. It could be that Trend as Cabinet Secretary set an example which Moon followed, while Hunt's comments were interpreted by Bridges as a green light for expressing his own opinion. Nonetheless, it is notable that Bridges did not make such robust comments anywhere else in the discussion about the EEC, so the issue of FCO involvement was clearly something about which he and his colleagues felt strongly.

There were other instances of giving advice or opinions, although this was often guarded and limited, but the effects on policy could sometimes be demonstrable. For instance, in March 1971 the FCO provided Moon with an extensive and secret report on the foreign policy Britain should pursue in the event of an unsuccessful bid for EEC entry. The report had been prepared by the FCO Planning Staff and had been seen by Douglas-Home and the Chancellor of the Duchy of Lancaster, both of whom agreed 'broadly with its conclusions', so Douglas-Home felt Heath should see it.[40] Moon then wrote to Heath on 10

March with a covering analysis of the document, highlighting what he felt were the key sections. Moon's comments broadly agreed with the report or were blandly neutral, but with regard to comments in the FCO's covering letter he was more forthright. This letter argued that if negotiations on EEC entry broke down Britain should announce that it would be consulting with its allies about the potential implications of this reverse. Moon, however, argued that 'it seems to me that the time for this kind of action is not the aftermath of the breakdown but in order to avoid breakdown'.[41] Superficially this was simply the provision of an alternative view so that the Prime Minister could weigh up the merits of different options, yet it provides solid evidence of the influence of the Private Secretary in Number 10. The report had been prepared by a team within the Foreign Office and had been approved by both Douglas-Home and the Chancellor of the Duchy of Lancaster, yet at the final stage on the route to Heath the intermediary between the FCO and Downing Street was able to impose his own view on the document and propose an alternative policy. Moon's intervention clearly made an impact because on 11 March he replied to his opposite number in the FCO and noted that 'the only comment' Heath had made referred to the section on consulting with allies in the event of a breakdown in the EEC negotiations. Moon wrote that 'the Prime Minister feels that the time for such action might be in an attempt to avoid a breakdown rather than in the aftermath of a breakdown', which exactly reflected Moon's advice.[42]

It should perhaps be re-iterated that the importance of any influence the Private Secretary might have been able to wield can be overestimated and most often advice to the Prime Minister and others took rather more bland and bureaucratic form. When Heath gave an interview to German and French newspapers *Die Zeit* and *Le Monde* in January 1972, for example, his comments on Britain's desire to take a full role in subsequent discussions with other EEC members were misinterpreted by or misrepresented to Pompidou as an attempt to influence the timing of a potential Summit Meeting. Containing the situation was clearly important and so Bridges wrote to Michael Alexander, Douglas-Home's Assistant Private Secretary, with the view that

> it is clearly desirable that this question should be cleared up at an early date, given the imminence of M. Pompidou's visit here, and if the Department agree [sic], I suggest that instructions are sent to Sir C. Soames inviting him to correct the misunderstanding of what the Prime Minister has actually said.[43]

Bridges could have been passing on Heath's instructions in this instance, but if so it seems likely that Bridges would have made this clear. Instead this seems to be an instance in which he acted as a door warden, filtering the issues to be dealt with by a busy Prime Minister. Moreover, in many respects Bridges' advice was simply stating the obvious and pushing the process along rather than expressing a personal opinion.

'Sound and comfortable men' 131

Perhaps the area where the influence of civil servants was most visible was in the drafting of speeches, telegrams and parliamentary answers. Such documents often received input from various parties, including civil servants from different departments and the politician responsible for giving the speech or signing the telegram. As a result there were usually multiple drafts but it is interesting to note Henderson's anecdote about Bridges advising a junior colleague 'that he should take great care with his drafting and never draft for himself but for the signature of others'.[44] The difficulties involved in this process are immediately apparent in Moon's attempts to produce a message in April 1971 from Heath to Pompidou outlining Heath's meeting with Brandt. Not only was the content and focus of the message highly delicate, but Moon's first draft of the message was revised by Armstrong in ways Moon disliked. Moon wrote to Armstrong on 8 April admitting that he was 'not very happy' with his own first draft, largely because he found it 'very difficult' to write a message which 'will be helpful toward the main purpose of starting the process for a meeting with President Pompidou'. Yet he felt Armstrong's version 'puts some of the most delicate points with considerable bluntness' which 'seems to me to risk doing serious damage'.[45] This was among Moon's most outspoken moments and it clearly made an impact because later that day Armstrong wrote to the Prime Minister with a new draft of the message 'which is a joint effort by Peter Moon and me' and copying Moon into the note. The role of various interested parties is highlighted by Armstrong's comment that he and Moon had 'drawn extensively' on a draft message prepared by the FCO and that if Heath approved it would then be sent to Nield at the FCO after which Moon would 'let you have a final version for approval early next week'. With so many people commenting and amending such a message, along with the desire to write drafts according to a ministerial voice, identifying the influence of an individual civil servant is again a difficult task.

This impression is further confirmed by the example of the draft of the Prime Minister's speech following the signature of the Treaty of Accession in January 1972. The Foreign Office provided Moon with the original draft, and although this was sent just five days before the speech was to be given it nevertheless underwent considerable re-writing. The first revise includes numerous corrections, changes and crossings-out in what appears to be Moon's hand. Whole paragraphs were removed, new sentences added and in some instances the additions were so considerable as to require pasting new pieces of paper over the top of the sections to be replaced. The tone of the speech became more positive, with an emphasis upon unity, European cooperation and looking to the future. The language was toned down slightly to make it more emollient both with regard to the other member states and the Soviet Union, while references to commitments on specific issues such as over-population and pollution were removed.[46] Two days later Moon supplied Heath with a much less heavily corrected second draft and asked for him to 'take an early opportunity to look at this'. It is notable though that Moon's covering note stressed the need to provide the final version of the speech in time for the

Foreign Office to send it to Brussels so that translations could be made into French, rather than specifically asking Heath for corrections.[47] Time was pressing and so further heavy editing by Heath would simply have complicated the situation further.

A further example is provided by the process for writing a message to President Nixon conveying Heath's impressions of the Paris summit in October 1972. As Britain's foremost ally this was an essential act of diplomacy and this made the wording of such a message particularly important. As a result Bridges's draft was commented upon by civil servants from various departments, such as the Treasury and the FCO. Peter Marshall at the Financial Policy and Aid Department discussed the wording of the draft with Bridges over the telephone and then wrote an extensive letter going into his suggestions in detail.[48] Bridges then discussed Marshall's response with Michael Armstrong at the FCO, again over the telephone, and Armstrong wrote a letter on behalf of the FCO effectively rejecting the substance of Marshall's suggestions.[49] The next day, 25 October, Bridges forwarded the final draft to Heath, along with the draft of another telegram to Japan, with the comment that 'it has taken longer than I would have liked to submit the drafts to you but I was anxious to ensure that the Treasury and FCO agreed with the texts'. Heath simply wrote 'both agreed' on Bridges' covering note and made no adjustments to the draft.[50] The version which was sent to Nixon reads as a personal note between friends and opens with the message that 'your own preoccupation with the obviously critical stage of the Vietnam negotiations must mean that you have little opportunity to consider other international matters just at present. But I thought you would like to have an account of my impressions of the Summit Conference in Paris, which I believe was of long-term importance'.[51] The message goes on to outline key areas of importance for the Americans, with an emphasis on giving a positive slant to Britain's entry into the EEC. Above all, Bridges had achieved the considerable feat of writing a message on someone else's behalf, making that message sound personal and individualised, and keeping multiple other agencies happy, notably Heath and various government departments. It is perhaps not difficult to understand why Bridges was held in such high regard by his peers.

Conclusion

Despite the difficulty of locating Moon and Bridges in contemporary accounts, the papers from the Prime Minister's Private Office held at The National Archives partially reveal their role. What emerges is necessarily an incomplete picture, especially because their verbal communication is lost forever, but it is clear that they helped to keep the wheels of government turning by processing information, gathering opinions, offering advice and quietly filtering the information landing on a busy Prime Minister's desk. With so many other actors in the process and such a partial view provided by the evidence one remains hesitant when it comes to the identification of influence over policy, but then of course this was not their role. The multifaceted nature of their positions nonetheless meant that they did play an active part in drafting, advising, writing reports and perhaps highlighting some views more than others, although again this is often impossible to demonstrate. The rare occasions when direct influence can be detected can hardly be called earth-shattering and, although both Moon and Bridges expressed opinions, only once did Bridges play an openly partisan role on behalf of the Foreign and Commonwealth Office. They were very different people, with Moon coming across as the more reserved and reticent of the two, but they both conformed to the Civil Service and Establishment ideal of 'sound and comfortable men'.

Notes

1. *Guardian*, 18 July 1991.
2. Quoted in Peter Hennessy, *The Great and the Good: An Inquiry into the British Establishment* (London: Policy Studies Institute, 1986), 4.
3. Uwe W. Kitzinger, *Diplomacy and Persuasion: How Britain Joined the Common Market* (London: Thames & Hudson, 1973); Simon Z. Young, *Terms of Entry: Britain's Negotiations with the European Community, 1970–1972* (London: Heinemann, 1973); Christopher Lord, *British Entry to the European Community under the Heath Government of 1970–1974* (Aldershot: Dartmouth, 1993); John W. Young, *Britain and European Unity, 1945–1999*, 2nd edn (London: Macmillan, 2000).
4. Edward Heath, *The Course of My Life: My Autobiography* (London: Hodder & Stoughton, 1998), 84, 312.
5. Lord Home, *The Way the Wind Blows: An Autobiography* (London: Collins, 1976), 248–9.
6. Douglas Hurd, *An End to Promises: Sketch of a Government, 1970–1974* (London: Collins, 1979).
7. John Campbell, *Edward Heath: A Biography* (London: Pimlico, 1994); Philip Ziegler, *Edward Heath: The Authorised Biography* (London: Harper, 2010), 265, 279, 546.
8. John W. Young, *Twentieth-Century Diplomacy: A Case Study of British Practice, 1963–1976* (Cambridge: Cambridge University Press, 2008), 26.
9. Marcus Collins, 'The Fall of the English Gentleman: The National Character in Decline, c.1918–1970', *Historical Research* 75 (2002): 93.
10. *Guardian*, 16 July 1991.
11. 'Moon, Sir Peter (James Scott), *Who Was Who*, online edn (Oxford: Oxford University Press, 2007).
12. *Guardian*, 18 July 1991.
13. *Who's Who 2012: An Annual Biographical Dictionary* (London: A & C Black, 2011), 276.
14. Nicholas Henderson, *The Private Office: A Personal View of Five Foreign Secretaries and of Government from the Inside* (London: Weidenfeld & Nicolson, 1984), 62.
15. Peter Hennessy, *Whitehall* (London: Secker & Warburg, 1989), 385.
16. Bernard Donoughue, *Prime Minister: The Conduct of Policy under Harold Wilson and James Callaghan* (London: Jonathan Cape, 1987), 17–18.
17. Henderson, *Private Office*, xiv.
18. Peter Hennessy, *The Prime Minister: The Office and Its Holders* (London: Allen Lane, 2000), 341.
19. Henderson, *Private Office*, 1.
20. Donoughue, *Prime Minister*, 18.
21. Quoted in Hennessy, *Whitehall*, 368.
22. See, for instance, Hennessy, *Whitehall*, 2–9 for an outline of many of the themes of this debate.

23 Henderson, *Private Office*, 113.
24 Home, *Way the Wind Blows*, 249.
25 Record of conversation, 21 April 1971, The National Archives, Kew [henceforward TNA]: PREM 15/370.
26 Record of conversation, 31 March 1971, TNA: PREM 15/370.
27 Hennessy, *Prime Minister*, 346.
28 Hennessy, *Whitehall*, 389.
29 Nield to Moon, 3 December 1970, TNA: PREM 15/62.
30 Young, *Twentieth-Century Diplomacy*, 129.
31 Note of a meeting, 15 July 1970, TNA: PREM 15/62.
32 Moon to Tickell, 23 March 1971, TNA: PREM 15/369.
33 Report of conversation, 21 April 1972, TNA: PREM 15/891.
34 Note by Bridges to Heath, 2 March 1972, TNA: PREM 15/890.
35 Hennessy, *Whitehall*, 238.
36 Tickell to Moon, 6 April 1971, TNA: PREM 15/351.
37 Note by Trend to Simcock, 5 May 1971, TNA: PREM 15/351.
38 Note by Hunt to Armstrong, 12 April 1973, TNA: PREM 15/1529.
39 Note by Bridges to Armstrong, 14 April 1973, TNA: PREM 15/1529.
40 Graham to Moon, 8 March 1971; report on 'Options for British External Policy if Our Application for Membership of the European Communities Fails', TNA: PREM 15/369.
41 Note by Moon to Heath, 10 March 1971, TNA: PREM 15/369.
42 Moon to Graham, 11 March 1971, TNA: PREM 15/369.
43 Bridges to Alexander, 8 February 1972, TNA: PREM 15/890.
44 Henderson, *Private Office*, 62–3.
45 Note by Moon to Armstrong, 8 April 1971, and 'Draft Message from the Prime Minister to President Pompidou', TNA: PREM 15/370.
46 'Draft: Prime Minister's Speech on the Signature of the Treaty of Accession, 22 January 1972', TNA: PREM 15/880.
47 Note by Moon to Heath, 19 January 1972 and 'Second Revise: Prime Minister's Speech on the Signature of the Treaty of Accession', TNA: PREM 15/880.
48 Marshall to Bridges, 23 October 1972, TNA: PREM 15/895.
49 Alexander to Bridges, 24 October 1972, TNA: PREM 15/895.
50 Note by Bridges to Heath, 25 October 1974, TNA: PREM 15/895.
51 Heath to Nixon, 30 October 1972, TNA: PREM 15/895.

References

Campbell, John, *Edward Heath: A Biography* (London: Pimlico, 1994).
Collins, Marcus, 'The Fall of the English Gentleman: The National Character in Decline, c.1918–1970', *Historical Research* 75(2002): 90–111.
Donoughue, Bernard, *Prime Minister: The Conduct of Policy under Harold Wilson and James Callaghan* (London: Jonathan Cape, 1987).
Heath, Edward, *The Course of My Life: My Autobiography* (London: Hodder & Stoughton, 1998).
Henderson, Nicholas, *The Private Office: A Personal View of Five Foreign Secretaries and of Government from the Inside* (London: Weidenfeld & Nicolson, 1984).
Hennessy, Peter, *The Great and the Good: An Inquiry into the British Establishment* (London: Policy Studies Institute, 1986).
Hennessy, Peter, *The Prime Minister: The Office and Its Holders* (London: Allen Lane, 2000).
Hennessy, Peter, *Whitehall* (London: Secker & Warburg, 1989).

Home, Lord, *The Way the Wind Blows: An Autobiography* (London: Collins, 1976).
Hurd, Douglas, *An End to Promises: Sketch of a Government, 1970–1974* (London: Collins, 1979).
Kitzinger, Uwe W., *Diplomacy and Persuasion: How Britain Joined the Common Market* (London: Thames & Hudson, 1973).
Lord, Christopher, *British Entry to the European Community under the Heath Government of 1970–1974* (Aldershot: Dartmouth, 1993).
Young, John W., *Britain and European Unity, 1945–1999*, 2nd ed. (London: Macmillan, 2000).
Young, John W., *Twentieth-Century Diplomacy: A Case Study of British Practice, 1963–1976* (Cambridge: Cambridge University Press, 2008).
Young, Simon Z., *Terms of Entry: Britain's Negotiations with the European Community, 1970–1972* (London: Heinemann, 1973).
Ziegler, Philip, *Edward Heath: The Authorised Biography* (London: Harper, 2010).

7 Patrick Wright and Bryan Cartledge

John Shepherd[1]

In February 1974 Harold Wilson returned to office, albeit leading a minority administration facing the most serious world capitalist crisis since the Second World War that ended the post-war boom. In 1973–1974 the OPEC oil embargo and the quadrupling of the international oil price, in retaliation for Western support of Israel in the Yom Kippur War, resulted in double-digit inflation and increasing unemployment (known as 'stagflation') that brought about a worldwide recession in the industrial world economies. In August 1975 the annual inflation rate reached more than 27 per cent – its highest peak in twentieth-century Britain.[2] In 2013, at age 95, the former West German Chancellor, Helmut Schmidt, James Callaghan's close ally on the international scene in the seventies, reflected on the oil crisis, a major turning point in world history. He echoed the words of former British Prime Minister Callaghan on losing office in 1979. Schmidt agreed: 'it was a sea change. It was an ebb tide after a flood tide. In my view it only needed one more step to a worldwide depression'.[3]

As Private Secretary (Overseas Affairs) to the Prime Minister, Patrick Wright and Bryan Cartledge (1974–1977 and 1977–1979 respectively) were key figures at 10 Downing Street. They served Harold Wilson during his final term from 1974 to 1976 and his Labour successor James Callaghan from 1976 to 1979.[4] For these two Labour administrations the seventies were a distinctive era in foreign and economic policy in European and international affairs. In 1985 at Blackpool, Margaret Thatcher in addressing the annual Conservative Party conference and the nation recalled the Labour Britain of 1979, trade union power and a country known as the sick man of Europe.[5] In the seventies Britain was often portrayed as 'Crisis Britain' with the energy crisis, the Heath Government's 'Three Day Week', the 1976 IMF financial crisis and the industrial disorder of British 'winter of discontent' of 1978–1979. In September 1975 Foreign Secretary Callaghan, previously Chancellor of the Exchequer and Home Secretary, had commented on the increasing association of foreign policy and diplomacy with British economic difficulties. He recalled how his famous Labour predecessor, the dominant Foreign Secretary Ernest Bevin, had proclaimed in the early 1950s: 'If Great Britain now had 40 million tons of coal to export my task would be much easier in dealing with the problems of the

Continent'.[6] Nicholas Henderson, British Ambassador, also recalled that British industry in the seventies appeared to be in a state of almost unalterable economic decline.[7] After the withdrawal from East of Suez, though Britain still remained an independent nuclear power, foreign policy was conducted in deeply troubled times and the loss of British status and power in the wider world.[8]

This chapter reviews the significant role played in the conduct of British foreign policy by two Private Secretaries for overseas affairs at 10 Downing Street, Patrick Wright (later Lord Wright) and Bryan Cartledge (later Sir Bryan Cartledge), who served under Labour in the 1970s.[9] Attention is also given to the important network of other civil servants who also contributed to British foreign policy in the seventies. In addition, this decade also witnessed the arrival in Whitehall of the political advisers to the Prime Ministers and departmental ministers. This mainly new group consisted of politically appointed aides whose main function was the provision of advice and policy support of a political and party-orientated nature.[10]

Patrick Wright and Bryan Cartledge

The Private Secretary for overseas affairs was one of a small group of senior aides in Whitehall who served the Prime Minister in the Private Office at 10 Downing Street. It was a key post in Whitehall at the centre of British government and was traditionally of counsellor grade in mid career in the Diplomatic Service, seconded from the Foreign and Commonwealth Office for three years.[11] The holder shared an inner office immediately adjacent to the Cabinet Room with the Principal Private Secretary, the Head of the Private Office (or Chief of Staff). In April 1975 Kenneth Stowe succeeded Robert Armstrong as Head of the Private Office and went on to serve Harold Wilson, James Callaghan and Margaret Thatcher. The overseas affairs Private Secretary was considered 'a high-flyer' destined afterwards for a very senior post, or even the top position, in the British Diplomatic Service. In 1976 Harold Wilson recalled that, besides Patrick Wright, then the current foreign affairs Private Secretary, out of around 300 diplomats of counsellor rank, several had worked with him during his time at Downing Street including Oliver Wright (then HM Ambassador in Bonn), Michael Palliser (then Permanent Under-Secretary of State) Edward Youde (then Ambassador in Peking), and Lord Bridges (then Commercial Minister at Washington).[12] Similarly, his successor James Callaghan later observed that during his premiership 'no fewer than four Permanent Secretaries and a brace of Ambassadors had acted as my Private Secretary in one department or another in the past'.[13]

Both Lord Wright and Sir Bryan Cartledge had joined the Private Office at Downing Street in mid career in 1974 and 1977 respectively. Their social and educational background of a public school and Oxbridge education were typical of the most talented officials entering the senior administrative grades of the Civil Service. In 1974 on re-entering Number 10 Harold Wilson judged that the Private Office was 'working far better than it ever did when I was here before' and invited Robert Armstrong and Tom Bridges to remain as Principal Private Secretary and foreign affairs Private Secretary.[14]

Educated at Marlborough School, Patrick Wright read Classics at Merton College, Oxford, before his national service as a gunner in the Royal Artillery. After joining the Foreign Service in 1955 he trained as an Arabist at The Middle East Centre for Arabic Studies (MECAS) in the Lebanon, which was then under the influential leadership of the Director, Donald Maitland, and its Principal Instructor, James Craig.[15] During the next 20 years Wright held posts as Third Secretary, British Embassy, Beirut, 1958–1960; Private Secretary to the Ambassador and later First Secretary, British Embassy, Washington, 1960–1965; Private Secretary to the Permanent Under-Secretary, FO, 1965–1967; First Secretary and Head of Chancery, Cairo, 1967–1970; and Deputy Political Resident, Bahrain, 1972–1974. From 1972 to 1974 Wright was Head of Middle East Department, Foreign and Commonwealth Office, in London, before being appointed as Private Secretary (Overseas Affairs) to the Prime Minister in October 1975.

Lord Wright's successor as overseas affairs Private Secretary at 10 Downing Street, Sir Bryan Cartledge, was educated at Hurstpierpoint College. He read History at St John's College, Cambridge and also gained a qualification in Russian, before national service in the Queen's Royal Regiment. He held research posts at Stanford University, 1956–1957, and a research fellowship at St Anthony's College, Oxford, 1958–1959. Cartledge initially wished to pursue an academic career at Oxford starting as research assistant to the former Prime Minister and Foreign Secretary, Sir Anthony Eden (later Lord Avon) helping him to prepare his memoirs. It was this memorable experience of studying Foreign Office documents that led eventually to Cartledge's decision to leave academic life and to take the Foreign Office entry examination in 1960. During the 1960s and 1970s, Cartledge then held a succession of posts in the Foreign Service (subsequently the Diplomatic Service): Northern Department, Foreign Office, 1960–1961; Stockholm, 1961–1963; Moscow, 1963–1966; Diplomatic Service Administration Office, 1966–1968; and Tehran, 1968–1970. During 1971–1972 he was at Harvard University and served as Counsellor in Moscow in 1972–1975. Finally, before his appointment to Number 10 Downing Street in 1977, Cartledge held the important post of Head of East European and Soviet Department at the Foreign and Commonwealth Office from 1972 to 1975.

Appointment to Number 10

In the seventies the Personnel Department at the Foreign and Commonwealth Office forwarded a short-list (usually two or three candidates) to Number 10 for the Prime Minister to select his Private Secretary (Overseas Affairs) though, as already noted, in March 1974 Harold Wilson had retained the personnel in Edward Heath's Private Office, including the overseas affairs Private Secretary

Tom (later Lord) Bridges who had served during Edward Heath's premiership from 1970.[16]

In December 1974 Patrick Wright's selection as the new Private Secretary to Harold Wilson suggests that he was already considered the outstanding candidate to succeed Tom Bridges. As it happened, Harold Wilson interviewed him at Downing Street *after* he had got the job. Lord Wright recalled he had first been taken to lunch at the Athenaeum Club in Pall Mall to be vetted by Robert Armstrong, the Principal Private Secretary, and Tom Brimelow, the Permanent Secretary at the Foreign Office.[17] The Prime Minister's new Private Secretary was a highly acclaimed Arabist and Middle East specialist, but his appointment still had to be defended against the remonstrations of a redoubtable opponent. Marcia Williams (later Lady Falkender), Harold Wilson's influential political and constituency secretary, was an ardent supporter of the Israeli cause.[18]

Sir Bryan Cartledge remembered that in 1977 he had been consulted about his name being put on the short-list to succeed Patrick Wright, though he personally didn't expect to get the job owing to a Diplomatic Service rumour about a strong field of candidates. When interviewed by Prime Minister James Callaghan, it was the first time Cartledge had stepped inside 10 Downing Street. Callaghan had asked him crucially 'whether there was anything political or otherwise which would make me uncomfortable about working for a Labour Prime Minister? I truthfully answered "No". There were no inhibitions of that sort at all. In fact, I had always voted Liberal, as it was then'.[19]

Yet it is not at all difficult to understand why Sir Bryan Cartledge was selected as the new Private Secretary at Number 10. After valuable diplomatic service in Sweden, the Soviet Union and Iran, he had returned to the Foreign Office in London. As Head of the East European & Soviet Department from 1975 and a close observer of the development of détente with the Soviet Union and East European countries, he was a significant aide to Callaghan as Foreign Secretary on East–West relations. In one of his well-received dispatches, Cartledge had perceptively commented on 'those aspects of Soviet policy which ... are in the forefront of Brezhnev's mind as he begins the run up to the 25th Congress of the CPSU'.[20] In February 1975 he was also a member of the British entourage accompanying the Prime Minister and Foreign Secretary to the Soviet Union, including the famous meeting between Harold Wilson and Leonid Brezhnev at the Kremlin Palace, Moscow, where the Soviet leader opened proceedings by joking with British Prime Minister about the recent election of a lady leader of the Conservative opposition in Britain, Margaret Thatcher.[21]

The role of the Private Secretary (Overseas Affairs)

In the seventies the primary task of the overseas affairs Private Secretary in the Private Office in Downing Street was to keep the Prime Minister fully up to date with foreign affairs on a worldwide basis. In an expanding era of modern communications, this remained a massive and unrelenting task. Since the Second World War, British foreign policy had been viewed in Churchillian terms of being at the centre of three overlapping circles of geopolitical power: the Atlantic alliance, the Commonwealth and Europe.[22]

However, during the Wilson and Callaghan administrations both Private Secretaries, Patrick Wright and Bryan Cartledge, did not describe their role in the Private Office at 10 Downing Street as the 'foreign affairs adviser' in policymaking to Prime Minister. Instead Lord Wright recalled that he saw his primary role as being the direct link between the Foreign Office and Number 10, passing on the Prime Minister's views and observations to the Foreign Secretary and in the same way conveying the Foreign Secretary's advice and opinions to the Prime Minister. Similarly, he was also the main line of communication between the Prime Minister and the Ministry of Defence and the Northern Ireland Office.[23] As Private Secretary (Overseas Affairs) Sir Bryan Cartledge held a very similar view of his role with a triple responsibility as the direct link between the Prime Minister and the Foreign Secretary, as well as the Defence and Northern Ireland ministries.[24]

It was essential that the Private Secretary (Overseas Affairs) also had 'to know the Prime Minister's mind', which entailed being close at all times, to keep up to date by attending Cabinet meetings, assisting with parliamentary questions and issuing most of the foreign affairs statements. However, it was also considered imperative that the Private Secretary should not get above himself nor in any role reduce the direct channel of communication link between the minister and the Prime Minister.[25] The Private Secretary undertook a variety of duties so that the Prime Minister could focus on important and essential business.[26] In this way, the role was seen as providing the 'extra hands, eyes legs, mouths and arms for the Prime Minister' to ease his work load in and to save time handling the vast amount of correspondence and communications that flowed in and out of Downing Street.[27]

By the seventies, Northern Ireland had become increasingly significant in the work undertaken by the Private Secretary with British troops in Ulster, the collapse of the power-sharing Sunningdale Agreement (established by the Heath government) and security issues arising from the IRA violence and the bombing campaign on the British mainland.[28] After attending the Ireland Cabinet Committee, Bernard Donoughue, Head of the Policy Unit at Downing Street, noted: 'I sat next to Patrick Wright, the nice new private secretary covering foreign affairs and replacing Tom Bridges. He is an 'Arab' [specialist] …'. His diary entry indicated the positive working relationship between two of the principal aides to the Prime Minister.[29]

Donoughue also that observed that:

> With the Principal Private Secretary (in the Private Office) sits the Foreign Affairs Private Secretary, usually a Foreign Office official who is expected to rise high in the ranks of the Diplomatic Service. In my time, the three occupants of the post were Lord Bridges (son of a former Head of the

Civil Service and later to be Ambassador to Rome), Bryan Cartledge (subsequently a predictably hawkish Ambassador to Moscow) and Patrick Wright, a marvellously amusing colleague who deservedly became head of the Diplomatic Service.[30]

Sir John Hunt, Cabinet Secretary during the Callaghan government was one of other senior civil servants who contributed to the conduct of British foreign policy. In a 1978 lecture at the Royal College of Defence Studies about decision-making in Whitehall, he made a number of observations about central policy advice and decision-making by civil servants and ministers. The Cabinet Secretary declared that the Cabinet Secretariat was not 'a Prime Minister's department … [and did not] push or develop policies of [its] own: in addition all members of the Secretariat [were] on short-term secondments from a wide spectrum of Government Departments'.[31] Instead, Sir John Hunt described an important role in steering policy across a number of ministerial fronts, including briefing Chairmen of Ministerial Committees on an ongoing or ad hoc basis on a variety of subjects where a different policy option might emerge. However, he repeated it was imperative 'that the Cabinet Secretariat should [not] start pushing policies on its own'.[32]

The overseas affairs Private Secretary recruited from the Foreign Office for normally two to three years needed to adjust to a new life and routine in the mainly invisible world of 10 Downing Street. According to Nicholas Henderson, Ambassador to Germany (1972–1975) and to France (1975–1979), this new identity and relationship with a different political master was quickly assumed. They soon 'had the ear and eye of the PM and that is enough to give them immense influence'.[33] However, secondment from a parent department to 10 Downing Street could result in divided loyalties. According to Lord Donoughue, the occupants of the Private Office 'were unreservedly the Prime Minister's men', but the overseas affairs Private Secretaries 'seemed a little apart from the rest of us at No. 10' and 'never ceased to be the Foreign Office representatives to the Prime Minister'.[34]

In the conduct of foreign policy, the key line of communication in Whitehall was between the Private Secretary (Overseas Affairs) and the Foreign Secretary's Principal Private Secretary (PPS). In the seventies Sir Ewen Ferguson held this post in the Foreign Office serving in succession three Labour Foreign Secretaries, James Callaghan, Tony Crosland and David Owen. Ferguson had worked for Jim Callaghan for the last six months when he was Foreign Secretary until he became Prime Minister in March 1976. He then became PPS to Tony Crosland until Crosland's death in February 1977 and finally served David Owen as the new Foreign Secretary until about April 1978. Ferguson later recalled the dedication needed for the role of PPS:

> You have one role in life and that is to ensure the interests of your minister are effectively interpreted and carried through. I had therefore to make a very different psychological shift between how I worked with

Jim Callaghan, how I worked with Tony Crosland, how I worked with David Owen, I have to say in retrospect it was quite an exhausting period.[35]

In turn, Foreign Secretary David Owen valued the personal qualities of the four senior members of his Private Office that were so important in twentieth-century diplomacy. The admirable Ferguson had the physique 'of a big, burly, Scottish rugby international forward, but it disguised a delicate mover within the Whitehall machine. He got on extremely well with every one – he was shrewd, holding firm opinions which he carefully hid in order to generate a climate of bonhomie'. His successor in 1978, the robust and loyal George Walden, believed 'that his prime duty was to serve the Foreign Secretary'. In addition, Kieran Prendergast was considered 'independent and tough-minded' in handling European policy; and Stephen Wall (a future Private Secretary to the Prime Minister) was 'imaginative, independent and hardworking' on African issues. As Diary Secretary for the Foreign Secretary, the impressive Maggie Turner (later Maggie Smart) was a vital member and highly diplomatic in handling the conflicting demands of Foreign Office, as well as the Cabinet Office, Parliament and the Plymouth constituency.[36]

At the British Foreign Office, the Private Office was a key part of the network of ministerial private offices in Whitehall. As Nicholas Henderson, British Ambassador to West Germany and then France from 1972 to 1979, observed: 'If you wished to know the pulse of Whitehall, I found that I had to keep in touch with the Private Secretaries'.[37]

The Number 10 Private Office

In the seventies the Private Secretary (Overseas Affairs) to the Prime Minister, based in the Private Office at 10 Downing Street, covered the gamut of international events from probably the most famous and widely recognised political address in the world. In 1924 the 8-year old Harold Wilson was photographed by his father, Herbert, in front of the Black Front door at 10 Downing Street, at the time the official home and office of Labour's first Prime Minister and Foreign Secretary, Ramsay MacDonald.[38] On reaching Downing Street as Prime Minister himself in 1964, Harold Wilson had five Private Secretaries in his Private Office; from 1976, six served his successor, James Callaghan, double compared to the three paid from public funds to assist Conservative Prime Minister Benjamin Disraeli, a hundred years before.

However, the principal function remained of ensuring an efficient channel of communication day and night between the Prime Minister and the Whitehall Civil Service machine in the policy and decision-making process as a central part of the premier's role in British politics.[39] This depended on the development of an important harmonious working relationship between Prime Minister and Private Secretary built on trust, loyalty, service and commitment to long working hours. After 1974 Harold Wilson gained a reputation for lethargy – a probable sign of his failing mental faculties, particularly his celebrated memory. One Downing Street aide observed that the premier undertook '… as little as he could persuade us to let him get away with'.[40] However, Lord Wright found Harold Wilson an easy man to work for – somewhat a workaholic who was at a loss once he had cleared his red boxes.[41]

Before becoming Prime Minister, Harold Wilson and James Callaghan had considerable experience at Westminster, as MPs and government ministers, as well gaining extensive knowledge of the British Civil Service. Both in 1945, at the ages of 29 and 33, were part of the large post-war intake of Labour MPs during the Clement Attlee premiership. Wilson had previously had been a civil servant during the Second World War – a working experience which he never forgot. From 1945 he held posts as Parliamentary Under-Secretary of State at the Ministry of Works and also at Overseas Trade before becoming President of the Board of Trade, the youngest Cabinet minister in the twentieth-century in 1947. Four years later, he was virtually the youngest to resign a Cabinet post when he left the Attlee government in the company of Nye Bevan and John Freeman. From 1959 to 1963, while in opposition, Wilson also chaired the Public Accounts Committee, providing him with seemingly valuable experience of the workings of Whitehall.[42]

James Callaghan had a similar political trajectory, albeit reaching 10 Downing Street in 1976, 31 years after entering Parliament compared with the 19 years it had taken Harold Wilson. In 1947 Callaghan's first two posts were Parliamentary Under-Secretary of State for Transport and then at the Admiralty. In the Wilson governments, 1964–1970 and 1974–1976, Callaghan then held the three main Cabinet offices: Chancellor of the Exchequer, Home Secretary and Foreign Secretary. As a result Harold Wilson and James Callaghan acquired first-hand knowledge of how the government machinery of policy making functioned at 10 Downing Street as well as in Whitehall in general, which is reflected in their written memoirs about the Labour administrations of 1974–1979.

James Callaghan regarded the Private Office as closer to the Prime Minister 'than the Think-Tanks, the Policy Unit or even the Secretary to the Cabinet'.[43] In his memoirs he described the quality of service provided

> Their tasks are limitless, bounded only by the number of hours in the day and the curiosity and interest of the Prime Minister. But a prime task is to sort out essential items for him to consider from the flood of reading matter that reaches the office in the form of Cabinet memoranda, correspondence from colleagues, resolutions from the Party, letters from the public, pleas from industrialists, seekers of honours, foreign telegrams and so on, in a never-ending forest of paper.[44]

As Callaghan put it, the Private Secretary was central to the Prime Minister's activities:

> ... they coordinate his engagements; take responsibility for assembling material for his speeches and usually have an important hand in drafting them; ensure he is properly briefed before Cabinet and other meetings at home and when paying official visits overseas; act as eyes and ears by maintaining a close liaison with other Ministers' Private Offices; act as the link with the Queen's Private Secretary; and act as a filter through which those who wish to see the Prime Minister must pass. They need to be diplomatic enough to pacify the untimely visitor ...

In addition to the Principal Private Secretary and the foreign affairs Private Secretary, who shared the Inner Private Secretaries Office (next to the Cabinet Room), there were three other senior Private Secretaries with responsibilities for economic affairs, non-economic domestic policy and the Prime Minister's parliamentary role (including dealing with Prime Minister's Parliamentary Questions). The other two members of this team were the Diary Secretary and the Duty Clerk.[45]

In particular, Donoughue emphasised that:

> the Senior Secretaries will periodically sit with him in the study or in the flat discussing how to respond to certain issues. Usually a close bond of trust builds up between the Prime Minister and his Private Office, which organises the whole routine of his governmental working day. Few people, inside or outside government, enjoy such a devoted and such an efficient service.[46]

Sir Bryan Cartledge provided an interesting view of his working life as a diplomat in the seventies after noting the Foreign Office hired out the Locarno Rooms (in 2007) for evening functions. He commented:

> If you go into the Foreign Office now at 6 o'clock/6.30, the place is like a tomb. When I was working there at 6.00 or 6.30 the corridors were teeming with people running hither and thither with boxes, getting submissions to the Secretary of State before he went home. A general atmosphere of buzz and activity and urgency. Now completely gone ... When I was working at No 10 I had arrived by 7.30 and I had to skim the newspapers before the Prime Minister had arrived ... I had to be aware of anything he or she ought to be aware of.[47]

Cartledge's observations also reveal how prime ministerial styles during the Labour governments in the seventies dictated day to day work routines of the Private Secretaries staff. While serving as a senior Private Secretary at the centre of Downing Street was an exhilarating experience in a diplomatic career, the daily routine was an unending and demanding treadmill.[48] Donoughue noted that while work routines might vary according to the personality and individual political style of Wilson and Callaghan, the senior staff in Downing Street spent more time with both Prime Ministers compared to anybody else. In his analysis of how the two Prime Ministers he served spent their time at 10 Downing Street, Donoughue commented:

> Pre-eminent among these [senior staff at Downing Street] were the Private Office Secretaries, who communicated with their boss many times a day. Often this was brief and informal (but some discussions required meetings to 'take the Prime Minister's mind') in the study or the flat at the beginning or the end of the day or at the Commons after Question time.[49]

Harold Wilson described Number 10 as 'a small village'. He also acknowledged that he intended to run the government in 1974 very differently compared with when he first took office as Prime Minister. In 1964, Wilson in a radio interview described his working style as 'a full time managing director or chief executive'. Ten years later, he resorted to a footballing metaphor:

> I told them [the Parliamentary Labour Party] '… whereas in the sixties I had played in every position on the field-goalkeeper, midfield, taking penalties and corners and bringing on the lemons – I was going to be an old-fashioned deep lying centre-half, lying well back, feeding the ball to those whose job was to score goals, and moving upfield only for rare 'set-piece' occasions.[50]

In 1974 Harold and Mary Wilson stayed each night in their home a short walking distance away in Lord North Street, rather than 'to live over the shop again'. According to Wilson, his daily routine was to read newspapers at home and be in Downing Street by 9.30 a.m. so that the Private Office could brief him on overnight developments.[51] Callaghan also acknowledged the qualities and professional expertise of the Private Secretaries which he described as part of a Rolls Royce standard in the British civil service.[52] 'They understand the mysterious ways of the Whitehall machine and how to make it respond', he observed.[53] During a long career in government since 1947, Callaghan, by the time he became Prime Minister 'no fewer than four Permanent Secretaries and a brace of Ambassadors had acted as my Private Secretary in one department or another in the past'.[54]

The appearance of the political adviser at Westminster and Whitehall was a significant feature of the Wilson and Callaghan governments during the seventies combined with the more general professionalisation of politics, the setting up of think tanks and other organisations that provided career opportunities for political aides.[55] The appointment of political advisers in Whitehall in Labour party politics had its roots in the Wilson's first two administrations in the sixties.

In 1964 Harold Wilson had entered Downing Street with far-reaching plans for the modernisation of Britain. Such innovations required significant changes to the machinery of government, the Civil Service and the bringing in outsiders with specialist expertise.[56] As the first Prime Minister since the Victorian period to write about the role of his office, Harold Wilson in 1976 had famously declared Number 10 would be turned into a 'powerhouse' compared to the 'monastery' under his predecessor, Sir Alec Douglas Home.[57] As well as strengthening his own position against rivals in his government and the Labour Party, as a former civil servant, Wilson was determined to secure political control and thwart any Civil Service weakening of Labour policy. During his first administration, Wilson brought into Downing Street a coterie of unelected political advisers and politicians — popularly known as his 'Kitchen Cabinet' — including Marcia Williams (later Lady Falkender), Joe Haines, Gerald Kaufman, Thomas Balogh (Economic Adviser to the Cabinet) and George Wigg MP (Paymaster General) who also advised on security issues.

According to Marcia Williams (later Lady Falkender), her extensive role as Harold Wilson's political and constituency secretary ranged from secretarial work, becoming the 'eyes and ears' within the Labour Party, accompanying him on visits abroad or keeping him up to date with developments in Britain while the Prime Minister was away.[58] She had first worked for Harold Wilson in 1956 and eventually accompanied Wilson to Downing Street to run his political office. Marcia Williams had much influence in advising the Prime Minister, especially during the 1966–1970 Labour Government.[59] On Labour's return to office in 1974, often working from home, she had markedly less influence on policy, though there were a number of occasions when she clashed with senior aides in Downing Street, including over access to the Prime Minister for visitors from abroad.[60]

While individual outsiders from time to time had been appointed by his predecessors, during his premierships Harold Wilson deliberately recruited political aides in greater numbers as a challenge to the official Whitehall machine. However, the Prime Minister's style in deciding matters was to first draw on the views of both his civil servants and his political aides.[61]

In May 1975, at the Commonwealth Heads of Government conference in Jamaica, Harold Wilson gave an early account of his experimental scheme to employ political advisers. He recognised it was a specific new development in government as traditionally 'Ministers take political decisions and civil servants carry them out'. At the time, there were about 30 such new advisers, with defined roles, based in about 15 departments.[62] Wilson argued that special advisers appointed from outside government were needed principally for two reasons. First, the pressure of work on ministers in modern government caused by 'the immense volume of papers, the exhausting succession of department committees, of party gatherings and meetings with outside interests' made a minister's role in departmental and government as a whole increasingly difficult. Second, as a Labour Prime Minister (and a former civil servant) he noted that, though the British civil service was renowned for its political impartiality and ability to serve administrations of different political colours, its critics maintained that senior mandarins, largely recruited from an elite educational and social background, can become cut off from changes in a rapidly developing British society.

While the Prime Minister recognised the possibility of tensions between civil servants and political advisers over working relationships and issues of confidentiality he was quick to point out that political advisers provided 'an extra pair of hands, ears and eyes and a mind more politically committed and more politically aware than would be available from the political neutrals in the established Civil Service. At the same time, Wilson concluded there was little danger of 'three dozen advisers [overturning] our powerful government machine' 'and that the most regular senior Civil Servants' welcomed his experiment.[63]

In 1964 Harold Wilson's most significant innovation was the creation of the Policy Unit at Downing Street under the leadership of Dr Bernard Donoughue, university lecturer, author, journalist and later government minister. He was recruited, aged 39, from his post as Reader in Politics at the London School of Economics. Staffed by a relatively small group of specialists, the Unit's primary task was to provide guidance to the Prime Minister on domestic policy, though Donoughue's close working relationship with the two Prime Ministers he served encompassed other areas, including at times foreign policy, the domain of the Private Secretary for overseas affairs. From the outset Donoughue had realised the importance of developing a harmonious working relationship the Prime Minister's Private Office and the network of ministerial private offices in Whitehall, and key civil servants, including Cabinet Secretary Sir John Hunt. 'I was urgently required to create a new institution in central government, against the scepticism and occasional hostility of some of the civil servants', he declared.[64]

Donoughue was a highly significant figure at the centre of Labour politics and policymaking. According to his friend Harold Evans, editor of *The Sunday Times*, Donoughue had 'an intellectual zest for manoeuvre matched by an emotional willingness to commit himself to a cause or person'. Evans observed that his loyalty to Wilson and Callaghan made him a good friend, but 'a poor source of news'.[65] As an insider he gained a highly perceptive view of key events in the seventies, including Wilson and Callaghan's renegotiation of the EEC terms of membership and the 1975 referendum during Wilson's final premierships. In 1976 on Wilson's retirement, Callaghan retained the Policy Unit led by Donoughue, the last survivor of Wilson's 'kitchen cabinet'. As a chief adviser to Callaghan, Donoughue witnessed at first hand the 1976 IMF crisis, the forming of the Lib–Lab Part, the collapse of Labour's Social Contract, the 'Winter of Discontent', as well as the downfall of the Callaghan government and its defeat in the 1979 general election. While having to liaise with central government as a whole (especially the Cabinet Office) he worked steadily to 'preserve the independence of the unit from the fatal embrace of the bureaucratic machine'. In fact, as Donoughue observed the Policy Unit survived under five different Prime Ministers, different political parties and directors, for 30 years.[66]

The main function of the Political Office was to keep the Prime Minister in contact with the Labour Party and the political world in general. In this respect, the members of the political office were not civil servants and were not paid from public funds. As political advisers, they were not restricted in participation in public political activity as were civil servants or ministerial special advisers.[67] While the members of the Private Office could survive a change of government, the political office appointments started anew with each Prime Minister.

In 1976, Tom McNally became the Prime Minister's chief political adviser as Head of the Political Office, after previously working with James Callaghan when he was Foreign Secretary from 1974 to 1976. McNally had been International Secretary of the Labour Party after an early career in student politics as Vice President of the National Union of Students, Assistant General Secretary of the Fabian Society and a full-time staff member of the Labour Party.

With a background in student politics and at the Labour Party's International Office, McNally had originally contacted Callaghan to offer his services *pro bono*. With Labour in opposition before 1974, Callaghan and McNally visited around 50 different countries in Europe, the United States, Africa, the Soviet Union and the Middle East. As well as foreign affairs, he advised Callaghan on domestic policy during the Callaghan government. While he became a political adviser, he confirmed that the role of the Private Secretary was as 'a link man – a facilitator ... making sure the [civil service] machine delivered what was needed ... linking [the Prime Minister] to the policy makers'.[68]

In 1972, he became a researcher for James Callaghan as Shadow Foreign Secretary – leading to his appointment as political adviser to Callaghan as Foreign Secretary in the Wilson Government of 1974–1976. In 1976, Callaghan became leader of the Labour Party and Prime Minister, 1976–1979 and took Tom McNally with him as Head of the Political Office, advising on both domestic and foreign policy. McNally advised on political appointments and was also one of Callaghan's speech writers. During the seventies, Lord McNally travelled widely with Callaghan on official visits to Presidents Ford and Carter, Dr Kissinger, Mr Brezhnev and Mr Gromyko, as well as to heads of government in the European Community countries and many political leaders in Africa and the Middle East. With the Principal Private Secretary, Ken Stowe, Tom McNally was James Callaghan's most influential adviser, though his advice to dismiss the left wing Tony Benn, to call a general election in October 1978 and possible party deals to survive the vote of confidence on 28 March 1979 were ignored by the Prime Minister. In the 1979 general election Tom McNally became the Labour MP for Stockport and eventually left Labour to join the SDP.[69]

Tom McCaffrey became Jim Callaghan's Press Secretary and took a different role to his predecessor Joe Haines, who had served Harold Wilson, not only as his press officer and public speech writer with an experienced knowledge of the media but also was always ready daily with frank political advice and guidance. Close to the Prime Minister, Haines also often clashed with Marcia Williams, as he set out in, at times in controversial terms, two sets of memoirs.[70]

When James Callaghan became Prime Minister in April 1976, there was a distinct change in the Press Office as Tom McCaffrey succeeded Haines. As a civil servant McCaffrey maintained a lower profile and did not seek to influence policy in the same manner as his predecessor. He had previously worked with the Prime Minister when Callaghan was Home Secretary and had been deputy Press Secretary in Downing Street during the Heath Government. He had a reputation for being professional and efficient, and was responsible for restarting the Press Lobby system in Downing Street. McCaffrey travelled widely with Callaghan, especially on overseas trips including the Guadeloupe summit in January 1979.[71]

Foreign policy: Continuity and change

During Labour's two administrations, James Callaghan had dominated Labour's conduct of international affairs as Foreign Secretary and Prime Minister. In his memoirs he penned his thoughts on the various opportunities and constraints that played a significant part in influencing Britain's role in the wider world:

> Foreign policy is a mixture of the old and the new. We may initiate but we also inherit; we may vote at the ballot box for changes in policy and personalities, but on acquiring office governments inherit an international situation on which the footprints of the past are heavily marked. We cannot wipe the slate completely clean. We become at once both instigator and recipient, actor and stage manager.[72]

On his return to 10 Downing Street for the third time in 1974, Harold Wilson at 58 was a noticeably changed politician from his premiership in 1964–1970. His celebrated 'white heat of technology' speech at the Labour Party conference at Scarborough in October 1963 had captured the public imagination with inspired rhetoric and in the 1964 election ended 13 years of Conservative rule. In 1966 Labour had been returned with an overall parliamentary majority of 96 – the first increased lead in the party's 36-year history.

However, during his final two-year term from 1974 to 1976, Wilson was no longer as sharp-witted, self-assured and full of vitality as earlier. According to Bernard Donoughue, Harold Wilson in the sixties was capable of 'working between fourteen to sixteen hours a day, often seven days a week and up to fifty weeks a year'. Yet ten years later, even the adrenalin of high office could not sustain this prodigious work rate, except on rare occasions.[73] At the same time Wilson suffered from poor health and noticeably often relied on brandy when stressed.

Patrick Wright observed that when he succeeded Tom Bridges as foreign affairs Private Secretary after the European Council meeting in Paris in December 1974, Wilson's doctor believed the Prime Minister had possibly suffered a slight stroke – perhaps a contributory factor to his decision to retire early in 1976.[74] Following a gruelling time in opposition during Edward Heath's premiership (1970–1974), and after medical advice, the Labour leader was secretly deciding on retirement from the political front line at 60.

In 1974 Harold Wilson, as previously observed, described his intention to play a different role as Prime Minister in footballing terms like 'a deep lying centre-half' rather than a goal scoring centre forward.[75] In this respect, in delegating matters more to experienced ministerial colleagues, Wilson was happy to leave the management of overseas policy to Callaghan who had built up considerable experience as Shadow Colonial Secretary in the late fifties and early sixties. As his biographer, Kenneth O. Morgan, has rightly recognised, foreign affairs had been the driving force of Callaghan's political career since his wartime experience and his earliest days in Parliament. Lord McNally also recalled an early visit with Callaghan to Africa in 1974 and the warm reception received from African leaders, including Julius Nyerere, Kenneth Kaunda and Jomo Kenyatta. Callaghan had supported them in their early struggles for colonial freedom.[76]

Wilson chose Callaghan as Foreign Secretary, rather than Denis Healey or Roy Jenkins, despite previous acrimonious relations owing to Callaghan's unflinching opposition to Barbara Castle's 1969 White Paper on trade union reform, *In Place of Strife*.[77] However, by 1974 Wilson and Callaghan had reached a *modus vivendi*. According to Lord McNally, 'They had decided it was better to be hanged together, than to be hanged separately'.[78] In fact, Callaghan as a result became almost deputy Prime Minister with a free hand in international affairs. On Friday mornings, he normally walked over to 10 Downing Street from the Foreign Office for private consultations with the Prime Minister and also with the Chief Whip, Bob Mellish, present from time to time to discuss the state of the party and the nation.[79]

In March 1974 Nicholas Henderson, British Ambassador to Germany, realised that the return of Labour to office meant a direct turnaround in the previous administration's policy on British membership of the Common Market. While the Heath government had taken Britain into Europe on 1 January 1973 and had joined with France and Germany in declaring that the European Union would be established by 1980, the new Labour Prime Minister and his Foreign Secretary would possess a different set of objectives in British diplomacy. The renegotiation of the EEC terms of membership had been a main plank in the party's election manifesto and at the party conference and would dominate Labour's agenda on regaining power. It was also a priority for Harold Wilson in his final term to keep open the possibility for a future Labour government to remain in Europe and particularly to preserve party unity.[80] Wilson had remarked to Henderson: 'They keep me there not because they love me but because there is no one else who can keep the party together'.[81]

Henderson also recorded that Callaghan had told his Private Office that:

> he wishes to put more muscle into the United Nations; he attaches great importance to the Atlantic Alliance and he wishes to have closer relations with the Commonwealth. He favours global rather than regional solutions, and America is, of course, vital to any global approach. Europe comes after this and the policy towards it is to renegotiate British entry to the EEC in keeping with the Labour Party's manifesto.[82]

With a very slim majority, Labour was defeated 29 times between March and July 1974. As a result, the question of Europe was seldom on the Cabinet agenda or discussed in Downing Street. However, Wilson did attend a European summit in Paris organised by French President Valéry Giscard d'Estaing where British EEC membership was discussed informally. In the October 1974 general election, despite an early lead in the polls, Labour secured only a majority of three, although there was a commitment to renegotiation of EEC terms to be followed by a Referendum which was held in Britain 6 June 1975.[83]

The renegotiation of EEC terms of membership in 1974–1975 throws some significant light not only on the role of the Prime Minister and Foreign Secretary but also the senior officials in the pro-European Foreign Office who briefed the Foreign Secretary and Labour ministers during the period of renegotiation. A determined Callaghan had issued a copy of Labour's manifesto to his Foreign Office aides. In response to the Assistant Under-Secretary for European Community Affairs at the Foreign Office, Michael Butler's remark of 'how was he going to explain this to his friends in Brussels?' brought Callaghan's retort that 'he had twenty-four hours to devise a plan'.[84]

Asked later in his career about the 1975 referendum, Sir Robert Armstrong revealed that:

> [if] Mr Wilson had taken a decision, or the Labour government of the day had taken a decision to leave the Community, I think I should have said to him, 'I had better not be your Principal Private Secretary … if I go into Europe … associated with a programme for coming out of Europe, I shan't be credible. I've just spent three and a half years doing the other thing. You had better have somebody who will have more credibility.[85]

Bernard Donoughue's view of Sir Robert Armstrong was that he 'comes professionally from the best civil service tradition of integrity and public duty'. He provided the 'Rolls Royce in Whitehall' Civil Service with the ability to switch easily from one administration to the next as in 1974.

In an interview with the journalist Hugo Young Sir Robert Armstrong also observed about the seventies:

> If you look back, on the whole what one government did tended to be left in place by another government. That government might change

direction, but it didn't try to undo what its predecessors had done. That's not quite as true as it was 30 or 40 years ago. And the polarisation has meant that the differences between – the gap between – the two main parties who provide the alternative governments is greater than it was. And I think that the business of being a professional, non-political civil service, serving governments of whatever political persuasion is more difficult because of this polarisation ... if the population changes ... then that problem will diminish in importance. I don't think it's impossible now. I think it makes the job a little more difficult to do.[86]

Patrick Wright was also among the officials who travelled to Dublin in March 1975 for the first briefing on the EEC re-negotiations. Others included Robert Armstrong, Pat Nairne and the Cabinet Secretary, John Hunt, as well as Michael Pallister, who had flown in from Brussels. This group briefed Harold Wilson on contentious areas for renegotiation: the budget, New Zealand and steel. They were joined by the Foreign Secretary, Jim Callaghan and his Foreign Office officials, for an extended discussion about shortening the time until the EEC Referendum and adopting a low profile campaign.[87] Two days later, a similar briefing took place to hear reports of the reaction in Dublin, Paris and Bonn. Donoughue was also present with Wright and Joe Haines, Wilson's Press Secretary, to advise on the Prime Minister's speech in Northern Ireland the next day.[88]

From Wilson to Callaghan

On 16 March 1976 in what appeared a bolt from the blue Harold Wilson announced his retirement to his Cabinet colleagues and the rest of the world. It was almost a unique event for a British Prime Minister still active in office to resign voluntarily. At the time Harold Wilson's resignation at age 60 apparently came as a complete shock to his colleagues, his opponents as well as the general public. In an interview with Peter Hennessy, Callaghan later revealed that in a car journey from the Commons Wilson had advised him to be ready to stand for the leadership as he saw him as his successor.[89] However, while at the time very few seemingly knew of Wilson's plans, his sudden departure from the front line of British politics was no surprise to Patrick Wright, his overseas affairs Private Secretary for 18 months. Lord Wright recalled that Wilson had reached his decision probably about two years before owing in part to family pressures.[90] Lord Owen, who as well as serving in government with Wilson and Callaghan was also a medical doctor, has written that Harold Wilson's decision to retire was an 'enlightened one' owing to the deterioration of his photographic memory and declining oratorical ability – probably due to Alzheimer's disease.[91]

As a result, for some time the Prime Minister's Private Secretary had found it increasingly difficult to plan overseas visits, including trips to Yugoslavia, Egypt, Israel and possibly Mexico. Eventually, in October 1975, Sir Ken Stowe secured Wilson's permission to inform Wright of his resignation pending in six months' time, which Wright had to keep secret up to the official announcement. Even so, Wright still had an extremely hard hand to play with the Foreign Office advising on overseas prime ministerial overseas visits. He recalled later that it had been a privilege to be in the know and he remained silent up to the final moment.[92]

One of Patrick Wright's last duties in serving Harold Wilson was to prepare a large number of communications with Ken Stowe and Joe Haines about the Prime Minister's resignation, which had to be approved by him before his announcement at the 11.00 a.m. Cabinet. Telegrams to the heads of foreign governments had to be delivered to Michael Palliser, the Permanent Under-Secretary at the Foreign Office. At this time Lord Wright remembered that the Private Office at Downing Street was inundated with phone calls asking about 'an extraordinary rumour going around that the Prime Minister has resigned'. It was excellent illustration of the Whitehall machine in action and the interplay of the network of Private Offices concerned with the conduct of government policy in 1976.[93]

According to Bernard Donoughue there was a different atmosphere at 10 Downing Street when Callaghan became Prime Minister, with a more authoritative style and a different routine to his predecessor. Patrick Wright, who stayed on as Private Secretary (Overseas Affairs) under Callaghan, was immediately involved in trying to resolve difficulties over Donoughue's visit to Israel. Callaghan had known Wright when he was previously Head of the Middle Eastern Department of the Foreign Office as well as Private Secretary to Harold Wilson. Wright continued to work closely with Callaghan as Prime Minister as part of a dedicated and industrious team at Downing Street that exemplified the phase that 'the Private Office never sleeps'.[94]

In selecting his Cabinet, Callaghan unexpectedly chose Tony Crosland, who had finished bottom of the party leadership poll in 1976, as his Foreign Secretary rather than Roy Jenkins or Denis Healey.[95] Tony Benn observed that Crosland had been appointed by Callaghan to prevent Roy Jenkins from taking the Foreign Office.[96] On Crosland's tragic early death in February 1977, Callaghan promoted David Owen at age 38 as the youngest Foreign Secretary since Anthony Eden, a reflection of Callaghan's advancing the next generation of leading politicians.[97] A highly supportive Prime Minister soon built up an excellent working relationship with his new Foreign Secretary.[98] James Callaghan's global outlook as Prime Minister now included Africa, the Middle and Far East and the Northern Atlantic alliance with specific interests in peace making in Rhodesia and the Middle East; progressing détente with the Soviet Union and strategic arms limitation. An Atlanticist, Callaghan worked hard after the neglect of the Heath years to restore Britain's relations with the United States – first with Henry Kissinger and from 1977 as an international broker in easing tensions between the new American President, Jimmy Carter and the European leaders, Helmut Schmidt and Giscard d'Estaing.[99]

The Private Secretary's many responsibilities included the planning and arrangements for overseas official visits by the Prime Minister, often accompanied by the Private Secretary himself and other officials. In occasional cases, officials concerned with the conduct of foreign affairs might travel with a different minister or by themselves. On Labour's return to office in 1974, the Cabinet Secretary, Sir John Hunt, had conducted preliminary talks in the United States with Dr Kissinger, the Secretary of State, on nuclear release procedures, the defence review, the British strategic nuclear deterrent, nuclear tests and the Nuclear Threshold Agreement. Sir John Hunt confirmed that the new Labour Government would not 'reverse the decision taken by the last (Conservative) Government. No formal decision could be reached, or announcement made, until the new defence review was completed but he expected that the decision to go ahead with the 'Super Antelope' project would be confirmed in due course'.[100]

Arranging the Prime Minister's overseas visits often raised thorny diplomatic issues in different parts of the world. On 19 September 1975, the Foreign and Commonwealth Office replied to Patrick Wright's letter of 11 September for the advice of the Foreign Secretary on whether the Prime Minister might pay a combined visit to Egypt and Israel after the European Council meeting in Rome. In replying, the Foreign Secretary pointed out this would create a precedent '… so far as we know no British Prime Minister has visited any Arab country while in office since the Second World War'. The proposal for a combined visit also raised important issues of timing, the need for a transit stop in a third country, as well as critical reaction in the Arab states. The Private Secretary, a Middle East expert, suggested visits to the Middle East which avoided a combined trip to Egypt and Israel.[101]

In December 1976, Patrick Wright contacted Ewen Ferguson at the Foreign Office about the difficulty of finding time for Callaghan to visit Egypt in the first six months of 1977. This followed correspondence from the Prime Minister's Chief Political Adviser Tom McNally, who had been handling the separate invitations from the Egyptian and Israeli ambassadors. Patrick Wright had advised the Prime Minister: 'The European Council meeting in Brussels is on 21/22 February. But that is likely to change … I think this would be an excellent idea. The Saudis would no doubt like you to visit them also, but would, I think understand the constraints'.[102]

McNally had sent the invitation 'via Mr Wright for his comments' adding 'with the thought that if you were so minded to accept the invitation, you could combine it with a visit to the Israeli Labour Party Conference which is being held from 22–24 February [1977]'.[103]

However, despite Callaghan's strong team of aides, their advice was not always heeded by the Prime Minister who at times kept his own counsel. On 7 September 1978, in a famous television broadcast James Callaghan told the nation: 'I shall not be calling for a general election at this time'. Callaghan's decision to defer the widely anticipated election was an extraordinary decision reached without consulting his Private Office, including Bryan Cartledge or his other senior political advisers, such as Tom McNally, who had been briefing the *Daily Mirror* on the election date, and Bernard Donoughue.[104] At his Sussex farm Callaghan had made his decision in mid August after analysing polling and other data, as well as a detailed memorandum from Sir John Hunt outlining the challenges of a third year in office, particularly on the international front and domestic policy. Hunt's memorandum indicated significant work to be completed that may have encouraged Callaghan to undertake the third year of his premiership.[105]

Similarly, one of Callaghan's most controversial decisions was the appointment of his son-in law, the economist Peter Jay, as Ambassador to the United States, replacing Sir Peter Ramsbotham. An angry Tom McNally burst into Tom McCaffrey's office to demand why he had been not been informed by the Prime Minister. 'Because he knew how you would react' was the Press Secretary's response.[106]

On 10 January 1979, at the height of the industrial unrest of the British 'Winter of Discontent', James Callaghan returned by VC10 to London from a three-day international summit on the French Caribbean island of Guadeloupe with President Carter, President Giscard d'Estaing and Chancellor Schmidt. In the last weeks of the Callaghan Government, the Guadeloupe summit was highly significant in terms of international diplomacy on the Strategic Arms Limitation Talks (SALT).

However, the summit is remembered far more for the banner press headlines about the industrial disorder in Britain of 'Crisis? What Crisis?' and 'The Ostrich Prime Minister' after Callaghan's complacent performance at the mishandled press conference at Heathrow Airport.[107] The Prime Minister had tried to convey he had been in touch with domestic affairs while abroad. About 'mounting chaos' caused by strikes in arctic Britain while he had been in the sunny climes of the Caribbean, he replied brusquely: '… perhaps you are taking rather a parochial view at the moment, I don't think that other people in the world would share the view that there is mounting [industrial] chaos'.

Guadeloupe was an important summit on international affairs, particularly concerning relations with the Soviet Union. At Callaghan's first Cabinet after his return, Lord Chancellor Elwyn Jones said: 'I wish the importance of these Guadeloupe discussions could be understood and explained to the public because you, Jim, had a very bad press when you were away'.[108] In particular, the Guadeloupe summit throws interesting light on the working relationship between the Prime Minister and his aides in foreign and domestic affairs at the end of the Callaghan premiership.

In Guadeloupe, the British Prime Minister was escorted by his wife, Audrey, and several senior officials, including Bryan Cartledge, Sir John Hunt, Tom McNally, Press Secretary Tom McCaffrey and Sir Clive Rose, Head of the Civil Contingencies Unit and Cabinet Office Deputy Secretary. Most had been with him since the beginning of his premiership in April 1976. In addition, the British press corps numbered around 50, though only about a third of those accompanying President Carter to the Caribbean.

156 *John Shepherd*

Hosted by the President Giscard d'Estaing with the President Jimmy Carter, Chancellor, Helmut Schmidt and James Callaghan, the three-day conference focused on defence, détente and disarmament in international affairs with a specific focus on the Strategic Arms Limitation Talks, which were nearing completion with Russia. At Guadeloupe Callaghan acted as an international honest broker helping to mend the diplomatic rift between Carter and Schmidt.

Even more important was the secret undertaking he secured from the American President that a future British government would be able to purchase, if required, the new C4 Trident system if the ageing fleet of Polaris submarines needed replacing. Callaghan recalled 'that the President said that he could see no objection to transferring this new technology [Trident C4 submarine with multiple independent re-entry vehicles] to the United Kingdom' and that 'it should be possible to work out satisfactory terms (about costs)'. Later Callaghan mentioned he only informed Sir John Hunt, though it is highly likely that Bryan Cartledge would have known. On his return Callaghan confirmed the arrangement in writing with Carter and sent two British experts on a follow-up visit to the States.[109]

Callaghan later recalled his discussion about Britain's future nuclear options with President Carter as follows:

> I walked the few yards across the grass to his hut next door and found him resting ... I then gave an outline of my view. For Britain, as a nation, the balance of advantage in procuring a successor to Polaris would be no better than marginal. There was a good case for ... strengthening our conventional forces ... but another factor weighed with me, namely that Britain had a responsibility not only for her own defence, but also a shared responsibility for the defence of Europe.
>
> The President heard me out. He said that like Helmut Schmidt he was also glad that Britain possessed the nuclear deterrent ... [and] that Britain would remain a nuclear power.[110]

According to David Owen, Sir John Hunt, the Cabinet Secretary, was influential in persuading the Prime Minister to employ his friendship with Jimmy Carter in securing this re-assurance from the American President. The Foreign Secretary also later recalled that Callaghan's initiative on Trident had not breached the Labour Party's manifesto commitment in 1974 not to replace Polaris as the Prime Minister was not committing a future Labour administration. However, on his last day in office, Callaghan left a minute which unusually and remarkably authorised the new Conservative Prime Minister his post-Guadeloupe Conference correspondence with President Carter. Also, Mrs Thatcher was given the extensive Mason–Rose Reports which Callaghan had commissioned on the different options for continuing the British independent nuclear deterrent.[111] However, British press coverage of the international summit focused instead on the Prime Minister and his wife strolling on a foreign beach under the Caribbean sun 4,000 miles away from the mounting industrial troubles back home.

In addition, on the return journey from Guadeloupe Callaghan and his party made a 36-hour official visit to Barbados for talks to see Prime Minister Tom Adams.[112] As Private Secretary, Bryan Cartledge had been responsible for planning the summit and briefing Callaghan, in conjunction with the Foreign and Commonwealth Office, especially about the visit to Barbados on the return journey.[113] After his return, Callaghan made a statement to the House of Commons about the Guadeloupe summit and the short official visit to Barbados.[114] As a result of the visit, Cartledge reported to the Foreign and Commonwealth Office for action on various issues, including the BBC Report on Barbados–Cuba relations, Barbadian fishing limits and sugar beet production.[115] The Guadeloupe summit in January 1979 was particularly significant for Jim Callaghan's informal discussions with President Carter on the question of replacing Polaris with Trident. Carter agreed that this nuclear technology could be made available in Britain.

Conclusion

Both Harold Wilson and James Callaghan readily acknowledged that their Private Secretaries Patrick Wright and Bryan Cartledge were destined for senior posts after their time at Number 10, including possibly reaching the summit of their profession.[116] After leaving Downing Street, Patrick Wright became Ambassador to Luxembourg, 1977–1979; Ambassador to Syria, 1979–1981; Deputy Under-Secretary of State FCO, 1982–1984; Ambassador to Saudi Arabia, 1984–1986; and was finally promoted to Permanent Under-Secretary of State and Head of Diplomatic Service, 1986–1991.[117] After his retirement from HM Diplomatic Service, Sir Patrick Wright was created a life peer in 1994 as Lord Wright of Richmond. In 2004 he gained *The House* magazine Award for the Best Parliamentary Speech of the Year.

After Labour's defeat in the May 1979 general election, Bryan Cartledge remained as Private Secretary to the new Conservative Prime Minister Margaret Thatcher. In 1980 he became Ambassador to Hungary and returned to Britain in 1983 as Assistant Under-Secretary of State at the Foreign and Commonwealth Office. From 1984 to 1985 Cartledge was Deputy Secretary of the Cabinet Office. During 1985–1988 he served as Ambassador to Moscow, including negotiations with the Soviet leader, Mikhail Gorbachev. From 1988 to 1996 Cartledge was Principal of Linacre College, Oxford. His publications include several books on environmental issues in the 1990s and *Will to Survive: A History of Hungary* (2006) and *Makers of the Modern World: Karolyi and Bethlen* (2009).

Any study of the close working relationship between a Prime Minister and the senior officials who served the premier at 10 Downing Street has to take into account the wider political context, particularly the constraints and opportunities, in which the different parties had to work. In many ways, the cultural, social, economic and political history of the seventies might be described in Dickensian terms: 'It was the best of times, it was the worst of times'. From 1974 to 1979 it was Patrick Wright, and his successor Bryan Cartledge, who held the post of Private Secretary (Overseas Affairs) – normally second to the Prime Minister's Principal Private Secretary, the Head of the Private Office at Number 10.

Both Wright and Cartledge served their Prime Ministers, Harold Wilson and James Callaghan, with consummate skill in difficult times. In the seventies Britain was beset by the most serious world crisis since the Second World War that ended the so-called post-war boom and Keynesian management of the British economy. In 1973–1974 the international quadrupling of the world oil price with the resultant double-digit inflation (at 27 per cent in August 1975 in Britain), combined with rising unemployment, produced the new phenomenon of 'stagflation'. The IMF Sterling Crisis in 1976, the 'Winter of Discontent' of industrial unrest in 1978–1979 also dominated the political news with Britain labelled as 'the sick man of Europe'. Yet, Britain arguably remained a world power with its independent nuclear weapons. Also the Private Secretary's responsibilities in overseas affairs had widened noticeably following the sectarian troubles in Northern Ireland and Britain's recent admission to the European Economic Community.

As the Private Secretary (Overseas Affairs), Wright and then Cartledge from similar public schools and Oxbridge backgrounds brought a wealth of experience and skills gained in diplomatic posts in different parts of the world to their new roles at Number 10. Clearly chosen as noted high-flyers in mid career, destined eventually to fill one of the most senior posts or the very top position (as they did), Wright was a distinguished Arabist and Middle East specialist and Cartledge an acclaimed expert on the Soviet Union. In particular, seconded for three years from the civil service, with they quickly demonstrated 'they knew the Prime Minister's mind'. As Ambassador Nicholas Henderson observed that they 'had the ear and eye of the PM and that is enough to give them immense influence'.

However, neither Private Secretary would describe his role as a 'foreign affairs advisor' but firmly believed instead his main task was to be the primary conduit between the Foreign Office and the Prime Minister in policymaking (with similar roles with the Ministry of Defence and the Northern Ireland Office). Particular attention was given in keeping the premier fully informed and up to date in an increasing busy world of global politics and international relations.

In the seventies Wilson and Callaghan were both notably experienced politicians who had built significant careers in British politics since 1945. Wilson had won more general elections than any Labour predecessor; Callaghan had the unique achievement of having held all the four major offices of state by the time he reached Number 10. However, from 1974 for five years, these two Labour premiers were at the helm of their minority administrations, often only kept in office only by electoral pacts and their parliamentary whips at Westminster.

In his final term in office from 1974 to 1976 Harold Wilson was in poor health and had privately decided to retire at 60 after only two years. He was no longer the Labour leader who had returned his party to power with his inspiring promise of 'the white heat of technology' conference speech. Instead, for example, he was happy to delegate much to Jim Callaghan (as in the renegotiation of the EEC membership terms in the run up to 1975 referendum). He appointed Callaghan as Foreign Secretary, allowing him much latitude in international affairs. Also, with weekly meetings on party business, he was almost deputy premier. As Prime Minister, Jim Callaghan brought a fresh working style, energy and authority (at least until the 'Winter of Discontent') He also acknowledged the work of his officials in terms of the 'Rolls Royce in the British Civil Service'.

Finally, as Jim Callaghan himself publicly acknowledged, the Private Secretary's 'tasks are limitless, bounded only by the number of hours in the day and the curiosity and interest of the Prime Minister'. Whether on overseas visits to Paris, Washington or Guadeloupe, or in liaison with British Foreign Office counterparts in London, making sure the Prime Minister was properly briefed before Cabinet or a million and one other unrelenting essential tasks in the Private Office behind the famous black door of 10 Downing Street, the Private Secretary's role was 'the best of times'.

Notes

1. I am very grateful for interviews about the 1970s to Charles Anson, Sir Bryan Cartledge, Lord Bernard Donoughue, Lord Peter Hennessy, Lord Tom McNally, Lord Owen and Lord Patrick Wright. Many thanks also to Mark Dunton, Contemporary Specialist, The National Archives (TNA). I am also indebted to TNA at Kew for permission to use copyright material and to the following for permission to quote from material for which they are the copyright holders: Lord Bernard Donoughue, Lord Peter Hennessy and Lord David Owen. I apologise unreservedly to any copyright holders who have been inadvertently overlooked.
2. Niall Ferguson, 'Introduction: Crisis, What Crisis? The 1970s and the Shock of the Global', in *The Shock of the Global: The 1970s in Perspective*, ed. Niall Ferguson, Charles S. Maier, Erez Manela and Daniel J. Sargent (Cambridge, MA: The Belknap Press of Harvard University Press, 2010), 6.
3. Helmut Schmidt, 'Britain Has a Problem; You Can be Hurt', *Guardian*, 23 December 2013. In April 1979 Callaghan told Bernard Donoughue, Head of the Downing Street Policy Unit: 'there has been one of those deep sea changes in public opinion. If people have really decided they want a change of government, there is nothing you can do about it'. Bernard Donoughue, *The Heat of the Kitchen: An Autobiography* (London: Politico's, 2004), 277. For a slightly different version, see Bernard Donoughue, *Downing Street Diary*, vol. II: *With James Callgahan in No. 10* (London: Jonathan Cape, 2008), 503.
4. For these Labour governments, see Harold Wilson, *Final Term: The Labour Government 1974–1976* (London: Weidenfeld & Nicolson and Michael Joseph, 1979); James Callaghan, *Time and Chance* (London: Politico's, 2006). In the Civil Service tradition, there are no memoirs by the Private Secretaries at Downing Street, but see Bernard Donoughue's illuminating two-volume *Downing Street Diary*

(London: Jonathan Cape, 2005–2008). For biographies of the two Prime Ministers, see Ben Pimlott, *Harold Wilson* (London: HarperCollins, 1992); Philip Zeigler, *Harold Wilson: The Authorised Life* (London: HarperCollins, 1995); and the magisterial Kenneth O. Morgan, *Callaghan: A Life* (Oxford: Oxford University Press, 1997).
5 *Daily Telegraph*, 12 October 1985.
6 James Callaghan, *Challenges and Opportunities for British Foreign Policy* (London: Fabian Society, 1975), 2.
7 Nicholas Henderson, *The Private Office Revisited* (London: Profile, 2001), 155.
8 Ferguson, Maier, Manela and Sargent, *Shock of the Global*.
9 Patrick Wright had succeeded Tom (later Lord) Bridges as the Foreign Affairs Private Secretary in October 1974. On becoming Prime Minister for the third time in February 1974 Harold Wilson had not changed the personnel in the Private Office who had served during Edward Heath's premiership. This was a practice first adopted by Ramsay MacDonald as Labour Prime Minister in 1924. Interview with Lord Wright, 13 July 2013; Harold Wilson, *The Governance of Britain* (London: Weidenfeld & Nicolson and Michael Joseph, 1976), 79–80.
10 See Andrew Blick, *People who Live in the Dark* (London: Politico's, 2004), chapter 6.
11 J. M. Lee, G. W. Jones and June Burnham, *At the Centre of Whitehall: Advising the Prime Minister and Cabinet* (Basingstoke: Macmillan, 1998), 44–5.
12 Wilson, *Governance of Britain*, 121–2.
13 Callaghan, *Time and Chance*, 406.
14 Interview with Sir Robert Armstrong, cited in Lewis Baston and Anthony Seldon, 'Number Ten under Edward Heath', in *The Heath Government 1970–1974: A Reappraisal*, ed. Stuart Ball and Anthony Seldon (London: Longman, 1996), 62. As a senior civil servant during the Second World War, including serving as Director of Economics and Statistics at the Ministry of Fuel and Power, Harold Wilson retained a deep respect for the British Civil Service. Interview with Lord Wright, 12 July 2013. For Bernard Donoughue's views on the changes in the Private Office in 1975, see Bernard Donoughue, *Downing Street Diary*, vol. I: *With Harold Wilson in No. 10* (London: Jonathan Cape, 2005), 545.
15 Interview with Lord Wright, 16 October 2000, Churchill Archive Centre, Cambridge [henceforward CAC]: DOHP 48.
16 Harold Wilson was the first Prime Minister to write about his office. He noted that his Labour predecessor, Ramsay MacDonald, despite opposition from his own colleagues, stopped the practice of changing the Principal Private Secretary and other senior colleagues on a change of government formed by a different political party. It strengthened the hold of the civil service on the Private Office at Downing Street. Wilson, *Governance of Britain*, 79.
17 Interview with Lord Wright, 11 July 2013.
18 For Marcia Falkender's views on Harold Wilson and Israel, see Marcia Falkender, *Downing Street in Perspective* (London: Weidenfeld & Nicolson, 1983), 177–8. See also Harold Wilson, *The Chariot of Israel: Britain, America and the State of Israel* (London: Weidenfeld & Nicolson and Michael Joseph, 1981), especially 374–8.
19 Interview with Sir Bryan Cartledge, London. 5 July 2013.
20 James Callaghan noted on this long minute: 'Very helpful thank you …' Minute from Cartledge to Morgan, 14 October 1975, in *Documents on British Policy Overseas*, ser. III, vol. III: *Détente in Europe*, ed. G. Bennett and K. A. Hamilton (London: Whitehall History Publishing in association with Frank Cass, 2001), 393–7.
21 The British party to the Soviet Union also included Sir John Hunt, Cabinet Secretary, Tom McNally, Chief Political Adviser to James Callaghan, and Joe Haines, the Prime Minister's Press Secretary. Record of meeting, 13 February 1975, in *Documents on British Policy Overseas*, ed. Bennet and Hamilton, 359. See also Interview with Cartledge, 14 November 2007, CAC: DOHP 115.

22 Interview with Lord Hennessy, 25 July 2014.
23 Interview with Lord Wright, 15 July 2013.
24 Interview with Sir Bryan Cartledge, 5 July 2013.
25 Interview with Lord Wright, 11 July 2013.
26 In important and influential part of the work of the Private Secretary included deciding on papers that needed the Prime Minister immediate attention (by highlighting key points in the margin) that required his attention or reply. Positioning in the Prime Minister's red box indicated relative urgency. 'Old Stripey' (a blue box with a red band) contained intelligence papers from the security service so confidential that only the Prime Minister, the Principal Private Secretary and the Private Secretary (Overseas Affairs) had keys. Interview with Lord Hennessy, 25 July 2013; interview with Sir Bryan Cartledge, 5 July 2013.
27 G. W. Jones, 'The Prime Minister's Aides', in *The British Prime Minister*, ed. Anthony King (Basingstoke: Macmillan, 1985), 76–8.
28 See Bernard Donoughue, *Prime Minister: The Conduct of Policy under Harold Wilson and James Callaghan* (London: Jonathan Cape, 1987), chapter 6.
29 Donoughue, *Downing Street Diary*, vol. I, 265.
30 Donoughue, *Prime Minister*, 18–19.
31 Lecture by Sir John Hunt, 1978, The National Archives, Kew [henceforward TNA]: PREM 16/1954.
32 Ibid.
33 Henderson, *Private Office Revisited*, 159–61.
34 Donoughue, *Prime Minister*, 19.
35 Interview with Ferguson, 2 December 1998, CAC: DOHP 35.
36 David Owen, *Time to Declare* (London: Penguin, 1992), 259–60. Interview with Lord Owen, 10 July 2013.
37 Henderson, *Private Office Revisited*, 155.
38 In 1924 Downing Street had no barriers and was open to the public. Herbert Wilson presented his son's photograph from the family album to the press on the day Wilson became Labour Party Leader. Pimlott, *Harold Wilson*, 18, photograph between 207 and 209.
39 The number of Private Secretaries varied during these years, for example, in wartime or when the Prime Minister took on additional portfolios. G. W. Jones, 'The United Kingdom', in *Advising the Rulers*, ed. William Plowden (Oxford: Basil Blackwell, 1987), 36–7.
40 Dennis Kavanagh and Anthony Seldon, *The Powers behind the Prime Minister: The Hidden Influence of Number Ten* (London: HarperCollins, 2000), 104.
41 When Wilson went on holiday to the Scilly Isles the Private Office would often speculate on how long before the Prime Minister phoned to ask if he should return. Interview with Lord Wright, 11 July 2013.
42 Donald Shell, 'The Office of Prime Minister', in *Churchill to Major: The British Prime Ministership since 1945*, ed. Donald Shell and Richard Hodder-Williams (London: Hurst & Company, 1995), 13–17.
43 Callaghan, *Time and Chance*, 405.
44 Ibid., 405.
45 For the other Private Secretaries, see Kavanagh and Seldon, *Powers behind the Prime Minister*, 10–13.
46 Donoughue, *Prime Minister*, 17–18.
47 BOHDP: Interview: Sir Bryan Cartledge.
48 Interviews with Lord Wright, 11 July 2013; interview with Sir Bryan Cartledge, 5 July 2013.
49 Bernard Donoughue, 'The Prime Minister's Day: The Daily Diary of Wilson and Callaghan, 1974–79', *Contemporary Record* 2:2 (1988): 16.
50 Wilson, *Governance of Britain*, 78.

51 Ibid., 83. Bernard Donoughue broadly confirmed the details of Wilson's daily routine, but noted that the Prime Minister 'lived at his house in Lord North Street and so, from Tuesday to Friday he was driven after breakfast the half a mile to Downing Street' to arrive usually by 9.00 a.m. Bernard Donoughue, 'Prime Minister's Day', 16.
52 Interview with Lord McNally, 15 July 2013.
53 Callaghan, *Time and Chance*, 405.
54 Ibid., 406.
55 Blick, *People who Live in the Dark*, 148–9.
56 Lord Bridges, Jo Grimond, Norman Hunt, Enoch Powell and Harold Wilson, *Whitehall and Beyond* (London: British Broadcasting Corporation, 1964), 11–19.
57 Wilson, *Governance of Britain*, 77.
58 Marcia Williams, *Inside Number 10* (London: Weidenfeld & Nicolson, 1973).
59 For the influence of Lady Falkender, see Donoughue, *Heat of the Kitchen*, 223–39.; Joe Haines, *The Politics of Power* (London: Jonathan Cape, 1977); Joe Haines, *Glitters of Twilight* (London: Politico's, 2003), 83–94.
60 Bernard Donoughue noted Marcia Williams's phone call to Patrick Wright that the Prime Minister's diary be kept free for dinner with the Israeli Ambassador. James Callaghan had not been consulted at a time of sensitive Foreign Office negotiations over the Middle East. Donoughue, *Downing Street Diary*, vol. I, 464–5.
61 Andrew Blick and George Jones, *At Power's Elbow: Aides to the Prime Minister from Robert Walpole to David Cameron* (London: Biteback Publishing, 2013).
62 However, Harold Wilson also readily acknowledged that previous administrations had occasionally employed outside advisers who were usually of similar political views. Wilson, *Governance of Britain*, 202–5.
63 Ibid., 202.
64 Blick, *People who Live in the Dark*, 148–9.
65 Harold Evans, *Good Times, Bad Times* (London: Weidenfeld & Nicolson, 1983), 86–7.
66 Donoughue, vol. I, 56.
67 Lee, Jones and Burnham, *At the Centre of Whitehall*, 86–99.
68 Interview with Lord McNally, 25 July, 2013.
69 When Lord McNally was ennobled in 1995, Lord Callaghan attended the ceremony sitting in the House of Lords so that he appeared on the video in support of his old friend. Interviews with Lord McNally, 11 and 25 July 2013. Kavanagh and Seldon, *Powers behind the Prime Minister*, 135–6.
70 Haines, *Politics of Power*; Haines, *Glimmers of Twilight*.
71 Kavanagh and Seldon, *Powers behind the Prime Minister*, 137–8; Donoughue, *Prime Minister*, 39–40.
72 Callaghan, *Time and Chance*, 331.
73 Donoughue, *Prime Minister*, 11–12.
74 Interview with Lord Wright, 11 July 2013.
75 In his constituency of Huyton in Liverpool he had remarked to Bernard Donoughue at the start of the February 1974 general election that if returned to Downing Street he proposed to be less 'Presidential' in style compared to 1964. Wilson declared: he would 'play as a sweeper in defence, not a striker in attack'. Donoughue, *Prime Minister*, 15.
76 Interview with Lord McNally, 25 July 2013.
77 In 1972 Roy Jenkins had resigned the Deputy Leadership of the Labour Party and was preparing to abandon British politics for the Chairmanship of the European Commission. From 1974 Denis Healey as Chancellor of the Exchequer became increasingly entwined in Britain's major economic problems. In 1976, on becoming Prime Minister, Callaghan chose Tony Crosland as Foreign Secretary. On Crosland's early death in February 1977, David Owen at 38 was appointed as

78 Wilson had also been impressed by Callaghan's successful handing of the Ulster situation as Home Secretary. Interview with Lord McNally, 25 July 2013.
79 Morgan, *Callaghan*, 408–9.
80 Bernard Donoughue, 'Harold Wilson and the Renegotiation of the EEC Terms of Membership, 1947–1945: A Witness Account', in *From Reconstruction to Integration: Britain and Europe since 1945*, ed. Brian Brivati and Harriet Jones (Leicester: Leicester University Press, 1993), 191–205.
81 Nicholas Henderson, *Mandarin: The Diaries of an Ambassador 1969–1982* (London: Weidenfeld & Nicolson, 1995), 72.
82 Ibid., 59.
83 Interview with Lord McNally, 25 July 2013.
84 Interview with Lord McNally, 25 July 2013; Interview with Sir Michael Butler, 1 October 1997, CAC: DOHP 25.
85 Quoted in Peter Hennessey, 'Sir Robert Armstrong: The Most Public Private Servant since Cardinal Wolsey', *Contemporary Record* 1:4 (1987): 28–9.
86 Ibid., 29.
87 Donoughue, *Downing Street Diary*, vol. I, 327.
88 Ibid., 343.
89 Callaghan also indicated that Harold Lever had given him a warning about Wilson's resignation some three months before. Peter Hennessy, *Muddling Through: Power, Politics and the Quality of Government in Post-War Britain* (London: Victor Gollancz, 1996), 279–81.
90 For a discussion of Wilson's resignation, including his reasons for retirement and those who knew or guessed in advance, see Paul Routledge, *Wilson* (London: Haus Publishng, 2006), 1–10.
91 David Owen, *In Sickness and in Power: Illness in Heads of Government during the Last 100 Years* (London: Methuen, 2008), 83–5.
92 Interview with Lord Wright, 16 October 2000, CAC: DOHP 48.
93 Ibid.
94 Returning to a 'quiet and dark' Downing Street on New Year's Day in 1975, Donoughue had found Patrick Wright (a few policemen and the duty clerk) at work in the Private Office. Bernard Donoughue, *Downing Street Diary*, vol. I, 270.
95 Susan Crosland, *Tony Crosland* (London: Jonathan Cape, 1982).
96 Tony Benn, *Against the Tide: Diaries 1973–1976* (London: Hutchinson, 1989), 555–6.
97 Interview with Lord McNally, 25 July 2014.
98 Interview with Lord Owen, 10 July 2014.
99 Morgan, *Callaghan*, 588–9; interview with Lord McNally, 25 July 2014.
100 Record of conversation, 26 April 1974, TNA: PREM 19/26.
101 Barrett to Wright, 19 September 1975, TNA: PREM 16/1074.
102 Wright to Ferguson, 21 December 1976, TNA: PREM 16/1077.
103 McNally to Callaghan, 16 December 1976, TNA: PREM 16/1077. See also, McNally to Callaghan, 11 December 1976, ibid.
104 On his return from holiday on 29 August, the Prime Minister had discussed the general election at Downing Street with Sir Ken Stowe, his Principal Private Secretary and Head of the Private Office. Note for the record by Stowe, 29 August 1978, TNA: PREM 16/1621. For a detailed commentary on Callaghan's decision to defer the 1978 general election, see John Shepherd, *Crisis? What Crisis? The Callaghan Government and the British 'Winter of Discontent'* (Manchester: Manchester University Press, 2013), chapter 2.

The beginning (before item 78) reads:

the new Foreign Secretary. Roy Jenkins, *A Life at the Centre* (London: Macmillan, 1991), 441–2; David Lipsey, *In the Corridors of Power: An Autobiography* (London: Biteback Publishing, 2012), chapter 5. Interview with Lord Wright, 11 July 2013; interview with Lord Owen, 10 July 2013.

105 Hunt to Callaghan, 3 August 1978, TNA: PREM 16/1621.
106 Interview with Lord McNally, 15 July 2013; interview with Lord Owen, 10 July 2013. For the Foreign Secretary's role in the ambassadorial appointment, see Owen, *Time to Declare*, 321–3.
107 Lord McNally recalled that he and Tom McCaffrey only disagreed once. On the flight back from Guadeloupe Tom McCaffrey had strongly advised the Prime Minister against holding a press conference at Heathrow, whereas he thought it was a good opportunity to be seized to speak to the country. *Guardian*, 26 July 2016. See also Shepherd, *Crisis?*, 127–8.
108 Tony Benn, *Conflicts of Interest: Diaries 1977–1980*, ed. Ruth Winstone (London: Arrow, 1991), 434.
109 Callaghan, *Time and Chance*, 554–6.
110 Ibid., 552–7; Peter Hennessy, *Cabinets and the Bomb* (Oxford: Oxford University Press for the British Academy, 2007), 325–6.
111 Interview with Lord Owen, 10 July 2013; Owen, *Time to Declare*, 403.
112 Adams to Callaghan, 22 December 1978, TNA: FCO 99/267.
113 Wall to Cartledge, 3 January 1979, TNA: FCO 99/267.
114 Cartledge to Walden, 16 January 1979, TNA: FCO 99/267.
115 Cartledge to Wall, 11 January 1979, TNA: FCO 99/267.
116 James Callaghan, *Time and Chance*, 405–6.
117 Interview with Lord Wright, 16 October 2000, CAC: DOHP 48.

References

Baston, Lewis and Anthony Seldon, 'Number ten under Edward Heath', in *The Heath Government 1970–1974: A Reappraisal*, ed. Stuart Ball and Anthony Seldon (London: Longman, 1996), 47–74.

Benn, Tony, *Against the Tide: Diaries 1973–1976* (London: Hutchinson, 1989).

Benn, Tony, *Conflicts of Interest: Diaries 1977–1980*, ed. Ruth Winstone (London: Hutchinson, 1990).

Blick, Andrew, *People who Live in the Dark* (London: Politico's, 2004)

Blick, Andrew and George Jones, *At Power's Elbow: Aides to the Prime Minister from Robert Walpole to David Cameron* (London: Biteback Publishing, 2013).

Bridges, Lord, Jo Grimond, Norman Hunt, Enoch Powell and Harold Wilson, *Whitehall and Beyond* (London: British Broadcasting Corporation, 1964).

Callaghan, James, *Challenges and Opportunities for British Foreign Policy* (London: Fabian Society, 1975).

Callaghan, James, *Time and Chance* (London: Politico's, 2006).

Crosland, Susan, *Tony Crosland* (London: Jonathan Cape, 1982).

Donoughue, Bernard, *Downing Street Diary*, 2 vols (London: Jonathan Cape, 2005–2008).

Donoughue, Bernard, 'Harold Wilson and the Renegotiation of the EEC Terms of Membership, 1947–1945: A Witness Account', in *From Reconstruction to Integration; Britain and Europe since 1945*, ed. Brian Brivati and Harriet Jones (Leicester: Leicester University Press, 1993).

Donoughue, Bernard, *The Heat of the Kitchen: An Autobiography* (London: Politico's, 2004).

Donoughue, Bernard, *Prime Minister: The Conduct of Policy under Harold Wilson and James Callaghan* (London: Jonathan Cape, 1987).

Donoughue, Bernard, 'The Prime Minister's Day: The Daily Diary of Wilson and Callaghan, 1974–79', *Contemporary Record* 2(1988): 16–19.

Evans, Harold, *Good Times, Bad Times* (London: Weidenfeld & Nicolson, 1983).
Falkender, Marcia, *Downing Street in Perspective* (London: Weidenfeld & Nicolson, 1983).
Ferguson, Niall, 'Introduction: Crisis, What Crisis? The 1970s and the Shock of the Global', in *The Shock of the Global: The 1970s in Perspective*, ed. Niall Ferguson, Charles S. Maier, Erez Manela and Daniel J. Sargent (Cambridge, MA: The Belknap Press of Harvard University Press, 2010), 1–24.
Haines, Joe, *Glitters of Twilight* (London: Politico's, 2003).
Haines, Joe, *The Politics of Power* (London: Jonathan Cape, 1977).
Henderson, Nicholas, *Mandarin: The Diaries of an Ambassador 1969–1982* (London: Weidenfeld & Nicolson, 1995).
Henderson, Nicholas, *The Private Office Revisited* (London: Profile, 2001).
Hennessy, Peter, *Cabinets and the Bomb* (Oxford: Oxford University Press for the British Academy, 2007).
Hennessy, Peter, *Muddling Through: Power, Politics and the Quality of Government in Post-War Britain* (London: Victor Gollancz, 1996).
Hennessy, Peter, 'Sir Robert Armstrong: The Most Public Private Servant since Cardinal Wolsey', *Contemporary Record* 1:4(1987): 28–31.
Jenkins, Roy, *A Life at the Centre* (London: Macmillan, 1991).
Jones, G. W., 'The Prime Minister's Aides', in *The British Prime Minister*, ed. Anthony King (Basingstoke: Macmillan, 1985).
Jones, G. W., 'The United Kingdom', in *Advising the Rulers*, ed. William Plowden (Oxford: Basil Blackwell, 1987).
Kavanagh, Dennis and Anthony Seldon, *The Powers behind the Prime Minister: The Hidden Influence of Number ten* (London: HarperCollins, 2000).
Lee, J. M., G. W. Jones and June Burnham, *At the Centre of Whitehall: Advising the Prime Minister and Cabinet* (Basingstoke: Macmillan, 1998).
Lipsey, David, *In the Corridors of Power: An Autobiography* (London: Biteback Publishing, 2012).
Morgan, Kenneth O., *Callaghan: A Life* (Oxford: Oxford University Press, 1997)
Owen, David, *In Sickness and in Power: Illness in Heads of Government during the Last 100 Years* (London: Methuen, 2008).
Owen, David, *Time to Declare* (London: Penguin, 1992).
Pimlott, Ben, *Harold Wilson* (London: HarperCollins, 1992).
Routledge, Paul, *Wilson* (London: Haus, 2006).
Shell, Donald, 'The Office of Prime Minister', in *Churchill to Major: The British Prime Ministership since 1945*, ed. Donald Shell and Richard Hodder-Williams (London: Hurst & Company, 1995), 1–29.
Shepherd, John, *Crisis? What Crisis? The Callaghan Government and the British 'Winter of Discontent'* (Manchester: Manchester University Press, 2013).
Wilson, Harold, *The Chariot of Israel: Britain, America and the State of Israel* (London: Weidenfeld & Nicolson and Michael Joseph, 1981).
Wilson, Harold, *Final Term: The Labour Government 1974–1976* (London: Weidenfeld & Nicolson and Michael Joseph, 1979).
Zeigler, Philip, *Harold Wilson: The Authorised Life* (London: HarperCollins, 1995).

8 Margaret Thatcher's Private Secretaries for Foreign Affairs, 1979–1984

Aaron Donaghy

Margaret Thatcher arrived at Downing Street in May 1979 as one of Britain's least experienced Prime Ministers in the field of foreign affairs.[1] By the time she left office eleven and a half years (and two more general elections) later, she was lauded as an international statesperson. Credited for helping to bring an end to the Cold War, her reputation in the United States and Eastern Europe, in particular, soared. Her role in overseeing an incredible feat of arms in the South Atlantic as Britain defeated an Argentine invasion of the Falkland Islands transformed her premiership domestically, while bolstering British prestige abroad. Despite later misjudgements, notably over the future of Europe and German reunification, it ensured her status as one of the most formidable political leaders of modern times.

Academia in recent years is suffused with studies of the Thatcher era, already served by an array of political biographies, interviews and a lavish biopic which preceded her death in 2013.[2] Memoirs of those who worked with or against Thatcher are also plentiful: Presidents, Prime Ministers, Foreign Secretaries and Cabinet ministers have written widely – and varyingly – on their experiences with 'The Iron Lady'.[3] Far less well known, however, are the recollections of colleagues and officials lower down the policymaking hierarchy (Alan Clark's diaries are a notable exception).[4] Those who operated alongside Thatcher on a day-to-day basis, in the Prime Minister's Private Office, are well placed to give a more nuanced appraisal of the longest-serving British leader of the twentieth century. Their story is rarely heard.

Thatcher's first two Private Secretaries for foreign affairs, Michael Alexander (1979–1981) and John Coles (1981–1984), witnessed a staggering amount of diplomatic traffic, encompassing foreign affairs, defence, intelligence, trade and 'intermestic' issues such as Northern Ireland and the Falklands. Their task, simply put, was to make the Prime Minister's life easier. This meant distilling vast quantities of papers from government departments – usually the Foreign Office – summarising complex subjects and the key factors involved. Ultimately, often on a cover note attached with a given paper, they had to outline to the Prime Minister the policy decisions that needed to be taken. Precisely how much advice a Private Secretary offered, and how much was merely descriptive, depended on the measure of the diplomat himself (for it was, almost exclusively, a male-dominated post). Their more mundane but no less hectic duties included the organisation of meetings, management of overseas tours, and keeping detailed records of conversations between Thatcher and a galaxy of foreign luminaries.[5]

Yet the roles of Alexander and Coles are important for other reasons. Firstly, Margaret Thatcher was a relative foreign policy novice when she assumed power. She had held only one Cabinet post prior to becoming Prime Minister (Secretary of State for Education and Science), and her overseas engagements were limited to her time as Leader of the Opposition. Nor did she, initially, show much interest in the subject. Thatcher's priority upon taking office was to revive Britain's flagging economy, bluntly telling officials that she did not intend to 'waste time on all this international stuff'.[6] She was, therefore, more open to suggestions and willing to 'delegate' on certain foreign issues during her first government. Secondly, her arrival as Prime Minister coincided with an uncertain time in international relations. Détente had given way to a new and more dangerous East–West confrontation, brought sharply into focus by the Soviet invasion of Afghanistan just months into her premiership. The 'Second Cold War', as the 1979–1985 era became known, was a stiff test of Thatcher's ability to learn and adapt quickly to the ever-shifting landscape of foreign affairs.

Thirdly, the relatively short spells of Alexander and Coles (though they would deem 30 months a normal timespan) stand in contrast with that of their successor, Charles Powell, whose stint as foreign affairs Private Secretary would last from 1984 to 1991. Powell became Thatcher's closest and most trusted foreign policy confidant – a feat in itself – and held similar views on the international stage. This led Percy Cradock (her de-facto 'foreign policy adviser') to remark that 'it was sometimes difficult to establish where Mrs Thatcher ended and Charles Powell began'.[7] Unsurprisingly in Thatcher's memoirs, *The Downing Street Years*, Powell appears on at least a dozen pages,[8] while Alexander and Coles are notable by their absence. Finally, the role of Private Secretary is important in lieu of the machinery of British foreign policy.[9] Thatcher's reign as Prime Minister has, after all, become synonymous with quarrels with the Foreign Office, the waning influence of Cabinet, and her tendency to rely on advice from 'outside' sources, notably the Centre for Policy Studies think tank.

Michael Alexander

Michael Alexander was perhaps always destined to become a foreign diplomat. His father Hugh, a famous mathematician and chess Grandmaster, was a leading cryptographer at Bletchley Park, where he helped crack the Nazi Engima code during the Second World War.[10] Hugh tried to persuade his son to become a businessman rather than a civil servant, but no one in the family had ever done anything except academic or clerical work, and Alexander Jr was resolved to boldness. His father's career and the heightening Cold War tensions had sparked an enthusiasm to engage with the wider world. This led Alexander to study history at Cambridge, and afterwards in the United States, as a Harkness fellow at Yale and Berkeley. As the fellowship's founders had doubtless intended, Alexander returned to Britain a committed Atlanticist. His interest in East–West relations, in particular, was sparked in 1956–1957 during his national service in the Royal Navy. Alexander was based in Kiel, northern Germany, where his job was to eavesdrop on the Soviet Baltic fleet. 'International relations were very much in my blood', he recalled;[11] 'I cannot remember having being seriously interested in any career other than that of diplomacy'.[12]

Though born in Winchester, England, in 1936 (to an Irish father and Australian mother), Michael Alexander was raised and schooled in Northern Ireland; an eclectic upbringing which helped shape his views on the 'The Troubles' during Thatcher's first term as Prime Minister. A tall, lean figure, he was a member of the British épée fencing team that won a silver medal at the Rome Olympics in 1960. Alexander joined the Diplomatic Service in 1962, just prior to the Cuban missile crisis, and a year later was posted to Moscow as Private Secretary to the British Ambassador, Humphrey Trevelyan. There he quickly discovered that his father's chess exploits – he once defeated the Soviet three-time world champion Mikhail Botvinnik – were a useful talking point with his diplomatic counterparts. But Alexander's two years in Moscow left deeper impressions which, to a large extent, shaped his approach to later Cold War issues during the 1970s and 1980s. The Russians, he reflected nostalgically, were an enigma. Alexander found them 'an enormously friendly, gifted, subtle, and intellectual people'. Conversely, they were also 'among the most devious, administratively incompetent, authoritarian, and instinctively secretive people' that he ever encountered.[13]

Alexander would spend the next few years in Singapore, where he operated in the joint intelligence staff. But his subsequent work during the 1970s made him ideally suited to the role of foreign affairs Private Secretary to Thatcher. After returning to the Foreign Office, where he dealt with defence and nuclear issues, Alexander became Private Secretary to two successive Foreign Secretaries, Alec Douglas-Home and James Callaghan. As his FCO colleague Sir Rodric Braithwaite observed, it was there that Alexander learned a truism: that even foreign policy is inevitably, at least in part, a function of domestic politics.[14] Perhaps his most significant work, however, was achieved as head of the political section of the British Mission at the United Nations in Geneva. There Alexander was at the heart of the East–West negotiations, and his fertile, inventive political mind helped contribute to the Helsinki Accords of 1975; a landmark agreement involving the Soviets which enshrined the principles of human rights. That marked the high point of détente. But four years later, when Alexander became foreign affairs Private Secretary to the Prime Minister (at the age of 43), East–West relations were again in peril.

'My two and a half years at No. 10 with her were the most strenuous of my life but not to have been missed', Alexander recalled. The beginning was hardly auspicious. Lord Mountbatten had been killed by the IRA the day before he joined Thatcher's staff – an early indication of the poor state of

Anglo-Irish relations, and the ongoing problem of Northern Ireland. Thatcher herself had been in office only three months, and many of the Whitehall 'cognoscenti' (who did not rate her highly) felt he had drawn the short straw. Sir Michael Palliser, head of the Diplomatic Service, for example, thought Alexander's priority as Thatcher's Private Secretary would be 'damage limitation'.[15] Overseas crises came in droves: Rhodesia, Northern Ireland, the EC budget rebate and the Cold War were all on the agenda from 1979 to 1981. Alexander, like Thatcher, relished political debate. On each of these issues he did not shy from stating his views to the Prime Minister – a trait that would continue in his subsequent roles during the 1980s.

Alexander and Thatcher had a dialectical relationship of mutual respect. They shared a broadly similar outlook on East–West relations, defence and the transatlantic alliance with the United States. But on other issues, notably those of Europe, Ireland, and the hunger strikes, their views diverged. This gradually dawned on the Prime Minister. Despite admiring his intellect, Thatcher sensed that the pro-European Alexander was not simpatico. 'His father is Irish and his wife is German', she once warned Hugh Thomas, a history professor and chairman of the Centre for Policy Studies (CPS).[16] The CPS, founded by Keith Joseph in 1974, remained Thatcher's favourite policy think tank. Though its *raison d'être* was to champion free market ideas and economic liberalism, it also served as an alternative source of foreign policy ideas, vying with the FCO, Ministry of Defence and the Cabinet for her attention. Once in power Thatcher consistently brought its assortment of academics into the government fold, much to the annoyance of senior ministers.[17]

The first overseas crisis emerged in late 1979, when an ailing Leonid Brezhnev authorised the Soviet invasion of Afghanistan. Hyped by US President Jimmy Carter (at the beginning of election year) as 'the most serious threat to peace since World War II', it marked a renewed period of hostility between the West and the Soviet Union.[18] Alexander and Thatcher were at the British Embassy in Luxembourg when the news filtered through. Though he agreed with Thatcher on the need 'to play the hand from strength' with the Soviets, he dissented from her views on the motives.[19] The Prime Minister viewed the invasion of Afghanistan as part of a wider pattern of aggressive Soviet expansionism, and of communist subversion in the third world, as the Kremlin exploited the 'western weakness and disarray' afforded by détente.[20] By contrast, Alexander saw the invasion as a reflection of Soviet *weakness* rather than strength. The Soviets, he believed, had resorted to military force against their neighbour precisely because of their inability to secure an acceptable regime in Kabul by other means.[21] 'On East–West relations … she was inclined to over-simplify and over-dramatise the issues', Alexander later mused.[22]

East–West relations were Alexander's forte and, unlike Thatcher, he had witnessed politics in Moscow at first hand. He wasted no time in offering some friendly advice – and a bit more – recalling a 'vigorous argument' with her about Soviet intentions. 'I must confess that I argued with her that night that the invasion was if anything an act of desperation on the part of the Russians – rather out of keeping with their usual caution', he recounts. 'The Russians were going in because they were unable to control the situation in any other way. That struck me as something over which we should not lose too much sleep. If the Russians were prepared to bleed themselves white in Afghanistan, good luck to them'.[23] Alexander was worried about the prospects for East–West relations in the 1980s even before Afghanistan had happened. It was he who had coined the term 'dangerous decade', subsequently used by Thatcher in her rousing speech to the Foreign Policy Association in New York – one week before the Soviet invasion. Alexander believed this danger arose because the Soviet Union, though a military superpower, was 'a nervous and uncertain giant, doubtful of its ability to compete successfully with the West, rather than because it was an "evil empire"'.[24]

As Charles Moore, Thatcher's biographer, notes, Alexander's views occasionally swung towards the Foreign Office line. But the Prime Minister held him in high regard. Clive Whitmore, her principal Private Secretary, recalled:

> Having seen the Russians at close quarters, Michael was under no illusions about how tough they were. She relied very much on his advice. He wasn't at all soft. But as a good member of the diplomatic corps he realised that we had to live with the Soviets, which was her approach too.[25]

There is more than a hint of truth to this. Despite her caricature as 'The Iron Lady' (which she quite enjoyed), Thatcher's views on how to deal with the Soviet government became more nuanced from an early stage in her premiership. Her willingness to listen to, and explore, new ideas – traits sometimes obscured by her rhetoric – was central to her relationship with future Soviet leader Mikhail Gorbachev, and (aided by US President Ronald Reagan) the easing of Cold War tensions.

Thatcher's response to the invasion was decisive and forthright. She pledged British support for the American-led policy of imposing economic and cultural sanctions to punish the Kremlin. The Prime Minister agreed with Carter's suggestion that a fine way of denting Soviet prestige would be a united Western boycott of the 1980 Moscow Olympics. But Thatcher's disappointment at being unable to deliver a British boycott (the UK sent more athletes than any other West European nation) was matched by her anger at the reluctance of the French and West German governments to impose significant sanctions on the Soviets.[26] As the British government prepared its longer-term strategy for East–West relations, Alexander found himself swamped in papers – mostly sent by the Foreign Office and the Centre for Policy Studies for the Prime Minister's viewing. The Private Secretary's handwritten exchanges with Thatcher show that this could be a delicate balancing act. It is an insight into the complex policy process and the Prime Minister's methods. Alexander passed a 35-page CPS report to Thatcher entitled 'Western Strategy in the wake of Afghanistan', at a time when the FCO were producing a paper on the very same theme. He suggested that, as Foreign Secretary, Lord Carrington be sent a copy of the CPS paper. Thatcher agreed but added, in bold black ink: 'I would rather it was NOT seen by the F.O. until they have finished theirs. I don't want one to influence the other'.[27] Subsequently, she expressed her gratitude to CPS chief Hugh Thomas for providing 'an independent measure against which to judge the proposals being put forward by [Foreign Office] officials'.[28]

With a Cold War back in motion, and having spent his adult life dealing with the subject, Alexander felt obliged to comment personally where he saw fit. On a telegram sent by UK Ambassador to Moscow Curtis Keeble – reporting on a visit to the Kremlin by the US Senate Foreign Relations Committee – he explicitly drew Thatcher's attention to the 'significant points in virtually every paragraph'.[29] He was also happy to form judgements on the proposals of Britain's NATO allies. On a letter sent by US Secretary of State Al Haig to his opposite number Lord Carrington about promoting Western policies and countering Soviet propaganda, Alexander advised the Prime Minister: 'I am not sure that Haig's ideas will cut much ice. Western "propaganda" initiatives can never, in the nature of things, be as well coordinated as those of the Soviet Union. It is our results – economic, technological, etc. – which impress'. However, he expressed his pleasure at seeing the new Reagan administration taking the lead. 'We should certainly back them', he concluded.[30] At other times Alexander could be blunt. When a new French proposal for an international conference on Afghanistan was announced by President Giscard d'Estaing on television (the Soviets were informed before Britain or the United States), the Foreign Office believed there was 'a strong element of electioneering' in the nature and timing of the move.[31] Alexander agreed. 'One gets a little weary of French gimmicks', he wrote to Thatcher,. 'I doubt whether this will run much further than its predecessors'.[32]

While East–West relations remained the prime concern, other overseas problems loomed large. The Rhodesian conflict was a long-standing one which, in retrospect, overshadowed a burgeoning crisis in the South Atlantic. On African issues Alexander had less input, yet his recollections are revealing. The 1980 agreement, he judged, was 'primarily, but not exclusively, Carrington's achievement'. Alexander believed that Thatcher's main contribution was to allow Carrington to conduct the negotiations at Lancaster House, while using her influence in the background at Number 10. This was done aggressively and effectively. 'We had sessions with the prime minister most evenings after the negotiating day was over', recalled Alexander.

> Her role was to be rather extreme, to criticise all the participants all the time. 'I won't have it; I won't do it' and 'absolutely not!' ... Peter would then go back to Lancaster House and say that the Prime Minister was giving him a hard time and that the participants had better agree to whatever he proposed 'for fear of something worse' ... I think that it was this good cop/bad cop relationship which made the Rhodesia success possible.[33]

172 *Aaron Donaghy*

Alexander was more involved in a crisis closer to home. The early 1980s saw mounting trouble in Northern Ireland, and relations between Westminster and Dublin were strained. Alexander, raised in the province of Ulster, knew the background well. But though he 'disagreed strongly' with Thatcher's policies over Ireland,[34] particularly the hunger strikes, Alexander was careful not to overstep his remit. Indeed, when the European Commission of Human Rights (ECHR) declared the protests of the 1981 hunger strikers at Maze prison admissible, he discovered just how steadfast was her position. The ECHR had invited the British government to send an official to Strasbourg 'for an informal meeting', and encouraged it to present new proposals to resolve the problems. Humphrey Atkins, Secretary of State for Northern Ireland, recommended 'seeking a way of responding positively' to the request, 'to maintain our good relations with the European Commission and counter PIRA propaganda'. Alexander appeared content with Atkins's line. But when he asked Thatcher if the Northern Ireland Office could proceed as proposed, the Prime Minister erupted. 'I am utterly dismayed and very angry that at no time was it raised with me even though the S. of S. [Atkins] knew how strongly I felt about it', she wrote. Instead, Thatcher proposed sending 'a highly skilled representative to Strasbourg who is fully conversed with the law'. While prepared to continue correspondence with the EC to help find a settlement, she instructed that the British government had 'no new proposals to make'.[35]

Although Thatcher's attitude towards the hunger strikes received much criticism (particularly in Ireland, and the United States, where a powerful Irish-American lobby remained prominent), Alexander believed the Prime Minister's policies were ultimately vindicated. 'She, on the whole, was right and I was wrong', he later admitted.[36] Thatcher's decision to sign the landmark Anglo-Irish agreement in 1985 meant recognising the legitimacy of the Irish government's role in the peace talks. Occurring just a year after the IRA's Brighton bombing which almost killed her, and in the face of staunch Unionist opposition, it again showed Thatcher to be more flexible in foreign affairs than has been popularly conceived.

Both during his time as foreign affairs Private Secretary, and in his subsequent diplomatic posts, Alexander held different views from Thatcher about Britain's role in Europe. Yet the extent to which their views diverged only became noticeable after Alexander had left the Private Office, when the Prime Minister's foreign policy approach became increasingly implacable. The thorn in British–European relations during Thatcher's first term was the EC budget rebate. Alexander remembered the European Council meeting of Dublin, November 1979, at which she famously, and bluntly, told European leaders: 'I want my money back!' 'I wrote speeches for her but not that one!', recalled Alexander.[37] In Dublin, Britain was offered a £350 million rebate, which Thatcher flatly rejected. At the Luxembourg summit in April 1980, the offer was upped to £760 million for two years, but this too was declined by the Prime Minister. Two months later Carrington and Ian Gilmour negotiated a three-year agreement which entailed ongoing repayments of Britain's budget contribution. But Thatcher, to the dismay of most of her diplomats, continued to stand firm, holding out for a better and more permanent solution. The issue was finally settled at the Fontainebleau summit in June 1984, when Britain received a 66 per cent refund, with a long-term rebate structure put in place.[38]

Carrington cited Thatcher's 'firmness and intransigence' as the key factors which had secured a better deal. But he felt that long-term relations between Britain and Europe were damaged as a result.[39] 'There was a good deal of tension on European issues', admitted Alexander. 'But, again, her actions and attitudes gave everyone else credibility. In my time [as foreign affairs Private Secretary] it was a single team whose members used, with conviction, the argument that "we have this lady who won't put up with that". It worked rather well'.[40] According to Alexander, the system began to break down later on, when colleagues became 'disloyal' and the Prime Minister became 'eccentric'. Foreign Secretary Geoffrey Howe, for example, was treated by Thatcher 'in a deeply unattractive manner'. Alexander recalled: 'On one occasion, during a NATO summit in Brussels, I found myself asking her to "lay off" him since I did not think it appropriate for the secretary of state to be criticised by the prime minister in front of his (and therefore my) staff'.[41]

In December 1981, at the age of 45, Alexander left his post to become UK Ambassador to Austria (1982–1986). After two and a half years in Thatcher's Private Office, Vienna seemed like a safe bet. There, and in his subsequent role as Ambassador to NATO (1986–1992), Alexander focused on the key issues of defence and security. He urged Thatcher to support the effort to intensify European defence cooperation within the Atlantic Alliance. Moreover, Alexander sought to persuade her to adopt a more sympathetic position towards the (increasingly inevitable) prospect of German reunification. In both instances, historian Keith Hamilton notes, 'he was disappointed by a prime minister whose leadership and pragmatism he otherwise admired'.[42] During the mid 1980s – the apogee of the Thatcher era – Alexander judged that Britain had 'missed, or rejected, more opportunities than we took'.[43] He added:

> Margaret Thatcher in 1985–1986 could have done more or less anything she liked to shape the political future of Europe – provided her starting point was seen to be pro-European. It is an enormous pity, given the opportunities available to her in those years, that she did not choose to take them.[44]

While in Vienna, Alexander used his successor in the Private Office, John Coles, as an intermediary to relay his policy ideas to the Prime Minister. A letter he sent in March 1984, following a particularly fraught period in East–West relations, concerned a new Western initiative to ease the risk of nuclear conflict. In some respects it mirrored the later US–Soviet negotiations that would help end the Cold War. The main thrust of Alexander's thinking was as follows:

> One possibility would be for NATO to state formally its readiness to see *all* American troops and weapons withdrawn from Western Europe provided that *all* Soviet troops and weapons were withdrawn from Eastern Europe; and its readiness to open negotiations to achieve this objective within a finite time span, say, by 1990.[45]

It was a bold paper, calling for an end to the large-scale US military presence in Western Europe – something Thatcher had always deemed essential for the stability of the continent. Consequently, Alexander had serious reservations about sending it to her. He thus passed it to Coles in the Private Office instead. 'I have not addressed the paper to the prime minister because I am uncertain whether or not you ought to show it to her', explained Alexander.

> Clearly, its thesis would not be unwelcome in the FCO and still more so in the MoD. What you can judge far better than I, is whether the concerns expressed and suggested course of action come into the category of ideas which are 'in the air' but not yet respectable, or whether they are still in the realm of the lunatic.[46]

Coles sent the paper to Thatcher, who placed it firmly in the latter. 'I am very unhappy about the idea', she wrote. 'The suggestion is unequal. The Russians could return within 48 hours and the threat would still be present in every East European country. Once the US had gone, they would never return'. To Alexander's mortification, Thatcher added: 'This proposal looks to me like a way to Finlandise the whole of Europe'.[47] In his memoirs, Alexander felt that Thatcher's comments were 'both reasonable and predictable', but deemed her remark about the Red Army to be 'a groundless nightmare'.[48]

Despite their differing views, Alexander and Thatcher remained on friendly terms. The Prime Minister bunked near the Alexanders at a mountain retreat above Salzburg in the summers of 1984 and 1985 (where he again tried to expose her to foreign policy ideas).[49] When asked about Thatcher's greatest qualities, he cited her 'unbelievable' energy and work ethic. 'Loyalty', meanwhile, was the characteristic that Thatcher most cherished. 'If you were part of the family, as one was as a private secretary, she was ferocious in your defence and would cover up for you if necessary. If you were outside the family, and above all if you were a potential rival, the situation was very different'.[50] Michael Alexander died in 2002, just shy of his sixty-sixth birthday. His worthy memoirs, *Managing the Cold War*, were published posthumously in 2005.

John Coles

Arthur John Coles succeeded Alexander as Private Secretary for foreign affairs in December 1981. His stint at the Private Office would run for two and a half years, a period which saw Margaret Thatcher traverse the highs and lows of international life: the Argentine invasion of the Falkland Islands, and a subsequent British military triumph; the dramatic worsening of East–West relations; Anglo-American rumblings over the Siberian gas pipeline, and the US invasion of Grenada; tempestuous struggles with the European Community. It was also the key transformative period of her premiership. Victory in the Falklands War, duly followed by a landslide re-election in 1983, substantially increased Thatcher's political self-assurance. This extended into the realm of foreign affairs, where plenipotentiary powers were further eroded.

Born in 1937, Coles's prelude to entering the Diplomatic Service included two years of national service (1955–1957), followed by a BA at Oxford University. While studying he developed a keen interest in foreign affairs, particularly the Middle East, a region emerging from the 1956 Suez crisis (which he regarded as 'a mistaken adventure'). Coles entered the Foreign Office in 1960. There he was asked to choose one of the 'hard languages', as defined by the FCO. Naturally Coles opted for Arabic, and soon found himself ensconced in Lebanon at the Middle Eastern Centre for Arabic Studies. A spell as THIRD Secretary in Khartoum followed (where his newly acquired Arabic was less useful), before he returned to the Foreign Office in 1964.[51]

Over the next decade Coles performed a string of unglamorous administrative roles, before becoming Head of the Chancery in Cairo in 1975. He subsequently became a counsellor at the UK Permanent Mission in Brussels (1977–1980), where his work focused on the relationship between the European Community and the 50-plus nations of Africa, the Caribbean, and the Pacific, with which it had a special treaty arrangement. It was Coles's first experience of dealing with the European political pillars. Not everything was to his liking and he formed similar, if less visceral, feelings about British–EC relations to that of Margaret Thatcher. 'I didn't have doubts about British membership of the European communities, but what I wanted to see was actually what advantages we were getting from this relationship', he recalled. 'By the time I left, in 1980, my overriding feeling was that in contrast to all the other member states, it was hard to see that Britain had gained strong, concrete advantages from its membership'.[52]

In 1980 Coles was appointed head of the FCO's South Asian department. However, his work focused almost entirely on the British response to the Soviet invasion of Afghanistan. Coles presented a proposal for an international conference on the Afghan question, 'to provide the Russians with a face-saving device for getting out of the mess they were in and bring the conflict to an end' (an approach which contrasted with that of Michael Alexander, as noted above). He recommended that Foreign Secretary Lord Carrington visit the Soviet Union to present the Afghan peace plan. At that time, Coles notes, Thatcher 'was very much against contact with Moscow', believing that little would come out of such a mission. She was proved right. Carrington was eventually dispatched to Moscow for an all-day meeting with the Soviet Foreign Minister, Andrei Gromyko, who would not brook the slightest interference in what was deemed a Soviet security problem. 'It had put pressure on him and had given Europe a clear and respectable position on Afghanistan', Coles later argued.[53] Yet the Soviet–Afghan War would drag on until the spring of 1989 – years after the reform-minded Mikhail Gorbachev became Soviet premier.

Coles could be candid about his life's work. 'I think I've had a very unusual career', he reflected.

> I've never been an assistant secretary at the Foreign Office. Apart from that one spell, lasting only a year, as head of the South Asian department, and that for a rather particular purpose, I've never been a head of department or an assistant head of department. I didn't have the classical route up.

Coles did have a small amount of Private Secretary experience: he worked, briefly, for Minister of State at the Ministry of Defence Lord Balniel in 1973, and for FCO Minister of State David Ennals in 1974. As Coles admitted, however, he did not progress through the departments in the orthodox fashion, and spent much of his career away from mainstream Foreign Office work.[54]

It is something of a surprise, then, that he was chosen to succeed Alexander as Thatcher's foreign affairs Private Secretary in late 1981. Coles was one of three candidates to be interviewed by the Prime Minister, and though he hardly knew her at all (they had met once in Cairo), soon discovered a stylistic quirk.

> Eventually I was interviewed by Mrs Thatcher and her principal private secretary … and talked for about an hour, at the end of which she said, 'I suppose you'd better come'. I said to her principal Private Secretary, 'Is that a decision?' and he said 'That *is* a decision'.

Later, Coles recognised the nature of Thatcher's comment. 'She really hated making changes, hated deciding on new people'. Although Coles did not believe that her remark was directed against him, it did little for his confidence at the time. 'It wasn't exactly the resounding, morale-boosting comment that you would hope for', he admitted, with charming understatement.[55]

Despite that uncertain beginning Coles grew fond of the Prime Minister. He had entered her Private Office, noted Charles Moore, 'with the usual somewhat anti-Thatcher prejudices of the civil service'. Soon, however, he became a very great admirer, praising her 'extraordinary courage and clarity'.[56] Unlike Alexander, his political views were more or less aligned with those of Thatcher. That, together with his relative lack of Foreign Office experience, may explain Coles's cautious, deferential style as Private Secretary. Recently declassified British government files display little evidence of Coles offering advice or opinions on foreign topics. His written notes for Thatcher on policy papers often amounted to a brief precis, whereby the FCO's recommendation would be stated, followed by: 'Agree?' Though the role of conduit was a primary function of all foreign affairs Private Secretaries, Coles seemed particularly careful not to overstep his remit. His overwhelming tendency to describe, rather than suggest or pass judgement, stood in contrast to both his predecessor and successor, who were willing to state a view where they saw fit. In short, Coles came to resemble a glorified correspondence clerk of the sort Chris Mullin had so despaired.[57]

By the time Coles entered Downing Street, divisions between the United States and Western Europe about how to respond to the Soviet crackdown in Poland were already evident. President Reagan described European leaders as 'chicken littles',[58] and duly ordered US companies to abandon work on the European-backed Siberian gas pipeline (much to Thatcher's annoyance). Well before the US pipeline sanctions were lifted, however, Thatcher was faced with Britain's greatest foreign policy emergency since the Suez crisis of 1956. The Argentine invasion of the Falkland Islands (a tiny dependency in the South Atlantic), provided the single sternest test of her leadership qualities. Thatcher's response and the subsequent, resounding British military victory, would transform and define her years as Prime Minister. It was, therefore, the most significant international issue that Coles witnessed from the Private Office.

Argentina's occupation of the Falklands was far less surprising or sudden than has often been construed. The sovereignty dispute had been simmering since Juan Perón first assumed power in 1946, and from the mid 1960s a series of bellicose Argentine threats had been directed at London. The Thatcher government had inadvertently contributed to the mess, making a series of miscalculations that had, in the eyes of Argentina's military leadership, reduced Britain's interest in keeping hold of the Falklands: the announcement of the withdrawal of Britain's South Atlantic vessel, HMS *Endurance*; the refusal to grant full British citizenship to the Islanders in the 1981 Nationality Act; financial cuts in the British Antarctic Survey, and the proposed closure of its base on South Georgia. Compounding all of this was the total absence of Cabinet meetings to discuss the dispute, and of regular updated intelligence reports.[59]

Coles was an intermediary in a chain of confusing events during the critical period prior to the occupation. On 29 March, four days before Argentina invaded, Thatcher travelled with Foreign Secretary Lord Carrington to Brussels for an EC summit. Coles, who accompanied them, maintains that even then there was 'no belief in her mind or that of Carrington that Argentina was about invade'.[60] That seemed odd, given that the Cabinet had discussed that very scenario just days earlier. Two weeks prior to that, Thatcher had spoken to Defence Secretary John Nott about dispatching Royal Navy ships to the region. Moreover, after a threatening Argentine communique on 3 March, the Prime Minister herself had minuted: 'We must make contingency plans'.[61] On 8 March – some five days later – this note was passed by Coles to John Holmes, who had just succeeded Roderic Lyne as Carrington's assistant Private Secretary. It was a brief but vital request from Thatcher: 8 March was effectively the latest date possible to arrange a British naval task force in time for its arrival in the South Atlantic before the invasion (a preventative manoeuvre implemented by the preceding Labour government during moments of Anglo-Argentine tension). On the same day, Carrington was informed of the 1977 British naval deployment to the region, but promptly dismissed the idea of launching a similar operation (honourably, he later regretted this decision).[62]

What happened to Thatcher's demand for contingency plans remains a mystery. Coles conveyed her exact words to the FCO but without any great conviction or sense of urgency. He tentatively stated: 'I understand that it may be the intention of Lord Carrington to bring a further paper on the Falkland Islands to OD in the fairly near future. You may think that this could helpfully contain an account of our contingency planning'.[63] Coles's minute was copied to the Ministry of Defence and the Cabinet Office. As the 1983 Franks Report points out, there was no response to the letter, 'because of the general expectation in Whitehall that it would be included on the agenda of an early meeting of the Defence Committee'.[64] Remarkably, this 'early meeting' did not take place until 1 April – just hours before Argentine ships docked at the Falklands. Historian Sir Lawrence Freedman noted that Thatcher's request 'does not appear to have reached any part of the intelligence community'.[65]

Once the invasion was a fait accompli, the British response was rapid and decisive. Argentine forces could either withdraw or else face military action. The Islanders, with their loyal, Anglo-Saxon, 'British' qualities, were to be liberated. For Thatcher, in particular, British sovereignty and the Islanders' right to freedom and self-determination were sacred principles that had been violated. Nothing less than a total Argentine withdrawal would suffice. The British position was in accordance with international law, and was sanctioned by the United Nations. Coles recalls that although these principles 'seemed obvious' when stated, they were less evident to British people at large in the aftermath of the invasion. 'It is to her [Thatcher's] everlasting credit that she saw them at once, publicly proclaimed them in the clearest terms and provided the nation with the clear moral justification for what was to follow'. The political establishment, too, had been uncertain in its response. Coles remembered a Foreign Office ill-prepared for war.

> We got into a frame of mind which suggested that negotiation was the answer to everything, and I think, psychologically, we found it very hard to cope with the fact that British troops were actually crossing the world to go into military action. It was a very novel experience for those in Downing Street too.[66]

Not least the Prime Minister, who had to learn on the job. However, as soon as the Argentine leadership made it clear that their forces would not withdraw from the islands, Thatcher was unswerving in her determination to dislodge the contingent by military might. Coles recalls that her 'clarity of vision, decisiveness and courage' formed his most abiding memories.[67] These Churchillian leadership qualities shone through in 1982, providing the political impetus that enabled the British military to succeed, resoundingly, in its campaign objectives.

The triumph in the South Atlantic was in every sense a turning point. Victory meant more than the liberation of the Islanders and restoration of British sovereignty. In the midst of a dangerous 'Second Cold War', it had to a considerable extent restored Britain's international standing, and sent a firm signal to Washington (and Moscow) that this was an able partner on which the West could rely. Domestically, it shored up an unsteady Conservative Party, and solidified Thatcher's position as an accomplished wartime leader, capable of fighting for, and securing, British interests. After the Falklands, the 1983 general election was won at a canter. The Prime Minister's self-confidence in foreign affairs soared. Thatcher, as biographer John Campbell noted, 'was ready to be her own foreign secretary'.[68] Coles recalled its wider significance: 'If Argentine aggression had succeeded the consequences for Britain would have been profound. The moral shock, the humiliation for a nation which has still not come to terms with imperial withdrawal, would have been unbearable. The national decline would have been irretrievable', he wrote in 1984. 'Instead, and largely thanks to her, the country was fired with a new sense of vigour and achievement, a feeling that Britain had not lost its former capacity for action in defence of freedom'.[69]

Coles performed his familiar duties in the Private Office throughout the campaign, but on an unprecedented scale. The volume of diplomatic traffic from ambassadors, the Foreign Office, and Ministry of Defence had increased tenfold. 'It was absolutely all-consuming', he recalled. 'From the time the Argentines invaded till the day they surrendered, very little else was done in Downing Street. We were at it all day, every day, so my experience was quite unlike that of any other Foreign Office private secretary, before or after'.[70] Subsequently, Coles was tasked with acquiring the documentation to prepare Thatcher for the Falkland Islands Review (the much-maligned Franks Report) – an enquiry into how Argentine forces were permitted to invade the Falklands unimpeded. This he did dutifully with the help of his predecessor, Michael Alexander. Though the report was criticised – important facts were omitted, and some conclusions appeared perverse – Thatcher was well briefed for both the enquiry and the ensuing Parliamentary debate, held after the report had been published in January 1983.

Of the American military intervention in Grenada in October 1983, Coles notes that Thatcher's reaction, in a similar vein to the Falklands, was guided by fundamental principles. Grenada, a former British colony and still a Commonwealth state, had been invaded by US forces in a bid to crush an attempted Marxist coup against the already-Marxist government of Maurice Bishop. Soon after he was killed, amid much hype of Cuban–Soviet influence on the ground, President Reagan authorised an invasion of the Caribbean island. This was done without consulting Thatcher (or anyone else in the British government) until it was too late to halt the American action. The Prime Minister had been angered and embarrassed. Thatcher was less bothered that the US had entered a member of the Commonwealth (for which she had little affinity) than she was by the fact that the actions of her closest ally had been taken completely unilaterally. 'She was humiliated by the revelation that her vaunted relationship with Washington was rather less close than she pretended', wrote Campbell.[71] The title of Foreign Secretary Geoffrey Howe's memoir on the episode, 'Humiliation in Grenada', captured the prevailing mood.[72]

Once again Coles was a first-hand witness. He recalls that Reagan sent a telegram on 24 October at 7.15pm, informing Thatcher that he was 'considering' taking action in Grenada, but without conveying any sense of urgency. The Prime Minister duly asked Coles to prepare a draft reply counselling caution and listing reasons why intervention might be unwise. He got to work, but within three hours a second letter had arrived from the US President, 'baldly stating that he had decided to intervene'.[73] As Private Secretary, Coles had the unenviable job of telephoning the Prime Minister to ask her to return to Downing Street and relay the news. Thatcher was seething. She dispatched a strongly worded message to Reagan and, rather than waiting for a response, called him on the hot-line about 20 minutes later to deliver an earful. 'At the time I felt let down by what happened', Thatcher explained. 'At best, the British government had been made to look impotent; at worst we looked deceitful' (the previous day Howe had told the House of Commons that he had no knowledge of America's intention to intervene in Grenada). It had been timed badly from another perspective: the British government was just about to present Parliament with details about the deployment of US Cruise missiles in the UK.[74]

Writing shortly after the episode, Coles revealed the conflicting principles over which the Prime Minister had agonised:

> The threat to freedom not just in Grenada but in the whole Caribbean was manifest. Was there not also a fundamental principle that the people of a country are entitled freely to choose their government? If that freedom is subverted by tyrants, with external support, is there not a point where Western democracies should intervene to protect freedom?

By the time Coles had left Number 10, Thatcher, he claims, had still not resolved these contradictions. In the months which followed, 'she was never certain that her attitude to the Grenada affair had been right'.[75]

The major international problem during Coles's stint in the Private Office was the Cold War. During 1983, arguably the most dangerous year of the crisis since 1962, a series of events plunged East–West relations into disarray: Reagan's 'evil empire' speech and the announcement of his Strategic Defense Initiative (SDI), a space-based missile defence system; the NATO deployment of medium-range nuclear weapons systems in Western Europe; the Soviet shooting down of a Korean airliner (62 Americans were among the victims); and harrowingly, a NATO military exercise (codenamed Able Archer) in Western Europe that was interpreted by Soviet leaders as a possible prelude to a US nuclear strike. But there was not unanimity within the British policymaking machinery. 'The FCO never really shared her [Thatcher's] attitude towards the Soviet Union', explained Coles. 'They were used to dealing with the Soviets and thought it was better dealing with them than not. I think they were frustrated that she was not supportive of having a relationship with the Soviet Union'.[76]

As was his wont, Coles did not present any particular advice or policy ideas on East–West relations. Unlike his predecessor he was not an expert in the subject. George Urban's memoirs show, however, that Coles was a fixture at

Thatcher's foreign policy meetings with the CPS, usually taking copious notes. On one occasion, to Thatcher's appreciation, he removed the term 'Thatcher Doctrine' from a CPS-inspired speech prepared for the Prime Minister (intended as a rejoinder to the 'Brezhnev Doctrine', and the Soviet crackdown in Poland).[77] As with the Falklands and Grenada, Coles believed Thatcher's views on the Cold War were strongly influenced by closely held principles:

> To understand her attachment to freedom in all its depth you had to visit a communist country. Whether China, the Soviet Union or Hungary (I accompanied her to all three), she could not suppress in private, and barely in public, her hatred of a society from which freedom was absent and which was afraid of liberty.[78]

John Coles left the Private Office in June 1984. He headed for the familiar, warmer climes of the Middle East, where he was appointed Ambassador to Jordan. Later, Coles would return to Britain to end his career as head of the Diplomatic Service (1994–1997). At his farewell dinner in 1984, Thatcher – not famed for her sense of humour – delivered a speech recalling Coles's fondness for whisky and cigarettes, and his disdain for the press, Treasury, and foreign affairs 'non-experts'. She also spoke of his taste for nightlife on the last day of overseas tours.[79] Coles in turn opened up about Thatcher, penning a lengthy appreciation of the Prime Minister soon after leaving his role. It was a favourable take on a political leader he clearly admired, though not fawning (he describes, for example, Thatcher's physical appearance as 'slightly dumpy', and 'not particularly good, apart from her face'). As with his predecessor, Coles was struck by her 'extraordinary' energy, unlike any he had seen in his diplomatic career. 'It was the habit of a lifetime', he wrote. 'She had been brought up to regard hard work as a virtue'. Determination, meanwhile, was the dominant characteristic. 'Time and again', Coles explained, 'when she was resolved on a particular course, she prevented the Cabinet or the party from wavering by refusing to waver herself. Not for her the "on the one hand … on the other" approach'. This resoluteness had earned Thatcher the title of 'Iron Lady'. But Coles felt that label was too simplistic. The Prime Minister's approach was usually more 'hesitant and cautious'. Too often, he believed, people mistook Thatcher's determination for dogmatism.[80]

Coles suspected that these were good times. 'The atmosphere was highly charged. You had to cope with strong emotions, strong statements, you could often work ridiculous hours. But I always look back on it with immense pleasure, which isn't to say that every day was enjoyable'. Like Alexander, he found Thatcher's treatment of her personal staff to be 'extremely considerate, almost to a fault', however she behaved towards anyone else.[81] On the policymaking side he acknowledged that Thatcher had personalised government – seeking advice from a particular person or department, while her staff attempted to 'smooth the feathers of ministers', who felt it was their role to channel advice. Their reactions, he recalled, 'disturbed her not one bit'. Coles carried out his duties faithfully and above all quietly. He bequeathed his position to Charles Powell, a different kind of Private Secretary. Powell would become Thatcher's closest and most loyal foreign policy adviser, remaining as Private Secretary in the final, troubled period of her premiership, when she was leader of an empty husk. 'She preferred people whom she knew and trusted to be in the key civil service posts', recalled Coles glumly. 'But she never showed the slightest interest in my own political views'.[82]

Conclusion

Michael Alexander and John Coles had each spent two and a half years as Margaret Thatcher's Private Secretary for overseas affairs. During this time they had witnessed her transformation from a foreign policy novice into a highly respected international leader. Both spoke of her personal kindness, limitless energy and resolute determination to fight for British interests – often guided by strong principles. They recognised too, however, that the 'Iron Lady' *could* be for turning. As her policies towards Rhodesia, Hong Kong, Northern Ireland and the Soviet Union show, Thatcher, for all her conviction and rhetoric, was above all a pragmatist. They had also, briefly, worked together. After bequeathing his position to Coles, Alexander used his successor as an intermediary through which he could feed policy ideas to the Prime Minister. Both cooperated in briefing Thatcher and providing her with documentation ahead of the Falkland Islands enquiry.

But Alexander and Coles performed their roles differently. The former was bolder in his approach, confident in his beliefs (particularly regarding Cold War issues), and liked an argument. Alexander was prepared to offer advice or arrive at a judgement when he thought it was for the benefit of the Prime Minister. Coles, less experienced in the great overseas challenge of the time (East–West relations), was not. As Private Secretary Coles usually confined his role to that of messenger, acquiring advice from the Whitehall departments and condensing their conclusions for Thatcher. Alexander and Coles also held different political views. The former's instincts on Europe and Ireland, for example, were notably different to those of the Prime Minister. Coles, though rarely expressing his personal opinions, was generally in accord with Thatcher's policies. Neither lasted very long in their role, finding their haven in Austria and Jordan, respectively, to take up ambassadorships.

Their successor Charles Powell, as memoirs and new government files indicate, would form opinions, question assertions, and highlight issues that needed addressing. He and Thatcher were of a similar mind on most issues and became 'exceptionally close'.[83] When in 1987 the head of the Diplomatic Service, Sir Patrick Wright, called on Thatcher to end Powell's secondment from the Foreign Office, the Prime Minister would hear none of it. 'She needed Powell', wrote historian Peter Hennessy. 'No one understood her thinking as he did. Nobody but him could write the kind of speeches she required'.[84] Powell was by no means a fusion of Alexander and Coles but they did share some commonalities. Like Alexander he was intelligent, confident, and forthright in stating his views. Unlike Alexander, however, Powell's political thinking was in complete harness with the Prime Minister. Coles for his part broadly shared Thatcher's policy instincts, but viewed the parameters of his role differently to that of his successor. In Powell, Thatcher had found the synthesis.

Notes

1. See, for example, John Campbell, *The Iron Lady: Margaret Thatcher: From Grocer's Daughter to Iron Lady* (London: Vintage, 2012), 138–9, 254; E. H. H. Green, *Thatcher* (London: Hodder Arnold, 2006), 146; Hugh Stephenson, *Mrs Thatcher's First Year* (London: Jill Norman, 1980), 77.
2. For an overview of foreign policy during the Thatcher era see Green, *Thatcher*, 146–85; Ben Jackson and Robert Saunders, eds, *Making Thatcher's Britain* (Cambridge: Cambridge University Press, 2012), 199–251; Robin Renwick, *A Journey with Margaret Thatcher: Foreign Policy under the Iron Lady* (London: Biteback Publishing, 2013). Insight into Thatcher's foreign policy in a wider context can be found in David Reynolds, *Britannia Overruled: British Policy and World Power in the 20th Century* (Harlow: Longman, 2000); John W. Young, *Britain and the World in the Twentieth Century* (London: Arnold, 1997).
3. Internationally, see particularly Ronald Reagan, *An American Life* (New York: Simon & Schuster, 1990); George P. Shultz, *Turmoil and Triumph: My Years as Secretary of State* (New York: Scribner's, 1993); Casper Weinberger, *Fighting for Peace: Seven Critical Years at the Pentagon* (New York: Warner Books, 1990); Mikhail Gorbachev, *Memoirs* (London: Doubleday, 1996); Anatoly Chernyaev, *My Six Years with Gorbachev* (University Park, PA: Pennsylvania State University Press, 2000); For British ministers, FCO diplomats, and advisers see Geoffrey Howe, *Conflict of Loyalty* (London: Pan Books, 1995); George Urban, *Diplomacy and Disillusion at the Court of Margaret Thatcher: An Insider's View* (London: I.B.Tauris, 1996); Nicholas Henderson, *Mandarin: The Diaries of Nicholas Henderson* (London: Weidenfeld & Nicolson, 1994); Lord Carrington, *Reflect on Things Past* (London: Collins, 1988); Francis Pym, *The Politics of Consent* (London: Hamish Hamilton, 1984).
4. Alan Clark, *Diaries: In Power 1983–1992* (London: Phoenix, 1994).
5. For first-hand accounts of the role during the Thatcher era, see British Diplomatic Oral History Programme (BDOHP) interviews with Sir Michael Alexander, Sir John Coles and Lord (Charles) Powell, held at the Churchill Archives Centre, Cambridge.
6. Campbell, *Iron Lady*, 139.
7. Renwick, *Journey with Margaret Thatcher*, 240.
8. Margaret Thatcher, *The Downing Street Years* (London: HarperCollins, 1993).
9. For analysis of the policymaking process and conduct of diplomacy, see John W. Young, *Twentieth Century Diplomacy: A Case Study of British Practice, 1963–1976* (Cambridge: Cambridge University Press, 2012); Reynolds, *Britannia Overruled*, 1–60; John Dickie, *The New Mandarins: How British Foreign Policy Works* (London: I.B.Tauris, 2004); Ludger Helms, *Presidents, Prime Ministers and Chancellors: Executive Leadership in Western Democracies* (Basingstoke: Palgrave Macmillan, 2005); Peter Hennessy, *The Prime Minister: The Office and its Holders Since 1945* (London: Allen Lane, 2001); Gaynor Johnson, ed., *The Foreign Office and British Diplomacy in the Twentieth Century* (Abingdon: Routledge, 2005).
10. *Guardian*, 27 June 2002.
11. Interview with Sir Michael Alexander, 25 November 1998, Churchill Archives Centre, Cambridge [henceforward CAC]: DOHP 34.

184 *Aaron Donaghy*

12 Michael Alexander, *Managing the Cold War: A View from the Frontline*, ed. Keith Hamilton (London: RUSI, 2005), 10.
13 Ibid., 14.
14 *Guardian*, 27 June 2002.
15 Interview with Sir Michael Alexander, 25 November 1998, CAC: DOHP 34.
16 Charles Moore, *Margaret Thatcher: The Authorized Biography*, vol. I (London: Allen Lane, 2013), 489–90.
17 Richard Aldous, *Reagan and Thatcher: The Difficult Relationship* (London: Hutchinson, 2012), 22.
18 Campbell Craig and Fredrik Logevall, *America's Cold War: The Politics of Insecurity* (Cambridge, MA: Belknap, Harvard University Press, 2009), 303.
19 Alexander, *Managing the Cold War*, 102.
20 Thatcher, *Downing Street Years*, 87.
21 Alexander, *Managing the Cold War*, 112.
22 Interview with Sir Michael Alexander, 25 November 1998, CAC: DOHP 34.
23 Ibid., 18.
24 Alexander, *Managing the Cold War*, 101.
25 Moore, *Margaret Thatcher*, 555.
26 Campbell, *The Iron Lady*, 143.
27 Note from Alexander to Thatcher, 14 March 1980, The National Archives, Kew [henceforward TNA]: PREM 19/137.
28 Thatcher to Thomas, 19 May 1980, TNA: PREM 19/238.
29 Keeble to Carrington, 29 November 1980, TNA: PREM 19/759.
30 Note by Alexander to Thatcher, attached to Haig to Carrington, 29 August 1981, TNA: PREM 19/759.
31 Richards to Alexander, 28 January 1981, TNA: PREM 19/387.
32 Note by Alexander, on Hibbert to FCO, 27 January 1981, TNA: PREM 19/387.
33 Interview with Sir Michael Alexander, 25 November 1998, CAC: DOHP 34.
34 Ibid.
35 Note by Thatcher, on Boys-Smith to Alexander, 28 May 1981, TNA: PREM 19/505.
36 Interview with Sir Michael Alexander, 25 November 1998, CAC: DOHP 34.
37 Ibid., 48.
38 Reynolds, *Britannia Overruled*, 249–50.
39 Green, *Thatcher*, 176.
40 Interview with Sir Michael Alexander, 25 November 1998, CAC: DOHP 34.
41 Ibid., 50.
42 Keith Hamilton, 'Introduction', in Alexander, *Managing the Cold War*, xix.
43 Quoted in ibid.
44 Interview with Sir Michael Alexander, 25 November 1998, CAC: DOHP 34.
45 Alexander to Coles, 14 March 1984, TNA: PREM 19/1494.
46 Ibid.
47 Note by Thatcher, on Coles to Thatcher, 16 April 1984, TNA: PREM 19/1494.
48 Alexander, *Managing the Cold War*, 129.
49 Interview with Sir Michael Alexander, 25 November 1998, CAC: DOHP 34; Alexander, *Managing the Cold War*, 130.
50 Interview with Sir Michael Alexander, 25 November 1998, CAC: DOHP 34.
51 Interview with Sir John Coles, 2 November 1999, CAC: DOHP 46.
52 Ibid., 17–18.
53 Ibid., 19–20.
54 Ibid.
55 Ibid., 21.
56 Moore, *Thatcher*, 752.

57 Chris Mullin, *A View from the Foothills: The Diaries of Chris Mullin* (London: Profile Books, 2009).
58 Reagan Library, NSC Country File Box 91283, Minutes of NSC meeting (Poland), 22 December 1981.
59 Leading works on the Falklands War include Max Hastings and Simon Jenkins, *The Battle for the Falklands* (London: Michael Joseph, 1983); Lawrence Freedman, *The Official History of the Falklands Campaign*, 2 vols (London: Routledge, 2007).
60 Moore, *Thatcher*, 664.
61 *Falkland Islands Review: Report of a Committee of Privy Counsellors* (Franks Report), Cmnd. 8787 (London: HMSO, 1983), para. 152.
62 For analysis of the naval task force sent by the Labour government in 1977, see Aaron Donaghy, *The British Government and the Falkland Islands, 1974–1979* (Basingstoke: Palgrave Macmillan, 2014).
63 *Falkland Islands Review*, para. 152.
64 Ibid.
65 Freedman, *Falklands Campaign*, vol. I, 160.
66 Interview with Sir John Coles, 2 November 1999, CAC: DOHP 46.
67 Appreciation of Margaret Thatcher, 14 June 1984, CAC: THCR 3/24.
68 Campbell, *Iron Lady*, 139.
69 Appreciation of Margaret Thatcher, 14 June 1984, CAC: THCR 3/24.
70 Interview with Sir John Coles, 2 November 1999, CAC: DOHP 46.
71 Campbell, *Iron Lady*, 267.
72 Howe, *Conflict of Loyalty*, 325–37.
73 Appreciation of Margaret Thatcher, 14 June 1984, CAC: THCR 3/24.
74 Thatcher, *Downing Street Years*, 328–32.
75 Appreciation of Margaret Thatcher, 14 June 1984, CAC: THCR 3/24.
76 Moore, *Thatcher*, 556–7.
77 Note by Coles to Thatcher, 30 January 1984, CAC: THCR 2/11/3/3.
78 Appreciation of Margaret Thatcher, 14 June 1984, CAC: THCR 3/24.
79 Notes for Margaret Thatcher speech (farewell to John Coles), 12 June 1984, CAC: THCR 1/17/114.
80 Appreciation of Margaret Thatcher, 14 June 1984, CAC: THCR 3/24.
81 Interview with Sir John Coles, 2 November 1999, CAC: DOHP 46.
82 Appreciation of Margaret Thatcher, 14 June 1984, CAC: THCR 3/24.
83 Renwick, *Journey*, 240.
84 Hennessy, *Prime Minister*, 405–6.

References

Aldous, Richard, *Reagan and Thatcher: The Difficult Relationship* (London: Hutchinson, 2012).
Campbell, John, *The Iron Lady: Margaret Thatcher: From Grocer's Daughter to Iron Lady* (London: Vintage, 2012).
Carrington, Lord, *Reflect on Things Past* (London: Collins, 1988).
Chernyaev, Anatoly, *My Six Years with Gorbachev* (University Park, PA: Pennsylvania State University Press, 2000).
Clark, Alan, *Diaries: In Power 1983–1992* (London: Phoenix, 1994).
Craig, Campbell and Fredrik Logevall, *America's Cold War: The Politics of Insecurity* (Cambridge, MA: Belknap Press, Harvard University Press, 2009).
Dickie, John, *The New Mandarins: How British Foreign Policy Works* (London: I.B.Tauris, 2004).

Donaghy, Aaron, *The British Government and the Falkland Islands, 1974–1979* (Basingstoke: Palgrave Macmillan, 2014).
Gorbachev, Mikhail, *Memoirs* (London: Doubleday, 1996).
Green, E. H. H., *Thatcher* (London: Hodder Arnold, 2006).
Helms, Ludger, *Presidents, Prime Ministers and Chancellors: Executive Leadership in Western Democracies* (Basingstoke: Palgrave Macmillan, 2005).
Henderson, Nicholas, *Mandarin: The Diaries of Nicholas Henderson* (London: Weidenfeld & Nicolson, 1994).
Hennessy, Peter, *The Prime Minister: The Office and its Holders since 1945* (London: Allen Lane, 2001).
Howe, Geoffrey, *Conflict of Loyalty* (London: Pan Books, 1995).
Jackson, Ben and Robert Saunders, eds, *Making Thatcher's Britain* (Cambridge: Cambridge University Press, 2012).
Johnson, Gaynor, ed., *The Foreign Office and British Diplomacy in the Twentieth Century* (Abingdon: Routledge, 2005).
Moore, Charles, *Margaret Thatcher: The Authorized Biography*, vol. I (London: Allen Lane, 2013).
Mullin, Chris, *A View from the Foothills: The Diaries of Chris Mullin* (London: Profile Books, 2009).
Pym, Francis, *The Politics of Consent* (London: Hamish Hamilton, 1984).
Reagan, Ronald, *An American Life* (New York: Simon & Schuster, 1990).
Renwick, Robin, *A Journey with Margaret Thatcher: Foreign Policy under the Iron Lady* (London: Biteback Publishing, 2013).
Reynolds, David, *Britannia Overruled: British Policy and World Power in the 20th Century* (Harlow: Longman, 2000).
Shultz, George P., *Turmoil and Triumph: My Years as Secretary of State* (New York: Scribners, 1993).
Stephenson, Hugh, *Mrs Thatcher's First Year* (London: Jill Norman, 1980).
Thatcher, Margaret, *The Downing Street Years* (London: HarperCollins, 1993).
Urban, George, *Diplomacy and Disillusion at the Court of Margaret Thatcher: An Insider's View* (London: I.B.Tauris, 1996).
Weinberger, Casper, *Fighting for Peace: Seven Critical Years at the Pentagon* (New York: Warner Books, 1990).
Young, John W., *Britain and the World in the Twentieth Century* (London: Arnold, 1997).
Young, John W., *Twentieth Century Diplomacy: A Case Study of British Practice, 1963–1976* (Cambridge: Cambridge University Press, 2012).

Conclusion
The Prime Minister's Private Office from John Martin to Chris Martin

Anthony Seldon

The foreign affairs Private Secretary

There were 25 Principal Private Secretaries (PPSs) to the Prime Minister between John Martin in 1945 and Chris Martin in 2015, and 27 foreign affairs Private Secretaries (PSs). The latter were the most senior of the team of three to five Private Secretaries who worked with the PPS and who together shaped, steered and guided the 14 Prime Ministers who served during the 70-year period.

For much of the time, the PPS and foreign affairs PS worked side by side in the small office in Number 10 through the double doors at the end of the Cabinet Room, a space later claimed by Prime Minister Tony Blair. The PPS and the foreign affairs Private Secretary were then relocated to a larger oblong room through more double doors on the opposite side to the Cabinet Room. They were not to return, even though Gordon Brown vacated the room for the large room in 12 Downing Street (the traditional home of the Government Chief Whip). The physical proximity mattered: 'We shared an office, we chatted away all the time, we'd hear each other on the phone and comment on what each other was doing', said Alex Allan (PPS 1992–1997), describing his relationship with the foreign affairs Private Secretary, with whom he worked alongside.[1] The PPS was the top dog, by dint of age, seniority in the Civil Service hierarchy, and in responsibility to the Prime Minster across the range of governmental activities.

The PPS and foreign affairs Private Secretary's room, 1945–1999

The relationship between these two high-grade people, the PPS often from the Treasury, the foreign affairs PS almost always from the Foreign and Commonwealth Office (FCO), is fascinating and intriguing, as will be seen.. The PPS rarely pulled rank on the foreign affairs PS, leaving them largely a free hand, apart from those areas, not inconsiderable, where foreign and domestic policy were inextricably combined. This chapter will examine the job and incumbents of the PPS position, before turning to the position of the foreign affairs Private Secretary, and concludes by looking at the factors that explain why some foreign affairs Private Secretaries have been far more influential on the formation of policy than even the Foreign Secretary, while others have been comparatively modest figures. But we begin by turning our attention to the landscape before 1945.

There were clear antecedents for the post-war foreign affairs Private Secretaries. Professor W. G. S. Adams, an Oxford political scientist, worked very closely on foreign policy with Prime Minister David Lloyd George after Lloyd George took office in December 1916. Ramsay MacDonald did not appoint himself Foreign Secretary when he became Prime Minister for the second time 1929 (as he had when he first became Prime Minister in 1924). Instead he appointed Arthur Henderson as to the Foreign Office, while leaning heavily on the advice of Robert Vansittart who had been a Private Secretary at Downing Street until 1930, when he was appointed Permanent Under-Secretary (PUS) for Foreign Affairs. Arthur Rucker was PPS to Neville Chamberlain as Prime Minister (1937–1940) and was very close to him on his foreign policy, including appeasement, as was another official on whom Chamberlain relied even more heavily, Horace Wilson. By the time Chamberlain arrived at Number 10 in 1937, the job of a Private Secretary specialising in foreign affairs had become consolidated.[2] However, it was only after the Second World War that the job of foreign affairs Private Secretary properly crystallised.

The Principal Private Secretary to the Prime Minister

All 25 incumbents of the role of PPS to the Prime Minister have been white and male. Of these, 21 (84 per cent) of the PPSs from 1945 to 2015 went to Oxbridge, including 12 to Oxford and 9 to Cambridge. Of the remainder, one went to King's College London, one to Cardiff, one to Bristol, while one was an external student at London University. Their school backgrounds were more catholic, with only one going to Eton (Robert Armstrong), while three attended Harrow (Jock Colville, Robin Butler and Alex Allan).

Eight of the 25 (32 per cent) appear to have come from a working-class or lower middle-class background. Notably these included Michael Halls, PPS to Harold Wilson 1966–1970, the son of a milk carrier and the most working-class of them all, and Ken Stowe, PPS to Wilson and James Callaghan 1975–1979, the son of a spectacle frames maker from Dagenham who won a scholarship to Oxford. The average age on appointment was 42 years old and the average length of service was three and a half years. The youngest appointee was Oliver Robbins, aged only 31, while the oldest was Michael Halls, aged 51, brought in because he had made a favourable impression on Wilson when he had been President of the Board of Trade (1947–1951) and shared his outlook on life. Over 60 per cent have come from the Treasury, with the department becoming more dominant as we move towards the present. Two came from the Foreign Office (Colville and John Holmes), two from the Dominions Office (John Martin and David Pitblado, who subsequently transferred to the Treasury), one came from the Colonial Office (Leslie Rowan, who transferred to the Treasury), while one came from the Ministry of Defence (Clive Whitmore).

The post of PPS to the Prime Minister is for the *crème-de-la-crème* of the Civil Service. The great majority went on subsequently to head departments, one becoming Head of the Civil Service (Laurence Helsby), and four additionally becoming Cabinet Secretaries (Armstrong, Robin Butler, Andrew Turnbull, and Jeremy Heywood). Halls and Stowe were appointed by Wilson expressly because they did not have a Treasury background. Helsby and Turnbull went on to become Permanent Secretaries to the Treasury. Stowe went on to become the Permanent Secretary at the Department of Health, while Clive Whitmore became Permanent Secretary at the Ministry of Defence, followed by the Home Office.

Not all rose to the top of Whitehall after leaving Downing Street. Jock Colville left the Civil Service with Churchill in 1955 for the City, feeling that the Civil Service could never offer him the same rich experience again. Colville is one of the very few PPSs to write books, a memoir called *Footprints in Time*, and his diaries, *Fringes of Power*.[3] John Holmes (1997–1999) published *The Politics of Humanity*.[4] More foreign affairs Private Secretaries have published books, most recently Tom Fletcher with *Naked Diplomacy*. Frederick Bishop, who had been such an influential PPS, resigned prematurely from the Civil Service in 1965 after Whitehall infighting, and became Director General of the National Trust. Derek Mitchell, whose Treasury background and outlook did not chime with Wilson's taste, left the Civil Service prematurely for the City in 1977. Two died in office: Michael Halls, whose widow sued the state claiming that he had died prematurely because of overwork at Number 10, and Chris Martin, PPS to David Cameron, who died of cancer in November 2015, aged 42. Alexander (Sandy) Isserlis was a very rare exception of an appointment that was unsuccessful; chosen by Wilson in 1970 to succeed Michael Halls, he failed to appeal to Edward Heath after he became Prime Minister in June 1970. Heath soon replaced him with Robert Armstrong.[5]

The Principal Private Secretaries can be divided into four categories.

Very powerful, who became too openly identified with their Prime Minister

The four key figures here are John Martin, Jock Colville, Frederick Bishop and Tim Bligh. Martin had been PPS to Churchill since 1940 and was a member of the inner political, as well as family, circle. He contributed to historian John Wheeler-Bennett's *Action this Day*, published in 1968 as a riposte to the image of Churchill as the sickly, ailing leader portrayed in the diaries of his doctor, Lord Moran.[6] Martin remained in the Civil Service, returning to the Colonial Office in July 1945. But his career did not blossom as did many other subsequent incumbents of the PPS post, finishing as High Commissioner of Malta in 1967. He subsequently worked with Martin Gilbert, Churchill's official biographer, who found him 'shy, diffident, and modest'.[7]

Jock Colville was brought back by Churchill as joint PPS alongside incumbent David Pitblado when he returned to power in 1951. Colville had served with Churchill as a junior Private Secretary during the war, and Churchill knew and trusted him. Colville was closer to Churchill than anyone in his last period in government from 1951 to 1955, and worked very much in a team with Cabinet Secretary Norman Brook and Parliamentary Private Secretary (and son-in-law) Christopher Soames to compensate for Churchill's deficiencies as a peacetime Prime Minster, above all covering up for his stroke during the summer of 1953. Colville concentrated in particular on foreign policy, as it pre-occupied much of Churchill's time. On 11 May 1953, Churchill delivered a major speech following the death of Soviet leader Joseph Stalin in March, suggesting a new era in Western–Soviet relations, instigated by high-level summit talks. Churchill deliberately went against the Foreign Office advice, from PUS William Strang and other senior officials, including Pierson Dixon, and Frank Roberts. Colville was dispatched by Churchill to hold secret meetings with officials at the Soviet Embassy without the knowledge of the Foreign Office.[8]

Frederick Bishop had made his mark as an Assistant Secretary to Norman Brook, the Cabinet Secretary, which explained Brook's recommendation that Bishop become Anthony Eden's PPS in 1956. Bishop was a forceful figure with Eden, shaping the domestic thinking of a man whose experience was almost entirely on foreign policy. Harold Macmillan kept him on when he became Prime Minister in January 1957. Bishop came to be a powerful influence also on foreign policy, notably being sent by the Prime Minister to Washington in 1957 for talks with John Foster Dulles, Secretary of State, who described him as 'genuine, intimate, and effective'. In 1959, he travelled with Macmillan to see Soviet leader Nikita Khrushchev in Moscow.[9] Bishop's influence was openly resented by the Foreign Office, as had Colville's been before. He became Deputy Secretary to the Cabinet in 1959, and continued to advise Macmillan on foreign affairs, including his attempt to join the European Economic Community in 1961. Bishop found life difficult after Labour returned to power in October 1964; in June 1965, after he let it be known that he wanted to resign from the Civil Service, Richard Crossman wrote in his diary 'he should be sent off as soon as possible'.[10]

Tim Bligh was another who came to see his primary loyalty not to the Civil Service but to his Prime Minister, and who became a close member of the tight political and family group that surrounded Harold Macmillan. Macmillan wanted Bligh on his epic African tour in 1960 which lasted six weeks, and equally wanted to keep him by his side until the end of his premiership in October 1963. Bligh came to public attention in 1962 during the Profumo affair. In June of that year it was to Bligh that Profumo first confessed his guilt, and it was Bligh who told Macmillan about Profumo's resignation letter.[11] When the high-powered Derek Mitchell, who had been PPS to the Chancellor of the Exchequer, was appointed his successor, Bligh refused to move out of Downing Street, feeling himself uniquely qualified to handle any change of government that would come in the general election which had to take place no later than the autumn of 1964. Mitchell turned to William Armstrong, Permanent Secretary to the Treasury, to complain that Bligh was refusing to move. Armstrong 'advised him to find a desk in a remote part of Number 10 and bide his time'.[12] It took fully four months before Mitchell was able to prise Bligh out, and take control of the PPS's desk in the traditional office beyond to the Cabinet Room. Bligh, like Colville, left the Civil Service when he ceased to be PPS, becoming a director of the Thomson, the media organisation, before becoming active in local politics as a Conservative, and dying in March 1969.

Very powerful, but correct

The second category were highly influential in their position, and close to their Prime Ministers, but saw themselves always as civil servants, and remained in the Civil Service after they left Number 10. It includes Leslie Rowan (1945–1947), who became Principal Private Secretary aged 37 in 1945 in succession to John Martin. Rowan had a dazzling career in the Treasury in the 1930s, and had joined the Number 10 Private Office in 1941, where he too became close to the Churchill family. He was close to Attlee during their two years together. Although Attlee had been Deputy Prime Minister since 1940, Rowan had much to teach him about the workings of Number 10. In 1947, he left for the Ministry for Economic Affairs, and then to the Treasury, before leaving the Civil Service aged 50 in 1958, for the private sector.

Robert Armstrong succeeded the ill-chosen Alexander 'Sandy' Isserlis in 1970, and became an all-powerful adviser to Edward Heath (Prime Minister, 1970–1974), while remaining correct and loyal to the Civil Service. So gifted was he that Harold Wilson, on his return to power in 1974, who had traditionally been so suspicious of the Civil Service, especially Eton-educated officials such as Armstrong who had spent their careers at the Treasury, decided to retain him on his return in March 1974. Armstrong did not return to the Treasury in 1975, but went to the Home Office, initially as Deputy, and then as Permanent Secretary (1977–1979), before becoming Cabinet Secretary.

Ken Stowe, his successor, was another formidably strong operator, serving Wilson for his last failing year as Prime Minister. He then served Callaghan throughout his three years, at his side throughout the IMF financial crisis in 1976, and remaining with Thatcher for her first weeks as Prime Minister, before becoming Permanent Secretary at the Northern Ireland Office in 1979, an unusual promotion directly so soon after giving up as the PPS.

Alex Allan became John Major's PPS in 1992, having spent his career in the Treasury, most recently for three years as PPS to Nigel Lawson as Chancellor of the Exchequer. Major's premiership was unusually troubled by opposition from his Conservative backbenchers, notably over Europe, and Allan provided tenacious support throughout, becoming close to him personally, and greatly trusted by Major's inner team. So effective was he that Blair retained his services until August 1997.

Jeremy Heywood, another Treasury official, served Blair effectively as PPS from 1999 to 2003, and became a still more influential figure when he returned to the more senior title of 'Permanent Secretary to Number 10', under Gordon Brown from 2008 to 2010, the highest-ranked PPS of the period. By this time, Heywood had acquired unrivalled knowledge and command across Whitehall, and his powerful presence in the two years did much to compensate for Brown's deficiencies as Prime Minister, in much the same way that Colville had compensated for the ailing Churchill (1951–1955), and Bishop for the tortured Eden (1966–1957).

Chris Martin, finally, was another to have spent his career in the Treasury, before coming into Number 10 as PPS and Director-General of the Prime Minister's Office, a new and slightly more junior title, on Heywood's departure in 2012. Martin had spent almost his entire career in the Civil Service working under Gordon Brown, and it was a mark of his exceptional diplomatic and personal skills that he quickly gained the trust of Cameron and his team, becoming a deeply respected and much loved figure until his untimely death in November 2015.

Effective and correct, but not personally close to the Prime Minister

Personal chemistry matters: it does not always mean that the PPS becomes part of the inner circle. The figures in this category were always highly efficient dispatching business, but not intimate with the Prime Minister. In this category come Laurence Helsby, who served Attlee from 1947 to 1950, Ivan Rogers, who served under Blair from 2003 to 2006, and James Bowler under Cameron from 2010 to 2011. Helsby was too austere, Blair had his own court with Jonathan Powell as Chief of Staff, and Bowler was too retiring and correct.

The PPS is not close to the Prime Minister, and the relationship is distant and not notably effective

In this category come David Pitblado, who served Churchill and then Eden from 1951 to 1956, and who suffered from being overshadowed by Colville, parachuted in over his head by Churchill in 1951; Derek Mitchell, who had to combat Tim Bligh in his first months, as well as Wilson's Political Secretary Marcia Williams; Sandy Isserlis, with whom Ted Heath did not bond; Nigel Wicks, a brilliant mind, who served Thatcher between 1985 and 1988 but was overshadowed by foreign affairs Private Secretary Charles Powell; and Tom Scholar, an equally talented Treasury official, who worked as PPS with Brown, 2007–2008, and who was unable to replicate the close relationship he had enjoyed with Brown when he had been PPS to him as Chancellor of the Exchequer (1997–2001).

The job of PPS changed when Blair brought in a new position of 'Chief of Staff', with powers of issuing instructions to civil servants, in the form of Jonathan Powell (1997–2007). It inevitably meant a downgrading of the position of the PPS, as he was no longer the key figure in Number 10 channelling information to the Prime Minister. Thatcher had appointed David Wolfson to the title of Chief of Staff from 1979 to 1985, but his was a very subordinate position. Brown appointed Stephen Carter as Chief of Staff in 2008, but it was not a success, and the position was revived by Cameron in 2010 with the appointment of Ed Llewelyn as Chief of Staff, concentrating largely on foreign affairs.

The five phases of the foreign affairs Private Secretaries

Five phases can be discerned in the evolution of the foreign affairs Private Secretary position, each new phase sparked by a particularly activist individual, an official or the Prime Minister. Over the 70 years, the core task of the foreign affairs Private Secretary has changed little – to connect the Prime Minister with Whitehall departments, notably the Foreign Office (FO), and the Foreign and Commonwealth Office (FCO) as it became known after 1968. Over the years after 1945, the volume of work emanating from the Empire and Commonwealth declined, while new activities, including defence, intelligence and security, overseas development, Northern Ireland and Europe were all added.

Phase 1: Restrained foreign affairs Private Secretaries, 1945–1963

Although the foreign affairs Private Secretary position had antecedents going back to David Lloyd George, it only became consolidated with the arrival of Neville Chamberlain as Prime Minister in May 1937. In this first period, a succession of five foreign affairs Private Secretaries, from Jock Colville through to Anthony Montague Browne in 1955, all relatively junior in rank, came to Number 10 from the Foreign Office, to provide Private Secretary support. Some, like Colville in 1945, and Montague Browne from 1952 to 1955 became personally close to the Prime Minister, but all were overshadowed by the Foreign Secretary, and saw themselves as conveyors of advice, and were seen by the Foreign Secretary and by the Foreign Office as purveyors of advice rather than as deciders themselves.

This began to change when Colville returned in 1951, though the position technically was as PPS. Then came Guy Millard, who had worked as a Private Secretary to Anthony Eden as Foreign Secretary during the war, who was asked by Eden to join him in Number 10 when he became Prime Minister in 1955. Millard became dragged into the Suez crisis. On 14 August 1956, for example, he was at Chequers with Eden when the French first suggested the plan for an Anglo-French force to separate Israeli invaders from the Egyptians. Eden told Millard 'there's no need to take notes'; Millard was deeply uncomfortable with the position in which he found himself placed.[13]

But it was Philip de Zulueta who brought this first period of restrained Private Secretaries to an end. De Zulueta had been brought in from the Foreign Office by Eden in 1955, alongside Guy Millard, unusually, so Eden had two foreign affairs Private Secretaries. Additionally, his PPS Frederick Bishop was heavily involved in foreign policy. Harold Macmillan kept de Zulueta on after Millard left in 1957. 'Philip knows my mind', Macmillan said of him, and the two men became exceptionally close, both personally and over policy. As Macmillan's friend and Private Secretary Max Egremont wrote, de Zulueta admired

Macmillan's 'style of government, intellect, and wit'.[14] Macmillan knighted de Zulueta in his resignations honours in 1963 – the first foreign affairs Private Secretary to receive such a high honour from a retiring Prime Minister. De Zulueta continued to work for Alec Douglas-Home (Prime Minister 1963–1964) but left the Foreign Office to become a merchant banker, joining Hill Samuel in 1965, as had Colville. It was clear that the Foreign Office was greatly disconcerted by the position that de Zulueta had obtained, as indeed was the Civil Service more generally by the power Macmillan's PPS, Tim Bligh, had acquired.

Phase 2: Heavyweight foreign affairs Private Secretaries, 1964–1991

After the de Zulueta saga, the Foreign Office powerfully reasserted its right to have its own figure in Number 10, who would not go native, but retain fidelity to the Foreign Office. In that quest, they came up with two high-flyers in a row: Oliver Wright (1964–1966) and Michael Palliser (1966–1969).

Oliver Wright was as solid a Foreign Office figure as could be found. He had entered the Civil Service in 1945 and was thought to have excelled as Private Secretary to Alec Douglas-Home as Foreign Secretary (1960–1963), who was thus keen that he follow him across Downing Street to Number 10 as foreign affairs Private Secretary in succession to de Zulueta. Wilson then decided to retain him after he became PM. Wright completed his career as Ambassador to West Germany, and finally to the United States from 1982 to 1986. He was succeeded by Palliser. The epitome of the establishment, he was educated at Wellington College, joined the Coldstream Guards, and married the daughter of Paul-Henri Spaak, Prime Minister of Belgium. He entered the Diplomatic Service in 1947 and served out his three years as foreign affairs Private Secretary, the traditional length of service, from 1966 to 1969. He went on to become an unusually long serving Permanent Under-Secretary at the FCO (1975–1982).

Three foreign affairs Private Secretaries succeeded them who were more akin to the officials in the first phase than the two stellar heavyweights who preceded them or those that followed. Edward 'Teddy' Youde joined in 1969. When he left prematurely, through ill health in early 1970, the Permanent Under-Secretary recommended the appointment of a promising young diplomat, Christopher Everett, on the grounds that he had accepted a job later that year to become a headmaster and would thus be there for only a short period until his successor took over. That successor, Peter Moon, succeeded after some ten weeks. It was an odd choice; Moon confessed to a colleague, 'I don't know why I am accepting this job!'

Moon continued as Private Secretary for foreign affairs at Number 10 until he had completed his allotted term in 1972, but he became less involved in European business than Palliser. When Ted Heath took office as PM in June 1970 the revival of negotiations for British accession to the EEC was top of his agenda. Cabinet Secretary Burke Trend, an experienced and convinced Atlanticist and committed to the support of Britain's role in the Commonwealth, did not share Heath's enthusiasm for a closer relationship with Europe and specifically for British accession to the European Economic Community (EEC). As a result, as Armstrong said: 'Heath used me for things to do with the negotiations for accession to the EEC for which he might in other circumstances have used the Cabinet Secretary, and I got deeply involved in Europe'.[15] Both Youde and Moon went on to successful careers in the Diplomatic Service. Youde's notably culminated as Governor of Hong Kong (1982–1986), where he died in office, while Moon finished his career as Ambassador to Kuwait (1985–1987).

The FCO was keen that his successor should claw back lost ground and nominated Tom Bridges, son of the former Head of the Civil Service, Edward Bridges (1945–1956). Armstrong supported the appointment of Bridges, having known him since school at Eton. They rapidly worked out a *modus operandi* with Bridges overseeing non-European foreign business, sharing Europe but leaving the lion's share of it to Armstrong. Relations with the FCO improved further still when Antony Acland became PPS to Foreign Secretary Douglas-Home in 1972; Armstrong, Bridges and Acland were all friendly: Acland too had been at Eton.[16]

Four Foreign Office heavyweights were appointed foreign affairs Private Secretary following Bridges: Patrick Wright, who went on to become Permanent Under-Secretary at the FCO (1986–1991), Bryan Cartledge, whose career culminated as Ambassador to the Soviet Union (1985–1988), Michael Alexander, who became Ambassador to NATO (1986–1992) and John Coles, who also concluded his career as Permanent Under-Secretary at the FCO (1994–1997). While the post of foreign affairs Private Secretary is nominally the choice of the Prime Minister, in practice, the premier choses from a short-list of carefully selected candidates put forward by the FCO. It was anxious to exercise maximum leverage over who was selected.

Charles Powell was ironically one such FCO nominee when appointed in 1984 to succeed John Coles. Little did the FCO know it, but the *status quo* was about to be shattered, as convincingly as it had been when de Zulueta had held the post. Significantly, they both served not the usual three years, but seven years and more in post. Ironically, Thatcher had initially resisted the appointment of the ultra-smooth diplomat Powell: she was very wary of the FCO, notably after what she saw as errors in the Falklands War build-up. But her PPS Robin Butler had been a neighbour of Powell in Dulwich in South London during the 1970s; Butler rated Powell, and swayed her. Butler indeed 'was puzzled at the resistance she put up to Powell's appointment'.[17]

Thatcher was responsible for another innovation. To bolster still further her advice and to balance that from the FCO, she made the unusual appointment in 1982 of Anthony Parsons, the British Ambassador to the UN, as her special adviser on foreign affairs. She had come to admire Percy Cradock, who succeeded Youde in 1978 as Ambassador to China, notably his work on the agreement with China over Hong Kong, resulting in the Joint Declaration of 1984. So she decided that she would bring him back after his retirement from the Diplomatic Service in 1983 as her 'Foreign Affairs Adviser' to beef up her advice in Number 10. In 1985, she asked him to combine that role with Chairman of the Joint Intelligence Committee (JIC), which he later said 'gave me a supporting staff of a kind that the Downing Street arrangements denied'.[18]

Cradock looked as if he would become her core adviser on foreign policy advice. But his influence was soon to be eclipsed by Charles Powell, though he nevertheless remained in position until 1992 when he was succeeded by Rodric Braithwaite, Britain's Ambassador to the Soviet Union, who held the joint post until 1994, after which the Foreign Policy Adviser role lapsed. After that, 'the JIC chairmanship was combined with the Cabinet Office post of head of the OD [Overseas and Defence] Secretariat'.[19]

When John Major first saw Powell in Number 10, his comment to him echoed Callaghan's to Patrick Wright: Major said 'I don't know if I can do this job'.[20] Major leant heavily on Powell, his consummate courtier, and was sorry to see him depart in March 1991 to be replaced by Stephen Wall, who had been his PPS during Major's brief tenure as Foreign Secretary in 1989.

Phase 3: Return to normality, 1991–2001

Normality returned with a series of four foreign affairs Private Secretaries, under whom a more regular relationship between the FCO and Number 10 was re-established. Wall had experience of working in the Number 10 Press Office in the 1970s when Patrick Wright had been foreign affairs Private Secretary. He had not been given direct instructions from the FCO to reclaim power, but had formed his own views. These were bolstered by talking to Cradock, who was far from an all-out admirer of Charles Powell, and who had pronounced views about how to conduct the job of foreign affairs Private Secretary. Wall had come to believe that Powell's *modus operandi*, especially in Thatcher's latter years, had restricted her access to key individuals, thus narrowing down her range of advice.[21] Wall's great expertise was Europe, which was timely as the Maastricht negotiations and their aftermath dominated his time at Number 10. But he and Major were close personally, liking and admiring each other, and Wall's support was crucial during Major's difficult years, including Black Wednesday, when Britain was ejected from the ERM in September 1992.[22] He described his job thus:

> It was the classic Private Secretary job of acting as the conduit for the Prime Minister into Whitehall, and offering the PM advice on a whole range of foreign and defence policy issues, and at the very end of the period, on Northern Ireland as well.[23]

After Wall departed to become Ambassador in Lisbon, he arranged for the Majors in the summer of 1993 to stay on a cousin's farm in the Douro in Portugal.[24] Major resented losing Wall in March 1993 in the midst of the Maastricht negotiations through Parliament. His successor, Roderic Lyne, was a specialist in Soviet affairs and security issues. Lyne, who had been a junior

Private Secretary to Peter Carrington as Foreign Secretary from 1979, was nevertheless adept at forging personal relationships. Major soon became as close to him, and as dependant on his sound advice, as he had been on Wall.

Major's time at Number 10 is indeed remarkable for a Prime Minister in his forging closer links in general with officials than with politicians.[25] Lyne's value to Major was across the board, including helping him through a difficult early relationship with new President Bill Clinton from January 1993, and during a turbulent period in history with post-Soviet Russia. But it was primarily in Northern Ireland that Lyne's expertise was to prove of salient value to Major, when he helped pave the way for a new era that led up to the Good Friday Agreement of 1998. Wall and Lyne both enjoyed a successful relationship with PPS Alex Allan, and both sides knew the frontiers: 'Formally, they reported to me', said Allan. 'I'm not sure though that I was *superior*, because they were the experts on the subjects they dealt with. I respected them as the professionals on foreign matters. If it was really big issues, then I'd be involved as well'.[26]

Lyne was succeeded in early 1996 by another FCO high-flyer, John Holmes, who had a more eclectic background as a specialist on the European Union, the Soviet Union, the Middle East and India. But Major's mind was not as much on foreign policy in his last year and a half when Holmes was at Number 10; he missed Douglas Hurd, who had been Foreign Secretary throughout Major's premiership until his departure in 1995. In his place came the highly proficient Malcolm Rifkind, whom he trusted to get on with the business.

Tony Blair's arrival in May 1997 set in motion the fourth transition in the foreign affairs Private Secretary's position, which eventually came in 2001. Jonathan Powell, younger brother of Charles, had left the Diplomatic Service to join Blair as Chief of Staff in 1995 while Labour were still in opposition. After the transition to Number 10, Powell was given a new title, 'Downing Street Chief of Staff', with the ability to give instructions to civil servants, unprecedented for a political appointee. Powell's particular expertise was the United States, having become close to the Clinton team from the time of his posting to the British Embassy in Washington in 1991. In May 1997, Powell moved into the Private Office alongside PPS Alex Allan and foreign affairs Private Secretary John Holmes. The initial plan was for Powell to take on part of the work Allan had been doing after he left, and John Holmes, promoted to PPS, would take on other aspects.

But Whitehall savvy was soon felt to be needed, so the practised Jeremy Heywood was brought in as PPS, and John Sawers joined in January 1999 as the traditional foreign affairs Private Secretary to the Prime Minister. Sawers was one of the brightest young officials in the Foreign Office, who unusually had experience of working for MI6. Whereas Major had found it perfectly natural to have officials as part of his inner circle, it took time for Blair to establish a close personal relationship with him:

> I was the first change to his inner team and he hadn't wanted John Holmes to leave. But over time I felt I became part of his team, helped by sharing

an office with Jonathan Powell and Jeremy Heywood, and the three of us worked very closely together as part of his office.[27]

Sawers saw himself very much in the lineage of Wall, Lyne and Holmes:

> It was the same job, in the sense that the line of communication was straight to the PM, and his Cabinet colleagues via their private offices. Crucially it meant being the point of contact with the White House, the Bundeskanzleramt, the Élysée, the Kremlin and other key Prime Ministerial and Presidential offices.[28]

It was a busy period, including the Kosovo War, the Northern Ireland agreement, Iraq sanctions, and building a relationship with the George W. Bush administration from January 2001.[29] Sawers went on to head MI6 (2009–2014).

Sawers wondered whether the traditional foreign affairs Private Secretary's role needed revision. He was pressing at an open door. Blair and Powell too had concluded that the structure for foreign, defence and security advice in Britain amateur and antiquated compared to the more streamlined structures they saw in the capitals of the US, France or Germany. Typically, one very senior figure there would coordinate policy advice on foreign policy and security matters, channel it up to the national leader, and have a role in ensuring it was implemented. This figure would be very senior – four-star rank – whereas the foreign affairs Private Secretary's role was only two-star equivalent.

Phase 4: Joint Number 10/Cabinet Office experiment, 2001–2010

Blair in his first term struggled to find an effective *modus operandi* to make his will felt in Whitehall on domestic and foreign policy: his and Powell's frustrations mounted over those years. Sawers made it clear he wanted to leave after the June 2001 election, and in his last few months started feeding into the system ideas for a fresh structure after his departure. He believed that the job of being the Prime Minister's closest official on foreign policy issues needed to be combined with the head of the Cabinet Office structures coordinating the Whitehall machine. These were overseen by two bodies, the Overseas/Defence Policy Secretariat and the European Secretariat in the Cabinet Office:

> It was partly the mix of issues that Tony Blair was dealing with, partly the way he liked to work, but also the growing requirement that Number 10 at the centre had direct authority over the diverse Whitehall machine that led him to believe a new structure was required.[30]

David Manning, who was to become a key figure in the new structure, agreed that after four or five years in office, the Prime Minister needed greater capacity in Number 10 to manage the frequent personal contacts between himself and other heads of government.[31]

Conclusion 199

Blair and Powell liked the proposals, which had the ready support of Cabinet Secretary Richard Wilson, keen to sidestep a more wholesale creation of a PM's Department. The new structure would see the replacement of the former foreign affairs Private Secretary's post by two far more senior officials, one overseeing European policy, the other all other international affairs. The choice of European head was straightforward – Stephen Wall, who held the foreign affairs Private Secretary's job under Major and who had been head of the European Secretariat in the Cabinet Office since 2000. Blair, a keen pro-European, anxious at that time to take Britain into the single currency, saw in Wall the perfect Europhile operator and ally. The choice of the head of the Overseas and Defence Adviser role was less obvious. David Manning had been appointed British Permanent Representative to NATO a few months before. Blair took him aside at a NATO summit and said to him 'I want you to come to Downing Street. Jonathan Powell will explain it to you'.[32]

Blair, by now, had himself moved his office into the traditional Private Secretary's office at the end of the Cabinet Room. Wall and Manning were accommodated in offices along the corridor connecting Number 10 to the Cabinet Office that turns to the right just beyond the famous black front door. But it meant for the first time since 1945, those responsible for advising the Prime Minister on foreign affairs were no longer sitting adjacent to his PPS. Because relationships were strong between Wall, Manning and Chief of Staff Powell, the new geography worked. The reporting line in the new regime was that Wall and Manning reported directly up to Blair, each taking pains to copy key papers into each other and Powell. Almost from the beginning of this new arrangement, however, the new structure did not work out as expected. The terrorist attacks of 11 September 2001 occurred within months of it being set up, focusing the Prime Minister's attention heavily onto Afghanistan, the relationship with Washington, security policy and Iraq. His hopes for the euro were stymied in part by lack of time, but also by the intransigent opposition of Chancellor Gordon Brown, Brown's key aide Ed Balls, and the Treasury.[33] Eventually, Wall decided to quit Number 10 'because it became clear that the Euro wasn't going to happen. I understood the *realpolitik*, but I felt that I had no more particular role to play, and didn't wish to see through another round of the EU presidency'.[34]

Wall is sceptical about the new arrangements:

> I was now thirty seconds away from the Prime Minister, because I had physically moved into Number 10, rather than 90 seconds away when my European secretariat office had been in the Cabinet Office, but it made little practical difference to my job. If anything, it was a disadvantage, because I rarely saw the Prime Minister, and I was cut off from my own senior staff who remained in the Cabinet Office.[35]

The Overseas and Defence (OD) Secretariat, too, continued to run very much as it had before the new arrangements came into being, albeit with more direct and regular input into Number 10 via the two key figures, Wall and Manning.

A clear benefit of the new system, though, stemmed from the peculiarly close relationships that Blair had with first President Clinton and then President George W. Bush, akin to Thatcher's relationship with President Ronald Reagan, as well as by the very high priority he chose to give international affairs after 9/11. Manning and Wall concur that the structure designed in the Blair and Powell period was very much what they personally needed. Cognisant of the errors of earlier periods, when Number 10 had moved too far away from the Foreign Office, as under Colville, de Zulueta and Charles Powell, Manning and Wall took trouble to ensure that the Foreign as well as Defence Secretaries were kept in close touch always about what was happening in Downing Street. 'Even then I knew that Whitehall looked on me with some suspicion', said Manning.[36]

Manning realised that Whitehall was apprehensive, so he tried to reassure the FCO, the MOD, Ministry of Defence and other departments and agencies by being as transparent as possible: copying letters, records and minutes as widely as security caveats allowed; and by briefing Secretaries of State and their Private Offices face to face and over the telephone.[37] In August 2003 Manning departed to become British Ambassador in Washington, to be replaced by Nigel Sheinwald, who had been UK Permanent Representative to the European Union in Brussels since 2000, one of the top posts. Having been selected several months before he took over, Sheinwald used the time to come to London from Brussels on Fridays to talk to key figures about the job, taking counsel in particular from Blair, Powell and Manning. 'The essential point for me was that it combined the ability to give personal advice to, and negotiate on behalf of, the PM, and ultimately the Cabinet as a whole', he said, 'but it meant that the person doing the job was rooted in the system himself, with the tradition of the Civil Service's ability to analyse impartially and bring together the best advice that Whitehall has to offer'.[38]

As with Manning before, he relished the Permanent Secretary rank of the job, which gave him far more power in Whitehall than the foreign affairs Private Secretary had in earlier iterations. It meant that the position was, for the first time, at least the equal of the Prime Minister's PPS in terms of clout, not just at the centre and across Whitehall but in overseas capitals as well. Sheinwald possessed a driving and buccaneering personality; he accumulated influence and responsibility around him by dint of his intellect. Under him, the job achieved an apex of influence, albeit, and almost counterintuitively, not more so than it had earlier under Colville, de Zulueta and Powell. Sheinwald's close contacts with the White House meant that he was the ideal candidate to be appointed Ambassador to the United States in succession to Manning in 2007.

The new joint structure of two senior foreign policy advisers to the Prime Minister might well have endured had it not been for Gordon Brown's arrival as PM in May 2007. By now, European specialist Kim Darroch had succeeded Wall as Foreign Policy Adviser heading the European Secretariat in 2004, while Simon McDonald had succeeded Sheinwald as the Foreign Policy Adviser heading the OD Secretariat. Brown retained the dual system, but moved both figures back into the Cabinet Office, and relied far more on the ever-present foreign affairs Private Secretary. The foreign affairs Private Secretary's position had continued in the Number 10 Private Office after 2001, albeit at a more junior position, with Francis Campbell succeeding Sawers from 2001 to 2002, followed by Matthew Rycroft until 2004, and Antony Phillipson from 2004 to 2007. All were highly capable, of course, but their position was eclipsed by the two big beasts above them. But then Tom Fletcher, a comparatively junior Foreign Office diplomat aged just 32, was appointed foreign affairs Private Secretary shortly after Brown's first visit to Washington in July 2007.[39]

In Number 10, geography is all important, and the fact that McDonald and Jon Cunliffe, Darroch's successor as head of the European Secretariat, were physically located in the Cabinet Office while Fletcher was just round the corner from Gordon Brown, was decisive. Then in 2008, when Brown moved his office into Number 12, Fletcher became physically part of the same space. Decisive too was Fletcher's unusually engaging personality, his vivid and self-confident opinions, and his reading of the PM. Fletcher was one of the more unusually gifted figures to have filled the foreign affairs Private Secretary's post, having the force of character to stand up to a particularly assertive, and at times aggressive Prime Minister in Gordon Brown, but also having the charm and intellectual skills to cope with apparent ease with the demands of the job and the relationships at home and abroad. 'When I came back in the summer of 2007, there was actually no one in Number 10 doing the Foreign Affairs job. If there had been a job description, I must have written it myself', he said.[40] Fletcher described the job thus:

> Providing Private Secretary support to the PM across the full range of foreign affairs activities, including foreign policy, defence, foreign aid and intelligence, as well as Northern Ireland. I supported the PM on his overseas visits, planning the trips, putting together deliverables and outcomes, planning the briefings and then travelling with him, supporting him in the meetings.

Brown felt comfortable with Fletcher: the FCO was an alien department to him, and he'd resisted Blair's moves to make him Foreign Secretary, whereas he knew the Treasury inside out. His relationship with Fletcher became extraordinarily close. Without Fletcher and Heywood, the deficiencies of Brown as Prime Minister would have become much more apparent.[41]

Phase 5: The foreign affairs Private Secretary under the National Security Council, 2010 onwards

The fifth and final evolution of the foreign affairs Private Secretary's role occurred with the creation of the National Security Council (NSC) in 2010. The story has been well told in the Institute for Government publication *The National Security Council*, by Joe Devanny and Josh Harris. The NSC evolution had a long pedigree, dating back to the Committee of Imperial Defence (CID) which preceded even the formation of the Cabinet Office in 1916. In 1963, the Defence and Oversea Policy Subcommittee of Cabinet took over its work, which was later replaced by the Defence and Oversea Policy Committee (DOPC). As Devanny and Harris make clear, 'rather than a completely new innovation, the NSC is the latest iteration in this process'.[42]

In 2007, Brown had renamed the DOPC as the Ministerial Committee on National Security, International Relations and Development (NSID), which also absorbed Blair's Ministerial Committee on Security and Terrorism. NSID operated closely with McDonald as head of the Foreign and Defence Secretariat, Cunliffe heading the European Secretariat, and Robert Hannigan overseeing the Intelligence and Security Secretariats.

Pressure for the creation of a new body, the NSC, came from a number of quarters. The Conservative Party had been talking about it since a policy paper in December 2006 produced by Pauline Neville-Jones, a former JIC chair, from the think tank world with an IPPR paper in 2009, and also from within Whitehall, not the least from Cabinet Secretary, Heywood.[43] Brown almost certainly would have created the NSC had he had won the election, but two senior figures in Cameron's team, Ed Llewellyn and Oliver Letwin, were strong enthusiasts as well.[44] Peter Ricketts, who had been Permanent Under-Secretary at the FCO since 2006, was duly appointed the first National Security Adviser (NSA).

Tom Fletcher remained as foreign affairs Private Secretary under this fifth and latest iteration. Even though he had been so identified with Brown, David Cameron asked Fletcher to remain at Downing Street. Despite the NSC structure being created, he found that his work remained largely the same:

> it wasn't hugely different after the NSC was established, to be honest. But it gave a stronger rhythm to the process of Cabinet Committees that had existed before, which the system often needed. I think the most important benefit the NSC gave was face time for the Prime Minister with his key security and senior foreign policy staff, which was greater than existed before.

Fletcher continued:

> David Cameron enjoyed the NSC, pulling the levers of power and having that group of people around the table. Key figures also had the chance to say 'Look, when I discussed this with the Prime Minister last week, he said XYZ', and doing that gave them authority and credibility. That is the most important benefit of the NSC, I believe.[45]

Fletcher left in November 2010, replaced as foreign affairs Private Secretary by John Casson, a Foreign Office Arabist, who had been recently overseeing seeing North Africa and the Middle East at the Foreign Office at just the moment when, with the Arab Spring, Cameron's attention was focusing on the region.[46] In 2014, with the focus switching heavily to Europe, Casson was replaced by diplomat Nigel Casey. His time was dominated under Cameron by five issues: the EU, Russia/Ukraine, Syria, migration and the terrorist threat. On the first in particular, Chief of Staff Ed Llewellyn played a major role, especially on EU renegotiation and referendum issues. Casson has three main colleagues; apart from an Assistant Private Secretary, at the end of the period, December 2015, he had also Jonny Paul from the Department for International Development on development, Middle East, Latin America and Asia; and one military assistant, Nick Perry, on defence, services and security matters.

Conclusion

Over these five different phases of the life of the foreign affairs Private Secretary, from Jock Colville to Nigel Casey, seven factors have explained the differing roles:

1   **Character and ambition of the Private Secretary.** Amongst the many formidably strong and able foreign affairs Private Secretaries, several of whom have gone on to head Whitehall departments, three stand out as being particularly independent of the FCO: John Colville (albeit not as foreign affairs Private Secretary, but as Joint Principal Private Secretary specialising in foreign policy), Philip de Zulueta and Charles Powell. These unusually powerful presences all precipitated change in the structure of Downing Street.

2   **Technology.** In 1945, the Prime Minister was travelling by propeller aircraft or even by ship, as was the case when Churchill returned as Prime Minister in 1951. Jet aircraft have transformed the ability of the Prime Minister to travel on short trips to the United States, and day trips to Europe, with a corresponding change and diminution in authority of the FCO and local ambassadors. The speed of communications with emails, video conferences and mobile phones make it easy for the Prime Minister to relate directly to his opposite numbers and foreign leaders without needing to go through ambassadors or Foreign Secretaries.

3   **The personality of the Prime Minister.** Some Prime Ministers formed particularly close personal relationships with their Private Secretaries, conspicuous amongst them Churchill with Colville (1951–1955), Eden with Guy Millard (1955–1956), Macmillan with de Zulueta (1957–1963), Heath with Robert Armstrong (PPS, 1970–1974), Thatcher with Charles Powell (1984–1990) and Gordon Brown with Tom Fletcher (2007–2010). Additionally, Blair came to rely heavily on Nigel Sheinwald in his position as Senior Policy Adviser, who brought so much power into the office that it was difficult for subsequent holders to recapture that same authority.

4   **The decline of empire and the rise of the European Union (EU).** After the decolonisation in the 1950s and 1960s, PMs continued to attend the Commonwealth Heads of Government meetings (CHOGMs), but they

ranked far less high in importance and regularity than European Councils. The insistent rhythm of European Councils has become a feature of the Prime Minister's life since Britain entered Europe in 1973, with the key focus in the EU being on the Prime Minister's relations with his or her opposite numbers, above all in Germany, France and Italy, rather than with the Foreign Secretary.

5 **Decline in influence of the Foreign Secretary.** In 1945, the Foreign Secretary, first Eden, then after Labour's election victory, Ernest Bevin, was the second most powerful figure in the government behind the Prime Minister. By 2015, the post had become third below the Chancellor, and the Treasury easily eclipsed the influence in Whitehall of the FCO. The downgrading of the Foreign Secretary did not happen suddenly, but 1964 is the best single date in the replacement. After it, the Foreign Secretary was more usually subordinate to the Chancellor, as economic policy came increasingly to dominate government thinking. With that transition, the post of PPS to the Foreign Secretary, which used to attract the major high-flyers, became a less important voice than the foreign affairs Private Secretaries at Number 10. Notably powerful PPSs to Foreign Secretaries include Pierson Dixon (1943–1947), Frank Roberts (1947–1949), Evelyn Shuckburgh (1951–1954), Nicholas Henderson (1963–1965), Antony Acland (1972–1975) and Brian Fall (1981–1984). Several went on to write books, notably Henderson with *The Private Office*.[47] As Sherard Cowper-Coles, PPS to the Foreign Secretary from 1999 to 2001, has noted, a stronger Foreign Secretary gave the PPS job the more power. But overall, the FCO, like the US State Department and Quai d'Orsay, have been in long term relative decline. Nevertheless, it was not until the mid to late 1980s, when Charles Powell was Private Secretary at Number 10, and Cradock/Braithwaite the Prime Minister's Foreign Policy Advisers, that the Number 10 job systematically outstripped in influence that of the PPS at the FCO. Many of the most powerful British diplomats in the post-war world held either the foreign affairs Private Secretary's job at Number 10 or the PPS job at the FCO. Some, however, held neither position because of timing, for example Denis Greenhill (FCO Permanent Secretary, 1969–1973). John Kerr (Permanent Secretary, 1997–2002) had been a PPS, but to the Chancellor of the Exchequer, while Michael Jay (Permanent Secretary, 2002–2006) missed out on either position because he joined the FCO late from the Overseas Development Administration (ODA).

6 **The personality of the Principal Private Secretary.** Some Principal Private Secretaries, notably Colville (1951–1955), Bishop (1956–1959), Bligh (1959–1963) and Armstrong (1970–1975), had pronounced foreign policy views of their own, which have meant that their advice either rivalled or eclipsed that of the foreign affairs Private Secretaries.

7 **Length of Service.** Undeniably, the longer the foreign affairs Private Secretaries are in office, the more power they acquire, none more so than the seven years of de Zulueta and the seven and a half years of Powell. For good reason does the FCO want to ensure that no incumbent is in position for more than two or three years.

Notes

1 Interview with Alex Allan, 10 May 2016.
2 Denis Kavanagh and Anthony Seldon, *The Powers behind the Prime Minister: The Hidden Influence of Number Ten* (London: HarperCollins, 1999), 51.
3 John Colville, *The Fringes of Power: Downing Street Diaries 1939–1955* (London: Hodder & Stoughton, 1985); John Colville, *Footprints in Time: Memories* (London: Century, 1976).
4 John Holmes, *The Politics of Humanity: The Reality of Relief Aid* (London: Head of Zeus, 2013).
5 Stuart Ball and Anthony Seldon, eds, *The Heath Government 1970–1974: A Reappraisal* (London: Longman, 1996).
6 John Wheeler-Bennett, ed., *Action this Day: Working with Churchill* (London: Macmillan, 1968). Lord Moran, *Winston Churchill: The Struggle for Survival* (London: Sphere Books, 1968).
7 Martin Gilbert, *In Search of Churchill: A Historian's Journey* (London: HarperCollins, 1994), 182.
8 Anthony Seldon, *Churchill's Indian Summer: The Conservative Government 1951–1955* (London: Hodder & Stoughton, 1981), 397–9.
9 Robert McNamara, *Britain, Nasser and the Balance of Power in the Middle East, 1952–1977: From the Egyptian Revolution to the Six-Day War* (London: Frank Cass, 2003), 100.
10 Richard Crossman, *The Diaries of a Cabinet Minister*, vol. I: *Minister for Housing, 1964–1966* (London: Hamish Hamilton and Jonathan Cape, 1976), 261.
11 Richard Davenport-Hines, *An English Affair: Sex, Class and Power in the Age of Profumo* (London: William Collins, 2013), 287–8.
12 Kavanagh and Seldon, *Powers behind the Prime Minister*, 63.
13 Interview with Guy Millard, Yale-UN Oral History Project, 20 April 1991.
14 Max Egremont, 'Zulueta, Sir Philip Francis de (1925–1989)', in *Oxford Dictionary of National Biography: From the earliest times to the year 2000*, ed. H. G. C. Matthew and Brian Harrison (Oxford: Oxford University Press, 2004), vol. LX, 1023.
15 Interview with Lord Armstrong, March 2016.
16 Kavanagh and Seldon, *Powers behind the Prime Minister*, 89.
17 Ibid., 181.
18 Percy Cradock, *In Pursuit of British Interests: Reflections on Foreign Policy under Margaret Thatcher and John Major* (London: John Murray, 1997), 43.
19 Joe Devanny and Josh Harris, *The National Security Council* (London: Institute for Government, 2014), 12.
20 Anthony Seldon with Lewis Baston, *Major: A Political Life* (London: Weidenfeld & Nicolson, 1997), 143.
21 Interview with Sir Stephen Wall, 21 May 2016.
22 Seldon, *Major*, 334, 740.
23 Interview with Sir Stephen Wall, 21 May 2016.
24 Seldon, *Major*, 392.
25 Seldon, *Major*, 739.
26 Interview with Alex Allan, 10 May 2016.
27 Interview with John Sawers, 1 May 2016.
28 Ibid.
29 Anthony Seldon with Chris Ballinger, Daniel Collings and Peter Snowden, *Blair* (London: Free, 2004), 607–10.
30 Interview with John Sawers, 1 May 2016.
31 Interview with Sir David Manning, 20 May 2016.
32 Interview with Sir David Manning, 20 May 2016.
33 Anthony Seldon with Peter Snowdon and Daniel Collings, *Blair Unbound* (London: Simon & Schuster, 2007), 404–14.

34 Interview with Sir Stephen Wall, 21 May 2016.
35 Ibid.
36 Interview with Sir David Manning, 20 May 2016.
37 Interview Sir David Manning, 20 May 2016.
38 Interview with Nigel Sheinwald, 24 April 2015.
39 Anthony Seldon and Guy Lodge, *Brown at 10* (London: Biteback, 2010), 27.
40 Interview with Tom Fletcher, 28 April 2016.
41 Seldon and Lodge, *Brown at 10*, 179, 187.
42 Devanny and Harris, *National Security Council*, 17.
43 Pauline Neville-Jones, *Security Issues Interim Position Paper* (London: Conservative Party, 2006). See also Devanny and Harris, *National Security Council*, 21.
44 Anthony Seldon and Peter Snowdon, *Cameron at 10: The Inside Story of 2010–2015* (London: William Collins, 2015), 61.
45 Interview with Tom Fletcher, 28 April 2016.
46 Seldon and Snowdon, *Cameron at 10*, 98.
47 Nicholas Henderson, *The Private Office: A Personal View of Five Foreign Secretaries and of Government from the Inside* (London: Weidenfeld & Nicolson, 1984).

References

Ball, Stuart, and Anthony Seldon, eds, *The Heath Government 1970–1974: A Reappraisal* (London: Longman, 1996).
Colville, John, *Footprints in Time: Memories* (London: Century, 1976).
Colville, John, *The Fringes of Power: Downing Street Diaries 1939–1955* (London: Hodder & Stoughton, 1985).
Cradock, Percy, *In Pursuit of British Interests: Reflections on Foreign Policy under Margaret Thatcher and John Major* (London: John Murray, 1997).
Crossman, Richard, *The Diaries of a Cabinet Minister*, vol. I: *Minister for Housing, 1964–1966* (London: Hamish Hamilton and Jonathan Cape, 1976).
Davenport-Hines, Richard, *An English Affair: Sex, Class and Power in the Age of Profumo* (London: William Collins, 2013).
Devanny, Joe, and Josh Harris, *The National Security Council* (London: Institute for Government, 2014).
Gilbert, Martin, *In Search of Churchill: A Historian's Journey* (London: HarperCollins, 1994).
Henderson, Nicholas, *The Private Office: A Personal View of Five Foreign Secretaries and of Government from the Inside* (London: Weidenfeld & Nicolson, 1984).
Holmes, John, *The Politics of Humanity: The Reality of Relief Aid* (London: Head of Zeus, 2013).
Kavanagh, Denis, and Anthony Seldon, *The Powers behind the Prime Minister: The Hidden Influence of Number ten* (London: HarperCollins, 1999).
McNamara, Robert, *Britain, Nasser and the Balance of Power in the Middle East, 1952–1977: From the Egyptian Revolution to the Six-Day War* (London: Frank Cass, 2003).
Moran, Lord, *Winston Churchill: The Struggle for Survival* (London: Sphere Books, 1968).
Neville-Jones, Pauline, *Security Issues Interim Position Paper* (London: Conservative Party, 2006).
Seldon, Anthony, *Churchill's Indian Summer: The Conservative Government 1951–1955* (London: Hodder & Stoughton, 1981).
Seldon, Anthony, and Guy Lodge, *Brown at 10* (London: Biteback, 2010).

Seldon, Anthony, and Peter Snowdon, *Cameron at 10: The Inside Story of 2010–2015* (London: William Collins, 2015).

Seldon, Anthony, with Chris Ballinger, Daniel Collings and Peter Snowdon, *Blair* (London: Free, 2004).

Seldon, Anthony, with Lewis Baston, *Major: A Political Life* (London: Weidenfeld & Nicolson, 1997).

Seldon, Anthony, with Peter Snowdon and Daniel Collings, *Blair Unbound* (London: Simon & Schuster, 2007).

Wheeler-Bennett, John, ed., *Action this Day: Working with Churchill* (London: Macmillan, 1968).

Appendix I: Private Secretaries to the Prime Minister with responsibility for foreign affairs, 1945–2015

1943–45	John Colville
1945–47	John Addis
1947–50	Laurence Pumphrey
1951–52	David Hunt
1952–55	Anthony Montague Browne
1956–57	Guy Millard
1957–63	Philip de Zulueta
1964–66	Oliver Wright
1966–69	Michael Palliser
1969–70	Edward Youde
1970–72	Peter Moon
1972–74	Thomas Bridges
1974–77	Patrick Wright
1977–79	Bryan Cartledge
1979–81	Michael Alexander
1981–84	John Coles
1984–91	Charles Powell
1991–93	Stephen Wall
1993–96	Roderic Lyne
1996–99	John Holmes
1999–2001	John Sawers
2001–03	Francis Campbell
2003–04	Matthew Rycroft
2004–07	Antony Phillipson
2008–11	Tom Fletcher
2011–14	John Casson
2014–	Nigel Casey

Appendix II: Principal Private Secretaries to the Prime Minister, 1945–2015

1945–47	Leslie Rowan
1947–50	Laurence Helsby
1950–51	Denis Rickett
1951–55	John Colville
1951–56	David Pitblado
1956–59	Frederick Bishop
1959–63	Tim Bligh
1964–66	Derek Mitchell
1966–70	Arthur Halls
1970	Alexander Isserlis
1970–75	Robert Armstrong
1975–77	Kenneth Stowe
1977–79	Clive Whitmore CVO
1979–85	Robin Butler
1985–88	Nigel Wicks
1988–92	Andrew Turnbull
1992–97	Alex Allan
1997–99	John Holmes
1999–2003	Jeremy Heywood
2003–06	Ivan Rogers
2006–07	Oliver Robbins
2007–08	Tom Scholar
2008–10	Jeremy Heywood
2010–11	James Bowler
2011–15	Chris Martin

Index

Acheson, Dean 14, 15
Acland, Anthony 125
Action this Day 9, 15, 24, 189
Adenauer, Konrad 71
Afghanistan, Soviet invasion 169–70, 175–6
Aldrich, Winthrop 41
Alexander, Michael 130; career 167–8, 173; *Managing the Cold War* 174; and Thatcher 168–72, 173, 174; on US/Soviet withdrawal from Europe 173–4
Allan, Alex 187, 191
Allen, Douglas 125
Alsop, Joseph 68, 70
Amery, Julian 64
Anglo-American Alpha Plan (1955) 60
Anglo-American relationship ('special relationship') 13–16, 70, 86; tensions 14–15, 16, 18, 82–3
Anglo-American talks, Nassau (1962) 70
Anglo-Irish agreement (1985) 172
Armstrong, Robert 118, 126, 151–2; and Wilson 191
Astor, David 47
Attali, Jacques 5

Barber, Anthony 124
Bay of Pigs (1961) 82
Bevin, Ernest 13
Bishop, Freddie 2, 5, 59; career 35–6; and Eden's legacy 47; and Macmillan 190; and Suez crisis 39–41; Washington mission (1957) 42, 190
Black Wednesday (1992) 196
Blair, Tony 3; Private Office, restructuring 198–200
Bligh, Tim 72, 82; career 190–1; and Macmillan 190; and Profumo affair 190

Bowler, James 192
Braithwaite, Rodric 168
Brandt, Willy 104
Bridges, Edward 11
Bridges, Thomas 118, 195; career 121; and Heath 127, 130, 132
British Diplomacy Oral History Programme (BDOHP) 119
British Guiana 85–6
Brook, Norman 8, 45
Brown, George 104
Brown, Gordon 200–1
Bruce, David 83
Bundy, McGeorge 85
Burnham, Forbes 86
Butler, R.A. ('Rab') 13, 14, 23, 26, 72, 88
Butler, Robin 195

Caccia, Harold 69
Cairncross, Neil 36, 42–3, 59
Callaghan, James 4, 143–4; on foreign policy 149; global outlook 153
Cameron, David 3
Campbell, Alan 81
Campbell, John 179
Cartledge, Bryan: and Callaghan 139, 156; career 136, 157; role 140; work routines 144
Casson, John 202–3
Centre for Policy Studies (CPS) 169
Chamberlain, Neville 8
Chief of Staff appointments 192–3
Churchill College, foundation 27–8
Churchill, Randolph 23
Churchill, Winston: 'Anglo-Saxonism' 14; Eden, relations 20–3; government (1951–1955) 9; health 24–7, 190; Private Office 10–13; work methods 11

civil servants: personalities of 127; politicians, relationship 122–3
Civil Service, *Code* 122
Clark, William 36, 42, 61
Cold War 10, 16–20, 37, 68; 1980s 180
Coles, John: career 175, 181; and Thatcher 174–5, 176, 177, 178, 179–82
Collins, Marcus 119–20
Colville, John (Jock) 8; and Churchill's health 24–7, 190; and Churchill's legacy 27–9; Eisenhower, distrust of 15; influence on Churchill 9–10; mediator, Churchill/Eden relationship 20, 21–3; resignation 13; works: *Footprints in Time* 9, 189; *The Fringes of Power* 9, 189
Common Market 67, 68, see also EC; EEC
Confrontation, Indonesia/Malaysia 89, 90, 92, 97, 106
Cradock, Percy, and Thatcher 195–6
Cuban missile crisis (1962) 69

Davies, Harold 103
de Courcel, Geoffroy 69
de Gaulle, Charles 68–9, 69–70
de Zulueta, Philip 36, 37, 43; ancestry 55–6; Catholicism 71; City career 72–3, 194; and Cyprus 64; early life 56–8; and Eden 59–62; and European affairs 67–70; and Iraq 64–5; and Macmillan 62–7, 73–4, 193–4; nuclear affairs 70–2; resignation 72; Russian language skills 60–1; and Suez crisis 61
Dean, Patrick 58, 88, 102, 103
Dewey, Thomas 15
Dixon, Pierson 69
Donoughue, Bernard 4, 118, 121–2, 147; on the Private Secretaries 140–1, 144, 145
Douglas-Home, Alec 124–5; *The Way the Wind Blows* 119
Downing Street, Policy Unit 140, 143; creation 147
Dulles, John Foster 15, 18, 42, 190

Eban, Abba 102
EC (European Community): UK budget rebate 172–3, see also Common Market; EEC
Eden, Anthony 2, 13, 18; Churchill, relations 20–3; health problems 20, 41, 47–8, 59; resignation 41

Eden, Clarissa 40
EEC (European Economic Community) negotiations 125–32, 195; civil servants 125; ministerial responsibilities 128–9; Treaty of Accession (1972) 131; and Wright 87; see also Common Market; EC
EEC (European Economic Community) Referendum (1975) 151
Egerton, Margaret 8
Egypt Committee, Suez crisis 39
Eisenhower, Dwight D. 15
Erhard, Ludwig 102
European Free Trade Association 67
Evans, Harold 62

Falkland Islands conflict (1982) 177–9
Ferguson, Ewan, on PPS' role 141–2
Fletcher, John, *Naked Diplomacy* 189
Fletcher, Tom: and Brown 201; and Cameron 202
foreign policy: Callaghan on 149
Forster, Oliver 100
Franks Report (Falkland Islands Review) 179
Freeman, John 103

Gaitskell, Hugh 63
Geneva summit (1955) 37
Gilbert, Martin 28
Good Friday Agreement, Northern Island (1998) 197
Gordon Walker, Patrick 86
Gore-Booth, Paul 105
Greenwood, Anthony 86
Grenada: US invasion (1983) 179–80
Guadeloupe summit (1979) 149, 155–6, 156–7

Haines, Joe 148–9
Halls, Michael 99
Hancock, P.F. 58
Harriman, Averill 85, 103
Heath, Edward 2, 69, 81
Helsby, Laurence 192
Helsinki Accords (1975) 168
Henderson, Nicholas 120, 121, 122, 137, 141, 142, 150, 151
Hennessy, Peter 44, 122
Heywood, Jeremy 191–2
Holmes, John 197; *The Politics of Humanity* 189
Horne, Alistair 67, 72
Home, Lord see Douglas-Home, Alec

Humbold, Anthony 23
Hunt, David 11–12
Hunt, John 125, 141, 154, 155
Hurd, Douglas: *An End to Promises* 119

Isserlis, Alexander 189

Jagan, Cheddi 86
Jay, Peter 155
Johnson, Lyndon B. 82, 89, 93
Jones, G.W. 10

Kaiser, Philip 97–8
Kelly, Denis 20, 24
Kennedy, John F. 67, 71
Kennedy, Robert 89
Kissinger, Henry 103
Komer, Robert 85
Kosygin, Alexei 84, 98, 101

Lee, Frank 69
Lennox-Boyd, Alan 64
Lloyd, Selwyn 42, 63, 66
Lyne, Roderic: and Major 196–7

McCaffrey, Tom, and Callaghan 148, 149
McDermott, Geoffrey 58, 72
Maclehose, Murray 100, 105
Macmillan, Harold 2, 38, 123; African tour (1960) 66, 190; and Suez crisis 39–40
McNally, Tom, and Callaghan 148
Maitland, Donald 100
Major, John 5
Malenkov, Georgi 19
Malik, Jacob 19
Manning, David 198, 200
Martin, Chris 192
Martin, John: career 189; and Churchill 189
Millard, Guy 2, 5, 36, 58–9; and Suez crisis 44, 45, 46–7, 49, 61, 193
Mitchell, Derek 82, 84, 190–1
Molotov, Vyacheslav 19
Monckton, Walter 39
Montague Browne, Anthony 10, 12, 20, 24
Moon, Peter 118, 119, 194; career 120; and Heath 120, 129–30, 131–2
Moore, Charles 170
Moran, Lord 24; *Churchill: The Struggle for Survival* 9
Morgan, Austen 85
Morgan, Kenneth O. 150

Mosaddegh, Mohammad 14
Multilateral Force (MLF): and Wright 87–8

Nairne, Pat 125
Nasser, Gamal Abdel 37
National Security Council (NSC), establishment 201–2
NATO (North Atlantic Treaty Organisation) 2, 14, 48, 174; French withdrawal from 97, 100, 107; naval command structure 84; nuclear weapons deployment 180
Nield, William 125
Northern Ireland 140; hunger strikes (1981) 172
nuclear deterrent: UK 156–7
Nuclear Test Ban Treaty (1963) 72
Nutting, Anthony 43, 44; *No End of a Lesson* 45

oil crisis (1973-1974) 136, 158
Owen, David 43, 47, 48

Palliser, Michael 2, 4, 5, 87, 126–7; career 97–8, 194; daily routine 100–1; diplomacy 101–4; and East of Suez withdrawal 106, 107; and EEC 106–10, 111, 112; and the Foreign Office 104–5; PUS, appointment 111, 194; and Wilson 98–9, 101, 102, 106; workload 105–6
Parr, Helen 92
Pitblado, David 10–11, 12, 13, 45–6, 58; career 35; view of role 36
Policy Unit *see* Downing Street, Policy Unit
political advisers 145–7
politicians: civil servants, relationship 122–3
Powell, Charles: and Major 195; and Thatcher 167, 182–3, 195
Powell, Jonathan, Chief of Staff 192, 197
PREM files 39, 119
Principal Private Secretaries (PPS) 1945–2015 209; age on appointment 188; backgrounds 188; 'civil servants' 191–2; 'distant' from PM 192–3; identification with PM 189–91; length of service 188; location 187; Private Secretary (Foreign Affairs), relationship 187–8; roles 141–2; subsequent careers 189; typology 189–93
Private Office (Prime Minister): restructuring 198–200; role 121–2

Private Secretaries (Foreign Affairs) 1945–2015 208; antecedents 188, 193; and EU prominence 204; and Foreign Secretary's diminished influence 204; 'heavyweights' 194–6, 203; and length of service 204; location 187; in National Security Council 201–3; phases 193–203; and Prime Minister's personality 203; and Principal Private Secretary's personality 204; 'regulars' 196–8; 'restrained' 193–4; roles 3–4, 5, 139–42, 166–7, 193, 201, 203–4; stereotypes 1; technology factors 203

Ramsden, John 9
Reid, M.H.M. 84
Reilly, Patrick 66
Rhodesia: conflict settlement (1980) 171; unilateral declaration of independence (UDI) (1965) 85
Rhys-Williams, Juliet 67
Rogers, Ivan 192
Romanov, Alex 69
Rostow, Walt 103
Rowan, Leslie 11, 191
Rumbold, Anthony 58
Rusk, Dean 83, 103

Salisbury, Lord 17, 22, 25–6
Sandys, Duncan 86, 88, 91
Sawers, John: MI6 Head 198; role 197–8
Scheinwald, Nigel 200
Seldon, Anthony 10, 12
Shuckburgh, Evelyn 48–9, 60; *Descent to Suez* 48, 49
Soames, Christopher 13, 19, 23, 111, 125
Soames, Mary 9
'special relationship' *see* Anglo-American relationship
Stalin, Joseph, death 17
Sterling crisis (1976) 158
Stewart, Michael 100
Stowe, Kenneth 137, 191
Strategic Arms Limitation Talks (SALT) 156

Suez Canal: nationalisation of 37
Suez crisis: *A Canal Too Far* (documentary) 47; Anglo-French intervention 38; and Bishop 39–41; Egypt Committee 39; and Millard 44, 45, 46–7, 49, 61

Thatcher, Margaret 2, 3, 4, 6, 7; priorities 167; *The Downing Street Years* 167
Thompson, Llewellyn 71
Thomson, George 98, 103, 107
Thorneycroft, Peter 87
Tickell, Crispin 125
Trend, Burke 82, 86, 89, 125; and Wilson 99
Truman, Harry S. 14, 15
TSR-2 aircraft 64

Walden, George 142
Wall, Stephen 142, 199; and Major 196; role 196
Williams, John 100
Williams, Marcia (Lady Falkender) 146
Wilson, Harold 2, 4, 73, 143; health 149–50, 159; 'Kitchen Cabinet' 146; resignation 152–3; work methods 145
Wilson, Richard 199
Woodfield, P.J. 84
Wright, Oliver 2; Ambassador posts 81, 93, 194; career 194; and Confrontation (Malaysia/Indonesia) 89; and Cyprus 91; and Douglas-Home 81–3, 87–8, 89–90, 92, 93, 194; and EEC 87, 93; and Multilateral Force (MLF) 87–8; and Northern Ireland 92; and Wilson 84–7, 92, 194; and Yemen 90
Wright, Patrick: and Callaghan 153, 154; career 138, 157; role 140; and Wilson 139, 152–3
Wyndham, John 62, 63

Youde, Edward, career 111, 194, 195
Young, Hugo 151
Young, John W. 126; *Twentieth-Century Diplomacy* 119

Taylor & Francis eBooks

Helping you to choose the right eBooks for your Library

Add Routledge titles to your library's digital collection today. Taylor and Francis ebooks contains over 50,000 titles in the Humanities, Social Sciences, Behavioural Sciences, Built Environment and Law.

Choose from a range of subject packages or create your own!

Benefits for you
- Free MARC records
- COUNTER-compliant usage statistics
- Flexible purchase and pricing options
- All titles DRM-free.

Benefits for your user
- Off-site, anytime access via Athens or referring URL
- Print or copy pages or chapters
- Full content search
- Bookmark, highlight and annotate text
- Access to thousands of pages of quality research at the click of a button.

REQUEST YOUR FREE INSTITUTIONAL TRIAL TODAY

Free Trials Available
We offer free trials to qualifying academic, corporate and government customers.

eCollections – Choose from over 30 subject eCollections, including:

Archaeology	Language Learning
Architecture	Law
Asian Studies	Literature
Business & Management	Media & Communication
Classical Studies	Middle East Studies
Construction	Music
Creative & Media Arts	Philosophy
Criminology & Criminal Justice	Planning
Economics	Politics
Education	Psychology & Mental Health
Energy	Religion
Engineering	Security
English Language & Linguistics	Social Work
Environment & Sustainability	Sociology
Geography	Sport
Health Studies	Theatre & Performance
History	Tourism, Hospitality & Events

For more information, pricing enquiries or to order a free trial, please contact your local sales team:
www.tandfebooks.com/page/sales

Routledge
Taylor & Francis Group

The home of Routledge books

www.tandfebooks.com

Printed in the United States
By Bookmasters